7-30-76

LEISURE RESOURCES:

Its Comprehensive Planning

JOSEPH J. BANNON

University of Illinois, Urbana-Champaign

PRENTICE-HALL, INC., Englewood Cliffs, New Jersey

Library of Congress Cataloging in Publication Data

BANNON, JOSEPH J
  Leisure resources, its comprehensive planning.

  Includes bibliographies and index.
  1. Recreation—Administration. 2. Cities and towns—
Planning—1945- I. Title.
GV182.15.B36   711'.4   75-30512
ISBN 0-13-528208-X

© 1976 by
PRENTICE-HALL, INC.
Englewood Cliffs, New Jersey

Printed in the United States of America.

10 9 8 7 6 5 4 3 2 1

PRENTICE-HALL INTERNATIONAL, INC., *London*
PRENTICE-HALL OF AUSTRALIA, PTY. LIMITED, *Sydney*
PRENTICE-HALL OF CANADA, LTD., *Toronto*
PRENTICE-HALL OF INDIA PRIVATE LIMITED, *New Delhi*
PRENTICE-HALL OF JAPAN, INC., *Tokyo*
PRENTICE-HALL OF SOUTHEAST ASIA PRIVATE LIMITED, *Singapore*

1924036

To My Mother and Father

CONTENTS

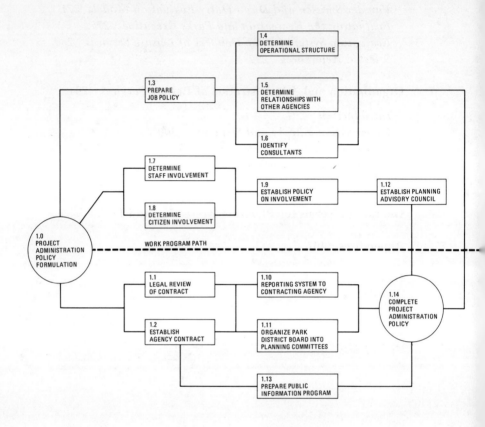

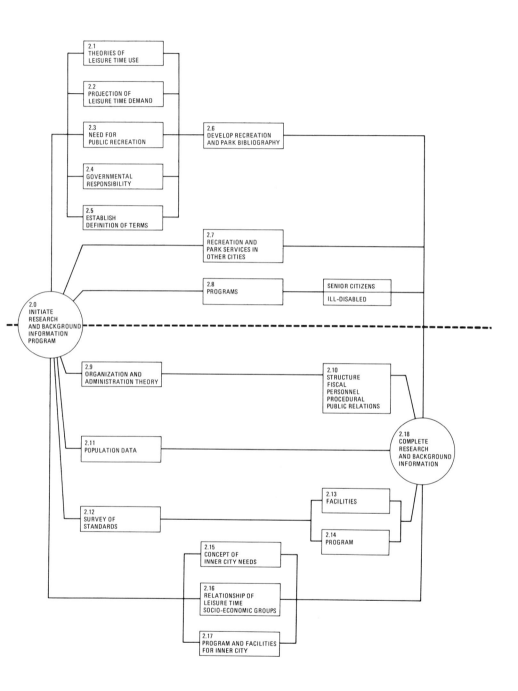

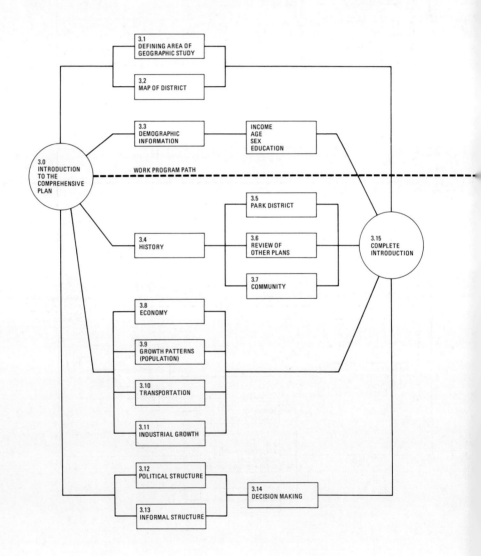

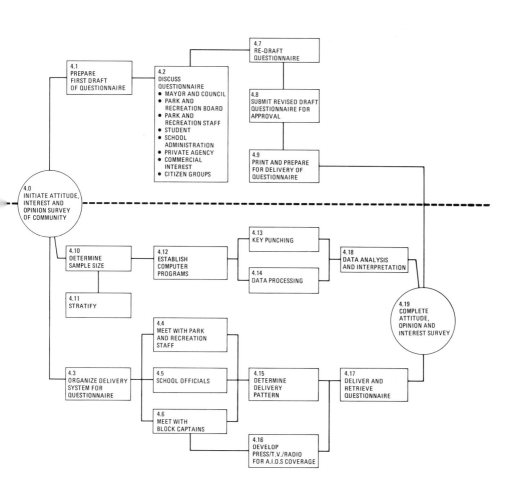

4.1 PREPARE FIRST DRAFT OF QUESTIONNAIRE

4.2 DISCUSS QUESTIONNAIRE
- MAYOR AND COUNCIL
- PARK AND RECREATION BOARD
- PARK AND RECREATION STAFF
- STUDENT
- SCHOOL ADMINISTRATION
- PRIVATE AGENCY
- COMMERCIAL INTEREST
- CITIZEN GROUPS

4.7 RE-DRAFT QUESTIONNAIRE

4.8 SUBMIT REVISED DRAFT QUESTIONNAIRE FOR APPROVAL

4.9 PRINT AND PREPARE FOR DELIVERY OF QUESTIONNAIRE

4.0 INITIATE ATTITUDE, INTEREST AND OPINION SURVEY OF COMMUNITY

4.10 DETERMINE SAMPLE SIZE

4.11 STRATIFY

4.12 ESTABLISH COMPUTER PROGRAMS

4.13 KEY PUNCHING

4.14 DATA PROCESSING

4.18 DATA ANALYSIS AND INTERPRETATION

4.19 COMPLETE ATTITUDE, OPINION AND INTEREST SURVEY

4.3 ORGANIZE DELIVERY SYSTEM FOR QUESTIONNAIRE

4.4 MEET WITH PARK AND RECREATION STAFF

4.5 SCHOOL OFFICIALS

4.6 MEET WITH BLOCK CAPTAINS

4.15 DETERMINE DELIVERY PATTERN

4.16 DEVELOP PRESS/T.V./RADIO FOR A.I.O.S COVERAGE

4.17 DELIVER AND RETRIEVE QUESTIONNAIRE

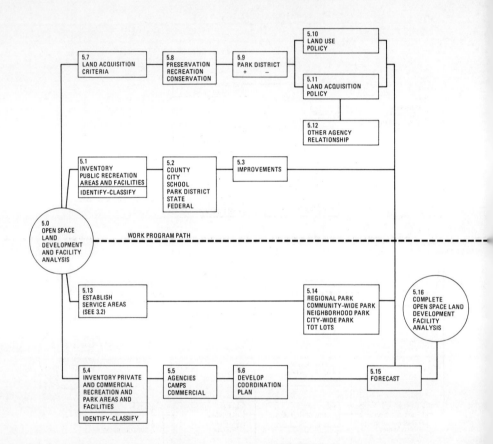

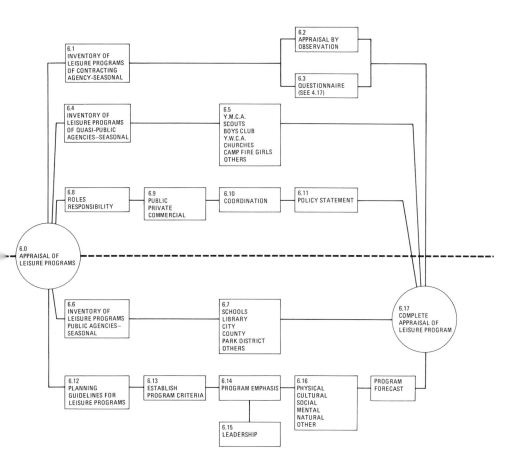

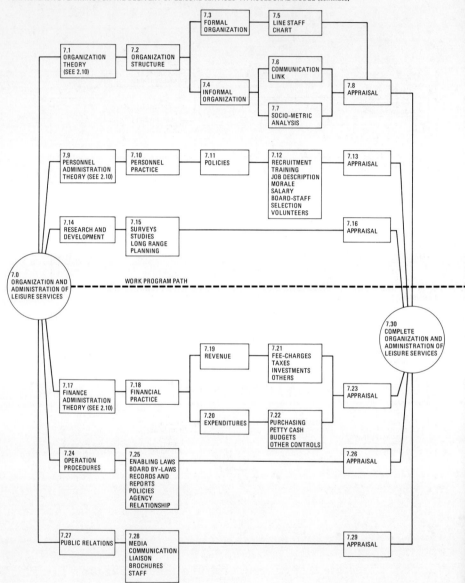

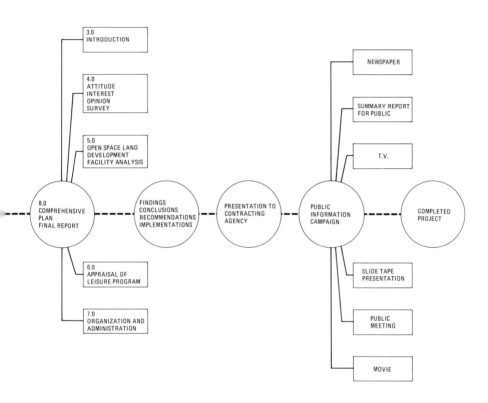

FOREWORD

The literature on planning is virtually staggering; one is easily overwhelmed by the broad coverage urban and community planning has received in academic and trade journals. But mere preponderance of coverage can be misleading: too much attention is given to the need and desirability of planning, too little to the limitations of planning, or how to undertake a comprehensive plan in a community.

These two omitted areas in the planning literature are of dire necessity for any recreation and parks agency seeking to undertake or effect a community-wide plan of leisure services. This book is not an attempt to say only glorious things about planning and then leave the practitioners to discover the shortcomings themselves.

While clearly premised on the need for planning, this book stresses as well a conceptual model to be used for the planning of leisure services at the community level. We must remember that communities vary greatly, from the tiny hamlet of several hundred people, to villages of several thousand, up to the unprecedented urban areas with their core city and outgrowths of suburbia and exurbia. "Community" has an intimate sound; in fact, as an adjective, community is often used to denote closeness, common feelings, mutual concern. But communities in reality vary greatly as to common concerns and interests, as to a sense of belonging or of alienation. Often this variance in a "spirit of place" is directly related in our minds to size: the larger a community, the more likely we are to feel displacement, fear, alienation, social fatigue, indifference; and the smaller a community, the greater likelihood of our feeling more involved, closer to our neighbors, informed, and aware. While this neat dichotomy of feeling can be blasted by images such as those presented in *Wisconsin Death Trip* or *In Cold Blood*, community and size are tightly related in our minds and in our approaches to planning. However inaccurate are our images of life in the country or in the city, these images nonetheless hold great sway over our dreams, plans, and forms of leisure and recreation.

It requires a great deal of imagination and effort for us to transfer to urban communities the benevolent compassion many of us have for the smaller community of our remote rural past. Yet the city is a community, not merely in sentiment, but in actuality. It is predominantly a community in comprehensive planning; if not, then community planning is a misnomer or intentionally misleading, when attempted in urban areas. Leisure services is itself a comprehensive term to include the wide variety of public and private, commercial or nonprofit, recreational services, pursuits, and facilities that have emerged in this country over the past 25 years. Thus, in urban areas, comprehensive planning by recreation and parks agencies must be taken seriously at two levels: it must seek depth first in the scope of people and institutions involved in planning, and second, in the variety of leisure services represented. Although this book is applicable for comprehensive planning in any size community, the focus is always clearly or implicitly on urban and city-wide planning.

This focus makes sense: this is where the people are. Of our current total population of almost 215 million, the U.S. Bureau of the Census reports that nearly 70 percent live in metropolitan areas. Metropolitan areas are central cities of 300,000 or more, surrounded by incorporated suburbs, with a substantial portion of this workforce commuting into the city daily. Of the 70 percent of the people who live in metropolitan areas, about 32 percent live in the central city itself and 38 percent live in the suburbs. Of the 24 million black Americans in this country, approximately 78 percent live in central cities. As of the 1970 Census, twelve metropolitan areas had populations of over 2 million residents. We must remember that all this metropolitan population, central city and suburb, is concentrated in less than *one* percent of the land area of this country!

Where the people are is where the needs are. Although nonurban communities feel the pinch of tightening municipal budgets for leisure services, it is the cities that suffer the most, for the simple fact that there are more people and a diminished tax base. Most of the people dwelling in the inner city are not there because of the "excitement" of city living; they are there because they have little choice, they are the immobile poor, or those barred from or in flight from suburban living. The greatest slums in our country have flourished, died, or been revived in the central city. Minorities live in tenements or overpriced apartments, artists and dropouts in lofts, the aged in welfare hotels or decrepit neighborhoods. And out of this profusion of people, their recreational needs, and the municipal constraints or incompetence rises the necessity to plan well, that is, comprehensively. In this book the desire and need for comprehensive leisure planning are viewed primarily from the viewpoint of the recreation and parks service, but the concepts are applicable to most other social services concerned with comprehensive delivery of a particular service.

Chapter 1 offers an overview to planning, with emphasis on the dangers of what is termed the spiral-binder approach to planning. This is simply planning that ends at the report stage, a fancy, impressive, forthright report that gathers dust on the shelf. Comprehensive community planning is not a one-step task; it is a continuous activity of which a plan report, fancy or not, is an essential phase, not the culmination. This chapter also discusses the crucial importance of citizen and professional involvement in planning, and the dilemmas such involvement poses for all involved in even the simplest efforts at participatory democracy. Finally, it touches somewhat on the environmental concerns of recreation and parks planning and the more specific social problems of planning for the inner city.

Chapter 2 focuses on the practical administrative and organizational needs for undertaking a comprehensive planning project. Basically, this chapter deals with the structure of the project—who will do what and why—as well as with the formulation of agency policies to guide the planning work, and the need for a public information program to keep the community apprised of what is happening. Planning often takes up to a year or more, and involves not only agency personnel, but often outside professional planners along with a wide array of other professionals and representatives from civic and various social agencies, as well as citizen participants. Some of the problems that arise when such a diverse group attempts to work together with resolutions for some of the more soluble problems, are covered in this chapter. Most importantly, it introduces the procedural model for the comprehensive planning and delivery of leisure services.

Although this model, like most procedural models, guides the planner through a series of clearly perceived steps, it is not truly indicative of the *complexity* and *ambiguity* of much of planning; for instance, it does not include any blank boxes for aspects of planning not yet grappled with or understood, nor do its components reveal the intensity of one area more than another. Even with the use of elaborate graphics, it is difficult for a model that summarizes the steps in an intricate and complex activity to truly reveal the specifics of that activity. Planning is difficult and models are not recipes.

Chapter 3 elaborates on the broad implications of population patterns in this country and their impact on planning. As noted above, the people of this nation are gathered (a kind word) onto one percent of our land; these people are affluent or poor, middling and content, or aspiring for more. They all produce effluence, including the massive industries that employ or serve them. The implications of population on community planning are widespsread and often puzzling. Some attempt is made in this chapter to cover the many viewpoints and controversies which clamor for our attention, as well as to conclude which viewpoints should earn our adherence as *responsible* recreationists.

Chapter 4 discusses the purposes and methods of survey research in a community plan and explains how to conduct an attitude, interest, and opinion survey for planning purposes. Surveys, properly conducted, are one way for a social service agency to study a community and to obtain current information on and responses from community residents. Survey research is a well-known research methodology, and because of its familiarity, most notably through public opinion polls, it can be badly misused. Hopefully, this chapter will at least bring moderation to those who undertake a community survey to aid in planning.

Chapter 5 devotes itself to a detailed discussion of open space, land development, and facilities analysis. It opens with a discussion of conservation, preservation, and recreation, their interrelation and overlap, and then covers methods of acquiring parkland, considerations for design of open space and recreation land, guidelines for planning recreation areas, suggested definitions for recreation areas, standards and their use in land and facility planning, estimating the demand for recreation services, leisure information retrieval systems, and trends in intergovernmental relations.

Chapter 6 concentrates on another important facet of planning— we might even say *the* most important—evaluation of the delivery of leisure systems. Evaluation in this chapter is twofold: it concerns evaluation of existing leisure services in a community, and evaluation of a plan once enacted. Since evaluation is an emergent research methodology, it is important not only that it be incorporated into planning from the very first, but that we realize the importance of carrying out an effective evaluation effort. Like survey research, this technique is not a hit-or-miss affair. It has as precise a methodology as experimentation and experience permit.

Chapter 7 presents a broad overview of the theoretical and practical aspects of the organization and administration of leisure services. This chapter differs from Chapter 2 in that it deals with theories and research on organization and administration rather than with organizing an agency for planning. The topics covered include organization theory and administrative science, personnel administration, board-staff relations in a recreation and parks agency, employee job placement and development, public relations and information programs, and modes of financial administration.

Finally, the volume closes with a glossary of terms on planning leisure services and related topics, and appendices of forms and questionnaires useful for the recreation and parks professional who wishes to undertake a comprehensive leisure services plan for a community.

This book is not intended exclusively for classroom use, but for practitioners and professional planners as well. It is our hope that this volume not only will stimulate interest in comprehensive planning among recreation and parks administrators, but will be of use to other professionals, notably planners in either the public or private sector who develop plans for recreation and park services. If it succeeds in its intention, it will show both the student and the field practitioner, the agency administrator and the academician, that comprehensive planning is the necessary involvement of *all* concerned with planning more livable communities with leisure services worthy of a progressive society.

This book is a result of my responding to hundreds of requests from communities primarily in Illinois, for information concerning the planning and administration of leisure services. For the past seven years, serving as Chief of the Office of Recreation and Park Resources at the University of Illinois, I became involved in many situations related to the planning and administration of leisure services. These gave insights to problems faced by community leaders and professional recreators charged with the responsibility of planning community programs. It is hoped that the information provided in this book will, in some way, assist these individuals in establishing more effective procedures in the planning process.

Acknowledgment is made of the many associations with practitioners in community settings who share with me their successes and problems. These provided reality for the content of the book. I wish also to thank the many departments who furnished photographs and artwork. I extend my appreciation to the authors and publishers who have permitted me to use their work to clarify and strengthen my ideas.

Sincere thanks are extended to my good friend and colleague, A. V. Sapora, who provided motivation and support for this work. Acknowledgment and thanks are also extended to Mary Vance, Head of the City Planning and Architecture Library at the University of Illinois. Her assistance in literature retrieval was above and beyond the call of duty.

Of course no acknowledgment would be complete without recognition of the typists, Connie Shaw, Karen Stayton and Vicki Smith. A special note of thanks is given to Jacque Nigg, who typed the final draft. I am also indebted to Mary Kelly Black for editing the manuscript, providing suggestions for organization and format and compiling the index, and to Teru Uyeyama of Prentice-Hall for her handling of the production. Naturally my students provided much reaction; for this I am grateful.

I wish to extend my love and appreciation to my wife, Ann, and sons, Joe and Peter, for their encouragement and patience with me throughout the development of this text.

JOSEPH J. BANNON

1

OVERVIEW
TO PLANNING PROCESS

*Don't be misled by a fancy report in a colorful spiral binder and
lose sight of the unmet needs which have been articulated on
paper only—another impressive report to grace our bureaucratic
bookshelves with only a printer's or consultant's bill demanding
any real attention.*

INTRODUCTION

In simple terms, planning is the recognition of an existing or anticipated need and the devising of specific steps for fulfilling that need.
The primary motivation for planning, as for problem solving generally,
is sensitivity to and awareness of a particular problem, dissatisfaction
with conditions as they presently are and a desire to change them. Planning should be initiated because of a real need for action in a given
situation. We live in a time when change for change's sake is often considered a virtue. The future beckons us, so we indiscriminately topple
the past in an effort to reach a millennium. An early stage of any plan
is to determine through preliminary examination whether change is
indeed needed. Once a planning administrator is assured of the necessity
for action, then it becomes essential to get everyone else involved.

Planners determine in a formal and detailed way what actions are
necessary to implement a particular leisure service or reach a certain
goal. Short-range plans are used to determine what a community's goal

might be for leisure services, and a long-range plan operates to implement these services. Whatever the type of planning need, the process is ongoing, not completed when a written report is submitted or a model closely followed. A written plan or any procedural model is the framework for action, not the goal.

We are too easily won by the seemingly completed task of a spiral-bound plan report. This situation has been encouraged by federal aid programs, with their stress on report-oriented planning and their insensitivity to how reports become an end in themselves, in essence the project goal. My advice is to throw away the binder and dig into the implications and prescriptions of the report itself. Don't be misled by a fancy report in an attractive binder and lose sight of the unmet needs which have been articulated on paper only—another impressive report to grace our bureaucratic bookshelves with only a printer's or consultant's bill demanding any real attention. Plan reports abound in every aspect of human services; unless they are used as guidelines for development, they are worthless.

How often, after a great deal of effort on a project, have you felt that distressing letdown of "nothing has really changed"? In some cases, elaborate and costly planning is intentionally undertaken as a smoke screen to preclude making any real changes. Of course, it is often difficult to know or admit to this device until the project has ended. Such a practice has to be condemned, or planning becomes purely an administrative game geared to alienate those who are supposed to benefit from it.

Planning usually encompasses everything from initial recognition of a problem to taking an action to solve the problem. Even though the model in this text leaves off at the point of implementation, the planning we propose is what is called *action planning*, not simply the writing of a plan report as the end product, a mere "paper solution" to community development needs.

Planning, to be effective, has to be ongoing. The procedural model in this book is not all-inclusive, but concentrates on the critical initial stages essential for formulating a work plan to determine a leisure services package for a community. This model is *not* a systems approach for determining and implementing leisure services, though it could easily be part of a systems design. Systems models usually entail *implementation* of whatever the plan recommends, *feedback* and follow-up on how the services are working, as well as formal *evaluation* of the plan. Our procedural model resembles systems analysis in most of its components, but is not as refined nor as all-encompassing as a systems approach to problem solving.

The model presented here is an investigative and integrated process for determining what a given community wants, needs, and can have in the way of leisure and recreation services. It is not intended to be a closed system, but offers the essential preliminary planning necessary to get a recommended leisure plan to the point of implementation. Implementation of an acceptable plan requires another model based on this model's recommendations. A written plan using this procedural model, but without a schedule for implementation and evaluation, is destined to be an unused report on a bookshelf. An overall planning or systems approach which might include this procedural model, along with provision for implementation, evaluation, and feedback, is graphically shown in Illustration 1.1.

Although it might be evident to most of us, the need for planning does require some justification. We are constantly bombarded with a multiplicity of stimuli and data which bend toward one conclusion: if any order is to be created out of social confusion, and if we are to avoid past errors, one solution lies in effective planning. Planning can offer one method for alleviating past mistakes, for preventing present mistakes from spreading, and for reducing future errors to some probabilistic minimum.

There has been a tendency not to study planning itself as a process or method, but to concentrate instead on problem-solving or decision-making processes. It is argued that planning is unique for each situation, and that every group of planners encounters different variables and conditions to invalidate any one approach. This is clearly not the case if planning is studied as a tool for coping with different variables and situations. There is much to be gained from studying planning as a tool or process, and there are more similarities among planning experiences than dissimilarities. A knowledge of the "rules" or guidelines for planning does not require a planner to rigidly adhere to them.

The procedural model offered here is a recommended approach to planning, but not the only approach. It is based on experience and research with systems analysis, and with problem-solving and decision-

COMPREHENSIVE PLANNING FLOW

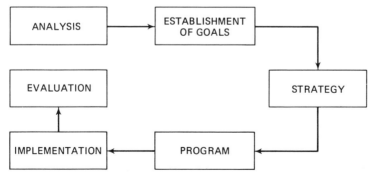

ILLUSTRATION 1.1

making techniques. It has a direct, and I hope a cogent, relation to the experiences of many of us who have employed more informal planning techniques at various levels.

Comprehensive community planning is an attempt by a public agency or organization to involve all those individuals and groups likely to be affected by some contemplated action in the decision making which precedes the action. The essence of such planning is to reflect the basic objectives, values, and desires of a community with regard to, in this case, leisure services. Community comprehensive planning is not merely planning with one agency or one program. It not only involves coordinating federal and state programs, but achieving social, physical, and economic goals at the community level through the participation of national, state, and regional groups, as well as neighborhood residents and special interest and civic groups.

Such a broad-scale philosophy of community planning is comparatively new to recreation and parks, although it has been used in most other human services during the past decade. The impetus for comprehensive community planning generally comes from two sources: (1) a demand from citizens, especially minority groups, that they be involved in all public policy-making decisions and plans which might affect their community or their communal lives; (2) a recognition by communities and municipalities that they must systematically prepare for and design any anticipated alteration in community services, since any modification in a community affects the future of that community.

CITIZEN INVOLVEMENT IN PLANNING

The issue of participation of the poor in our political system has been raised in the most compelling way by black Americans in urban areas. This major demand for reform through participation has had an important impact at all levels of public administration.[1] Citizen involvement in decision making, at the local level especially, flourished during the past decade through the concept of Maximum Feasible Participation [MFP] for the poor. The philosophy of MFP, and all the gradations and variations of it, was increased involvement of citizens in those decisions which affect their lives, primarily decisions made by social service agencies. This philosophy of citizen involvement in decision making had earlier roots in the community development projects undertaken by the United States in underdeveloped countries. It was transferred to domestic programs to permit local residents to get involved in public decisions that directly affected them.

Through the Office of Economic Opportunity (OEO) and its War

[1]Dale Rogers Marshall, "Public Participation and the Politics of Poverty," in Peter Orleans and William Russell Ellis, Jr., eds., *Race, Change, and Urban Society* (Beverly Hills, Calif.: Sage Publications, 1971), pp. 450–82.

on Poverty, this concept developed into a national strategy known as Community Action Programs, funded through the 1964 Economic Opportunity Act (EOA), the Demonstration Cities and Metropolitan Development Act, and the Neighborhood Service Pilot Program.[2] With Title IIA of the Economic Opportunity Act of 1964, Congress sought to involve local residents in programs designed to "break the cycle of poverty." To qualify for 90 percent federal financing of projects, a community had to develop a planning and administration structure known as Community Action Program (CAP).[3] While Title IIA was only one of several titles of the EOA, it is the most well known and controversial, since it strove to involve the poor in planning and implementing programs to attack their own poverty. The inducement to agencies and communities to participate was not any great desire for citizen involvement, but rather the 90 percent federal financing.[4]

When we talk of citizen involvement in community decision making, we primarily mean the poor, minority groups, and lower-class people who have been effectively prevented from having much to say about decisions that affect them. Although comprehensive planning is intended to involve all strata of a community, the above-mentioned groups are the ones most likely to be excluded. Middle-and upper-class whites or powerful minority groups are usually involved in planning through a myriad of connections and interactions with the policy makers, or they are themselves the policy makers. While such involvement is important and laudable, citizen participation in public planning must include *all* citizens,. or planning will become merely another device for continuing to exclude the disenfranchised. One planner has suggested just that: "Contrary to popular mythology, planning did not bring socialism—in fact, it became a sophisticated weapon to maintain control under a mask of rationality, efficiency, and science."[5] And, we might add, under the guise of participation as well.

The Community Action Program's *mandatory* requirement that funded programs enlist the active participation of local citizens in decisions which involved their own welfare sought to blend social action with community development. CAP listed four rationales for this mandatory requirement: (1) it would give citizens a realistic perspective of social services; (2) it would be the foundation of a power base in community affairs; (3) it would develop the unused or latent administrative and social talents of residents; and (4) it would come closer to achieving

[2]Joseph J. Bannon *Outreach: Extending Community Service in Urban Areas* (Springfield, Ill.: Charles C Thomas, Publisher, 1973), p. 39ff for a summary of the history of MFP.

[3]See Public Law 88–452, sec. 202–a, in *Community Action Program Guide* (Washington, D.C.: Office of Economic Opportunity, February 1965).

[4]Ralph M. Kramer and Clare Denton, "Organization of a Community Action Program: A Comparative Case Study," *Social Work*, October 1967, pp. 68–80.

[5]Robert Goodman, *After the Planners* (New York: Simon and Schuster, 1971).

our national creed of participatory democracy. Poverty, as perceived by OEO, was the inability of certain groups to obtain, maintain, and exercise the power vital to effective political involvement.

Paradoxically, although community participation in public decision making has generally been a failure, it has had a profound impact on society in general, and on the poor and the agencies who serve them in particular. It is not our purpose here to determine exactly *why* this concept failed; however, we should stress the importance of making this concept operable for community planning.

Moynihan offers a succinct explanation for the failure of community action programs: The substance of their failure was that CAP expected to use the conflict strategy of Saul Alinsky while also receiving large sums of public money—a sort of cake-and-eat-it objective.[6]

Others believe that OEO did not emphasize citizen participation enough and that little money was provided for self-help at the local level. There was no method or preplan to provide for individual or community growth. Such a method might have offered intensive training programs affecting all levels within all agencies, which would also have developed the ability of personnel to make effective demands on community groups.[7]

As public planners, we have to strive for citizen participation; its impact still reverberates through most aspects of our national life. The failure of CAP is clearly indicative of how radical and refreshing a component of national and community life this philosophy can be. The seed of the concept has taken deep root in many people, and among civic groups and public and private agencies. In fact, it is one of the potentially major political shifts of the generation. It is more than a fad; it speaks right to the heart of control over our own lives, attainment of political power, and the creative use of the skills and talents of our diverse citizenry. It also speaks to the more troublesome matter of relinquishing power or sharing it with those who have none. It will not be easy. For comprehensive planning to be effective, and not be a mere diversionary tactic as Goodman suggests it can be, the involvement of citizens has to be substantive.

Although community action projects often involved creating and funding neighborhood corporations directly, in recreation and parks such participation is likely to be through community policy groups or through citizen members of park-board planning committees. A literature review of the Maximum Feasible Participation experience indicates a preference for thinking of citizens as "community policy boards" rather than simply "advisory groups," because citizen participation is meant

[6]Daniel P. Moynihan, *Maximum Feasible Misunderstanding: Community Action in the War on Poverty* (New York: The Free Press, 1969).

[7]David Borden, "Participation on the Block," in Edgar S. Cahn and Barry A. Passett, eds., *Citizen Participation: Effecting Community Change* (New York: Praeger Publishers, Inc., 1971), pp. 184–99.

to be more than advice-giving: citizen groups or boards should have clear policy-making power on those issues which affect community residents.

The Model Cities program experienced a problem which is no doubt indicative of citizen participation in general. In each program, responsibilities were shared between a city administration and an elected citizens' group—the citizens to approve policy, the administration to carry it out. The theory behind this was that local residents knew their needs best; however, there were difficulties:

> Being elected representatives from a target neighborhood, they tended to favor visible, quick projects like rehabilitation or construction. Agreement between citizens' board and the city administration was not easy to reach. The poorer, less educated citizen often resented the city hall professionals. Moreover a board of 12 to 20 laymen meeting infrequently and at night cannot help but impede efficiency. Typically, the laymen tended to leap from a visible need to a program idea without regard to the need of intervening planning or budgeting. However valuable the citizens' groups, there is no doubt they got on the nerves of results-oriented administrators.[8]

Another problem with citizen boards is that often the so-called "representatives of the poor" are actually middle-class neighborhood politicians or their carefully selected "community leaders" who out-maneuver the poor for positions on these boards.[9] The War on Poverty has given rise to professional poverty workers of all sorts, a lot of them "free-lance" types who become quite effective at putting themselves in the center of any action remotely related to "power to the people." While there is no sure way of detecting and preventing such misrepresentation, it is something we have all seen and must be alert to.

While such misrepresentation can be a potential outrage to the concept of citizen participation, we must not forget the larger outrage which denies power to various groups in the first place. We should not malign the idea because it can easily be abused. Those who keep decision-making power exclusively to themselves will always be the far greater threat. It is important not to lose sight of relative abuses when we judge the value of any planning concept.

Citizen participation in planning, when those citizens are middle class and white, does not ensure good social planning. Such planning only manages to reinforce the old private-interest zoning patterns; for instance, the new planned city of Irvine, California, "is a social scandal—an all white, upper-middle-class enclave. It is exactly the sort of project that

---

[8]Dudley Post, "The End Comes Too Soon: Requiem for Model Cities," *The New Republic*, April 14, 1973, p. 14.

[9]Irving Lazar, "Which Citizens to Participate in What?" in Cahn and Passett, *Citizen Participation*, pp. 92–109. Also Frances Fox Piven, "Whom Does the Advocate Planner Serve?" *Social Policy*, May–June 1970, pp. 32–37.

at once shows the high potential of the new metropolis and its bigoted, class-bound failure to realize that potential."[10]

An attempt at broad involvement in community planning was recently reported by the New York City Planning Commission, who invited "350 representatives of civic groups, architectural firms, developers, financial institutions and officials at all levels of government to the first comprehensive planning workshop on neighborhood preservation."[11] This workshop discussed the $45 million budgeted by the Commission to prevent the deterioration of five residential neighborhoods in "once-flourishing sections" of the city. The workshop is part of a decentralization effort throughout the city's municipal services to open up the planning process to residents affected by the Commission's actions. It is too soon to judge how successful the Commission's apparently sincere effort to involve local residents and other groups will be, but the attempt is what interests us.

It is difficult to involve people other than planning professionals and officials in any substantive way. Certain people are excluded from decision making for several reasons: (1) through oversight or ignorance by professionals; (2) because they have elected or selected another to proxy for them; or (3) because they are intentionally denied power and control over some aspect of their lives. There are certainly other reasons, subreasons of these if you will, but generally these three represent the spectrum. As recreation planners, we have to confront all three. The first is the easiest to resolve: we simply *begin* the process of inviting and seeking those local groups and individuals who have not participated before. The second and third reasons are where we face difficulty, resistance, or outright threats.

It is not my intention to lightly recommend "citizen participation in planning" without acknowledging how impossible a goal this can often be. Unless we want to be hypocritical in our aims, we will have to examine very closely the stakes involved in the truly radical notion of citizen participation. Participatory democracy is very, very powerful in concept, and that is why a veritable labyrinth of diversions to this goal have been and will be created by those with power.

If we seek citizen participation in the planning of leisure services—and I believe it a vital need—then we have to get more than a "warm body" from the community on the planning committee. Too many poverty corporations and programs have had community representatives either whom the community never heard of or whom they considered incompetent.

Finally, a major task of a planner is to keep the desire for action

[10]Sam Bass Warner, Jr., *The Urban Wilderness* (New York: Harper & Row, Publishers, 1972).

[11]Glenn Fowler, "Residents Advise City on Housing," *The New York Times*, December 9, 1973, p. 40.

prominent in the minds of citizens, while working through the less exciting and more exacting aspects of formal planning:

> Two interrelated factors are necessary in any successful process of working-through of group problems.... The necessaries are a group with a problem severe and painful enough for its members to wish to do something about it; but also of a sufficient cohesion of purpose, or morale, to render them capable of tackling it and of seeking and tolerating necessary changes.[12]

HUMAN BEHAVIOR AND PLANNING

Any professional planner who desires to reflect the impact of people in a plan must try to learn as much as possible about people and organizations, especially human needs and desires for leisure and for community involvement. Comprehensive planning, while seeking the involvement of a wide array of people, often simplifies the human element—the inscrutable and unpredictable behavior of people involved in any plan no matter how well devised. Any systematic plan for leisure services must recognize and reduce the mistakes others have made in designing comprehensive planning models which simplify human motivations or which overlook certain people. Of course, this is more easily said than done, especially when planners seek to involve community residents in deciding what comprehensive leisure services to offer. In addition to the problems of staff behavior, a planner is now confronted with the behaviors of community residents.

When we begin to deal with community residents, either as participants in formulating a leisure services plan or as those for whom the services are being designed, it is essential to perceive people *as* people, not as humanoids or as statistics. Indeed, how often have we heard people discussed as objects, whether with scorn or benevolence, as things or numbers? A doctor coming onto a ward looking for "the foot" or the "the head" that has just been admitted may be an excellent doctor, but the *total* person requires consideration and recognition, not merely an injured part. As recreators, we often commit a comparable offense by perceiving those we serve as lumpen citizens who should be delighted and responsive to what we decide to offer them—the professional-knows-best arrogance.

Human behavior research is replete with wisdom and with dead ends. Not only should we be able to discern what is useful in the behavioral and social sciences, or in humanistic psychology in particular, we should also systematically determine what the recreation needs and

---

[12]Jacques Elliot, *The Changing Culture of a Factory* (London: Tavistock Publications, 1951), p. 310.

desires of a community's residents are. Since we are professionally trained to know what to offer in the way of leisure services and how to offer them, it will be difficult to pause and reflect about the "nonprofessional" recipient of these services. In fact, the word recipient is part of the difficulty: one who receives a social service does not necessarily benefit from that service.

The best example of this distinction is one given by Charles Hamilton, Professor of Government and Urban Political Science at Columbia University (also co-author with Stokely Carmichael[13]). Professor Hamilton makes a clear and critical distinction between welfare recipients and welfare beneficiaries. In a talk given at the University of Illinois in spring 1973, Dr. Hamilton defined as a class of welfare beneficiaries those landlords and others who receive money from welfare recipients for goods and services. For instance, Dr. Hamilton indicated that in housing alone, approximately $329 million in New York City annually goes to pay rent for welfare recipients, mostly for substandard housing. These recipients, Dr. Hamilton further argues, are merely a *conduit* for funds from federal and state administrators ("colonial administrators") to slumlords and welfare-hotel owners, who obtain "venture capital" from recipients' subsistence incomes.

Professionals in the human services are perpetually puzzled about how to ensure that those for whom services are intended receive them. Now Dr. Hamilton introduces the unnerving suggestion that receipt of a service is far from the goal. It didn't require the insights of the Association of Black Social Workers to tell city officials what was wrong with guaranteeing housing subsidies to pay for inhuman housing; any welfare recipient could tell any planning committee within moments what was missing: the right of the poor to have something to say about their own life has been systematically denied.

Another example, a bit afield, but also indicative of differences between receiving something and benefiting from it, has to do with truck drivers. A stoppage of trucks on some of our nation's highways in the winter of 1973, to protest the so-called "energy crisis," actually opened a Pandora's box of grievances by drivers. As recipients of one of the highest blue-collar wages in the country, truck drivers argue they have few of the benefits that accrue to others with comparable or even lower incomes. In addition to being the butt of innumerable jokes and insults, drivers claim they are unable to obtain loans or credit easily, are treated as beneath most other blue-collar workers and, as one driver said, they get the scruffiest-looking waitresses in out-of-the-way truck stops to serve their meals! What is sad about this issue is that no one had asked truck drivers what their gripes were. Their complaints about reduced fuel and high gasoline prices were only symptoms of a more pervasive

13Charles V. Hamilton and Stokely Carmichael, *Black Power: The Politics of Liberation* (New York: Random House, 1967).

discontent. Union leaders rarely reflect their constituencies, and this outburst by drivers further emphasizes the need to work directly with those affected by whatever we are planning to offer.

The need for comprehensive planning in recreation and parks is most pressing because of the central role leisure is assuming in the lives of many Americans. As a nation, we are undergoing profound change: our discretionary time is increasing, the traditional work ethic has lost much of its ability to stimulate personal development and interpersonal relations, and employment and mobility have put strains on family and community ties. Many feel a strong need for a sense of individual identity and self-worth which is no longer supplied by work. A growing number of people feel trapped in unfulfilling, repetitive jobs and feel dehumanized by their workplace, invariably becoming dissatisfied with themselves and their lives.

In the past, people found personal satisfaction in their work. However, for many people the work ethic no longer suffices, and for others, such as the aged, youth, minority groups, and some handicapped persons, it has little meaning at all. Yet we have not evolved any complementary leisure ethics to meet a deep and basic need for challenge, creativity, and commitment. We are uniformly uneducated in how to use discretionary time: our education has been primarily for work.

Some people experience personal and collective guilt with the increased leisure available to them, plus considerable social and peer pressure to make "constructive" use of their free time. Constructive, of course, is defined as productive; inactivity and nonproductivity are not sanctioned as being equally essential to mental and physical well-being. We are told, play hard as you once worked hard.

The term "recreation" is beginning to refer to all the things people do that involve use of discretionary time. It is not simply outdoor or indoor recreation, not merely fun and games; those terms connote facility-oriented activities. There are other kinds of recreation, involving museums, libraries, cultural and performing arts, crafts, volunteer work, nonschool or nondegree education, or various forms of meditation. These forms of recreation are rarely considered in leisure planning. A comprehensive approach must include educational, cultural, and esthetic aspects as part of the overall leisure needs of people.

Illustration 1.2 offers a simple model of one method for determining what a community's citizens—all of them—want in the way of leisure services. As shown in this illustration, we have to examine the connection between a person's preferences for leisure activities and the values that underlie such preferences. These values, which are labeled in Illustration 1.2 as a *leisure ethic*, are intrinsic to a person's selection of leisure pursuits. The leisure ethic is not simply the obverse of a work ethic, it is a component of it. For most of us, leisure activities are what we do in the time free from work and other duties.

Of course, other broader values comprise a leisure ethic. In this

HUMAN BEHAVIOR
RECREATION NEEDS AND DESIRES

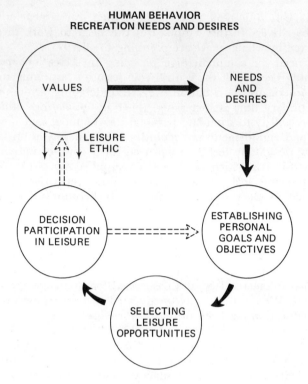

ILLUSTRATION 1.2

book, however, we are not so much interested in the etiology of a leisure ethic (though that in itself is a fascinating subject) as we are in the impact of any leisure ethic on the needs and wants of people for leisure pursuits, and on their decision to participate in leisure activities. As our work ethic shifts from the view that hard work is necessary for fulfillment of physical and emotional needs, to a more ambiguous viewpoint, so too any leisure ethic reshapes itself. While there are, of course, many attitudes toward work and leisure, we tend to generalize about American attitudes toward work and play. While such generalizations have a seed of truth, we should be careful about generalized policies emanating from these assumptions. That is, we should determine what various community groups hold as a general leisure ethic.

Forced leisure from unemployment or underemployment is becoming a part of many Americans' lives; heretofore it had been confined to the poor, minorities, handicapped, women, and the like. Walter Heller, chairman of the Council of Economic Advisors under President Kennedy, recently commented on the probable impact of the energy shortage on employment. Professor Heller, who is presently Regents Professor of Economics at the University of Minnesota, said in a 1975 radio interview that he did not see how unemployment could ever be kept below 6 percent because of anticipated reverberations from the energy shortage. For many groups the figure is already higher and could soar.

Although it is difficult to treat these speculations as predictions, we need to recognize the likelihood of such "free" time becoming a way of life for more Americans. Thus, a change in economic realities forces a shift in work and leisure ethics; these ethics are not immutable foundations of our culture. Other economists suggest that our economic status and options determine our views and behaviors in most activities much more than any so-called "instinct." That is, the economic realities of a person's experiences are deeply entwined in their decisions to engage in leisure pursuits and the kind of lesiure they prefer. For example, if someone used to a limited income and hard labor gains "free time" through unemployment, he or she is rarely prepared in any sense to enjoy that leisure, because of a harsh and limiting economic history.

If we impose our leisure ethic—of free time away from labor as deserved and enjoyable—then we will misunderstand the cause of leisure for many people in a depressed economy and insult them in the process. If free time is not *free* of guilt, discomfort, anxiety about survival, or a broader concern for the fate of a culture, then throwing a ball around a court might not be a true leisure need or want. Even with people who are fully and enjoyably employed, there is little sense in imposing a presumptive leisure ethic on them.

If our economy continues in its precipitous recession, there is a good possibility that our seemingly abandoned work ethic could re-surface in a more virulent form as people become overly grateful for jobs, much as in the Depression. Americans have deep puritanical and economic drives, so we should beware of any facile theorizing about how we are entering an age of expanding leisure. Cut off the power and we'll be re-entering an age of barbarism soon enough.

Lack of employment is not leisure; the latter presupposes some degree of release and contentment for its enjoyment. The only way such "free" time can be reinterpreted as leisure is through reshaping the national idea about labor and nonlabor; such is the task of the ideologues—and likely it is already underway, and it may be easier than we think if it serves national policy.

In any event, when we are attempting to elicit ideas about a community's leisure needs we do have to scrutinize the responses we receive. Surface responses to basic questions are often not indicative of deeper values and needs. Discovering these may require some probing, and that is where a good grasp of behavioral and social sciences can be quite useful. For example, community residents might suggest more play-grounds—these make a community look more leisurely, more socially conscious—when in actuality they may crave more demanding activities for children, more "constructive" programs rather than the transporting joy of a good ride on the swings. If residents, when probed further, actually prefer an arts and crafts program for children or a mobile library, do we come along and banter about the fun kids have on swings?

If there is conflict of values, the residents must predominate, for it is their community. If, as professionals, we feel they have been misled by a fad or fashion to want some facility or program we believe to be dubious, then we should struggle for supremacy on that issue. Professionals should not be self-effacing servants to a community, but on the other hand they should not impose their ideas unless called on for that express purpose. It is easy to visualize communities that do not wish to participate in planning leisure services. They expect and pay professionals to do it for them. It is then up to the professional to decide how much they are able to do alone. A professional planner can certainly *demand* participation in such cases.

Once we have established the *personal* goals and objectives of leisure services—developed out of definition of a community's leisure needs and desires—then we have to select various leisure opportunities that satisfy those goals (see Illustration 1.2). Often the goals and objectives are themselves specific leisure services, so this aspect of our method may not be a separate step. Finally, as shown in the illustration, the decision to participate in leisure activities is related to a leisure ethic for reasons already discussed.

This process is one way to identify the basic values which underlie the availability and demand for leisure services. As planners, we need to understand the leisure ethic (or ethics) which stimulate various recreation demands in a community. Once this ethic is specified, (1) the definition of particular desires and needs, (2) the statement of goals and objectives, (3) the selection among various leisure options to meet these goals and objectives, and (4) the choice of a specific leisure service or services should be based as much as feasible on current knowledge of human behavior. Illustration 1.2 offers one method for discovering these human needs.

Public recreation and park officials may soon find themselves as managers and operators of comprehensive leisure services. It is certainly conceivable that a community, through its department of recreation and parks, will own lands far from the central city. Rapid transit can provide fast and efficient transportation to these areas of recreation and leisure at a reasonable cost and at a price that most may be willing to pay. For this reason, the future recreation and park director will exercise greater control over human behavior and leisure experiences.

BROAD INVOLVEMENT IN PLANNING

In addition to citizen participation in planning, we need to involve a great many other groups and individuals as well. These are shown in Illustration 1.3. The vital importance of involvement and coordination

INVOLVEMENT IN THE PLANNING PROCESS

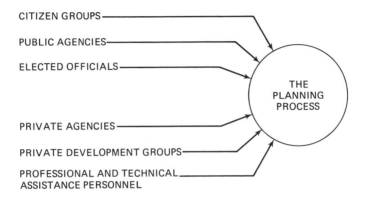

CITIZEN GROUPS

PUBLIC AGENCIES

ELECTED OFFICIALS

PRIVATE AGENCIES

PRIVATE DEVELOPMENT GROUPS

PROFESSIONAL AND TECHNICAL ASSISTANCE PERSONNEL

THE PLANNING PROCESS

ILLUSTRATION 1.3

among professionals, laymen, private and public agencies, as well as community and city officials, cannot be overemphasized. Of course, it is one thing to graphically outline a necessary aspect of planning; it is quite another to achieve and sustain it.

Interdisciplinary coordination among professionals is an essential ingredient for a successful plan. In addition to coordination, professional respect and cooperation are needed. Because of specialization and the departmentalization of disciplines, professionals can often get into squabbles or build up resentments. All sorts of conflicts can arise between professionals of different persuasions, so it is best to be prepared for these.

Goodman notes that at the onset of urban renewal, many architects became "urban designers" and "city planners" overnight.[14] Many planners are recognized not only through professional affiliations but through membership in the American Institute of Planners. There are others who do not have such credentials—elected officials, planning board members, department heads, budget officers, civic leaders, and community representatives. This lack of certification does not necessarily mean lack of skill.

While all professionals who move into planning are far from charlatans, it is easy to conceive of planning so narrowly or so simply that the results are the same. Charlatanism and incompetence are not very different. It is, therefore, important to discern conflicts between the precepts of each discipline and conflicts that arise over sloppy planning. You do not criticize, say, a sociologist merely for a heavy reliance on sociological concepts—that is why he or she is on a planning board in the first place—but you most assuredly take any professionals to task for incompetence as planners, regardless of their discipline.

[14]Goodman, *After the Planners.*

The administrator or official responsible for planning community leisure services requires the expertise of many professionals outside recreation and parks; planning such services can no longer be the insular concern of recreation and parks specialists. A community planner needs to draw on the accumulated knowledge of planning from other professions, most notably urban and regional planning, where most planning of the type we are concerned with occurs. Illustration 1.4 indicates various professionals who should be involved or reflected in planning leisure services.

A basic problem which can develop with planning committees stems from the sudden juxtaposition of professional and layman as co-workers. Having community residents, professionals, and private groups and agencies serve on a planning committee will *not* suffice if the professionals assume a distance from the laymen. Such artificial distance only amplifies the suspicion many citizens, especially minority groups, have of public officials and professional planners. Professionals should become participants in the planning process rather than outside experts for cultural change.[15]

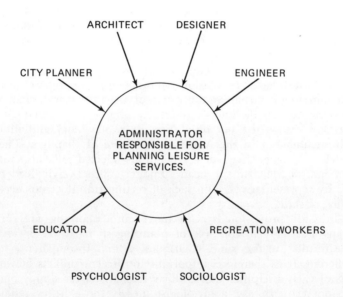

PHYSICAL RESOURCES

ARCHITECT   DESIGNER

CITY PLANNER   ENGINEER

ADMINISTRATOR RESPONSIBLE FOR PLANNING LEISURE SERVICES.

EDUCATOR   RECREATION WORKERS

PSYCHOLOGIST   SOCIOLOGIST

HUMAN RESOURCES

ILLUSTRATION 1.4

[15]Ibid.

This is not to simplify or ignore the difficulties encountered with informal policies like Maximum Feasible Participation. However, false professionalism is one thing professionals can do something about. It is by no means *the* decisive factor in group planning, but is indicative of the many obstacles encountered by community groups trying to obtain and maintain some power over their daily existence. Professional distance has a dual effect: it not only denies laymen access to professional skills, it insulates professionals from the often-perceptive criticisms of their discipline by nonprofessionals. The latter is an advantage that will not be lightly relinquished, but it has to be if joint planning committees are to be more than farcical.

The almost instinctive objection to reducing professional distance in such planning groups is that one is sloppily equating professional expertise with laymen's insights; that is, in a desire for a semblance of participatory democracy one is willing to risk the rigor necessary to any profession. This objection is certainly valid. How to meld professional and layman skills continues to be a dilemma in most attempts at citizen involvement in social planning. There are those who concentrate on this aspect of community planning as the prime dilemma: how to resolve the obvious conflict between a desire to involve community residents in a professional endeavor and the all-too-pervasive uncertainties and disabilities of citizens engaging in such activities.

There is a real threat to professionalism in participatory democracy; one might even say these are incompatible aims. If someone has had a great deal of training in a field and has been told that a professional attitude and respect from nonprofessionals are implied rewards of training, then it is no doubt difficult to thrust off the false attributes of professionalism. If distance from nonprofessionals is merely protective—so one is not confused with or rudely approached by "the people"—it is a false attribute. On the other hand, if a professional acts like one of the boys, slurring over differences in training and background, this is just as artificial and equally insulting to nonprofessionals.

Any person can respect your knowledge if you are approachable, considerate and reflective of criticism, and willing to readjust any false aspects of a professional attitude or of inapplicable knowledge. It is unfortunate that various professions inculcate these false attributes, some even offering courses on such attitudes under the guise of professional ethics.

Since this is a book for professionals, it will not get into the negative attitudes of nonprofessionals, especially the Philistine who feels anything that smacks of the academy is *prima facie* suspect. However, let us not forget that often the most conventional, the supreme Philistine of narrow imagination, can be safely lodged behind a professional title.

To criticize a professional for all sorts of nonsense and quackery is no easy matter and rarely successful. On the other hand, issuing primers on decision making and planning to a community does not make planners of amateurs. The simple fact is that you do not create expert planners by the free distribution of little booklets on "Community Planning For Everyman." Participation in planning, without some qualifications on what is *expected* of the expert and what is *hoped for* from citizen groups through some training program, is foolish, even dangerous. Each group has different functions which might shift and change as planning goes through its various stages, but there is no reversal of roles or some egalitarian blending of skills of a nondistinctive sort.

Although some recognition is given to private leisure planning, recreation planners usually ignore private leisure planning. The investment of large amounts of capital in campgrounds, golf courses, amusement areas, recreation vehicles, and ski areas are examples of how industry, private investors, or what are now called "leisure time entrepreneurs," are creating and meeting a variety of demands in recreation and leisure.

It has been suggested that recreation activities may be one aspect of our national life to suffer disproportionately from the energy shortage. Fuel and energy are deemed wasteful for leisure pursuits in view of their necessity for more important needs. If the demand for recreation does diminish, especially in the private sector, good planning by public agencies now can help to coordinate the response of the wide-ranging leisure industry and recreation profession to this anticipated slackening. If people do not use their autos to drive to a private resort, or no longer use power-driven recreation vehicles, these same people are likely to turn to public recreation resources in their own community. The recreation and parks profession has virtually ignored the growth of the private leisure industry, letting each tend his own garden. This doesn't make sense. It is especially wasteful and foolish if we wish to conserve energy. Good planning, with all involved, can be the first step.

ECOLOGY AND PLANNING

When any decision is made on the use of a community's land—whether for commercial, private, or public use—the future community is being shaped for a long time, and so recreation planning, or any planning for that matter, is more crucial. If these decisions are disparate, arbitrary, and not integrated, the chances for a community to reflect some foresight and creativity in its development are slim.

The overall objective of any leisure plan is to add to the total welfare of a community, not to enhance leisure services in a social vacuum. Although the focus of a plan will remain on leisure services, the planners have to be aware of the broader ecology of a community. The physical, social, and economic aspects of community life must be viewed as a total organism inseparable from any one aspect of community development. It is the function of planners to provide the insight *and* prevision for comprehending this totality.

While most recreation and park specialists acknowledge the importance of perceiving recreation and leisure services within a broader ecological framework, too often this recognition is superficial or naive. If this recognition is not reflected in the planning base of leisure services, such services will be determined by others outside our profession. Not only will other professionals solve recreation and leisure problems, they will be the first to recognize and define our problems as well. This is already happening, for instance, with economists.

The rapid increase in the demand for leisure services, brought about by growth in population, leisure time, income, and increased mobility and urbanization, has developed widespread interest in resource allocations:

> When we speak of environmental aspects in parks and recreation demand, we are basically talking about the purity of air and public waters; preserving the variety and vitality of natural landscapes, their fauna and flora; and ensuring the existence of certain other natural features, such as wildlife areas, beaches, even swamps, bogs, and marshes, as well as the critical issue of land use in general.[16]

Land use is a major issue in this country today. We would have to have our heads in the sand to be uninformed about the enormous political and private machinations that are going on about land use:

> An important battle that has attracted too little national attention is being fought in Congress over the future use of this country's remaining undeveloped land. Lobbyists for land developers, the National Association of Realtors and the U.S. Chamber of Commerce, are working hard . . . to kill or cripple a bill [by Senator Henry M. Jackson] that would push the fifty states to take over regulation of major land uses within their borders.[17]

Although the broad implications of land use to recreation and parks are covered in Chapter 5, it is mentioned here as one of the major resources recreators are concerned with in any ecological discussion. A classic book on the design of more livable communities, and the political context in which community planners operate, had as its premise that human needs should govern the planning of communities, not the needs of real estate developers and corporations.[18]

Environmental economists interested in amenity rights—our right to clean air and water, privacy and quiet—are seriously working on demand models for outdoor recreation, models that seek to determine the value

[16]*Illinois Association of Park Districts: A Prospectus for Tomorrow.* Report on the Purpose, Program, and Organization of the IAPD (Champaign: Office of Recreation and Park Resources, University of Illinois, October 1973), p. 13.

[17]Leonard Downie, Jr., "National Land Use: A Move to Save What Is Left," *The Nation,* December 17, 1973, p. 649.

[18]Percival and Paul Goodman, *Communitas—Means of Livelihood and Ways of Life,* 2nd rev. ed. (New York: Vintage, 1960).

of water-based recreation vis-à-vis other uses of water. To such economists, if a waterway is partially polluted and does not attract much recreational use, then its *relative* value to a community might be to allow pollution to continue rather than to "save" the water. This is especially so when another waterway might be totally relieved of pollutants that are diverted instead to an already polluted lake or river. In the past, pollution was considered needless and irresponsible; now it is likely to be planned for and intentional.

Amenities are those natural resources or stimuli which bring on "feelings of comfort, pleasure, or joy...."[19] Using Maslow's hierarchy-of-needs concept, amenities often satisfy basic needs of survival, safety, and security as well as higher-level satisfactions of comfort, joy, or pleasure.[20] For instance, we need air to breath, but we also require fresh air and expansive skies to achieve a feeling of intensity, of joy. We can see that economists and others studying environmental quality are deeply involved in matters of pertinence and value to the recreation profession.

The point of this discussion is not that recreation professionals should become economists, or seek to usurp the demand models from economists; it is that we must be aware not only of the findings and researches of economists and other environmental specialists, but of why they have undertaken such broad-based studies. Their viewpoint is beyond recreation and leisure, naturally, but since our profession is now encompassed by these other fields, it behooves us to at least know what is going on. Merely talking about environmental concerns, while other professions directly concern themselves with matters intrinsic to the provision of leisure services, is a waste of time on our part. While it may not be the concern of recreation professionals to determine the relative cost-effectiveness of land and water resources, or to present theoretical arguments for amenity rights, it is the concern of our profession to understand how such cost-benefit and amenities judgments affect recreation.

Few Americans are happy with the physical environment they see developing around them. We have only to get into our cars or to take a walk to see places that make us shudder with distaste and helplessness: Where did that hamburger stand come from? Who allowed the parking lot takeover of downtown? Even a person who is fortunate to have a

---

19Arthur A. Atkinson and Ira M. Robinson, "Amenity Resources for Urban Living," in Harvey S. Perloff, ed., *The Quality of the Urban Environment: Essays on "New Resources" in an Urban Age* (Baltimore: Johns Hopkins Press, 1969), p. 183.

20A. H. Maslow, *Motivation and Personality* (New York: Harper & Row, Publishers, 1964). Maslow suggests that people's motives can be seen as an ascending hierarchy from lower-level needs for survival, safety, and security to higher-level needs for self-actualization. Once lower-level needs are satisfied, higher-level ones are valued more. Resources that are threatened affect all levels of needs, high and low—dirty air, for instance.

hideaway in fairly attractive surroundings has to travel occasionally to other localities which quickly threaten the esthetic and physical well-being obtained in the hideaway.

A drive on the Los Angeles expressway exposes one to gaudy signs, junk yards, pollution from jetliners, and literally hundreds of cars waiting to exit. Who were the planners who created this diabolical mess? Remember Los Angeles is a *planned* city: it remains an "outstanding example of regional and national planning." Yet this city, according to Warner, is no better than most cities when it comes to racial discrimination, segregation, and disadvantages for its poor."[21] Warner's book not only is a strong plea for more planning, but offers a good discussion of past national planning—mostly a disgrace—and of our potential as planners, if we learn from the past.

It would be difficult to find much disagreement with the fact that our cities and communities are becoming uninhabitable. Ironically, this is happening at a time when the importance of communities is vital, as more intimate family ties loosen and people seek leisure fulfillment in nonfamily pursuits. Also, it would be difficult to find a more suitable place than a community to serve as a center of business, cultural, and social activity. In every way community life is vitiated and repudiated by a lack of *comprehensive* planning.

In a midwest campus town a high-rise building was constructed with almost total disregard of those affected by it. It was discovered after this 21-floor structure had been built that a zoning permit had never been obtained! In addition to disrupting the skyline of the campus area, which had been graced by one-storied Georgian buildings, the building blocks the sunrise for an adjacent neighborhood. The birds have left or behave erratically; the building's floodlights and lack of a distinct sunrise confuse daylight and twilight for them.

Astronaut Joe Engle once described the beauty of his 240,000-mile trip to the moon. He did *not* describe the beauty of the moon—its mountains, craters, or the soft landing of the spaceship with its precision and accuracy. Instead he described the beauty of the earth as he looked back—its sparkling lights, land contours, waterways, the movement of various land-launched satellites in its ionosphere. There was much on the earth he did not describe—polluted rivers, massive concrete cities, poverty—all the problems we have seen for decades. As planners, we cannot afford the perspective of the astronaut, no matter how lyrical; it obscures the realities of life on our "spaceship earth." We have a lovely country that is being destroyed by ruinous attempts to have it yield its resources to the greed of the moment.

Even though many Americans feel that poor planning or no planning is a prime cause of the ugliness around them, Illustration 1.5 shows one situation where such agreement would not necessarily prevent

[21]Warner, *The Urban Wilderness.*

ILLUSTRATION 1.5

ruinous community development. In June 1962 the Recreation Commission of Leonia, New Jersey, recommended that Highwood Hills, an undeveloped hilly wooded area of about 14 acres, be retained and dedicated as a park, rather than zoned for residential development. The intrinsic value of this area was not that Leonia needed another park, but that this was a wild, natural area in the midst of an otherwise highly developed area, not far from New York City and Palisades Park, New Jersey, with a busy highway nearby. This wood offered a unique opportunity for Leonia and nearby residents to enjoy what is now a luxury long lost to most Americans—wilderness.

An independent citizens' committee was quickly formed to save Highwood Hills; the local government with few exceptions did not see the value of retaining this rare and unusual site even though most of it was borough-owned property. The mayor and council told the citizens' group that the burden of proof was on them, that they had to demonstrate interest and use for Highwood Hills. Despite what seemed self-evident to the citizens' group, and what had received lip service from borough officials and other "ecology lovers," conservation and preservation of unique, natural settings were not prime values to all community residents, particularly not to those interested in generating a high tax return from such lucrative property.

The principal objections to preserving Highwood Hills, coming from the town government, business groups, and private citizens interested in stimulating residential development, were that nobody was interested in going to such a place, that it was not beautiful (wilderness is not sculptured or neat), that it was simply too good a tax ratable to pass by, and that Leonia already had plenty of recreation facilities. In other words, Leonia didn't need Highwood Hills, so it could be destroyed. Point by point, the citizens' group protested each objection by offering contrary information or enlightenment. They were especially surprised to learn that many people considered a wilderness messy or ugly, and had to familiarize Leonia residents with the often disheveled charms of nature. Leonia, a small residential town, had so lost a taste for wilderness that it had to be re-educated to its transcendent beauty and value.

A 1963 economic study of the area by professional planners, in response to the tax-ratable argument—in reality the prime objection—indicated that private-home development of Highwood Hills *might* bring a small net income to the town, but this was far outweighed by the property's future "intangible" value to the town as a permanent park. The question, therefore, should not be one of income but of priority; what is more important, increasing the tax base of a town or preserving a unique area for present and future residents? A Master Plan drawn up by the town government in January 1966 offered to save two to three acres of Highwood Hills for park purposes, but with the remainder zoned for residential development. This compromise, since it flew in the face of the conservation argument, was clearly unacceptable to the citizens' group, and they continued their fight to preserve the entire tract.

After almost ten years, the Borough Council of Leonia agreed to preserve the 14-acre tract in its entirety as a park, as well as to buy some adjacent privately owned acreage to increase the park's domain. This citizens' group was successful because of the interest they alone had sustained over a decade to preserve the area. They had the prevision so essential to balanced community development—and the tenacity to fight until they had convinced enough Leonia residents and politicians that preservation of Highwood Hills as an "endangered" resource was indeed in the best interests of the present and future community life.

These few examples, while perhaps more outrageous than others, are painfully familiar to anyone who has lived in this country for the past few decades. American cities are ugly, and a great deal of their ugliness stems from lack of imagination, from individual and corporate greed, distorted value systems, and a remarkable absence of any systematic planning at the local or national levels.

Although there is not necessarily a correlation between lack of social planning and mental health, still the pervasive ugliness of our environment is a legitimate concern for those involved in improving psychological well-being:

> The gaudy and garish commercial areas of our cities are a disgrace to a supposedly civilized people.... If the mental health and social well-being of our civilization are to survive, we must do a better job of community organization. If our communities are not to be bankrupted by

wasteful and uncoordinated development, we must have practical plans for the future; if we are not to be overwhelmed by man-made ugliness, we must see to it that our plans work.[22]

In 1970 the Citizens' Advisory Committee on Environmental Action published a booklet entitled *Community Action for Environmental Quality*, which gave practical advice on how citizens might save or enhance their environments. This same group more recently published seven case studies of citizens who were successful in their strategies:

> They [the case studies] reflect the wide diversity of recent citizen action, at the local level or even greater in scope, which has reaped substantial benefits for the environment. Determination, perseverance, and imagination run as a common theme through each story, whether a struggle to save a mountain or a park, a harbor or a river, or the air from filth and noise. While prospects for success were often bleak indeed, with individuals pitted against organizational giants and opponents with immeasurable resources, citizens did in the end make the difference.[23]

What is disturbing about all these case studies, and that of Leonia, is their similarity: people against power, forces that wish to malign the environment for profit rather than preserve it for ecological and communal survival. While it must give an enormous sense of achievement to win these fights, some of which often drag on longer than the ten-year Leonia resistance, still the question arises as to why we are pitted against such powerful forces time after time. Why do we avoid analysis of who controls these resources, or has the power to affect them, and repeatedly pit ourselves against "opponents with immeasurable resources"?

The lesson of these case studies is not that citizens can win, but why did they have to fight alone against almost insuperable odds? As each new environmental issue arises, another citizens' group has to arise to combat destructive interests. Although these groups have much to learn from earlier groups, they are still weak. Even with national or international support, if the interests of business or what are deemed broader national interests are jeopardized, the citizens' groups are virtually helpless. A good example of this was the recent Alaska pipeline controversy, or the head-on collision of ecology and the energy crisis:

> ... with national survival said to be on the line, environmental quality goes to the wall ... environmentalists ... cannot remain a dedicated few if they want to change legislation and keep corporations under reign. That level of effectiveness requires a popular movement. What has happened to the near-unanimous call for environmental quality from every section of society just a few years ago?[24]

22Herbert H. Smith, *The Citizen's Guide to Planning* (West Trenton, N.J.: Chandler-Davis Publishing Co., 1961), p. 10.

23Citizens Advisory Committee on Environmental Quality, *Citizens Make the Difference: Case Studies of Environmental Action* (Washington, D.C., CACE, 1973), p. 1.

24Robert Sommer, "Ecology and the Energy Shortage," *The Nation*, December 10, 1973, p. 615.

"Fill 'Er Up, Check the Oil, and Remove the Bumper Sticker!"

ILLUSTRATION 1.6

Editorial cartoon by Pat Oliphant. Copyright, *Washington Star*. Reprinted with permission, Los Angeles Times Syndicate.

In the environmental movement, especially in conservation, victories are only temporary but defeats are final. Therefore, although it is useful to read and learn from citizens' groups, we must also begin to analyze and understand why ecology, presumably agreed to be the key to our survival, can be tossed aside by the threat of a fuel shortage. Undoubtedly environmentalists will offer a counteroffensive once we have all recovered from the shock of the "energy crisis."

A recent counteroffensive was undertaken by the National Sierra Club's legal defense fund, requesting "a temporary restraining order to enjoin the [U.S.] Interior Department from selling Gulf of Mexico oil leases off Florida, Alabama, and Mississippi.[25] The leases cover about 817,000 acres of the Outer Continental Shelf off these three states, an area the Sierra Club says provides one-third of our nation's commercial fish.

If environmentalists put their energies into single battles, without also fighting the propaganda issuing from large oil companies and the federal government about energy shortages, we may no longer have many successful case studies to read for inspiration.

One possibly positive effect from the fuel shortage involves a more judicious use of land. Because of the constraints put on a variety of products and fuel needed for building homes, and because buyers are more hesitant about new homes which they may not be able to heat and

[25]"Sierra Club Requests Ban on Oil Lease Sale by U.S. in Gulf," *Wall Street Journal*, December 17, 1973, p. 3.

for which they must pay high interest rates, the building trade has experienced sharp cutbacks: "Some think the energy crisis could mean a reemphasis on development in central cities and older nearby suburbs. Builders will have to use land that was hopscotched in the rush to the suburbs. . . . The days of building helter-skelter in the suburbs are over for a while."[26] Of course, this setback doesn't mean that developers see the wasteful folly of unplanned suburban sprawl; it just means they have to stop it for a while.

Past attempts at planning and ordering communities have been anything but systematic and effective. Policy making at the community level is disparate, filling our communities with fragmented pieces of a puzzle which never properly fit. So many public and private agencies pride themselves on autonomous power that they overlook the obvious failings of such autonomy and continue to prize their separateness as an achievement in itself. If there is to be separate *or* coordinated efficiency by social agencies, there will have to be a great deal of planning at all levels of government. Even in agencies where the recognition of planning has taken hold, such planning is virtually impotent if other pieces of the communal puzzle are overlooked.

> The type of planning with which most organization and agency people are most extensively involved today is planning for and within their respective organizations or agencies. Since organizations and agencies are usually a major part of the community functioning process, this type of planning is a very important part of the total community planning process. It is very important, therefore, that organization and/or agency planning be in support of and not contradictory to, the community planning process in both areas of concern.[27]

A comprehensive plan must be coordinated to reduce conflicts or duplication among social services. Recreation, park, and open-space planning must be interrelated with similar planning in transportation, housing, water and sewer service, and so forth. To be effective, planning must deal with people in all aspects of their life, and not simply concentrate on what are considered traditional leisure concerns.

With the increasing malfunction of social institutions, new methods are needed to improve communication, to develop relevant programs, and to provide a means for resolving conflicts among groups. Most hardcore social problems are interrelated, and any human resource planning has to be linked with other human needs. The need to deal with social symptoms as indicative of larger problems was strongly pointed out

[26]Terry P. Brown, "Money and Fuel Woes Plunge Housing Market into Full Recession," *The Wall Street Journal*, December 14, 1973, p. 1.

[27]Frederick Wileden, *Community Development: The Dynamics of Planned Change* (Totowa, N.J.: Bedminster Press, 1970), p. 159.

by John F. Kennedy in his campaign speeches and by the Kerner Commission Report in 1968.[28]

Most of the problems we face are within the scope of public action—poor housing, poverty, unemployment, economic recessions and layoffs, racism, crowded or inadequate schools, obsolete hospitals and libraries, inadequate recreational facilities, poor or threatened mass transportation systems, pollution of all sorts, crime, drug addiction, and the rest we all know so well. These problems are compounded in many communities, especially in urban areas. There is no way to deal with any one of these problems in isolation from the others. In fact, past programs that have attempted to do so have almost invariably failed—for instance, building low-rent housing projects in the inner-city and slum areas, while ignoring the persistent effects of racism and the isolation from the outer community of people with the same economic troubles.[29]

The probable future for most public housing projects is that of the Pruitt-Igoe Development in St. Louis—thirty buildings, eleven stories each—which is to be torn down after only twenty years because of the deterioration of the buildings and the intolerable crime rate. Initially, public housing projects had been designed for Depression victims as a way station for economic recuperation, for upward-bound persons temporarily in a bad situation. "In 1956, 52 percent of the families there [Pruitt-Igoe]... were self-supporting. By 1972, that figure had fallen to 22.1 percent. In Pruitt-Igoe, a scant 15 percent are not on welfare."[30] The people who live in such projects are predominately black, in broken families, experiencing horrendous levels of unemployment.

The concept of public housing for the upwardly mobile is a cruel joke for poor people invariably crushed by the forces of racism and welfare myopia. While there were only about 350 of the 2,800 apartments still occupied in late 1973, the problem of those displaced by the failure of Pruitt-Igoe has not only not been solved, it has never been properly identified. The U.S. Department of Housing and Urban development finally gave up, even though they will be paying back bondholders until the beginning of the next century.

It is not at all unlikely that the property of the razed project, or any other central city property for that matter, will be redeveloped for

---

[28]*The Speeches of Senator John F. Kennedy, Presidential Campaign of 1960,* S. Res. 305, 86th Cong., 1st sess., 1961; U.S. National Advisory Commission on Civil Disorders, *Report* (New York: Bantam Books, 1968).

[29]There are only a few public housing projects which have been successful, primarily because they have not isolated poor, broken families in slum neighborhoods, nor ignored their other needs in addition to housing. For a good summary of public housing successes, see J. S. Fuerst, "Hidden Successes of Public Housing," *The Nation,* November 12, 1973, pp. 493–96.

[30]"City Life: St. Louis Project Razing Points Up Public Housing Woes," *The New York Times,* December 16, 1973.

people in the suburbs who, because of energy shortages and gasoline prices, may want to migrate back to the city. I am not the first to suggest that the inner-city poor may wind up in our deserted suburbs, while the middle-class whites drift back to the central cities *because it is advantageous for them to do so.* Again, the poor blacks and other minorities in the city become pawns. Planning is political, it determines who gets what, when, and how. "The planning process and the implementation of plans also determines who is denied what, how long they are denied, and the methods by which they are prevented from having what they want."[31] Most planners, of course, would be uncomfortable with the label "politician," much preferring a safer and more objective professional title, while ignoring the political and social implications of their work.

Planning that truly reflects the total needs of a community's residents would be one step toward limiting the outrageous displacement of powerless people whenever it suits those with power. Soon enough we'll hear stories of slum suburbs that have gone to pot since the poor and minorities moved in. And once again we'll exclaim how "such people" have no respect for property, completely ignoring that most of us have little respect for these people if they are persistently displaced at our convenience. Such an approach to community development is irresponsible, unethical in the extreme, and costly. Pruitt-Igoe's deficit in 1972 was $1,659,399; the human toll, of course is never calculable.

Another defeated concept is Model Cities, which received 50 percent funding until mid-1974, after which it will be dead. As former presidential aid John Ehrlichman said—much as HUD said about Pruitt-Igoe—"We have run out of patience with model cities." This is an ironic comment, since:

> [The Model Cities program] was one of the first examples of the comprehensive local planning that will be required if the administration's revenue sharing ideas are to work; it tested and demonstrated the concept of decentralized power which the President favors. . . . Decentralization means a changed power balance, means measuring results at the end of the year instead of proposals at the beginning, measuring services delivered. Successful decentralization demands increased management expertise in cities and states, and given the rudimentary level of competence in many of Model Cities' urban hosts, it's quite possible that no first attempt would look good after four years, even if it had been strongly supported by Washington. One would think that a five-year program such as this deserves five years before being called to account.[32]

Too often federal and local governments treat these social problems in isolation, deny their importance and interrelations, or refuse to

---

[31]John C. Ries, "Planning and Politics," Working paper, Institute of Government and Public Affairs, University of California at Los Angeles, December 1969.

[32]Post, "The End Comes Too Soon," pp. 13ff.

recognize them as government concerns at all. John F. Kennedy almost fifteen years ago stressed the need for federal and state governments to deal with these problems as a totality:

> I propose that we create a new and vital partnership between the National Government and the communities of America. Each community will plan its own future, but it will be helped to get there by the combined resources of cities, States, and Nation.[33]

There have been innumerable program responses to the social problems of cities and communities; some have been successful. On the other hand, many solutions have been programmatic rather than systematic, so no matter how ambitious a program is, the effect is bound to be piecemeal. Until a community is viewed as a unit, its problems will be resolved as isolated trouble spots in what is actually an interdependent unit. One of the difficulties with maximum participation of the poor was the bewildering effect all the new programs based on citizen participation had on the community. These programs were funded by several agencies and administered by a variety of federal employees. There was little if any coordination among them.[34]

In addition to not really solving problems, programs too often compound problems: Public welfare, intended to help the poor, is now considered part of the problem the poor endure. Even though it may have been potentially useful, a lack of systematic planning for reviewing and modifying it, for examining its relation to other social services and needs for making a prognosis of its effectiveness over time, has proved disastrous.

In all communities, and in most social services, there had been a proliferation of local, state, and federal legislation involving a great many programs, agencies, and institutions. In some cities the number of programs were so numerous as to be almost impossible to tally. In addition to the bureaucracy needed to dispense such programs, these public-sector services often wound up competing with each other for limited public monies.

The dismantling of the Office of Economic Opportunity, which represents a strong political distrust of centralized programmatic efforts to aid the poor, still in no way helps poor people; ending OEO programs and grants, without systematic solutions for seemingly intractable social problems, is throwing out the proverbial baby with the bath water. It is a deceleration of government assistance to communities under the guise of decentralization and revenue sharing. Nonetheless, revenue sharing only accentuates the need for long-range coordinated planning.

At the 1973 annual conference of The National League of Cities,

---

[33]*The Speeches of Senator John F. Kennedy.*

[34]Stanley J. Brody, "Maximum Feasible Participation of the Poor: Another Holy Grail?" *Social Work*, XV, 1 (January 1970), 68–75.

an association representing 15,000 U.S. municipalities, President Thomas Bradley (Mayor of Los Angeles) issued the following statement:

> [The cities] share a growing national sense of frustration with the deceleration of the Administration's domestic program and the inability of the Congress to provide adequate alternatives.... This has left cities squarely in the vise of reduced Federal outlays for domestic programs with no clear prospect of new tools to help us do our job....
>
> We shall support legislation which decentralizes community development planning and decision making into broad flexible block grants but retains reasonable national standards and equitable protection of our vital interests.[35]

While the League favors simplification of the morass of federal and local programs, it does not desire a "total withdrawal" of the federal government.

Planning is needed to coordinate the human service activities of local, state, and national governments in a given community; this coordination should reflect the social, physical, and economic goals of the community and also ensure the participation of public officials and private citizens in the plan. To dismantle uncoordinated programs is not the solution.

To be most effective, planning must occur at all levels of society and within a reasonably short time period. If community planning is to be effective, the decisions of various organizations and agencies, and the decisions made at county, area, state, regional, or national levels must be in some agreement. This is not to say that planning is perfect, or should be. Planning needs to reflect some worked-out consensus of what the views and needs of a community are at a particular time and a prognosis of what future resources are likely to be:

> If the original predictions of the ecologists are correct, and no one has proved them wrong, similar shortages [like fuel] will occur with almost every other resource. At present rates of consumption, copper may last twenty, fifty or seventy-five years. Nickel and manganese are similarly limited. No matter how the figures are juggled, we are talking about periods within the lifetime of children already born.... The fuel shortage is the result of an excess of demand over supply. All our resources are finite and unable to service spiraling worldwide demands. We must learn to live within finite resources.[36]

Planning for social needs has raised real and imaginary "Big Brother" accusations, and modern planners will continue to receive similar criticisms. American skepticism of elitist planners is healthy, but planning to many public officials and citizens smacks of socialism

[35]William E. Farrell, "Cities Ask Funds, Assailing Census," *The New York Times*, December 9, 1973, p. 37.

[36]Sommer, "Ecology and the Energy Shortage," p. 616.

(a dirty word), stifling free enterprise, or limiting individual expression. These critics confuse a framework for community development with *constraints* on such development, and view planning as simply an imposition of orders from the top down. Even when people are in favor of it, planning from the top down is usually ineffective. Therefore it is imperative that critics of planning be shown the value of community participation in any plan, as well as the importance of planning itself, and be assured that planning does not mean harsh controls or a diminishment of free expression. Planning seeks to fetter license, not freedom.

For example, at the community level, a comprehensive leisure plan can enable communities to make the best decisions at the most propitious time. The plan can provide data on land use, transportation, or other recreation facilities. These data aid the community planners in making rational decisions. In this sense, a plan is a tool to enhance sensible development, not a coercive instrument to limit private or public development. As communities and cities become more complex, and as populations and social demands increase, the necessity for planned social development must be recognized, or we may lose any say in how our future will be shaped.

Planning does not always involve a thrust into the future; often it is needed to catch up with where we are, and to act on more immediate and pressing needs. One doesn't need a crystal ball to realize that some

A boy looks to the future. Will our streams and rivers be clean in 1980? Only with proper planning and control.

comprehensive plan involving transportation would be useful in a community with widely spaced yet varied recreation facilities. The plan would not concentrate on future recreation needs as such, but would study travel patterns and possibilities for neighborhood interchange and use of existing facilities.

The planner who produces a comprehensive leisure plan for both the short and long range has, of course, done an outstanding service. Such a scope of planning can ensure that transistions to the future will be smoother, albeit somewhat uncertain. Planning cannot be precise about future leisure needs, but it can instill in a community the *need* to plan continuously for the future. If we are flexible in our planning philosophy and do not view the formal plan as an ultimate dictum, planning can help us know more quickly when we are planning badly.

Planning is one mode of grappling with the apparent confusion and haphazard growth that often pass for community development. As citizens or professionals, we should never assume we have little control over the shape of our immediate or broader environment. With planning as a tool, we can hope to rationally *and* imaginatively affect the kind of communal atmosphere now being arbitrarily created for us. As a society we live with massive repercussions from poor planning in the past; it is ludicrous to perpetuate this kind of passivity in the face of yet more accelerated changes.

For example: the automobile is not a problem simply because we don't have the "juice" to run them any longer; in our efforts to make money and to be active consumers, we have permitted our lovely landscape and our personal well-being to become secondary to the automobile:

> Since World War II, for example, the profligate American highway program has provided more or less stable profits to its sponsors in the automotive industry and its various satellites, including the energy companies. But it has also created such profound structural changes in American society as to have made most American transactions, whether public or private, hostage to a diminishing energy supply. The social price of American energy profits are not only an irrational system with its clogged highways, excessive horsepower, and bankrupt railways, but social structures that can neither be sustained by current energy supplies nor altered without catastrophic political and economic consequences.[37]

Because of poor planning, and our persistent wish to ignore the prevision of the few social critics who knew what an automobile-dependent economy was likely to lead to, we now face an almost insurmountable dilemma, one that will also burden later generations.

The coming decades will be characterized by sweeping changes in living and cultural standards, social patterns, and industrial productivity. Americans will have to change their habits, desires, motives,

[37]Jason Epstein, "The Big Freeze," *The New York Review of Books*, December 13, 1973, pp. 33–34.

satisfactions, level of demand, and value systems. The energy crisis has shown us that government planning can require us to curb our demand for products and services:

> The interesting problem that follows is to anticipate the corresponding political transformations that may arise in various democracies, including our own, as these limitations become increasingly apparent and oppressive —as the restriction of demand for the sake of national survival becomes an essential public policy.[38]

With this in mind, all the techniques of planning—fact gathering, analysis, judging alternatives, selection of goals—must also be applied to decide the form of government we desire as citizens, the functions for our government, and the areas for government to handle.

The consequence in present-day America is that recreation and parks must seek to be a new and compelling priority. It must resist being regarded in times of need as a frill or luxury. It is a vital human requirement, especially during times of stress, one which touches a root cause of much personal and civic discontent. Planning must reflect these needs and create the systems needed to meet them; it must even anticipate such needs and not let recreation be subsumed in the clamor for the "necessities" of life.

SELECTED REFERENCES

ALTSHULER, ALAN A. *Community Control: The Black Demand for Participation in Large American Cities.* New York: Pegasus, 1970.

BALDINGER, S. *Planning and Governing the Metropolis—The Twin City Experiences.* New York: Praeger Publishers, Inc., 1971.

BANNON, JOSEPH J., AND EDWARD H. STOREY. *Guidelines for Recreation and Park Systems.* Urbana: University of Illinois, 1970.

BARNES, PETER. *The Sharing of Land and Resources in America.* Compilation of articles, *The New Republic,* June–October, 1972.

BOLLENS, JOHN C. *The Metropolis: Its People, Politics and Economic Life.* New York: Harper & Row, Publishers, 1970.

COX, DAVID, ed. *How Does a Minority Group Achieve Power: Case Study of Black Americans.* New York: John Wiley & Sons, Inc., 1969.

GREENSTONE, J. DAVID, AND PAUL E. PETERSON. *Race and Authority in Urban Politics: Community Participation and the War on Poverty.* New York: Basic Books, 1973.

LE BRETON, P. P., AND D. A. HENNING. *Planning Theory.* Englewood Cliffs, N.J.: Prentice-Hall, Inc., 1961.

---

[38]Ibid., p. 34.

RABINAVITY, F. F. *City Politics and Planning.* New York: Atherton Press, 1969.

SPATT, B. M. *A Proposal to Change the Structure of City Planning.* New York: Praeger Publishers, Inc., 1971.

U.S. CONGRESS. Senate Subcommittee on Urban Affairs, Joint Economic Committee. *Urban America: Goals and Problems.* 90th Cong., 1st sess., August 1967.

WEBBE, M. M. "Comprehensive Planning and Social Responsibility." *Journal of the American Institute of Planners,* XXIX, 4 (November 1963).

———. *Planning and Delivery of Social Service.* Center for Community Planning, Department of Health, Education and Welfare, National League of Cities, April 1969.

2

ORGANIZATION AND ADMINISTRATION OF COMPREHENSIVE PLANNING

It makes little sense to hire a consultant to confirm what we already know or agree is correct. They are an outside stimulant, not a validator of pet ideas, and the more open-minded we are to their ideas and suggestions, the less likely we are to force abstract concepts into poor application.

1924036

INTRODUCTION

Now that we have touched on some of the broader concerns and overviews of planning in Chapter 1, we turn to the practical aspects of organizing and administrating a planning project for a leisure delivery system in a community. The major task of project administration is twofold: to determine the organizational structure of the project—who will do what, where, and at what time—and to carefully formulate and articulate the policies that will guide all those involved in the planning project.

Any procedural or theoretical model is useful only for defining the major tasks to be performed from start to completion of a planning project. Most social models rely on a simple problem-solving approach, outlining for the decision maker steps to solve a problem, the steps necessary to implement a chosen solution, as well as feedback and evaluation of the selected solution or solutions. Although our procedural model necessarily involves the rationality and common sense used in problem-solving models, its emphasis lies more in the creation of an administrative structure and the steps necessary for undertaking a comprehensive plan, and somewhat less on the implementation of the plan's outcome.

It is not our intention to slight any aspects of problem solving as much as to magnify the detailed activities in the links between problem definition, implementation, and evaluation. Too often, because a method is logical and sounds easy, we skip over the multiple details and effort necessary to achieve a seemingly "logical" progression from start to finish. Planning appeals to administrators because, like Mom and apple pie, it seems wholesome: at face value it sounds so good that it must be easy to undertake, simply a matter of following predetermined, foolproof steps. But anyone who has done the slightest bit of planning, at any level, knows it is rarely a simple progression from start to finish, but a more complex and often contradictory process from that outlined in any model:

> Some [planning] theorists and practitioners stress only the implementing aspects, assuming the goal is given. Others include in planning the process of determining the goal as well as devising and/or implementing the means to carry it out.[1]

Another method or philosophy of planning, which has been given the unfortunate label of "muddling through," breaks away from the rational approach and uses a more interactive process instead: "planning in this view establishes processes of interaction out of which both goals and methods of achieving them will be generated. ... It [is] built on the notion that there is no single rational solution to a stated problem, but that issues of evaluation arise at every point among people who are working toward the solution of a problem."[2]

Muddling through is a very important philosophy in social planning, especially for comprehensive planning, which involves not only the agency that seeks to do planning but most likely professionals from planning firms, representatives from other relevant social agencies, and community citizens and private groups. While the burden for defining the need and purpose of the project (i.e., the problem statement) rests squarely with the agency director and park board, interaction with all these other groups and individuals necessarily brings on the "processes of interaction" so integral to the muddling through philosophy of planning.

The term "comprehensive planning" immediately brings to mind one of two images—centralized planning or coherent planning. Comprehensive planning is not equivalent to either centralized control or co-

---

[1]Robert Perlman and Arnold Gurin, *Community Organization and Social Planning* (New York: John Wiley & Sons, Inc., 1972), p. 49.

[2]Charles E. Lindblom, "The Science of 'Muddling Through'" *Public Administration Review*, Spring 1959, quoted in Perlman and Gurin, *Community Organization*.

ordination. Its aim is to achieve *improved coherence* among all relevant components "[calling] for a process of looking outward from one's own focus of activity in search of relations to other activities and in an attempt to fit the one to others."[3]

Even with such modifications, planning still remains a rational process, but subsumed in the activities of planning is now the recognition that comprehensiveness does not mean central control or rigidity, nor does "muddling through" indicate an abdication of *responsibility* for planning to anyone other than the agency. Thus when an administrator considers comprehensive planning and the way to convince others of its values and importance, knowledge of these philosophical variances is invaluable. Not only can an administrator define types of planning, the use of procedural models as guidelines, the necessary interactive processes of "muddling through," and the coherence of comprehensive approaches, he can also intelligently reply to criticisms about centralized control, supposed lack of rationality, or any presumed indifference by the agency to what those outside may have to offer.

The procedural model in this book defines the steps necessary to carry out a planning process for a problem that has basically been defined; that is, part of the preplanning that precedes this model has to be spent on clearly defining the problem as perceived by the recreation agency desiring to undertake comprehensive planning. Preplanning is for the most part an informal procedure, often involving the agency director and board, and sometimes even a planning consultant at the earliest stages. During this prelude to planning, the administrator is trying to formulate various descriptions or perceptions of the problem. Although an administrator can call on others to aid in problem definition, more often than not this is the "lonely" part of planning, where one's earliest interests and inclinations toward comprehensive planning, or any other planning for that matter, take shape. Though a lonely, task, preplanning even in its vaguest shape does not and should not occur in a vacuum. The administrator can draw on as much expertise and insight as possible to help define more clearly the possibilities of planning and the kinds of objectives sought.

The more scrupulous the attention given to preplanning, the more likely the administrator will be able to justify the need and value of planning, including the value of contracting with professional planners to handle the project. The more complex the effort, the keener the need for professionals eventually becomes.

[3]Melvin M. Webber, "Systems Planning for Social Policy," in Ralph M. Kramer and Harry Specht, eds., *Readings in Community Organization Practice* (Englewood Cliffs, N.J.: Prentice-Hall, Inc., 1969), p. 424. See also James Q. Wilson, "An Overview of Theories of Planned Change," in Robert Morris, ed., *Centrally Planned Change* (New York: National Association of Welfare Workers, 1964), pp. 12–29; and Ronald Lippitt, Jeanne Watson, and Bruce Westley, *The Dynamics of Planned Change* (New York: Harcourt Brace, 1958).

RATIONALE FOR USING PLANNING CONSULTANTS

Since few recreation and park agencies are likely to have professional planners on their staff (or even if they do they are not likely to want to involve them full time on a lengthy planning project), the procedural model was designed with the supposition that outside planning consultants would be used. Professional planners can either handle the entire project or supplement the work of any agency planners, providing the special expertise necessary for effective and complex planning. Although professionals in parks and recreation may have a good grasp of leisure service possibilities and of the needs of a particular community, they often do not have effective planning talents as well. Even if they happen to be good planners, the demands on their time for other agency work may not allow a thorough concentration on a comprehensive planning project.

There is no strict gauge for determining when an agency or department should seek outside consulting services and when it could use its own staff to perform such tasks. Even with a substantial and talented staff, outside help is often preferable, since it can usually devote its energies almost exclusively to the planning project; this is rarely the case with in-house staff.

Some agencies may have access to the services of a zoning board or commission. The only drawback here is that planning boards and commissions usually do not have time to work extensively with other agencies. In any event, there should be close involvement between a parks and recreation agency and these groups to reduce any duplication of effort.

Too often agencies work not only independently of one another but often ignorant of what others are doing. In some cases planning commissions have designed parks and recreation plans for entire counties without the express knowledge or advice of the parks and recreation agency. In other cases, even after such a plan had been completed, the parks and recreation agency was still unaware of its existence. In smaller communities, where extensive social and other informal links exist among agency personnel, this may not be a problem, but one cannot be too certain. Therefore, even if a plan or zoning commission is not able to help much with the details of comprehensive planning, it is important it be kept informed of agency activities. A liaison committee from the park board might be set up, or a member from these commissions might sit on any planning council that the agency establishes.

Many state governments offer consulting services to public agencies, ranging from giving simple advice to conducting comprehensive plans and surveys. It is best to determine the scope, quality, availability, and *legality* of such state services. Legality is especially important if a stipulation in federal or other governmental funding requires liaison with a state consulting agency. In addition, some colleges and universities offer professional consulting services through their park and recreation departments, as well as student researchers who can undertake a variety of planning assignments. Such services are often free except for out-of-pocket costs or a slight overhead.

Hiring outside consultants precludes the necessity of hiring additional professional staff for only one project, people who may have to be let go or given "filler" work once the planning project is completed. Although agency staff are usually able to devote time and energy to planning projects at the start, when everyone is fresh and optimistic, the demands of ongoing agency preoccupations act as a countervailing force to planning, even if these staff are relieved of some responsibilities. Planning has to be a major concern for the duration of the project; it is difficult for staff members to sustain this sort of concentration alone, nor should they be expected to.

Because of the complexity of comprehensive planning, even if an agency has an extensive planning staff, there is still a necessity for hiring planning consultants. It is the contention of many involved in social planning that the professionals who carry out planning in the human services are coming to represent a "new breed" that cuts across all fields:

> More and more, this new breed of practitioner is coming to utilize similar methods and techniques. But something more fundamental provides a common base for their efforts. Social needs and problems are so inextricably interrelated and intermingled that traditional boundaries between fields and disciplines are being everywhere breached.[4]

Although a professional planning education is important, this should not be the exclusive criterion for selecting a consultant:

> Many professionals in allied fields such as architecture, engineering, social or political science, have achieved a high level of excellence in planning on the strength of many years of relevant experience. Impressive academic credentials alone ... without planning experience, usually should not be considered a substitute for such experience.[5]

Planning is not a sacred skill imparted to none but the chosen, but there are times when outside help is not only essential but beneficial. Of course, if the consultants are themselves ineffectual, then outside help may only confound the efforts of any agency planning staff.

Nonetheless, an agency staff planner, no matter how desirous of instituting an interdisciplinary approach, would be hard put to bring the necessary expertise to the task. Since this new "breed" of planner

---

[4]Perlman and Gurin, *Community Organization and Social Planning*, p. 3.

[5]American Institute of Planners, *Selecting a Professional Planning Consultant* (Washington, D.C.: AIP, 1971), p. 2.

is in evolution, and no single profession as yet encompasses all facets of social planning, it is necessary that recreation professionals work *with* planning consultants but not delegate the project in its entirety to them. It is to be expected that the agency personnel will know more about recreation than the consultant (unless one contracts with a firm that has specialized in recreation and parks planning); on the other hand, it is likely that the consultant will more likely resemble this new breed of planner than any agency staff, especially if the firm is reputable and competent.

The major concerns in recreation and parks quickly affect and impinge on other professions—social work, economics, psychology, political science, sociology, education, and so forth. Even the most myopic view of recreation and parks leads one into other disciplines. Comprehensive planning calls for close collaboration among social scientists and their applied disciplines. This collaboration is best secured through a planning firm that either employs or itself has contractual links with such professionals. Unless a recreation agency has established itself and tested such links, it is best to rely on firms who have. An interdisciplinary approach to planning is not achieved by any simple potpourri of professionals, but by a conceptual approach to social planning; this approach is not presently the province of any single profession.

Another value of professional consultants is that they are usually not imbued with the inner workings of an agency, involved in its personal politics, nor overly affected by what agency personnel and board members might consider constraints, and they can often bring a much-needed objective viewpoint to the problem at hand:.

> the practitioner in the service agency looks outward from the vantage point of his responsibility for that service toward the environment in which his agency operates; he deals with that environment in such a way as to pursue the purposes to which his agency is committed. In planning organizations, that perspective is reversed.[6]

Planning in the human services field is oriented (or should be) toward an examination and discovery of needs in the social environment, as the basis for determining how resources can best be mobilized and allocated to meet those needs.

One of the first issues a consultant has to determine, in view of the above, is whether to accept a problem as identified by the agency, or to define the situation more "objectively" based on newly acquired or freshly analyzed information:

> The planner is frequently enmeshed from the outset in a variety of prejudgments and constraints that stem from the auspices under which he is operating and various other factors.... The exercise of appraising the problem with as much freedom from predefinition as possible pro-

6Perlman and Gurin, p. 185.

vides an opportunity to consider a range of alternatives in addition to those that may already exist in the minds of [others]. . . .[7]

For this reason, although it is essential that an administrator define the problem and project scope in advance, there should be no constraint on project redefinition by a consultant, at least for reconsideration by the administrator and board. In order to reappraise the problem situation, a consultant must have a grasp of the relevant research in social planning and recreation, as well as an ability to relate this to the present situation. Kahn calls this a "knowledge-organizing scheme," which in a sense then becomes the intellectual framework for planning.[8]

It is this kind of knowledge-organizing ability one values in a social planner, for such a skill brings to the agency viewpoint either support and validation of its own thinking or a new and modified way of assessing the community situation. A good analytical planner will enter the situation critically, question decisions already made, consider other possibilities that experience and training may have exposed him to, and untangle the value assumptions and operational preferences that are usually subsumed in any problem statement.

Some planners do not desire to redefine problems, but exist to help clients identify their own needs and the ability to meet them. This is often known as the "enabler role." At the other extreme is the "advocate," where a planner is committed to a specific social policy or philosophy and desires to work with clients who share this perspective. Whereas the enabler is virtually neutral, the advocate is not. All these roles require skill. It is the agency's responsibility to clearly determine what it is looking for in a planner: does it want a planner who has no programs or prescriptions of his own (the enabler); a planner who has command of the subject matter and literature being considered (analytical planner); or one who practices with a particular philosophy or social cause (the advocate). Often it is possible to elicit all three roles or traits in one planning firm, but the agency would have to have a fairly good grasp of the intellectual and social issues which affect social planning, as well as what aspects of the planning project might require which of these three roles.

However, it is up to the agency administrator and board to decide on *the role* of the consultant, not the other way around. It is not merely a question of choosing one role for a consultant over another, but choosing a sufficient role for the project under consideration. It is up to the project administrator to select or rank-order the appropriate roles. The administrator must also be sure none of the determined roles transcends or defeats the goals of the agency itself. For example, an administrator may judge client-advocacy important, but may be unable

---

[7]Ibid., p. 63.

[8]Alfred J. Kahn, *Theory and Practice of Social Planning* (New York: Russell Sage Foundation, 1969), p. 79.

to undertake such work with agency staff or within the framework of agency responsibilities. Hiring an outside consultant in the hope of advocating change can lead to disastrous results. Although we may hire consultants to do things we cannot, they are not to be hired to do things we should not. If an enabler or advocacy role is desirable, such action should be officially and clearly designated by the policy-making board. Nor, on the other hand, should an administrator drift in such directions merely because of the philosophy of a consultant.

Although we say that an objective viewpoint is achieved with professional planners, this does not mean they are so removed from leisure service knowledge as to be worthless. While it might be interesting to obtain the viewpoint of, say, a civil engineer, this is not the kind of refreshing viewpoint referred to here. The professional planner is someone attuned to or trained in one or several of the social sciences, including recreation and parks. Even if the planner is educated and trained in another profession, the experience in recreation and parks, and more notably in leisure systems designs becomes important. But, again, experience has to be carefully assessed on its own merit, not according to where it has been acquired.

Many different professionals can be involved in planning: recreation and parks professionals, architects, landscape architects, foresters, psychologists, engineers, economists, sociologists, and so on. If a team of professionals is involved, the professional that has primary responsibility is held accountable to the agency.

In some cases, consulting firms intentionally keep their technical and professional staffs small, themselves subcontracting with outside experts as needed to suit a particular project. Subcontracting gives flexibility to the consulting firm and increases the likelihood that their fees will not reflect a disproportionate amount of permanent professional overhead charges. These firms can then expand the base of their services without expanding their permanent staff or overworking them by spreading them too thin. Another prominent pattern of organization is the small firm which continues to specialize in only one or two services, not increasing or decreasing their staff or their capabilities to fit a contract.[9]

Objectivity does not come from remoteness to a planning subject as much as from a degree of psychological detachment from the agency undertaking the planning. Objectivity can mean theorizing or undertaking a project without a strong desire for a particular outcome but with *an interest* in some outcome. Such work "is exceedingly objective if it means that every step in the process of thinking is based on critically sifted evidence, and furthermore if it takes a critical attitude toward commonsensical premises."[10]

[9]In addition to these outside professionals, retired parks and recreation administrators can often be useful for consultation, but on a more limited basis, usually for administrative and organizational matters.

[10]Erich Fromm, "Introduction," in Ivan Illich, *Celebration of Awareness: A Call for Institutional Revolution* (New York: Doubleday & Co., Inc., 1969), p. 9.

Most agencies seek consultants not only for their expertise but also because they can handle delicate and touchy issues much better than those involved in day-to-day operations. This involves a bit of buck-passing on the part of administrators, but the advantages to be gained make the delegation worthwhile. However, consultants *must* be apprized of delicate matters if they are expected to smooth them over. An administrator has to be candid with outside consultants even if it means admitting to personal or professional shortcomings. Consultants are often called trouble shooters; giving them a good target can save a lot of shooting in the dark, a lot of money, and hopefully, hurt or abused sensibilities by all involved. If an administrator begins acting cagey with consultants, for whatever reason, then impressive contracts and rhetoric will be meaningless. If consultants are hired to help, there must be a real *and* acknowledged need for them, and the agency must fully intend to cooperate. Naturally, there are problems an administrator cannot point out, their presence or urgency may not be so evident to him, or they may in fact be the reasons why a consultant is sought. In such cases, the consultant can describe these problems for administrative scrutiny and *joint* deliberation.

One aspect of objectivity is a consultant's interest in whether you take his advice and directions. Consultants are not hired to soap box their viewpoints but to present them to a purportedly receptive group. Of course, any competent consultant is interested in seeing his or her recommendations implemented, and many consultants are contracted to handle the public relations aspect as well.

A consultant's lack of personal interest in the agency or in the community should be valued for what it is; complaints from staff or citizen groups about bringing in outsiders should be anticipated and sensitively handled. The advantages of those outside the immediate concerns of the agency should be indicated to all involved. Community participants, too often considered outsiders themselves, will probably see the value of consultants, especially if the latter are receptive and competent. A poor reputation or behavior by consultants will, of course, preclude any efforts by the project administrator to show the obvious gains from their services.

Although the consultant can bring a fresh angle to agency perspectives, he is still an adjunct of the agency: he is not independent of the agency as, say, a social critic might be, since he is hired to serve that agency. The scope of work that he eventually performs is ultimately determined by the functions and objectives of the agency. Therefore, although a fresh viewpoint is sought, it is not a viewpoint that ignores the agency's purpose, no matter how illuminating it might be. An agency still requires very practical advice and help, for which it is willing to pay.

In addition to analytical expertise and objectivity, an outside consultant has usually had a great deal of experience in working with local residents. Consultants can familiarize residents with the workings of the agency far more effectively than can the agency staff, for consultants themselves are outsiders and more aware of what needs to be acquired for meaningful participation. As we all know, too many reports and studies by experts, without the involvement and participation of community residents, wind up collecting dust because local residents were not involved in planning for *their* community. Only when professionals and local citizens work together can a plan be effectively implemented. If a consultant does not agree with this precept, his competence and experience are called into question unless he can defend his position based on experience.

For example, one planner who has had experiences with the concept of citizen participation in social planning may feel it is a hopeless objective, time consuming, frustrating, and so forth. Another consultant may feel citizen control is the only answer, with anything less mere pussy-footing. Before discarding any firm from further consideration because they question the concept of citizen participation or seem cynical about its efficacy, hear what they have to say. It would be wiser to draw on their experience than to hire a yea-sayer only to run into all sorts of difficulty later because of a naive assumption by both parties that citizen participation is not only self-evident but easy.

It makes little sense to hire a consultant to confirm what we already know or agree is correct. They are an outside stimulant, not a validator of pet ideas, and the more open-minded we are to their ideas and suggestions, the less likely we are to force abstract concepts into poor applications. Experience can bring complexities and ambiguities to light. If we are interested in experienced planners, then we need to know what experience has taught them.

For example, if the dynamics of community involvement and change are not viewed in a compatible fashion by the consultant and the administrator, there will be conflict. Much of this conflict surrounds the issue of citizen involvement in planning—should it be citizen control, participation, or merely citizens acting as respondents or interviewers in a community survey? If a consultant is not happy with the degree of community involvement ultimately decided on by the agency, such discrepancies in planning philosophies should be known as soon as possible. It is not that we would avoid such a consultant, but that we would examine together how much any disparity of views is likely to affect the overall project. If viewpoints appear irreconcilable, by all means look elsewhere, or else reassess your position on citizen involvement.

We must remember that citizen involvement to whatever degree, in public and private agencies, is a justifiable demand but it is also a fad. If an agency is going along with the fashion of including citizens or responding to their demands without scrutiny and analysis of the concept itself or without the intention of relinquishing any power, then superficial relations with community residents are inevitable.

The veterans of the 1960's, those citizens involved in community control or participation efforts, as well as the myriad of professionals involved, should be approached for their viewpoints. There is a voluminous literature on what was originally called Maximum Feasible Participation of the Poor in community decision making. Even if an administrator is not conversant with the trends and findings of this literature, at the least he should listen to the veterans, especially when conflicting reports are received. To accept the concept as justifiable or self-evident may be laudable; it will not, however, prepare an administrator for the dissensions and conflicts that can arise. Consultants should be listened to, for they often have gained their experience under fire.[11]

Although the task of planning can be delegated to a consulting firm, the administration *and* control of the planning project rest clearly with the agency. The design and structure of the project, as well as the policies for everyone's responsibilities, duties, and probable role, can only be determined by the agency director and the park board. Even when the bulk of the project can be handled by others, project administration must remain with the director. This might become difficult to sustain once the project is under way and other agency matters claim attention. For this reason, the director should plan for sufficient assistance and delegation before the project begins.

There is probably nothing so distressing as the necessity for adding staff or delegating tasks while under pressure. An early understanding of the *scope* of the project can help avoid, although not prevent, administrative modifications during a project. Some have suggested adding a policy advisor to the agency, someone who would identify and qualify problems, advise the chief administrator, and make all contacts with professional planners. While such a position can lessen the work pressures of the administrator, it in no way diminishes the necessity for administrator involvement in planning.

The administrator, with the concurrence of the park board, now begins to think about the feasibility of hiring professional planners. Implicit in this search for a consultant is an antecedent agreement with the park board that a comprehensive plan is indeed necessary for the community. Such agreement itself often requires energy and dedication by a director and of citizen groups. Since planning connotes socialism to many people, resistance to its use can be deeply entrenched. Even though this book does not suggest ways to convince a board of the value of comprehensive planning, other than the arguments presented above, this in no way diminishes its critical importance; without board consent, planning never leaves the preplanning stage.

---

[11]For a broad discussion of working with citizens in various capacities, see Joseph J. Bannon, *Outreach: Extending Community Service in Urban Areas* (Springfield, Ill.: Charles C Thomas, Publisher, 1973), especially Chapters 2 and 3, "Community Outreach in Recreation" and "Role and Function of the Outreach Program."

Clavel discusses problems which can arise when professional planning consultants or administrators have to advise nonpartisan laymen boards in semirural communities.[12] Because of a limitation of resources, time, training, and experience, there has been little involvement of semirural community boards with professional planners. In addition there is a tendency in smaller nonurban communities to distrust "experts" and reassert "traditional rural institutions." Planners have to relate not only to citizens on planning advisory councils, but more importantly in parks and recreation agencies, to commissioners or board members who are almost always laymen. Clavel believes that difficulty or lack of rapport can develop when there is a high percentage of "locally oriented board members of generalist status, and less likely when board members have specialist status and cosmopolitan orientation."[13] This distinction between types of board members is, of course, the well-known cosmopolitan/local typology of sociologists.[14]

In any event, it should be clear that the need for outside help is not an admission of failure but recognition of the complexity of most social needs. Professional planners are, at this time, the most qualified to advise on or undertake comprehensive planning in the human services. They themselves may specialize in one field, but through experience and the demands and exigencies of social planning, they have come to resemble the new breed of professional planners described by Perlman and Gurin.[15]

If an agency cannot afford to pay for consultants, it should be remembered that they are far from mandatory. In such cases, even for long-range, comprehensive plans, a sufficiently able and conscientious staff, with the involvement and cooperation of community residents, can often bring impressive skills to planning. It is desirable to have professional planners if possible, but an agency should not be immobilized if it cannot afford a consultant.

[12]Pierre Clavel, "Planners and Citizen Boards: Some Applications of Social Theory to the Problem of Plan Implementation," *Journal of the American Institute of Planners*, XXXIV, May 1968, pp. 130–39.

[13]Ibid., p. 130.

[14]An excellent review of the applications of role theory to an analysis of various social roles is given in Alvin W. Gouldner, "Cosmopolitans and Locals: Toward an Analysis of Latent Social Roles," *Administrative Science Quarterly*, Parts I and II, December 1957 and March 1958, pp. 281–306 and 444–80. For those who are interested, a critique of Gouldner's original work can be found in: Andrew J. Grimes and Philip K. Berger, "Cosmopolitan-Local: Evaluation of the Construct," *Administrative Science Quarterly*, December 1970, pp. 407–16.

[15]In addition to Perlman and Gurin already cited, for an overall coverage of the emerging discipline of social planning, see Kahn, *Theory and Practice of Social Planning*; also see Joan Ecklein and Armand Lauffer, *Community Organizers and Social Planners* (New York: John Wiley & Sons, Inc., 1972); Robert Morris and Robert Binstock, *Feasible Planning for Social Change* (New York: Columbia University Press, 1966); and W. G. Bennis *et al.*, eds., *The Planning of Change* (New York: Holt, Rinehart and Winston, Inc., 1961).

Finally, it is important for an administrator to know as much as possible about how to contact professional planning consultants, what to look for and expect in their services, and what the functional and legal aspects of contractual arrangements with them are. While making arrangements for consultants, the project administrator is simultaneously concerned with establishing the overall structure of the project— the internal relations with staff, the external relations with public and private agencies, both local and national, and contacts with citizen and civic groups. While these aspects of administration can also involve the consultant, our discussion is premised on a consultant entering the project *after* the preplanning phase, though there is little sense in preventing any retroactive assessment of the project statement or definition by consultants.

SELECTING A PLANNING CONSULTANT

The overall administrative and operating structure of a planning project is primarily determined by the relationship the agency establishes with a planning consultant. The goals of a plan have to be formulated by the agency before they contact any consultant. The expertise of a planning consultant can be useful from the very earliest stages, so the earlier the consultant is chosen the better, though this does not reduce the necessity to clearly define and detail the planning project as perceived by the agency. Once selected, a consultant should be immediately involved in all aspects of project administration and policy formulation, or at least those facets in which he has expertise or worthwhile experience.

To evaluate a consultant properly, it is necessary for the administrator and the board to be as clear as possible about what they expect to obtain from a comprehensive plan, with a sure understanding of what comprehensive planning entails. These should be specified before seeing a consultant, otherwise the tail might be wagging the dog from the start, or consulting firms might be reluctant to try to support ambiguously or poorly defined services. One consideration that has to be determined early, and which any consultant needs to know, is how much assistance and resources within the agency, the community, or in related agencies, are available and in what form. This information often has direct bearing on how much work a consultant may have to do and hence what the fee will be.

For example, statistical or survey data on various demographic aspects of a community might be available, or could be compiled for a consultant. The consultant would need to see samples of the data, to determine their complexity, their currency, whether they have been analyzed or evaluated, who prepared the data, what the method and suppositions of data collection were. It is not enough to list "data on hand";

these must be specified and judged for their applicability to the plan. This can only be done if the administrator has a good grasp of what a comprehensive plan requires, the complexity of data needed, and possible limitations or deficiencies in data that are on hand.

Planning consultants are usually advised by professional associations *not* to accept assignments unless the prospective client has sufficiently analyzed the planning problem or has adequate information available that will aid the consultant in doing such analysis himself. An administrator should have thoroughly reviewed the proposed planning project, its purposes and objectives, before a consultant is sought. For it is only after the planning problem has been properly defined that a correct choice in a consultant can be made. It should not be the consultant who determines his inability to handle the project, but the administrator, who is thoroughly familiar with the planning problem and should be able to confidently judge who is qualified or not.[16]

There are generally four types of parks and recreation planning that private consulting firms handle: (1) *comprehensive park and recreation systems plans*, (2) *master site plans* (specific park or recreation area), (3) *detail site planning* (construction and development of projects and facilities indicated in a master site plan), and (4) *special studies or projects* (a catch-all for consulting services that are not included in the above types). In addition to determining the leisure needs of a community, a consultant can also evaluate and make recommendations on the internal organization of the contracting agency, its financing and programs, and its relation to other public and private institutions and agencies.

Comprehensive park and recreation systems plans, or leisure delivery system plans, usually involve an inventory and evaluation of existing local facilities and lands, often using comparisons with well-established national standards. A pamphlet of the National Recreation and Park Association defines comprehensive park and recreation systems plans as follows:

> An inventory and evaluation of existing conditions with recommendations for proposed acquisition, development, organization, finance and programs for the future, covering a given geographical area. Too often the plan adheres to political boundaries which can stifle its effectiveness. Every effort should be made to plan by region or total service area. An important feature of the comprehensive system plan is a projection of recreation demands as determined by population, time-distance factors, physical and man-made barriers, income, education and other socio-economic factors.[17]

[16]For an extensive discussion of problem-solving approaches in recreation and parks, see Joseph J. Bannon, *Problem Solving in Recreation and Parks* (Englewood Cliffs, N.J.: Prentice-Hall, Inc., 1972).

[17]Robert D. Buechner, *The Use of Consultants: A Manual for Park and Recreation Officials* (Washington, D.C.: National Recreation and Park Association, 1970), p. 10.

Comprehensive plans for a town, city, county, special district, or a community are often part of a more comprehensive overall plan for a larger political division. Often included in these plans are projections of recreation demand by demographic factors such as population, education, income, and other socio-economic factors. The following items are usually determined for a comprehensive leisure plan:

- Inventory of existing areas and facilities
- Inventory of potential resources
- Population profile
- Deviations from national standards
- Demand and activity analysis
- Organization and administrative review
- Role of private and commercial recreation
- Financial considerations
- Priorities and plan of action
- Summary and recommendations

In general, consulting fees are based on the scope and complexity of the work, usually measured by the time of professional personnel on the project. In addition, the experience, education, and reputation of the firm's personnel, and the quality of its service, are usually reflected in the fee. There are no standard fee schedules as yet for professional planning firms, nor are there likely to be because of these intangibles and the trend in most professions not to have fee schedules at all. Four factors that do affect fee determination, however, are: (1) specific services to be performed, (2) types of financial arrangements, (3) additional cost factors, and (4) guidelines of professional ethics.

SPECIFIC SERVICES

Below are the kinds of services offered by planning consultants:

Surveys and work development programs. Surveying needs and opportunities relating to physical, social, or economic development and outlining a work program with the kinds of planning activities to be undertaken.
Agency organization and administration. Advising an agency on staffing, organizing, and developing programs to carry out a variety of planning or development activities.
Long- and short-range plans, policies, and programs. Analyzing development problems in depth, establishing objectives, shaping alternative policies and programs, and evaluating their impact as a basis for preparing comprehensive community plans.
Technical assistance and special planning studies. Providing advice on urgent development problems or on intergovernmental relations and federal aids.

Project planning. Preparing specific plans for areas under unified control, such as new communities, shopping centers, college campuses, industrial parks, urban renewal, and similar projects.

Assistance and testimony in court. Preparing cases on zoning and planning-related litigation and providing testimony.

TYPES OF FINANCIAL ARRANGEMENTS

There are several forms of compensation that consulting services can take:

1. *Fixed fee or lump sum.* This is used most often when construction projects are involved, but also for comprehensive plans and studies.
2. *Percentage of construction cost.* The fee varies, where accurate cost estimates can be made.
3. *Time.* Fees are on an hourly or per diem basis, when the exact scope of the work is uncertain.
4. *Fee as fixed percentage of expenses.* Compensation is based on the firm's technical payroll, multiplied by an agreed-on factor.
5. *Contingency fee.* The compensation is determined later, based on the benefits from the service. This form is not recommended and could in some cases be unethical.
6. *Retainer fee.* Payment is for services over a long period of time, usually a fiscal year, not requiring separate negotiation for each project. A retainer contract usually includes: maximum allowable time or money to be spent by the consultant's per diem or hourly rate; travel and subsistence expenses; provisions for termination or cancellation of contract; frequency of payment; and payment of other miscellaneous costs.

Although comprehensive planning is usually expensive, it should be remembered that it is an enormously time-consuming, skillful, and difficult process. If the technical expertise of the consultant is to be of any value, many hours need to be devoted to preparation, direction, and fulfillment of the planning task. Also, the most important aspect of a consultant's contribution may not be readily evident; "it may be the achieving of community agreement on an issue or method, a decision reached on a governmental reorganization matter, or a process instituted to help the community meet future needs."[18]

ADDITIONAL COST FACTORS

Other cost factors which might be reflected in a fee are:

Personnel, other than professionals
General overhead costs
Other miscellaneous project expenses

[18]Illinois Department of Business and Economic Development, *Choosing a Planning Consultant* (Springfield: IDBED, May 1969), p. 7.

PROFESSIONAL ETHICS

"Acceptance of a contract and the manner of compensation impinge directly on the ethics of the planning profession and subject both contractors and consultants to the penalties provided by such codes."[19] These penalties usually concern the prohibition of competitive bidding by consultants, any requirements for future work, "free" services promised in view of future work, or commissions from the sale of related products.

Some sources for locating consultants to do recreation and parks leisure planning might be recommendations of other parks and recreation agencies who have used professional planners, the National Recreation and Park Association, or the American Institute of Planners, and the American Society of Consulting Planners. The American Institute of Planners is the national professional society of urban and regional planners whose members meet established standards of education and/or experience. The American Society of Consulting Planners is a national organization of planning consulting firms whose members have met stringent criteria based on professional planning experience. Members of both organizations are governed by complementary codes of ethics. Membership in these organizations offers some assurance of professional responsibility.

Some states require licensing or registration before certain professionals, such as landscape architects, architects, and engineers, can practice. Codes of ethics for professional behavior can be obtained directly from the national professional organizations which represent planning professions. In addition to a code of ethics, ask these organizations if they have any (1) guidelines for selecting consultants, (2) lists of consulting firms, (3) sample contracts, or (4) manuals and bulletins on consulting services.

For example, the American Institute of Planners (AIP) has listed seven broad guidelines for the selection of a planning consultant. These guidelines themselves are a straightforward, problem-solving approach to consultant selection:[20]

1. Define the nature of the planning work or development problem sufficiently to permit proper choice of consultants to be considered for the work.
2. Consider the general qualifications of a number of firms which appear to be capable of meeting the requirements of the assignment. There will be some consultants who are quite interested in taking on a planning program for comprehensive leisure

[19]American Institute of Planners, *Selecting a Professional Planning Consultant,* p. 5.

[20]Ibid., pp. 1–2.

services. However, since these firms will vary in capability, a general consideration of several should serve as a screening device for those whom you think it worthwhile to pursue further negotiations with. The size of a consulting firm is no indication of competence or suitability for the particular planning work or project being considered. Some firms intentionally stay small, either because they wish to specialize in only a few services, or to subcontract with other professionals depending on the needs of a project, keeping their permanent technical staff to a modest size.

3. Choose for interviews one or more firms (but not more than three) which are believed to be the best qualified for the particular project in mind.

4. Interview the selected firms, explaining fully the proposed assignment and the selection procedure to be followed. Carefully examine the qualifications of each firm by interviewing not more than one at a time, scheduling at least an hour for each interview, and spacing interviews to allow adequate time for deliberation on each firm by the administrator and board members in attendance. At this point, it is also useful to check with the consultant's other clients to determine their satisfaction with his work or for any suggestions.

5. List these firms in order of desirability, based on capability for carrying out the planning assignment, taking into consideration their reputation, experience, special qualifications, personnel available, whether the workload already carried by them will permit good service, and any other pertinent factors.

   At this point in negotiations you should have a pretty good idea of what each consultant's strengths or weaknesses are for undertaking a comprehensive plan for community leisure services. It should also be determined whether the consultant with whom you have been negotiating will stay on the project or delegate the project to another staff member. If the planner in charge is to be someone else, he or she should be present at this interview so their qualifications and personal attributes can be assessed. Clarifying who from the firm will actually be in charge can save a lot of later disgruntling about responsibilities. It must be clearly determined whether a consultant, in view of other work they may be handling, will be able to accomplish the project "promptly and effectively."

6. Choose the firm having the greatest capability for carrying out the assignment and then agree upon a detailed program of work and mutually satisfactory fee. *This would be the first time there is any discussion of fee.*

7. In the event that it is impossible to agree on the work program, the fee, or other contract details, notify the firm in writing that

negotiations are being discontinued and go on to negotiate with the next firm. Unless an agreement has been made, a dismissal in writing may not be necessary, since the lack of any contractual arrangement is tantamount to dismissal. However, some written ending of negotiations may be valuable when negotiating with other consultants to show them the final status of your negotiations with any other firm.

The AIP "Code of Professional Conduct" prohibits its members from competitive bidding on identical work programs; therefore, fees are not discussed until a firm is tentatively chosen to carry out the planning project. It is likely that even in dealing with nonmembers this procedure will prove best, though it can make the selection procedure somewhat cumbersome.

> Clients are advised not to deprive themselves of competent professional assistance by insisting on a bid in competition with others. . . . This should not be deemed to preclude the consultant from citing cost experience elsewhere on projects of similar magnitude and complexity or from discussing a likely cost range, it being understood that the final cost will be a function of the final scope of services agreed upon. If the client is subject to budgetary constraints, he should make them known to all pre-selected consultants.[21]

Nonetheless, too often a consultant is eventually selected solely on the size of his fee. Although cost is important, it should not be the deciding factor no matter how habitually it becomes a prime criterion in decision making. It is important that cost be only one of several factors considered, such as the competence of the consulting firm and the range of services it offers.

> But, most important, remember that your community is buying a service and that the quality of the service—even when it is offered at identical prices—can vary considerably. It is essential that the services accepted be right for the community; price is only one consideration.[22]

Epperson suggests that consultants be listed in order of preference, using the following six criteria:

1. Length of time in business
2. Background of planners
3. Reputation for integrity and practical results
4. Ability to communicate and cooperate with local groups
5. Experience applicable to the problem
6. Reasonable cost and time estimates[23]

[21]Ibid., p. 2.

[22]Indiana University, Division of Community Planning, "Choosing Planning Consultants," *The Indiana Community Planning News*, I, 2, February 1965.

[23]Arlin Epperson, "Use of Consulting Services for Park and Recreation Programs," *Considerations for Community Decision Making* (Columbia: University of Missouri, Extension Division, July 1971).

Below is a list of interview questions that are useful for conducting the initial meeting with consultants. If it appears too time-consuming to ask all of these questions of two or three firms (though this time is *well* spent), then whatever questions are asked of one consultant should be asked of the others so meaningful comparisons can be made.

Interview Questions

1. Outline as best you can the steps you believe should be taken to develop the basic planning work.
2. Describe the most critical issues of the work as you perceive them.
3. Tell us about your firm.
4. What work does your firm presently have under contract? Would any of this be in conflict in any way with the proposed project?
5. Discuss the staffing that you would offer:
   A. Who in the firm would be responsible for the work?
   B. What other members of the firm would be included in the work project?
   C. Would you need any other consultants for other aspects of the work?
6. Would it be possible for your staff to remain in the community for a relatively long period of time? How long?
7. How long will it take your firm to do the work?
8. Is your current workload flexible enough to provide sufficient time for the project?
9. How long has the firm done recreation and park planning?
10. Will you permit us to review other studies and reports completed by your firm?
11. What references can you provide?
12. What professional organizations do your staff belong to?
13. After the study has been completed, what follow-up will your firm provide?
14. What experience do you have in working with community groups?
15. Will your firm provide a prospectus that will describe the consultant's ability to do the work?
16. Does your firm have a particular approach to planning? Is there a philosophy or emphasis your firm uses for planning problems?
17. Is your firm basically a planning firm, or is planning a division of an architectural or engineering firm?
18. Will the personnel from your firm attend monthly planning meetings of the board?
19. What help will the firm provide in the implementation of the recommendations?
20. Will you provide advice and procedures for proceeding with the next phase of planning when the project is completed? What form will this take?

The Division of Planning, Massachusetts Department of Commerce, lists some other factors that should be determined in an interview or at some point:

> What kind of a staff does the consultant have available? (professional, clerical, drafting.) What is the consultant's background? Membership in professional organizations? What is the background of staff members? Competence in a field related to planning does not necessarily mean competence in planning.
>
> Is the consultant's full time devoted to planning or is consulting a "second job"?
>
> The interviewer should ask for references and then contact clients in other communities where the consultant has worked. What is their reaction to his work? Persons both nearby and in towns and states further away should be checked. Has the consultant been prompt in completing work?
>
> Does the consultant have examples of other planning work, studies, reports? Do these seem stereotyped, impractical? Are they imaginative yet reasonable? Are the final planning reports understandable, providing material that is both interesting and useful? Remember the consultant will not always be available for advice. The material should provide a continuing guide.
>
> What is the consultant's approach to public relations? How does he prepare press releases? Display materials? Is the consultant effective in presenting plans and recommendations to the Board? To the public?
>
> What is the consultant's personality? Is he liable to work well with a planning Council and Board? What about dealing with the public?[24]

The Indiana University Division of Community Planning adds some additional questions:

> What about the size and depth of the consulting staff? Does it include specialists in economics, design, statistics, law, etc., who can be consulted on certain problems? Does the firm have its own printing and drafting facilities?
>
> Which member of the firm will be the planner on the project? Will he or she have full responsibility or will someone be supervising their work in the firm?
>
> Is the consultant familiar with state and federal planning legislation, programs, procedures, etc.? Other programs affecting community development? State and local government? Will he be likely to work well with local officials and be accepted by the public?
>
> What is the consultant's philosophy about planning and its relation to local government? How well does he know the community? Does he see in it the same characteristics, problems, qualities, and potential as you? How well is he qualified, staffed, and equipped to handle special local problems?

[24]Massachusetts Department of Commerce, Division of Planning, "Suggestions as to Selecting a Planning Consultant," mimeographed memorandum, May 1960.

How does he feel about involving local citizens in planning decisions? In what ways would he approach this? How does he feel about the use of citizens' committees?

If his office is located some distance from your community, how will communications be handled? Will he be available on short notice for consultation on an urgent problem?[25]

Those consultants who are to be considered further after this initial interview should be invited (again, separately) to make a preliminary visit to the agency and give a presentation to the board. At this point the consultant should advise the board what information and data will be necessary if the contract is awarded. At the same time, the consultant submits in writing the scope of work to be performed, the fee, and the method of payment. This written statement should also include all information and services to be supplied by and at the expense of others:

> Complex planning programs may require special expertise which a given firm may prefer to subcontract or perform in association with another. In such instances, the availability and reputation of all subcontractors or associate team members should be as carefully considered as that of the principal contractor.[26]

For example, if consultants will supervise various stages of the project, be sure both parties have the same conception of what supervision entails. In terms of any data to be collected or compiled by consultants, be sure they agree to interpret these, especially for statistical data. Analysis of data can be handled by both parties, if that is initially agreed on, but data interpretation first has to be provided by the data-gathering team.

Make few assumptions about what might seem generally agreed-on terms or responsibilities. There is no need to be mistrustful of consultants, but do not presume their competence and abilities, and the terms of an agreement, to be self-evident or free of ambiguity. One can have an incisive attitude in such negotiations without being suspicious or ill-mannered toward consultants. Not for a moment should an administrator or board be intimidated by a professional consultant, especially if he or she comes on with a hard sell. Remember you offer the contract and control the project.

At this stage in negotiations, since the contract is usually outlined, it is important to concentrate on specifics. For instance, assess the presentation of the consultant's recommendations to the board carefully: Is it merely a front-man pitch with attractive audio-visuals, but low on content, or is it a professional, well-prepared, useful presentation of how

25"Choosing Planning Consultants."

26American Institute of Planners, *Selecting a Professional Planning Consultant*, p. 2.

the project would be conducted? It cannot be emphasized too strongly that one must watch out for the fancy presentation, impressive and dazzling, which fizzles out when contracts have been signed and the detail work begins. Learn to spot the phoney if you can; if you have doubts, carefully check the firm's other work, probing as much as you can beyond mere compliments or vague assessments from other clients.

Fancy audio-visuals do not necessarily indicate a sophisticated, knowledgeable, and effective consultant, nor do they indicate for certain a front-man approach. However, since we rely so much on appearances, the firm's emphasis may be more on a sophisticated image than on the skills of planning. The initial presentation should include illustrations and documents to serve as a basis for discussion, not be a one-way demonstration. These materials should be thoroughly understood and reviewed by the board. Such materials could then be revised or modified in terms of the outcome of this preliminary visit.

The contract proposal should be read very carefully (as would be the contract itself). Be sure the fees and method of payment are precisely stated and understood. A firm might have a mandatory, but not always evident, stipulation about guaranteed involvement in future aspects of the project or in its implementation:

> Clients who select planning firms to do planning work should avoid supporting the practice of "loss-leader services." This practice seeks to provide cut-rate planning services in anticipation of securing future contracts for other types of professional services.[27]

Loss leaders are risky and most likely unethical stipulations and should be avoided.

If you are prepared to pay a fair price for the services—avoiding a bargain-basement mentality—then be sure you know *precisely* what the fee includes and what it does not. As with any major purchase or service contract, the more assiduously the agreement is examined before "purchase," the less misunderstanding or resentment there will be later. An assessment of the contractual proposal, and of the contract itself, rests solely with the contracting agency and its attorney.

After the tentative selection of a consultant has been made, and details on what the contract would include are specified, the administrator and consultant have to determine the reporting system and communications that will exist between their firms. It is important that arrangements be made for a reporting system between the prime consultant and the project administrator. One important rule is that the consultant *not* work with or report to the park board or any of its members without the express knowledge of the project administrator. A subcommittee of the board can be set up to work with the administrator on liaison matters. It is simply too cumbersome and generally a waste

27Ibid., p. 3.

of time to have a consultant report to too large a group. The reporting scheme should be worked out in advance, but is certainly amenable to any later modifications that improve communications.

The consultant should report directly and frequently to the administrator or a delegated assistant. The administrator then reports to the board, as often as seems necessary, bringing the consultant in for special or summary presentations, or preparing joint presentations or status reports for the board. The board can get information to the consultant either through the director or at board meetings where the consultant is in attendance, or through its liaison subcommittee. It is not a good idea, and in fact should be discouraged, to have board members convey informal information to the consultant.

Definite problems can arise if there is confusion about a reporting scheme (especially about who is in charge of the project) and about the formal channels established for communication. While working out the reporting system, the administrator will also be specifying the degree and kind of agency staff involvement in the project, especially staff relations with the planning consultants and with citizen representatives. Separate policies and guidelines are needed for staff participation and citizen involvement in the project which clearly delineate the functions of each. It is important to clarify, before any contract is prepared, the relationship and functions of the consultant with the planning council, especially with the community representatives and other groups and agencies who are members of the council. It is simply not enough to accept the judgment of the firm and its other clients that the consultant "works well" with local citizens. What is specifically expected of a consultant in his association with all council members has to be specified clearly beforehand.

In addition, the relation of the consultant (and his staff) to agency staff members requires specification, especially where the consulting staff and agency staff would be working on the same aspects of the project. Detailed task or job schemes should be discussed or prepared on what the interactions are likely to be. A framework for this might be garnered from discussions with the agency staff on what their questions, or apprehensions, might be. Any agreed-on details of a reporting scheme should be included in the contract.

Although we have argued for the value of objectivity in a consultant, we should subjectively evaluate his personal characteristics. Since an agency will be working closely for a long time with the consultant, it is important that he be fully acceptable as a person to all agency staff and the board. Don't diminish the critical importance of liking those you work with, unless you happen to be one of those who works well in a negative atmosphere!

Since a good assessment of a consultant's qualifications might not be evident in the first interview, or even in the initial visit and presentation, it is a good idea for the administrator, some local citizens, or even a delegation from the board, to visit the consultant's office. This same group might visit other communities where the firm has worked to obtain a more informal, and perhaps more candid, assessment of their work.

So far we have concentrated on the responsibilities of the consultant to the agency, but the agency has responsibilities to a consultant as well. Below are some of these responsibilities, over and above those which might be expressed in a formal agreement:

> As mentioned, the agency should clearly know what type of planning is to be undertaken and what its general emphasis should be.
>
> The agency should have available for consultants existing technical and engineering studies, and data, and be able to show what other materials are available, since these may affect the fee charged.
>
> When selected, the Park Board should reserve one night a month *exclusively* for the consultant.
>
> The agency should not expect the consultant to work in a vacuum. The administrator should introduce him and his staff members to town officials and interested citizens. If the Board members have valid suggestions as to sources of materials, persons to contact, etc., they should be made.
>
> Once the consultant is contracted, work wholeheartedly with him. If you do not understand his proposals, seek explanations. Once agreed on a course of action, stick with it, but do not expect him to fight *your* battles. Have him prepare the plans and studies needed for your town; have him assist and advise you.[28]

It is essential to have a written agreement or contract which accurately describes the services and responsibilities to be undertaken by the consultant. "Unwritten orders, duties, and terms not defined will often lead to misunderstandings, dissatisfaction on the part of the client, consultant or both, and possible legal action."[29] The contract should be formalized and signed *before* the start of any work, and should be specific on the precise nature of the services, the responsibilities of each party, the amount of fee, the method of payment, the time limits involved, and any other pertinent points.

Many of the details in a contract have already been discussed, and would of course come out in initial discussions with a consultant. However, for a formal agreement, certain items require specification in the contract. Gentlemen's agreements are not enough, even on apparently minor issues. At the very least, include such issues in a letter or in some written form to which both parties have access and prior understanding.

The major elements to be specified and described in a contract are the scope of the work, and who will be responsible for the identi-

[28]Massachusetts Department of Commerce, "Suggestions as to Selecting a Planning Consultant."
[29]Ibid.

fiable units within the planning work.[30] As much detail as possible should be included in the contract or appended. The more time spent on who will do what, when, and where, the smoother the flow of work will be. In addition to the scope and responsibility for project tasks, the contract should specify when these identifiable tasks are to be completed. If you are attracted to Program Evaluation and Review (PERT) techniques, are guided by other management techniques, or follow the model in this book, these can serve to indicate deadline dates as well as identify the work to be done.

Since a planning council will be formed to participate in decision making, it should be clearly determined what the consultant's responsibilities for the council will be. If working with the council is the consultant's responsibility, this should be specified in the contract, and provisions should be made for introducing the consultant to the necessary contacts and personnel as needed. Many agencies also expect the consultant to prepare or assist in presenting the results of the study at any public hearings, meetings, through the media, or whatever. If consultant involvement or responsibility for a public information campaign is desired, this fact should be included in the contract. Naturally, it is expected that a competent consultant will strive to have his recommendations implemented, but how this is to be achieved should not be left for later consideration.

The contract should also specify the fee if at all possible, leaving no open-ended agreements on possible costs for later determination. The fee arrangement might be any of those six previously listed or a combination of elements from them. The total cost for the project, as well as how and when it is to be paid, must be clearly delineated and adhered to. Remember: if before any contract is signed you cannot agree on the fee or the method of payment (or any other aspect, for that matter), the consultant must be dismissed in writing, especially if written agreements and details have been exchanged.

The information to be supplied by the agency, in what form, by what deadlines, and how frequently, must be detailed in the contract. If these are *not* articulated in the scope of work to be performed, any information to be supplied by or subcontracted by the consultant must also be detailed. The contract should specify those who will represent the agency and the consultant in the reporting system by name and/or title, or their delegates. The number of meetings a consultant is expected to attend, which meetings these are (in addition to the recommended monthly meeting with the board), should be indicated, as well as what would be expected of the consultant at each meeting. For example, much more might be required of a consultant at a board meeting than at a planning council or any other meeting. There should not be a "wait-and-see attitude," but the information should be clearly detailed in the contract, with a list of meeting dates appended if possible.

[30]See Appendix A for a Sample Agreement between an Agency and a Consultant.

After the contract has been approved by an agency attorney, and has been signed and agreed to by both principals, work can begin according to the predetermined work schedule. During the project the consultant is required to keep the agency informed of progress, not only on an informal day-to-day basis but more formally and explicitly at the pre-arranged meetings cited in the contract.

There are several problems that can arise with consultants once a project is underway which, if anticipated, might be avoided. Many agencies find that consultants have a tendency to put too much emphasis on national standards when evaluating land and facilities; these standards are not always applicable to every community, as is discussed in Chapter 5. "The local community should make every effort to advise all consultants as to local conditions, goals, demands, and the general economic capacities of the community."[31] Since this is an anticipated problem area, it would make sense to clarify it in early discussions with the consultant. A logical time would be during the discussion of planning philosophies, since one's attitude toward national standards reflects a philosophy of planning.

Although a consultant may have been hired because of "objectivity," too often he begins to be overly influenced by local or agency bias. It is important to be alert to any tendency in the consultant to become "one of the boys," losing sight of the broader perspective and expertise for which he was originally hired. Many consultants have difficulty meeting time schedules. In some cases this is due to an overload of work on other contracts. For this reason, it is essential that realistic and appropriate emphasis be given to deadlines.

Once the consultant has been selected, news releases should be issued describing the comprehensive plan, with background on the consultant. After the broad policies and structures of the project have been decided on, and as soon as work begins, a public information campaign is needed to inform the public about the purpose and status of the project.

This section has highlighted the ways of contacting and selecting a consultant, as well as the contractual obligations to be determined. Needless to say, depending on the particular planning project and the details of a plan, these items will vary and should not be considered as exhaustive of the topic.

The administrator, often with the help of the consultant, establishes a planning council, consisting of local citizens, representatives from other agencies, professionals with a specialization or interest in community leisure services, agency staff, a subcommittee of the park board, the consultant, and the agency administrator:

> The choice of those to be represented . . . rests on such considerations as who can bring experiential and expert knowledge of the problem under discussion; who can articulate the ideological positions and the interests

[31]Epperson, "Use of Consulting Services for Park and Recreation Programs."

of the various groups; and who can speak . . . for the organizations that will ultimately be called on to support the proposed program.[32]

Regardless of its success or lack of success, the 1970's has seen the practice of "community representatives" become an accepted part of planning in the human services.

CITIZEN AND STAFF INVOLVEMENT IN PLANNING

Chapter 1 summarized some of the recent history and rationale behind citizen involvement in human services delivery. This concept has expanded into demands that private and business organizations also involve consumers in their policy-making and decision-making mechanisms. However, our emphasis is primarily on public service agencies. We are concerned with the practical applications of citizen participation as a philosophy, and with amplifying some of the general statements made about this concept in Chapter 1.

Why has citizen participation become important, both to community residents and to the public agencies that serve them? At its root, citizen participation is a prelude to citizen involvement and ultimately to citizen control over social agencies. Of course, movement along such an easily conceived continuum is not itself simple, but represents a major political tendency of our time. Yet success in such a movement is by no means ensured:

> community action . . . failed because the organizations of the poor did not amass sufficient influence on their own or through alliances to make lasting changes in the social structures they were trying to affect.[33]

When citizen participation in the policy-making and planning activities of social agencies is resisted—and it can be resisted in a score of ways—what is ultimately at stake is control of that agency and its services.[34] It is recognition of this on the part of many career bureaucrats, politicians, and professionals that causes the basic conflict over citizen involvement. On the other hand, these career professionals espouse the need for community and democracy, knowing that:

> a true community is *itself* a creative, initiating, and synthesizing agent, with the power to determine the architectural unity of its living and

[32]Perlman and Gurin, *Community Organization and Social Planning*, pp. 215–16.
[33]I bid., p. 5.
[34]See, for instance, Arnold Gurin and Joan Levin Ecklein, "Community Organization for What?—Political Power or Service Delivery," *Social Work Practice* (New York: Columbia University Press, 1968), pp. 10–15; special issue on "Citizen Participation," *Journal of the American Institute of Planners*, XXXV, 4, July 1969; J. David Greenstone and Paul E. Peterson, *Race and Authority in Urban Politics: Community Participation and the War on Poverty* (New York: Basic Books, 1973); and David Cox, ed., *How Does a Minority Group Achieve Power: Case Study of Black Americans* (New York: John Wiley & Sons, 1969).

working spaces and their coordination, the power to allocate community property to social uses such as participatory child-care and community recreation centers, and the power to insure preservation and development of its natural ecological environment. This is not an idle utopian dream. ... even in a technologically advanced country the potential for decent community is great, *given the proper pattern of community decision mechanisms.*[35]

Determining the "proper pattern" of community decision mechanisms is not as difficult, of course, as attaining and sustaining these mechanisms. Too often citizen clamor for better, improved, or more humane services leads only to aggrandizement of the professionals who offer such services, with a trickle of services into the community, perhaps a few paraprofessional jobs, or in more "radical" cases, a warm body or two on an advisory board. Most of us in the human services know that too often institutionalized (i.e., professional) forms of providing services "are organized far more effectively to serve and perpetuate the interests of these trained providers, and those who train them, than to meet the needs that they ostensibly exist to serve."[36]

A nice distinction has been made between national and local decision mechanisms in the federal manpower program: Derthick defines the difference between *administrative decentralization*, where certain operational responsibilities are delegated from higher to lower levels, and *decentralization of authority*, which enlarges the influence of the public on the programs being conducted.[37] Administrative decentralization presumably allows greater flexibility in modifying national programs for local needs, whereas the decentralization of authority allows local governments to decide whether they want a program in the first place. The same distinction could also apply to service agencies and local residents.

Citizen participation in community planning would ultimately require decision mechanisms that are the results of a decentralization of authority from professionals and planners to local citizenry. If one follows the precepts of democratic thinking, then logically the authority or power should rest with the citizens, who would then delegate some power back to professionals, making the concept of "public servants" more accurate than it has ever been.

Since we are talking about an eventual power base for the poor and other disenfranchised groups, we should make some distinction

[35]Herbert Gintis, "Toward a Political Economy of Education: A Radical Critique of Ivan Illich's *Deschooling Society,*" in Ivan Illich *et al., After Deschooling, What?* (New York: Harper & Row, Publishers, 1973), pp. 45–46.

[36]Sumner M. Rosen, "Taking Illich Seriously," in Illich *et al., After Deschooling,* p. 97.

[37]Martha Derthick, *The Influence of Federal Grants* (Cambridge, Mass.: Harvard University Press, 1970), cited in Daniel P. Moynihan, *The Politics of a Guaranteed Income: The Nixon Administration and the Family Assistance Plan* (New York: Random House, Inc., 1973), p. 211.

between the concepts of citizen participation and community control: the first is to give advice to those in power or with authority; the second is to gain a share of power over social institutions:

> Involving local groups in elaborate planning procedures guides them into a narrowly circumscribed form of political action for which they are ill equipped. Not only are low-income groups severely handicapped in planning activities, they are diverted from the political action that may most increase their political power.[38]

We can see that citizen participation, while a laudable concept, can frustrate the political actions of citizens.

Citizen involvement, which is of greater depth than citizen participation, can take several forms: working as paraprofessionals, serving on an advisory board or council, sitting as an equal member on a policy-making board, or undertaking social actions related to or developing from an agency. Advocacy or social actions, of course, are the most controversial, but are also the ultimate route to building a power base for a community.

Since we are not in an ideal democratic state, we must deal with the power/control nexus as it exists—securely in the hands of those who determine and those who offer services, not those who require or demand them. It has been effectively argued that if citizens had control over decision mechanisms, or control over basic social decisions, there would be no need for social services in the first place. The acceleration of social services reflects not merely a more humane attitude by government, but an increase in social awareness and commensurate demands by those who suffer from the inequalities of our social and economic systems. Our smorgasbord of social and human services are indeed responsive, responsive to the demands and threats of the disenfranchised, vocal minorities.

Citizen participation in community planning developed from threats to the "very social order" of communities, not from professional interest in laymen power. As far back as a hundred years ago Charles Loring Brace, in his *The Dangerous Classes of New York*, was urging that something be done about juvenile delinquents.[39] Why? Not because these children of "poverty and vice" might be victims of social inequalities and dysfunctions, but because these kids represented a terrible danger to society. "Let the civilizing influences of American life fail to reach them, and, if the opportunity offered, we should see an explosion from this class which might leave this city in ashes and blood."[40]

[38]Bannon, *Outreach*, p. 48.

[39]Charles Loring Brace, *The Dangerous Classes of New York, and Twenty Years' Work Among Them* (New York: Wynkoop and Hallenbeck, 1880).

[40]Quoted in Lawrence M. Friedman, "Society and Its Enemies: The Tolerance Level for Crime," *The Nation*, April 6, 1974, p. 424.

One form of extending civilization to the disenfranchised is through the benign form of social services. From the very start social services have been in reaction to citizen demands, rarely in anticipation of them, and this reaction has too often been to protect the status quo, not to serve the community. And you can bet that a growing number of people are aware of that distinction. If you help me after I threaten you, can you be called a humanitarian?

Service and welfare bureaucracies, which for the most part frustrate and deflect citizen participation, often so compound the problems of those they exist to serve that the solution is usually to offer more or newer services, thus causing the agency to grow (become more bureaucratic), further accelerating the inability of citizens to affect the maze, and so on:

> teachers, doctors, and social workers realize that their distinct professional ministrations have one aspect—at least—in common. They create further demands for the institutional treatments they provide faster than they can provide service institutions.[41]

Social services too often become a *symptom* of the problem rather than its solution:

> Most social work has not directly attacked social problems. In many instances, professionals have been solely concerned with handling individual manifestations of larger problems. Social workers have attempted to help "maladjusted" people *adapt* themselves to society, rather than trying *to change* those aspects of society which hurt people. This is the crux of the revolt in social services today.[42]

All of this is well known to those in the human service professions. It is reiterated here because of the relation of these failures in social services to the concept of citizen participation. When we consider the involvement of community residents in planning community services, be these leisure services or any other, we should first be aware of the broader framework of the concept. This concept is not merely a gesture to "bring in" the community; it is more a mandate for social action. As mentioned in Chapter 1, this mandate was reflected in the requirements and guidelines of the federally sponsored community action programs in the War on Poverty, and later in the Community Development Agencies of the now defunct Model Cities program.[43]

---

[41]Gintis, "Toward a Political Economy of Education," p. 35.

[42]Bannon, *Outreach*, p. 29.

[43]See, for example, U.S. Department of Housing and Urban Development, "Citizen Participation in Model Cities," *Technical Assistance Bulletin No. 3* (Washington, D.C.: Government Printing Office, December 1968); Dudley Post, "The End Comes Too Soon: Requiem for Model Cities," *The New Republic*, April 14, 1973, pp. 13–15; U.S. Office of Economic Opportunity, *OEO Instruction, Participation of the Poor in the Planning, Conduct and Evaluation of Community Action Programs* (Washington, D.C.: Government Printing Office, December 1, 1968); U.S. Office of Economic

Attempts at more comprehensive social planning were evident in the United States during the 1960's, most notably in the Kennedy administration and the legacy of that administration which was inherited and expanded by the Johnson administration. All the demonstration programs in low-income neighborhoods sought to be comprehensive in their approach to social problems; of these, the Model Cities program was by far the most ambitious. The bulk of the planning in Model Cities concentrated on inner-city housing, transportation, and environmental development. The image of Model Cities was intended to be: "a high-level, centralized planning body that is an integral part of city government and has a general mandate to plan for the model neighborhood in a way that will integrate all facets of the city's planning and program resources in a concerted attack on the problems of that neighborhood."[44]

One of the more relevant aspects of Model Cities was authorization to help organize and finance nonprofit corporations of citizens in the model neighborhood. The Model Cities' staff was to act as a liaison between these citizen corporations and government resources. The City Demonstration Agency (CDA), established by the city government where Model Cities funds were granted, handled the planning, budgeting, and administering of some programs, while it subcontracted programs to other agencies, to the citizen corporations, and to various indigenous groups. Therefore, one tenet of the Model Cities philosophy was not only to obtain and improve services for community residents, but to involve them in the planning by helping them organize their own nonprofit community corporations.

Even if involving citizens in the planning of a community's leisure services is not a funding requirement, the precepts of the Community Action Programs (CAP) might be useful to planners and agency staff in efforts to work with local citizens. In the first U.S. Office of Economic Opportunity Community Action Guide (CAG), four rationales for resident participation were given.

First, resident participation should be undertaken with the aim of giving local citizens a realistic perspective on the effectiveness of social services. This aim goes beyond public relations since it seeks to convey realistic information, not a flattering or persuasive image of an agency. The broad aim of the CAP, as of most programs in the

---

Opportunity, *Participation of the Poor in the Community Decision-Making Process* (Washington, D.C.: Government Printing Office, 1969); Hans B. C. Spiegel and Stephen D. Mittenthal, "Neighborhood Power and Control, Implications for Urban Planning," Report prepared for the U.S. Department of Housing and Urban Development, November 1968; Edward M. Kaitz and Herbert Harvey Hyman, *Urban Planning for Social Welfare: A Model Cities Approach* (New York: Praeger Publishers, Inc., 1970); and Roland L. Warren, "Model Cities First Round: Politics, Planning, and Participation," *Journal of the American Institute of Planners*, XXXV, 4, July 1969.

[44] Perlman and Gurin, *Community Organization and Social Planning*, p. 251.

War on Poverty, was to combine social *action* with social *development.*

In attempting this dual aim, the agency administrator and consultant have two objectives: they have to educate community residents; and they have to involve their representatives in the planning council of the agency, perhaps even in the governmental body to which the agency itself reports. One of the reasons given for the failure of community participation was that little money (hence time) was provided for educational purposes, either for personnel in agencies or for citizens.[45] Both sides have to be educated and prepared for this new partnership of effort. A great deal of resistance and antagonism to citizen participation comes from the very agencies established to serve citizens. Comprehensive planning has to include more than outsiders sitting on a planning council who may or may not be heeded.

When we formulate staff involvement in comprehensive planning, we need to consider staff and citizens almost in one breath. The project administrator has to make some clear and terse policies about what he expects from staff in the planning project, their prescribed interactions with the consultant, and their relationship with citizens on the planning council. Often the project administrator and the board need to be educated as well, especially when citizen participation is mandatory or where a vague philosophy of involvement needs substantiation and "teeth." As former President Nixon said about federal Manpower Training, it had a "fine ring and an imprecise meaning," we must give precision and applicability to citizen participation in leisure planning.

Educational efforts to ensure development of community awareness, and the involvement of community residents in leisure planning, can take many forms: preplanning sessions for both staff and citizen representatives, short courses, or simple "warm-up" discussions at planning council meetings.[46] The educational effort should be determined by specific needs in each community. Information for educating staff and citizens can come from their own experiences, those of the consultant, the administrator, or any other source:

> The purpose of the initial organizational efforts . . . is basically educational —to expose potential participants in the project to the problem situation in a way that may arouse interest and concern. Study committees frequently serve this type of educational purpose. . . .[47]

If a community leisure plan is undertaken for a community with residents sophisticated enough and comfortable with governmental

---

[45]David Borden, "Participation on the Block," in Edgar S. Cahn and Barry A. Passett, eds., *Citizen Participation: Effecting Community Change* (New York: Praeger Publishers, Inc., 1971), pp. 184–99.

[46]See, for example, Harvey S. Perloff, *Education for Planning: City, State, and Regional* (Baltimore: Johns Hopkins Press, 1957); and F. B. Gillie, *Basic Thinking in Regional Planning* (The Hague: Mouton & Co., 1967).

[47]Perlman and Gurin, *Community Organization and Social Planning,* p. 68.

agencies and planning, then preplanning education can be less intensive. In most cases, the community members who need to be involved the most, or who are demanding a voice, are those without political sophistication, having been excluded from or apathetic to such involvement. Any effective educational program will require a great amount of time, energy, and money.

If we accept much of the criticism of social services as perceptive, but some of it as inaccurate, then we should make every attempt to give community representatives a more realistic perspective on the agency. If planning for leisure services is centered in a recreation agency, it is that agency's responsibility to define recreation vis-à-vis other social services for the community representatives. This perspective must be conveyed or reemphasized to agency staff as well; make no assumptions about a broad-minded staff. Recreation should be placed in a leisure services context, a social and human services context, and a social, political, and economic context as well.[48] Do not try to avoid the political aspects of placing recreation within a social framework: We are a political force whether we like it or not. Envisioning recreation at some innocent remove from the political life of a community is not only naive but untrue.[49]

The second precept of the Community Action Programs was creation of a power base for the poor so they could direct their own lives. Since most social service agencies are themselves without a power base, it would be ludicrous to pressure them to yield power they may not themselves have. This would be like storming the Bastille—a *symbol* of power but not the *source* of power. However, social service agencies can yield some control, or decentralize their authority, so community groups can participate in leisure or other planning. One method of decentralizing authority is creation of a planning council, consisting of local citizens, the planning consultant, agency staff, liaison members from other community agencies involved in the comprehensive plan, and professionals and experts from fields other than parks and recreation who have contributions for leisure planning. These experts might be subcontracted by the consultant or invited by the project administrator.

The selection of citizens to serve on a planning council can be a delicate matter, unless there are citizens' organizations which represent the segments most likely to be overlooked. Most efforts at formal community participation have been through community corporations or councils, which are usually funded by community residents, foundations, and federal grants:

48The discussions in Bannon, *Outreach*, should be useful for this purpose.

49For a study of community power structures, see Floyd Hunter, *Community Power Structures: A Study of Decision Makers* (Chapel Hill: University of North Carolina Press, 1953); and Nelson W. Polsby, *Community Power and Political Theory* (New Haven: Yale University Press, 1963).

These are private, nonprofit organizations governed by resident-selected boards who control their own funds. The first generation of community corporations appeared in 1966 as part of the CAPs. The advisory committee has long been used by government agencies, but not until CAP was it broadened to include the poor, as well as middle- and upper-class city leaders and community workers.[50]

In a community where such a corporation already exists, that corporation's board would be the most likely group to select community representatives. Of course, as also warned in Chapter 1, we have to be very careful that we are not getting old-time or middle-class politicos who claim to represent those without representation.[51] Where there is no organized group whom the planners can approach for council representatives, the agency and the planning consultant will have to seek out—using their intuition and best judgment—the sources of viable community representatives.

The third precept of the Community Action Programs was to use the administrative and psychological potentialities gained from citizen involvement. By involving residents in planning—assuming they are prepared to take full advantage of such involvement—we can obtain a great many insights on the project, while also enhancing the morale of the community. Naturally, if the motivation for having citizens involved in leisure planning is merely to boost their spirits, or to take administrative shortcuts through otherwise intractable issues, then we are likely to fail. The psychological and administrative gains must be secondary to the primary necessity for participation.

The fourth CAP precept, and one we will not comment further on here, was the general value of participatory democracy, especially at the local level. This seems self-explanatory.[52] These four community action rationales are, of course, not the only ones; there are many reasons for having citizens participate in leisure planning, from the more pragmatic desire to assuage citizen demands to the more visionary ones of policy-making control.

A planning council is simply *one* way of involving citizens; it is far from the only way, nor is it necessarily the most effective. It is recommended because it seems the best way to introduce citizens to planning in the social and human services.

> Citizens often wanting to have a word or hand in decision making and program determination feel inadequate when confronted with profes-

50Bannon, *Outreach*, p. 43.

51See, for example, Irving Lazar, "Which Citizens to Participate in What?" in Cahn and Passett, *Citizen Participation*, pp. 92–109; and Ecklein and Lauffer, *Community Organizers and Social Planners*, Chapter 12, "Selecting A Model Cities Board."

52See, for instance, Harold H. Weissman, *Community Councils and Community Control: The Workings of Democratic Mythology* (Pittsburgh: University of Pittsburgh Press, 1970).

sional superiority and techniques, a feeling produced not totally from lack of education, but more from lack of experience.[53]

The best way to gain such experience is, of course, through involvement, with education and thoughtful preparation available from the agency.[54]

The policy formulations on citizen involvement, and also on staff involvement, have to be made *prior* to any planning work and must be clear and specific. To open up an agency's decision-making or policy-making mechanisms to the public is not achieved by generalities about the value of participatory democracy. If at any point in our professional careers we crystallize our thinking about citizen involvement in social agencies, it is at this stage. Broad and generous statements about citizen involvement have their place, but not in policy formulation. All those involved in a planning effort—either a simple or large-scale project—should undertake it with a *clear* understanding of their part, their scope of responsibility, and the role of those they work with. This goal is not achieved by well-intentioned statements about how we are all in it together, etc. A fault of many planning guidelines is that generalization masks uncertainty: the planners hope to sidestep the need for specificity by using glowing yet vague language. One reads these guidelines, lulled by the language into believing that something substantive has been stated, and of course it has not.

The degree of citizen involvement—advice giving, policy making, working for the agency as a paraprofessional, or being involved in policy making—has to be detailed as a policy, not as a preference. It has to mesh with and be reflected against staff involvement, to anticipate tasks or areas of responsibility where confusion or conflict might arise between both groups. A good many suggestions and insights will come from the very people to be involved: from the consultants, who have valuable experience (presumably); from staff members, who are concerned with and preparing for their planning role; and from the citizen representatives themselves.

When inaugurating citizen participation, there is no need for the administrator to try to anticipate all conflicts. When everyone is involved

---

[53] John G. Williams, "Administrative Problems Inherent in the Outreach Program," in Bannon, *Outreach*, pp. 133–34.

[54] See, for example, William W. and Loureide J. Biddle, *Encouraging Community Development: A Training Guide for Local Workers* (New York: Holt, Rinehart and Winston, Inc., 1968). In this book the authors describe "the more sensitive ethical conduct necessary to help people become competent to contribute to the solving of their problems" (viii). See also Arthur Hillman, *Community Organization and Planning* (New York: Crowell-Collier and Macmillan, 1950); Clarence King, *Working with People in Community Action* (New York: Association Press, 1965); William J. Platt, "Individuals: Neglected Elements in Planning," *International Development Review*, V, 3, September 1963; and "Planning and Politics: Citizen Participation in Urban Renewal," *Journal of the American Institute of Planners*, November 1963.

in the preplanning, it is surprising how soon the administrative and psychological potentialities of democracy become evident. So also the headaches of democracy. If our interest in citizen participation is genuine, and if involvement is to succeed, then time, patience, and inefficiencies are all required.

Attempts at community involvement must, of necessity, concentrate on participation, responsiveness, and power-sharing for the community, rather than on economy and efficiency for the agencies.

> Citizens who try to cooperate with planners should realize that these professional people also suffer from confused motivations and ambivalences. They want to evolve plans that are a credit to their profession and are workable. Yet they want to have democratic participation in the evolving and adoption of their plans, lest their blueprints remain forever in dusty files . . . . they want people to be a part of the planning process, but do not want to be bothered with the troubles of seeking people's participation.[55]

If citizens need to learn about planning, planners need to learn how to work effectively with community representatives.

There is an understandable tendency for citizen representatives to give more attention to the most *obvious* community needs and problems, while resisting the routine, often boring and frustrating planning tasks. Since attacking the most obvious problem is too often an attack on symptoms of a deeper dysfunction, this tendency has to be resisted. "This tendency toward immediacy is good for the beginning, but it normally leads to poor planning if in the process citizens are persuaded to undertake more and more difficult tasks."[56]

It is the responsibility of the agency director or project consultant— whoever has the responsibility of working with the planning council— to encourage and lead citizens into progressively more complex and difficult tasks. The policies for such tasks must, of course, be determined *prior* to the start of planning. While it is not sensible to rigidly adhere to policy guidelines, it is also not sensible to keep modifying these guidelines based on success or failure with local residents. The range of possibility should be stated in the original guidelines, from advisory functions to advocacy planning, if the latter is the desire of the agency.[57]

Once the poor or other minorities are given a say in planning

---

[55]Donna E. Shalala, *Neighborhood Governance* (New York: American Jewish Committee, 1971), p. 137.

[56]Ibid., p. 136.

[57]For a discussion of advocacy in planning, see Earl M. Blecher, *Advocacy Planning for Urban Development* (New York: Praeger Publishers, Inc., 1971); Lisa R. Peattie, "Reflections on Advocacy Planning," *Journal of the American Institute of Planners*, XXXIV (March 1968), 80–88; and Paul Davidoff, "Advocacy Pluralism in Planning," *Journal of the American Institute of Planners*, XXXI, 4 (November 1965), 331–39.

leisure services, or any service for that matter, they will begin to eventually operate as a "quasi-political" force in the community.[58] Although the aim of citizen participation on a planning council may not be a political gesture, in essence it is. That is why it is important, as noted earlier, not to forget the political implications of community planning. Although social service agencies do not take on the task of developing citizens into a quasi-political force, one result of a good working relationship, and of an effective educational effort, is greater political awareness and expertise among the residents involved; often the professionals themselves are politicized in the process. Since increased awareness often leads to conflict between the agency and community residents, it is best to anticipate its emergence and consider useful ways of dealing with it.

Community representatives on planning councils and advisory boards are sometimes so affected by the experience that their participation in the political system rises, their personal and political effectiveness increases, and they begin to view themselves as leaders. "Leaders for social change are being created where they did not exist before."[59] It is at this juncture that many professionals argue we should go beyond citizen participation in planning and move toward ensuring their political and social self-reliance.[60] It is not our purpose here to resolve this dilemma, but it should be recognized that this is a logical outcome of citizen participation in any social planning. Often citizens groups, rather than waiting passively to be asked to advise a public agency or private institution, demand involvement and control, or what has been recently called a "radical form of populism," an effort "to build a power base to force existing institutions to change."[61] It is important when preparing policies for citizen participation to anticipate receiving very clear citizen demands on what *they* want participation to be. To believe we are doing citizens a favor by "letting" them participate denotes an astonishing lack of political awareness.

Arnstein offers a typology or classification of the degrees of citizen participation and citizen control as they existed in federal programs.[62]

---

[58]Edgar S. and Jean Camper Cahn, "Maximum Feasible Participation: A General Overview," in Cahn and Passett, *Citizen Participation*, pp. 9–66.

[59]Dale Rogers Marshall, *The Politics of Participation in Poverty* (Berkeley: The University of California Press, 1971).

[60]Paul A. Kurzman and Jeffrey R. Solomon, *Beyond Advocacy: A New Model for Community Organization, Social Work Practice* (New York: Columbia University Press, 1970).

[61]Derek Shearer, "CAP [Citizen's Action Program]: New Breeze in the Windy City," *Ramparts*, October 1973, pp. 12–16. See also, Alan A. Altshuler, *Community Control: The Black Diamond for Participation in Large American Cities* (New York: Pegasus, 1970). The rise of Citizen Action Projects, most notably in urban areas, has shown again that not only public agencies and institutions are under fire but private institutions, businesses, and corporations as well.

[62]Sherry R. Arnstein, "A Ladder of Citizen Participation," *Journal of the American Institute of Planners*, July 1969, pp. 216–24.

Illustration 2.1, devised by Arnstein, shows the degrees of citizen participation on an eight-rung ladder. As is evident from this illustration, citizen involvement has ranged from nonpartcipation—where individuals might be involved in clinical group therapy or other therapy to divert their energies and anger from the demand for control[63]—to varying degrees of citizen control beyond tokenism and placation.

"*Placation* is simply a higher level of tokenism because the ground rules allow have-nots to advise, but retain for the power-holders the continued right to decide." *Manipulation* is when citizens are placed on "rubberstamp advisory committees or advisory boards for the express purpose of 'educating' them or engineering their support." On the other hand, *consultation* is usually seeking information from community residents (most often through surveys, meetings, or public hearings), whereas *informing* is advising citizens of their rights, responsibilities, and options.[64]

Any policy formulator on citizen participation should keep this ladder in mind, since it simply and bluntly testifies to the kinds of loopholes that surround resident participation in professional organi-

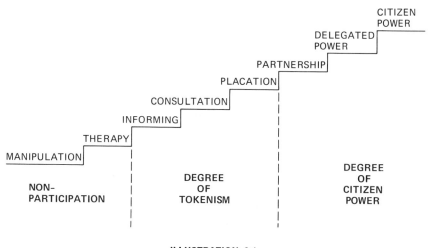

ILLUSTRATION 2.1
Citizen Participation Ladder

Source: Sherry R. Arnstein, "A Ladder of Citizen Participation," *Journal of the American Institute of Planners* (July 1969), p. 217.

[63]Ms. Arnstein cites Robert Coles, "Social Struggle and Weariness," *Psychiatry*, XXVII (November 1964), 305–15, to elucidate the use of therapy; see also Jerome Agel, *The Radical Therapist* (New York: Ballantine Books, Inc., 1971); and William H. Grier and Price M. Cobbs, *Black Rage* (New York: Bantam Books, Inc., 1968).

[64]Arnstein, "A Ladder of Citizen Participation," pp. 217–18.

zations. The essence of Ms. Arnstein's message is that participation without a redistribution of power is "an empty and frustrating process for the powerless." In *partnership*, the citizens can to some extent "negotiate and engage in trade-offs with traditional power-holders." Nonetheless, she does feel that:

> ... employment of the have-nots in a program or on a planning staff could occur at any of the eight rungs and could represent either a *legitimate* or *illegitimate* characteristic of citizen participation. Depending on their motives, power-holders can hire poor people to coopt them, to placate them, or to utilize the have-nots' special skills and insights.[65]

Most of the literature on community involvement in planning has dealt with three forms of planning: *consensus, cooptation,* or *centrally planned change:*

> *Consensus* refers to the traditional "council" model, criticized in the literature on the ground that "participation of all" leads primarily to trade-offs and the protection of the status quo. *Cooptation* is associated with the type of structure in which representatives of a minority view or interest are included within an organizational framework dominated by others but render legitimacy to the latter's purposes.... "Tokenism" would be the popular term for [such] a structure.... A *central planner*—individual, group, or organization— ... organizes a structure designed to maximize his opportunity to achieve that purpose.[66]

In the Model Cities programs many communities had created citizens' policy boards and committees which had no policy-making function whatever. A HUD analysis of City Demonstration Agencies indicated that:

1. Most CDA's did not negotiate citizen participation requirements with residents.
2. Citizens were extremely suspicious of this new panacea program.
3. Most CDA's were not working with citizens' groups that were genuinely representative of model neighborhoods and accountable to neighborhood constituencies.
4. Residents were unaware of their minimum rights, responsibilities, and options available under the program.
5. Most of the technical assistance provided by CDA's and city agencies was third-rate, paternalistic, and condescending.
6. Most CDA's were not engaged in planning comprehensive enough to expose and deal with the roots of urban decay.
7. Residents were not getting enough information from CDA's to review CDA-developed plans or to initiate their own plans as required by HUD.
8. The training of residents, which would enable them to understand federal-state-city systems, was not even considered by most CDA's.[67]

[65]Ibid., p. 218.

[66]Perlman and Gurin, *Community Organization and Social Planning*, pp. 68–69.

[67]U.S. Department of Housing and Urban Development, "Citizen Participation in Model Cities," cited in Arnstein, "A Ladder of Citizen Participation," p. 221.

Such evidence shows that people are being planned *for* rather than with.

Burke, in a discussion of citizen participation, indicates five degrees of resident involvement comparable to Arnstein's ladder: education-therapy, behavioral change, staff supplement, cooptation, and community power. He concludes, not so surprisingly, that:

> Planning agencies must be more precise about what they mean by citizen participation, how they intend to organize and involve citizens, and what voice citizens will have in planning decisions. This may mean a redefinition of planning agencies' goals toward a new focus where a citizen group assumes the responsibility for defining the goals and aims of the planning agency. But it also may mean less contentious citizen participation.[68]

For these reasons, a clear policy and intent of involvement by citizens, with the motivations for seeking such involvement understood by all concerned, can help reduce later recriminations about deception or cooptation. Whatever form citizen participation is intended to take should be reflected in the title of the committee, council, or board. Of course, if citizen demands change or rise in the course of a planning project, a strict interpretation of agreed-on guidelines might antagonize them unnecessarily; a policy must be well thought out and articulated, but it must also remain flexible.

The following checklist summarizes the aspects to be reflected in a policy for citizen involvement:

- Do not establish a rubber stamp council.
- Prepare extensive training and orientation for citizens.
- Be willing to encounter and reflect a different value system than that of most professionals.
- Remember that citizens are skeptical of the "establishment."
- Ensure an atmosphere that encourages citizens to speak freely.
- Do not preclude items for discussion as "for policy board only."
- Listen to what citizens have to say.
- Have enough resources—money, personnel, and power—to make participation effective.
- Have a complete understanding of the participatory relationship *before* undertaking planning.

Members of the park and recreation board also have to be involved in the planning process. This is the group who often determine and who must approve all policies; thus their function is integral to planning. In addition to their consultation on the formulation of staff and citizen participation policies, and their role in selecting a planning consultant, the park and recreation board will also be organized into planning committees, which will reflect various aspects of the planning program:

---

[68]Edmund M. Burke, "Citizen Participation Strategies," *Journal of the American Institute of Planners*, XXXIV, 5 (September 1968), 294.

- Finance
- Land acquisition and development
- Personnel
- Program
- Community involvement
- Public information
- Agency relations

Finally, after policies on staff and citizen participation have been established and agreed to, attention has to be given to informing the community about the consultant, the scope of work to be done, the public's involvement in the project, and the aims and objectives of planning. For these a public information program needs to be designed and carried out.

PUBLIC INFORMATION PROGRAM

A public information campaign has to be designed before the project starts, since public information and news releases are used throughout. News releases should be prepared not only at the start of the project, announcing the consultant, scope of work, and deadlines, but should be prepared throughout the entire project. These releases, in addition to keeping the public informed on the status and details of the comprehensive plan, also help to raise public awareness and interest in the plan, most critically in its implementation. Sometimes these releases stimulate the flagging interests of those directly involved in the plan itself.

A public information campaign to present the recommendations of the plan, and the suggestions for implementation, has to involve as many media and forms of communication as feasible. Too often the task of channeling information to the public is left to the news media. With little or no planned information from the agency, the community is kept unaware of what a comprehensive community plan entails. In such cases, if a public hearing is held at some point during the project, the meeting could become a forum for people to "blow off steam" rather than serve as an opportunity for an *informed* group to discuss whatever is at issue.

Of course public information programs cannot ignore the reportage function of the media, but they cannot rely entirely on newspapers, television, and radio to gather and prepare the information on an agency project, carefully and correctly, emphasizing what needs to be emphasized, and giving a progress and status report of the overall project. Since the media are interested in news events, and since so much of comprehensive planning is tedious and time-consuming, reporters will either ignore the activity altogether or look for news angles; these "angles" are not always accurate nor germane, though they may provide interesting tidbits.

Only by preparing and distributing news releases can an agency have some control over what is released and in what form. If the atmosphere seems to require, or if there is enough interest, press conferences or panel discussions can be set up for open-ended evaluation and discussion of the entire plan. These can be stimulating whether on television, radio, or at public meetings. It is up to the project administrator to *influence* public opinion on the comprehensive plan through public education, and tasteful, accurate, and well-designed information releases, films, summary reports, open meetings, and any other mode.

If the consultant is to be involved in a public information program, he or she will be concerned with both its design and implementation. Since the consultant has to prepare information for various purposes on the status of the project, and must make a presentation at the plan's completion, he is an excellent choice to handle most public information tasks. Many consultants include such skills in their services. Of course, whatever the consultant is to handle must be specified in the written agreement. As noted earlier, in considering the competence of a consultant in this area, ask for samples and copies of public releases and other presentations he has made; also check with former clients. It may not be too useful to check with current clients of the consultant, since the bulk of public information work comes at the end of a plan and may not be readily determined for ongoing projects.

Information, whether flattering or not, must be disseminated to the public. Local citizens, especially those on the planning council, usually take part in information gathering and presentation. This ensures that all information of interest to the community is released, and that face-saving or other expansive gestures are kept to a minimum. If citizen representatives begin to identify too closely with the agency and if joint efforts to embellish information releases occur, intentionally or not, then the media reporter can be valuable in breaking any collusive web hiding or disguising information. While the media can easily distort or oversimplify information on the one hand, they can also help to expose attempts by the planners to distort or embellish information. For example if one of the Community Development Agencies of the Model Cities program had been releasing false information on citizen participation, an alert reporter would have served a real public service in broadcasting this fact.

Public information applies not only to dissemination of information to the community, but to its distribution to the park board and members of the planning council as well. How many have had the not-too-pleasant experience of hearing news on radio or television that we should have been privy to in advance?

Information programs, to be valuable, have to allow for two-way communication, in which those receiving the information can comment on it if they choose. The best way to achieve a two-way public discussion is to hold small public meetings. If groups are too large the presentation tends to be formal and the responses from the audience nonexistent or mere harangues. If the interest is there or can be cultivated, everyone should be encouraged and have ample opportunity to express their views.

Although its applications are not clarified yet, the development of cable television, especially rulings about citizen access to channels, might offer one way to ensure such two-way communication.[69]

Public education should raise the community's awareness of the distinctions between information that is available to them and information that is not available (and why). A public information campaign must judge the proper information for a release, raise the public's interest in such information, and give them all the information necessary to achieve informed participation. As part of its educational effort, the agency can bring citizens to a point where they will know the kinds of information they desire, will recognize poor or distorted information, and will be able to demand lucid information when needed. For the community to be informed as much as their selected representatives on the planning council, they too will require an access to skills for assessing information, as well as the right to affect and influence the information disseminated.

One of the prime aspects to come out of the agitations over the "Pentagon Papers," the Anderson tapes, and the entire Watergate affair is not only the public's right to know, but their ability to judge and weigh what they do know. We have been often described as "over-informed and underreflective America."[70] Access to information is only part of a public information program; the ability to understand the value of what is being conveyed is critical to any two-way communication. Unless one is keenly trained in what to look for in seemingly innocuous releases, information of import and value is often missed. The gripe about the Pentagon Papers is not that they were released, but how they were released—with a skill for getting the public's eye, front page in *The New York Times*, which has probably the best qualified readership in the world.

The public's ability to get a message quickly and accurately is partly dependent on their ability to weigh information. If we support the public's *right* to know, then vague, distorted, or "hidden" information does not serve that right, at the local or at any other level. It is a pleasure to present information to an audience who can readily determine its worth. Their interpretation of the information need not be that of the planning agency. As letters to the Editor columns in

[69]For a summary of Federal Communication Commission Rulings on this new broadcast system, see Steven R. Rivkin, *Cable Television: A Guide to Federal Regulations* (Santa Monica, Calif.: Rand, March 1973).

[70]Most recently in Jean-Louis Servan-Schreiber, *The Power to Inform: The Business of Information* (New York: McGraw-Hill Book Company, 1974).

newspapers attest, the readership is not always in agreement with the purveyors of information. An agency does not seek consensus from a public information campaign (that's the task of press agentry); it desires an informed, enlightened, and responsive audience. Part of the task of assuring these qualities in any community rests with the planning agency.

SUMMARY AND CONCLUSION

Planning is far from simple, no matter how logical its various steps might seem:

> It is a demanding process . . . and without complete understanding and a disciplined approach, planning may fall far short of our expectations. The point is that planning is not an automatic thing. It may result only in wasted time, for difficulties abound in its implementation.[71]

Cited in the literature are several administrative reasons why planning fails:

1. The planning project is not integrated into the agency's administrative structure.
2. The various aspects of planning have not been sufficiently understood by those involved.
3. Planning has been done *solely* by a planning unit or specialists, causing the rest of the agency staff and community to abdicate any responsibility for it.
4. The agency administration and board expect the plan to come out as anticipated with no unforeseen problems or surprises.
5. Too much is attempted at one time.
6. The administrator or planners fail to follow the plan's model or guidelines.
7. Inadequate information is used.
8. Too much emphasis is given to one aspect of planning to the neglect of others.[72]

Another reason for planning failure, which goes beyond administrative difficulties, is the unwillingness of the planning leadership to challenge the status quo where necessary:

> The often disastrous results of the [urban] planners' work are a function of . . . their adherence to the conventions of a repressive social structure which is biased against the people their plans are supposed to serve.[73]

[71]Stephen J. Knezevich, *A Resource Allocation Decision System for Education: Program Budgeting (PPBS)* (Berkeley, Calif.: McCutchan Publishing Corporation, 1973), p. 35.

[72]See K. A. Ringbakk, "Why Planning Fails," *European Business.* Reprinted in *Notes and Quotes* (Hartford: Connecticut General Life Insurance Company, 1972).

[73]Robert Goodman, *After the Planners* (New York: Simon and Schuster, 1972), quoted in Robert Woods Kennedy, "Insistent Patterns of Repression," *The New Republic*, March 18, 1972, p. 28.

If we intend not to "rock the boat," or if we feel the present situation requires drastic change, either principle must be stated in the planning policies formulated. If one of the reasons for planning in the first place is dissatisfaction with a situation, then to solve the problem while also avoiding conflicts with established or dominant factions seems an exercise in futility. If we are hypocritical, saying one thing in our policies, little expecting to practice them, we must remember that hypocrisy imposes its own obligations and restrictions. By being hypocritical we in no way avoid the demands of the situation; in fact we may compound them. Planning fails because we have been unable *or* unwilling to reflect in policies our true positions on social planning.

As noted by Sherry Arnstein earlier, involvement of citizens at any level of planning can be either legitimate or illegitimate, depending on the motivations of those with power. If we wish *not* to yield any power to citizens, then the policies formulated for their involvement should not belie this wish with rhetoric on shared decision making, delegation of authority (there are those who argue that power cannot be delegated), and the like. On the other hand, if citizens are to share in policy making for planning, they should be involved in drawing up the very policies governing their own involvement. It has always amused me to hear bureaucrats and administrators say, "We are interested in shared policy making, and here is *our* policy on this issue." A policy invariably drawn up in the recesses of some board room!

Policy formation, be it for citizen or staff roles or any other aspect of planning, has its roots in the values and goals of the agency. In fact, policies are usually considered concrete statements of these abstract values. Policies attempt to incorporate (in writing) some continuity of attitude and operations over time, the laws and regulations of an agency, and guides for future actions. Like all aspects of administration and planning, policies involve a choice—choice among the values and goals of the agency and among those of the community. *"A methodology of policy analysis is therefore a technique for making choices clear and explicit and for using data in order to achieve that purpose."*[74]

In formulating policies, the administrator or planner should have in mind a theory or an opinion about the long-run interests of the community, comparing these to the goals of the agency for any possible contradictions or ambiguities.[75] Policy formulation is not an objective practice, in that it involves both the values of the agency and what are felt to be the best long-run goals for serving the community. Since policies involve a choice among several goals or values, an administrator can use various management techniques to help in policy formulation.

[74]Perlman and Gurin, *Community Organization and Social Planning*, p. 71.

[75]See John W. Dyckman, "Societal Goals and Planned Societies," in H. Wentworth Eldridge, ed., *Taming Megalopolis*, Vol. I (Garden City, N.Y.: Doubleday & Company, Inc., 1967), p. 258.

These techniques can be useful for the decision making that occurs throughout the entire planning project; their use in preplanning can give the administration a better idea of their possible applications later on.

In the methodology that has developed for policy analysis, the following approaches have been useful:

- Ends-means analysis
- Systems analysis
- Cost-benefit analysis
- Resource analysis
- Policy strategy

Since policies involve both *ends and means,* and the values implied in both, an attempt should be made to distinguish between ends and means for policy statements. If the goal is for citizens to share in policy or decision making, and the means is membership on a planning council, the administrator should relate these to the long-run concerns of the community. If decision-making power is to be viable and to extend beyond the duration of the planning project, this goal has to be reflected in the policy.

Systems analysis can be useful for specifying the structure and relationships of the planning project and the structures and relationships outside the agency that the project might affect. The alternatives that are considered would be comparable to those in ends-means analysis.[76] *Cost-benefit analysis* can help to determine the benefits of various alternatives. *Resource analysis* is used to determine available funds, manpower, and expertise, and how and to what extent each of these relate to each alternative. Finally, a *policy strategy* would be the foundation from which all policies would develop. Based on the above methods and the alternative(s) that survive analysis, a policy strategy would be selected. All policies then written would derive from the policy strategy decided on.[77]

[76]Yehezkel Dror, in "Prolegomena [Introduction] to Policy Science," *Policy Sciences,* I, 1 (Spring 1970), 135–50, argues that systems analysis is too limited for use in the human services because it does not take into account political realities and other "irrational" elements. Among these elements he lists values, ideologies, and the charisma of the people involved. Furthermore, systems analysis only deals with alternatives that are known and does not uncover unknown alternatives. Although policy science is in the infant stage, it tries to reflect these qualitative elements in its analysis. See also K. A. Archibald, "Three Views of the Expert's Role in Policymaking: Systems Analysis, Incrementalism, and the Clinical Approach," *Policy Sciences,* I, 1 (Spring 1970), 73–86, who argues for more comprehensive approaches to policy making than relying on any one technique.

[77]See, for example, Bannon, *Problem Solving in Recreation and Parks,* op. cit., and Perlman and Gurin, "Policy Analysis and Choice" in *Community Organization and Social Policy,* pp. 70–73.

Naturally, for most agencies a policy strategy might already exist, either implied or explicit. In that case, the policies formulated and devised for the planning project would have to be consistent or complementary to the overall strategy; otherwise planning will fail or the agency will experience serious upsets and confusion. Policies should be reassessed throughout a project, but if the basic purpose and philosophy of an agency are undermined in the process, the conflict must be resolved.

If contradictory policies are formulated, it is impossible for both the agency *and* the planning project to succeed. One or both will suffer. Serious thought and time given to policy formulations and analyses during preplanning can help diminish possible failure. If policies are weakly assessed, no matter how good the administration of the project itself, these weak policies will ultimately undermine the entire plan. The literature and our own experiences abound with lessons in this simple precept.

SELECTED REFERENCES

American Society of Consulting Planners. *Administrative Manual for Consulting Planners*. Washington, D.C.: ASCP, 1970.

Guides for Planning Your Community. Department of Business and Economic Development, State of Illinois, 1966.

KNITTEL, R. E. *Organization of Community Groups in Support of the Planning Process and Code Enforcement Administration*. U.S. Department of Health, Education and Welfare, Public Health Service, Bureau of Community Environmental Management. Washington, D.C.: Government Printing Office, 1970.

KOTLER, M. *Neighborhood Government*. Indianapolis: Bobbs-Merrill Co., Inc., 1969.

LIPPITT, G. L. *Organization Renewal*. New York: Meredith Corporation, 1969.

NISBET, R. A. *Community and Power*. New York: Oxford University Press, 1962.

Planning Administrative Personnel in Local Governments, A Pilot Study. U.S. Department of Labor, Bulletin 1631. Washington, D.C.: Government Printing Office, June 1969.

TOMSON, B. *It's the Law*. New York: Channel Press, 1960.

Using Consultants. U.S. Department of Housing and Urban Development, Management Assistance Program, No. 11. Washington, D.C.: Government Printing Office, 1971.

3

POPULATION IMPLICATIONS FOR PLANNING

The basic social situation is very simple. The deterioration of the environment in the United States has been accelerated by the expansion of our population at too rapid a rate and far beyond a beneficial maximum level. Furthermore, the prospect of additional population growth will necessarily complicate, if not made impossible, the task of improving or even maintaining the present level of environmental quality.

THE POPULATION CONTROVERSY

As a nation we are in the grips of an enigma, or at least a paradox: as the rate of our population growth drops, the actual number of people seems to remain alarmingly high. To paraphrase Moynihan, in his assessment of the 1960's in general, things get better and worse.[1] There are multiple explanations for the so-called "population explosion," as well as a myriad of solutions offered to cope with that explosion in this country and throughout the world. This chapter will discuss many of these solutions and some of the controversies surrounding them, and in particular will relate the implications of population and its attendant social issues to community planning for leisure services and to recre-

---

[1]Daniel P. Moynihan, *The Politics of a Guaranteed Income: The Nixon Administration and the Family Assistance Plan* (New York: Vintage Books, 1973), p. 38: "The 1960's was a period of marked demographic change, curiously parallel to and interconnected with changes in income and employment. Things got better and worse."

ation in general. There is probably no current issue with as many implications for our patterns of leisure as population and broad demographic change.

Although the discussion here centers primarily on the United States, if we have learned anything these past few years, we should realize how delicately related our well-being is to that of the rest of the world. Aside from our diminished hegemony over countries with resources essential to our voracious society, the biological hegemony of man over nature is disintegrating. Of course, philosophical arguments can be made that man never dominated nature but only abused and mutilated her. Nonetheless, the result is the same. The term "rape" is often applied to what we have done to our national surroundings—the animal and vegetative life, the land, waterways, and air that constitute our essential biosphere. All aspects of our ecosphere—life on earth, in the atmosphere, and in the waters—are threatened, damaged, or already destroyed by the puzzling alienation and accelerating disharmony of humans with all other life.

Field naturalists at the turn of the century had already seen man's distance from nature: "There is no doubt that men are very ignorant about Nature. . . . We are not *in* Nature; we are out of her, having made our own conditions; and our conditions have reacted upon and made us what we are—artificial creatures. Nature is now something pretty to go and look at occasionally, but not too often nor for too long a time."[2] We have reached the point where even these occasional glimpses at nature are severely threatened. Land, water, and air are endangered elements, which sadly need to be protected from mankind, as so many animal species have been. The most prominent cause of such destruction is thought to be burgeoning populations:

> The U.S. Forest Service estimates that 60 million people now live within a day's drive of the White Mountains. To them must be added at least 5 million Canadians. Their combined numbers will increase to perhaps 110 million by the turn of the century, making the WMNF [White Mountain National Forest] one of the most important and most vulnerable green belts in the world.[3]

In addition to its recreational use, these White Mountains yield trees to commercial loggers, their waters to the Eastern megalopolis, and minerals to miners: "At present the loggers degrade the forest most seriously. Even a tourist can view the degradation—great geometric shapes cut out of the hillsides, making the ski resorts look like conser-

---

[2]W. H. Hudson, *The Book of a Naturalist* (New York: G. H. Doran, 1919), Quoted in Walter De La Mare, *Pleasures and Speculations* (London: Faber and Faber, Ltd, n.d.), pp. 48–49.

[3]Daniel Ford, "The White Mountains: Must We Close Them to Save Them?" *The Nation*, January 19, 1974, p. 80.

vation areas by comparison."[4] Even if the loggers were gone and the park confined only to backpackers, Ford does not believe the White Mountains could tolerate that limited usage either: there are simply too many backpackers. As open space becomes more of a premium, even if the present fad for backpacking in this country subsides, the vulnerability of the White Mountains remains. These mountains would still constitute the most lucrative, albeit damaged, green belt in the East. No one is quite sure how to save such areas from destruction by "nature lovers." "Trails die, just as campsites do: the soil is now dead along the beautiful Ammonoosuc Ravine Trail, on the western slope of Mount Washington. It can be healed, but only if the traffic—and the destruction—are diverted."[5]

As we think about planning leisure services for the future, of which outdoor recreation is the most threatened aspect, there is no way we can ignore the vulnerability of such green belts to people and to commerce. Ford's solution for the White Mountain National Forest is radical and poignant:

> Close it carefully, step by step, but close it. . . . If it is not possible to maintain the White Mountains in a condition approaching nature's, and still allow free access to everyone who claims to love nature, then its lovers must be kept out.[6]

Although most of us would agree that population expansion is a real problem, not all accept its unquestionable link to environmental pollution. Although Ford admits to the greater damage done by commercial loggers, it is ultimately people whom he fears more, those millions of tramping boots.

> Ehrlich [author of *The Population Bomb*] believes that population is the most pressing problem posed by environmental pollution. But it is questionable whether reduction of population in the United States, for instance, would do much to alleviate environmental pollution. As Barry Commoner, the ecologist, points out, much of the stress that caused pollution began at the end of the Second World War. During that period there was tremendous growth in per capita production of pollutants. . . . This suggests that technology and industry, not the increased numbers of people, increased pollution. . . . The most severe population explosion exists in India. But India contributes little or nothing to environmental pollution.[7]

Others feel that if we want to control pollution, we should attack

[4] Ibid., p. 81.
[5] Ibid., p. 83.
[6] Ibid., pp. 83–84.
[7] James Ridgeway, *The Politics of Ecology* (New York: E. P. Dutton, 1970), pp. 190–91.

it directly and not via diversionary concern with population control: "The two problems of population pressure and pollution abatement are, both conceptually and in practice, quite separate and distinct."[8]

In the White Mountain National Forest, even though it is the loggers that degrade the forest the most, it is tourists and visitors who will receive the brunt of the criticism and the greatest loss. Plans for "Management Areas" in the park call for 60 percent of it to be given over to the loggers! It is much easier to focus criticism on abstract numbers of heedless park visitors than to examine the implications of the commercial rape of the environment. We all carry some blame for the careless and abusive attitudes we have toward the natural environment. However, some are more to blame than others, and it little serves our purpose as recreationists to fault the unborn for problems created well before the expansion of population.

Concern over population growth is basically a political and economic concern about the distribution of the world's natural and monetary wealth. That is why the major impetus for population control comes from the richest and among the least populated countries in the world, the United States: "The 'Population Explosion' within the United States is not as depressing as the Neo-Malthusians claim. The U.S. has a current population of about 215 million. The people are spread over 3,615,123 square miles of land, for a density of approximately 55 persons per square mile."[9] Our population at present growth rates is projected to be perhaps 280 to 290 million by the year 2000, although predictions vary quite widely depending on who is issuing them and what premises are used.

The interest in population control stems primarily from white, middle- and upper-class groups, and the movement is often sponsored by the wealthy. For instance, during the 1950's the Rockefellers first financed the Population Council, Planned Parenthood, and the Population Reference Bureau. A committee of population experts from the Rockefeller Fund, the Conservation Foundation, and Planned Parenthood in 1957 argued that the United States had an overall balance between population and resources. This admission came in a report otherwise dedicated to convincing people of the dangers of population—"Population: An International Dilemma."[10]

The attitude of many developing countries toward birth control programs, emanating largely from the United States, is one of suspicion. Although we do not spend a great deal of money disseminating birth

---

[8]Edwin G. Dolan, *TANSTAAFL (There Ain't No Such Thing As a Free Lunch): The Economic Strategy for Environmental Crisis* (New York: Holt, Rinehart and Winston, Inc., 1971), p. 69.

[9]Ridgeway, *Politics of Ecology*, p. 189. In comparison, Mexico has 60 people per square mile; England, 588; Switzerland, 382; Nigeria, 174; and Holland, 975.

[10]Ibid., p. 183.

control information abroad, it is still an implied facet of our foreign policy, through AID programs and developmental loans via the U.S.-dominated World Bank.[11] Developing nations fear that environmental control is a method to retard economic growth among the poorer countries, to reduce the possibility of competition or self-sufficiency in world markets and trade.[12]

Such controversy should give us pause before we assume that people, especially poor people in the United States and those of undeveloped countries, are indeed the problem. The major problem regarding worldwide population growth is the increasing demand for limited resources; the concern in the United States is to ensure that other countries don't grow to such horrendous proportions that they might threaten our affluent status in some way. China, the most populated country in the world, is remarkably self-sufficient and virtually unpolluted. Its interest in population control is to maintain that internal equilibrium. People are not the only problem; other factors, such as heedless drive for profits, senseless development, a disproportionate demand for world resources from industrial nations, and economic growth for its own sake, have to be faulted and examined as well.

A well-known statistic confirms this: It is estimated that the United States, which has about one-sixteenth of the world's population, consumes between 35 and 50 percent of the world's goods and services. Our interest, or at least that of many elected and business leaders, is not to redistribute our disproportionate share of the world's booty, but to ensure it for future demands. The unbelievable political and corporate intrigue surrounding the "energy crisis" is a good example. Although there was some soul searching about our consumption of fuels during the recent "crisis," there is little likelihood that we will significantly reduce our consumption of resources if we have the choice. Most of the soul searching came, unfortunately, from household users, while the big oil companies continue their conglomerate tactics to ensure control over world supplies of fuel, as well as over the demand and price for these resources.

There are those who believe limited population growth is the solution, whereas others see this as a ploy by politicians and corporations to distract us while they expand their control over our economy. Most programs, efforts, and viewpoints reflect the proposition that population growth is the demon, others that there are multiple factors which contribute to environmental degradation, while still others argue cogently about the political and economic motivations which have created our fear of the population bomb. As we discuss the population issue, these controversies will be kept clearly in view.

11Ibid., pp. 184–86.

12Marshall L. Goldman, "Pollution International: Has the Environment a Future?" *The Nation*, October 18, 1971, pp. 358–61.

THE STATISTICAL ARGUMENT

If it is possible to discount population growth in the rest of the world for a moment, the question simply becomes one of how many people we desire to have in this country—that is, the quality of life question:

> Even with the birth rate at its all-time low, we must each year incorporate into the pattern of life in the United States 1.5 million additional Americans, a number large enough to fill a metropolis the size of Minneapolis/St. Paul with all its surrounding suburbs. This means stretching our resources each year, to accommodate this many more people with all the demands for housing, roads, automobiles, airports, shops, schools, recreational facilities that Americans have come to regard as indispensable.[13]

If predictions for the turn of the century are for a U.S. population of 300 or even 400 million, and if this level is considered undesirable, for whatever reasons, then social planning has to be undertaken now with couples who may procreate. If every family in the United States has an average of two children, and if immigration rates remain constant, then by the turn of the century our population will be only about 266 million over the approximately 215 million we have in 1975. On the other hand, if families have three children each, the population will reach 320 million by the same period.[14] We must remember that the children born in the 1970's will be parents to those born by the year 2000. It is even more startling when these statistical inferences are carried still further: "One hundred years from now the two-child family would result in a population of 340 million persons; the three-child average would produce nearly a billion."[15]

For the U.S. Commission on Population Growth, the question was simply: Do we wish to expand our population or concentrate instead on improving the quality of life at our present level of population? In terms of the effect of population on social services, for instance, if families average three children each, in the year 2000 elementary school enrollment will be 50 percent higher than if families have two children; secondary school enrollment will be 43 percent higher, while college enrollment will be 34 percent higher. Overall educational costs are predicted to be $30 billion higher for three-children families, or a 30

[13]U.S. Congress, House Committee on Government Operations, *Effects of Population Growth on Natural Resources and the Environment, Hearings before a subcommittee of the House Committee on Government Operations*, 91st Cong., 1st sess., 1969, p. 77.

[14]U.S. Commission on Population Growth and the American Future, *An Interim Report to the President and the Congress* (Washington, D.C.: Government Printing Office, 1969), p. 2.

[15]Ibid.

percent increase in educational expenditures for every working person, with a demand for one million extra teachers.

For health care, it is anticipated that the three-child pattern would bring an annual increase of $14 billion more by the year 2000; if health costs continue to rise as they have in the past decade, the difference could be as high as $30 billion. The same would be the case for most other social services. With the possible exception of health care, these predictions do not reflect any inflationary spirals such as experienced in the past few years.[16]

In considering the opposing views on population and social problems, the Commission on Population Growth believes that "population growth of the magnitude we have had since World War II has aggravated many of the nation's problems and made their solution more difficult."[17] Nonetheless, the Commission is reluctant to blame population growth alone for present-day social problems:

> We are not saying that population growth continued at current rates portends an immediate crisis for the country. There is little question that the United States has the resources, if it chooses to use them, to meet the demands of a population growing at the current rate as well as to correct various social and economic inequities.... And it is equally true that our social and economic problems would not be solved by stabilization of population alone.[18]

A good example of this point is Harlem, the largest U.S. ghetto, where there are 167,000 people per square mile![19] "By the end of the 1960's black Americans were living in a state almost of population seige."[20] Are the problems of Harlem the result of population growth— all those minority groups crushed into such a small tract of land? Or does the problem have roots elsewhere, say, in confining certain groups to ghettos, economic migrations from devastated life styles, and the pervasive racism that virtually precludes mobility for the poor and lower-class black and Puerto Rican into less-populated regions or better neighborhoods?[21] If one concentrates on population control among such groups—which have, by the way, received most of the attention, as

[16]Data are from U.S. Census Bureau, *Current Population Reports*, Series P-25, No. 448, "Projections of the Population of the United States by Age and Sex (Interim Revisions): 1970 to 2020" (Washington, D.C.: Government Printing Office), 1971.

[17]U.S. Commission on Population Growth, *An Interim Report*, p. 4.

[18]Ibid., p. 5.

[19]Paul Goodman, *Like a Conquered Province: The Moral Ambiguity of America* (New York: Random House, Inc., 1966).

[20]Moynihan, *The Politics of a Guaranteed Income*, p. 37.

[21]For a quota system established on the number of blacks permitted to live in a Chicago suburb, see Michael Kirkhorn, "Oak Park Toes the Color Line," *The Nation*, January 26, 1974, pp. 109–10.

if they alone constitute the fuse to the population bomb—without also examining the forces that have led to their impoverished, crowded lives, one would be seeking to solve the problem of poverty by reducing the number of poor. Wouldn't this simply be a modification of the old saw, "The poor will always be with us, only now let's reduce the number of babies born into poverty families so they won't be with us quite so much"? For those who are poor and also dependent on the state for support, this pressure can be enormous: "Mrs. Carol Brown, a welfare mother pregnant with her fifth child, publicly charged that she had visited three doctors to find one who would deliver her baby. None would perform the delivery unless she first agreed to be sterilized."[22] Can anyone imagine this stipulation for a middle-class white woman?

Sterilization is rarely simply a therapeutic or surgical decision; it invariably contains a social judgment of whether a person should be allowed to bear children. Compulsory sterilization has been legally practiced in the United States since the beginning of this century, although most of us are unaware of it. The most famous Supreme Court case, *Buck* v. *Bell,* judged that sterilization of a feeble-minded woman was constitutional. In his decision to permit sterilization of a woman who was the third generation in a feebleminded family, Justice Oliver Wendell Holmes said that "Three generations of imbeciles are enough." By a slight extension of such ethical and genetic logic, we can easily perceive a social judgment that three generations of poverty are enough. That is, if a family, by some magical force, has not lifted itself from poverty after three generations (maybe less since time is running out), then all women of childbearing age or younger would receive compulsory sterilization, or have the family's public assistance withdrawn. Fortunately, for this aspect of population control there is some indication that the Supreme Court may rule the *Buck* v. *Bell* decision unconstitutional, primarily because the genetic theories on which Justice Holmes based his decision have since been disproved.

After presenting population statistics, and their conceivably harrowing implications, the U.S. Commission on Population Growth then voices concern that if our rate of growth continues to decline, as it has over the past few years, we may actually wind up worrying about too little population in the United States. Surely, we can't have it both ways; either population is a planetary problem or it is not. Insular concern with national growth seems to contradict our supposed concern with "spaceship earth." If the United States uses a disproportionate amount of world resources, then a stable or reduced population would seem beneficial in view of the rising populations elsewhere. However, isn't our concern really with what groups increase, not so much with

22See, for example, Richard Babcock, Jr., "Sterilization: Coercing Consent," *The Nation,* January 12, 1974, pp. 51–53, on the coerced sterilization of black women *and* children who receive public assistance.

overall world population? The idea of more Americans doesn't seem as unsettling as that of more Asians.

Regardless of what motivates our interest in population control, population has its own momentum no matter what national or ethical policies we adopt:

> Thirty years ago, in 1940, we had a population of 132 million people. After all the births, deaths and new immigrants over the following 30 years were balanced out, by 1970 we had a population of 204 million and a net gain of 72 million. Because of the baby boom, the number of persons now moving into the childbearing ages is much larger than previous generations of parents. In 1975 there will be 5½ million more people in the prime child bearing ages of 20 to 29 than there were last year [1968]. By 1985, the figure will have jumped still another 5½ million.[23]

The population of the world in 1974 was about 3.6 billion; of this about 1.1 billion people lived in areas that are experiencing a declining birth rate—North America, Europe, Japan, Oceania, and the Soviet Union. Even with such declines, however, these populations will still be 30 to 60 percent larger by 2000. Without for a moment worrying about the pervasive damage to the environment from population growth in richer nations' expansion, there is the greater problem of growth in those countries which are not experiencing a declining birth rate. For the most part these countries are already poor—Southeast Asia, Africa, and Latin America:

> Southeast Asia, for example, is growing at a rate that will double its numbers in less than thirty years; the African continent as a whole every twenty-seven years; Latin America every twenty-four years. Thus, where we can expect that the industrialized areas of the world will have to support roughly 1.4 to 1.7 billion people a century hence, the underdeveloped world, which today totals 2.5 billions, will have to support something like 40 billions. . . .[24]

Even if undeveloped countries were to reach a zero population rate by the year 2000, within fifty years they would still have increased by two and a half times, simply because of the steady increase of people in their fertile years.[25] The gruesome methods for controlling population in these countries are predicted to be those of the past—famine and disease; indeed they already are. Heilbroner foresees an ironic twist to this otherwise gruesome prediction:

[23]U.S. Commission on Population Growth and the American Future, *An Interim Report*, p. 8.

[24]Robert L. Heilbroner, *An Inquiry into the Human Prospect*. Copyright © 1974 by W. W. Norton & Company, Inc. By permission of W. W. Norton & Company, Inc.

[25]Tomas Frejka, "The Prospects for a Stationary World Population," *Scientific American*, March 1973, p. 22.

the fact that population control in these countries is likely to be achieved in the next generations mainly by premature deaths rather than by the general adoption of contraception or a rapid spontaneous decline in fertility brings an added danger to the demographic outlook. This is the "danger" that the Malthusian check will be offset by large increases in food production that will enable additional hundreds of millions to reach childbearing age.[26]

Things can get worse, then better, then worsen again. If efforts were made to limit world population immediately, and if these efforts were successful, world population would be stabilized by 2000. Nonetheless, "Barry Commoner has estimated that the earth's population at that time will be from 6 to 8 billion, or about twice the present world population.[27] This is basically the same as the prediction of Paul Ehrlich on the population bomb.

However, for U.S. population at least, these predictions may not be as dismal as anticipated. As noted, the national birth rate in our country has dropped sharply. The overall fertility rate, which is considered a sophisticated demographic measurement, had by 1972 almost dropped to the replacement level of 2.11—the number of children women must bear to replace themselves, their mate, single people without children, and women who die without having had children. In 1972 the U.S. rate was 2.14, the lowest since the Depression.

> Reaching the threshold to zero population growth is not the same as no growth, however. For the population to stabilize firmly, very low fertility rates would have to persist for some thirty years. No authority believes that this situation is even conceivable. For example, there have been substantial fluctuations in U.S. fertility rates in the past: In 1937 the rate was 2.23; in 1947, 3.27; it was 3.77 in 1957, and 2.57 in 1967.[28]

Whatever the rate, let us not forget what the average American baby means:

> Every 8 seconds a new American is born. He is a disarming little thing, but he begins to scream loudly in a voice that can be heard for seventy years. He is screaming for 56,000,000 gallons of water, 21,000 gallons of gasoline, 10,150 pounds of meat, 28,000 pounds of milk and

[26]Heilbroner, "The Human Prospect," p. 23.

[27]Donald N. Thompson, *The Economics of Environmental Protection* (Cambridge, Mass.: Winthrop Publishers, 1973), p. 4; see also Barry Commoner, "Is There an Optimal Level of Population?" Paper presented to the Annual Meeting of the American Association for the Advancement of Science, Boston, December 29, 1969.

[28]Thompson, *Economics of Environmental Protection*, p. 5. For a general discussion of trends in mortality and fertility, see Donald J. Bogue, *Principles of Demography* (New York: John Wiley & Sons, Inc., 1969); and Ralph Thomlinson, *Population Dynamics: Causes and Consequences of World Demographic Change* (New York: Random House, Inc., 1965).

cream, 9,000 pounds of wheat, and great storehouses of other foods, drinks, and tobaccos. These are his lifetime demands on the economy.[29]

What has primarily helped lower fertility rates in the United States and other countries has been the emphasis on birth control programs as well as all sorts of information and propaganda about the dangers of unexamined, uncontrolled population growth.

In the United States the major impetus for access to birth control devices and information has come from women, as it has historically. This drive for more and safer forms of birth control was dramatized by the 1973 Supreme Court ruling on legal abortion. Like all legal decisions, this one is subtle and full of loopholes, some of which have been taken up by Right-to-Life groups in an effort to rule the abortion decision unconstitutional because it does not protect the rights of the unborn. This ruling, with perhaps the exception of *Brown* v. *Board of Education* on the desegregation of schools, has been one of the most controversial in our legal and social history.

> As recently as ten years ago it was inconceivable that such a decision could have been handed down. What are the prerequisites for such a reversal of attitude at the highest judicial level? For one thing, there must be a special constituency, imbued with zeal, packing the force of reason, and pushing hard for change in the law. . . . In the matter of abortion, Planned Parenthood, Women's Lib, liberal gynecologists and other groups provided the motive power.[30]

Also there is little doubt that the possibility of curbing the birth rate of the poor and those on public assistance ensured support from those usually less liberal about such constitutional measures. As with most social benefits, there was gross discrimination against the poor, especially black women, in obtaining even a safe illegal abortion before this decision. Obtaining abortions for the rich had never been much of a problem. The idea that we might ever return to back-alley septic abortions, at exhorbitant rates, now seems as inconceivable.

> The religious aspect remains unchanged by the Supreme Court decision. Those who wish to have children, a few or many, can still have them. They are free to try to convince their fellow citizens that "the right to life" is indivisible and paramount.[31]

To be in favor of legalized abortion does not mean to prefer it as a method of birth control; any woman will testify that it is the least

[29]Robert and Leona Rienow, *Moment in the Sun, A Report on the Deteriorating Quality of the American Environment* (New York: Dial Press, 1967), p. 3, cited in Dolan, *TANSTAAFL*, p. 69.
[30]"Jane Roe and Mary Doe," *The Nation*, February 5, 1973, p. 165.
[31]Ibid.

desirable method. What the abortion struggle represents is an effort to reduce the wholesale death or disabling of women which so often occurs with illegal medical or badly mangled home abortions. Furthermore, it stresses the right of women, in consultation with their mate if they so desire, to decide whether to bear a child after conception has occurred. The Supreme Court has acknowledged this right, at least for the first trimester of a pregnancy. After that the state, except for extreme cases, can deem abortion illegal and unconstitutional.

Many women who support abortion legislation would never consider an abortion themselves. However, they support *the right* of other women to have access to this extreme method of birth control if they so desire. The moral decision remains with the individual, where it rightly belongs. The moral burden for this decision also rests with the individual (or couple) as well. The state has not adjudicated a moral issue as much as it has permitted access to the simple (and safe) medical techniques of abortion for those who are willing to resort to that form of birth control in order not to have a child.

Such a decision kills at the root the black market in abortions, with its exhorbitant fees and questionable hygienic and medical practices. Unfortunately, there is some evidence that referral agencies and clinics, which have sprung up since the Supreme Court and other state-level decisions, are themselves not as ethical nor as proficient as one might wish:

> Abortion is big business now, and a woman who needs an abortion is just as subject to exploitation as she ever was—though maybe safer physically. . . . A woman who needs an abortion is almost helpless legally.[32]

Ironically, even though the Supreme Court decision might seem to be a gross invasion of the privacy of couples, it is not. If abortion had not been legalized, and if our population continued to increase with unwanted births, it is easy to conceive of the state intervening at a more brutal level of, say, forced sterilization to control fertility. This would be most probable among the poor and the black, where the highest rates of unwanted pregnancies occur and where coerced sterilizations have also occurred. As the U.S. Commission on Population Growth notes, "Unwanted fertility is highest among those whose levels of education and income are lowest." The Commission also "believes that all Americans . . . should be enabled to avoid unwanted births. Major efforts should be made to enlarge and improve the opportunity for individuals to control their own fertility, aiming toward the development of a basic ethical principle that only wanted children are brought into the world."[33]

---

[32]"Abortion Referral Services," *Off Our Backs: A Woman's News Journal*, August 1973, p. 10.

[33]U.S. Commission on Population Growth and the American Future, *Population and the American Future* (Washington, D.C.: Government Printing Office, 1972), pp. 97, 98.

Even though the Supreme Court has ruled first-trimester abortions permissible, the reduction in fertility within any group still is and ought to remain a voluntary and private decision. The accelerating increase in use of contraceptives, abortions, sterilization, those remaining single or marrying late, working women, as well as greater concern about over-crowding and the environment, have brought about reduced fertility rates in virtually all developed nations.

For those who like to think futuristically, several "other" schemes for birth control have been recommended. Kenneth Boulding has suggested that each woman be required to obtain a permit before having a child. Each child, male and female, would be given such a permit at birth, to use as they saw fit when they got older; thus each couple would automatically have two birth permits when they mated. Any person who did not want to use his or her permit could sell it to someone who did. Biologist Ehrlich, on the other hand, has suggested various incentives for not having children: taxing families with more than two children, putting sterilants in the water systems, imposing taxes on baby products; in addition, he would give "responsibility prizes" to couples who married late or who went five years without having a baby, or would hold special lotteries only for those without children. Garrett Hardin, also a biologist, thinks the freedom to breed oneself will have to cease or be curtailed.[34] So much for the future.

Predictions of population growth can now be projected indefinitely into the future through the use of what is known as system dynamics, or models of doom.[35] The studies of Jay Forrester and of Donnella and Dennis Meadows present widely publicized computerized analyses of population and resources. They assure us, with their growth models, that by the turn of the century our society, in fact "civilization" itself, will be damaged unless we take steps now to restrain population and economic growth.

In a critique of these social-system growth models, economist Boulding argues that we cannot know the limits to growth, no matter how sophisticated our computer technology, because we cannot know what the future state of knowledge will be:

Insofar as the social system is set in a mechanistic framework of an

[34]Kenneth Boulding, *The Meaning of the 20th Century* (New York: Harper & Row, 1964); Paul Ehrlich, *The Population Bomb* (New York: Ballantine Books, 1968); and Garrett Hardin, *Population, Evolution, and Birth Control* (San Francisco: W. H. Freeman and Company, Publishers, 1969).

[35]H. S. D. Cole *et al.*, eds., *Models of Doom: A Critique of the Limits to Growth* (New York: Universe Books, 1973). [This was published in Britain under the title *Thinking About the Future.*] See also, Ralph E. Lapp, *The Logarithmic Century: Charting Future Shock* (Englewood Cliffs, N.J.: Prentice-Hall, Inc., 1973); John Maddox, *The Doomsday Syndrome* (New York: McGraw-Hill Book Company, 1973); Jay W. Forrester, *World Dynamics* (Cambridge, Mass.: Wright-Allen Press, 1971); and Donnella H. and Dennis L. Meadows *et al.*, *The Limits to Growth* (New York: Universe Books, 1972).

ultimately exhaustible earth, and indeed an ultimately exhaustible sun, we are able to detect certain future limits within which the social system must operate. Where these limits are, however, and how long it will take to get there we really do not know.[36]

A somewhat more superficial critique of Forrester and Meadows comes from two younger economists, who feel that a scarcity in resources, brings about a higher price and thus less demand for that resource, and meanwhile technology and science seek a substitute.[37]

Without totally dismissing the models of Forrester, Meadows, and Stanford biologist Paul Ehrlich—who extrapolates a doubling of the world's population in 37 years—Ulmer feels that economic growth at least might be continued but in a different way:

> Almost without question, if growth persists through the next generation, it will have to be more economical in its use of materials, less tolerant of waste.... For the developed countries and for the rich in general, this implies a greater relative role in their total consumption for services, as in education, the arts and recreation.... Everywhere it would require strict mandatory rules avoiding pollution.... And that means planning.[38]

THE SOCIO-ECONOMIC APPROACH

Whether the population of the United States remains at a steady state of zero population growth (ZPG), whether we ultimately reach the stupendous predictions of the three-child family given by the U.S. Commission on Population Growth, or whether some unforeseen element arises, we still have to consider the effects of population on society. For instance, if there were too few people, as in the early days of our republic, then we would be quite interested in importing or even enslaving labor. Too few people can be a problem as well as too many. One of the major debates to develop from the concern over population has been over economic growth and expansion as the guiding premises of our society, that is, as ends in themselves.

The problem of economic growth, and how this affects the environment, is a present-day problem. Although the future predictions are impressive enough, for the moment we can dwell in the present. For those who are interested, the report of the U.S. Commission on Popu-

---

[36]Kenneth E. Boulding, "Zoom, Gloom, Doom, and Room," *The New Republic*, August 11, 1973, p. 26.

[37]Peter Passell and Leonard Ross, *The Retreat from Riches: Affluence and Its Enemies* (New York: The Viking Press, Inc., 1973).

[38]Melville J. Ulmer, "Doom or Boom," *The New Republic*, April 7, 1973. pp. 32–33.

lation Growth and the American Future presents economic predictions based on their two-child/three-child estimates.[39]

It is a professional and laymen's "catchword" that we are now in the post-industrial age; this seems especially ironic since industries are touted as the major cause of environmental degradation. As soon as we begin to focus on goods-producing corporations as the villains, we are told that they represent a past era.

The post-industrial society—which some theorists believe we have already entered—is a society in which the supremacy of business and industry is replaced by a meritocracy of scientists and technologists. This theory develops quite naturally (though one is uncertain how accurately) from the pervasive belief that we are heading toward a new kind of society and that the evidence indicates it will be a post-industrial age. This concept, most recently given weight by sociologist Daniel Bell, was a major topic of the American Academy of the Arts and Sciences Commission on the Year 2000, of which Bell was chairman.[40] In industrial society, economic values predominate, Bell argues, and in the post-industrial society, more communal, noneconomic concerns predominate. In his prediction for the industrial nations, based on present tendencies in our society, Bell foresees a radical transformation of technology, the economy, and occupations. Industrial economies would shift from the production of goods to the production of services, a shift which has been perceived or recommended by others.

Since recreation and parks are service producers, these theories and their offspring are worth examining:

> The economy will change over from goods-producing to service-dispensing, the commanding position passing from manufacturing and processing to trade, finance, transport, communications on the one hand, and health, recreation, education, research, government on the other—with the latter category proving the decisive one. The process is already under way. Today about 60 percent of the American labor force is engaged in services; by 1980, the figure will have risen to 70 percent. The service economy has already changed the nature of the work force so that the white-collar occupations outnumber the blue-collar occupations for the first time in the history of industrial civilization.[41]

Another writer states that even though the proportion of industrial blue-collar workers is declining, in absolute numbers they are increasing. "The 1980 projections are that 35 million workers will man Bell's post-industrial service sectors of the economy; there will still be

[39]U.S. Commission on Population Growth and the American Future, *Population and the American Future*, Chapter 4, "The Economy."

[40]Daniel Bell, *The Coming of the Post-Industrial Society: A Venture in Social Forecasting* (New York: Basic Books, Inc., Publishers, 1973).

[41]Bert Cochran, "Paradise, Dystopia, or Just More of the Same?" *The Nation*, July 30, 1973, p. 85.

nearly as many workers—33 million—in the old industrial areas of manufacturing, construction, and mining.[42] Thus, rather than a 70/30 ratio between industrial and service workers, Featherstone sees more of a 50/50 ratio.

Such statistics also say nothing about the rise of scientists and researchers, especially in terms of economic or political power. For our purposes, we can keep in mind the growth of the public sector of the economy toward service production, and discount the probable merit-ocracy of scientists over politicians and corporate owners. Even though Bell's analytical construct seems to weaken under scrutiny, what has not dissolved is the growing importance of social services in the economy, nor the arguments of some economists that these *should* continue to increase.

To simplify the argument on economic growth: unplanned or uncontrolled economic growth will ruin the environment and must be curbed very soon, if possible.[43] Regardless of what viewpoint one has toward economic growth, the fear is that we will be unable to sustain the trend of economic growth we have experienced in the United States very much longer. The recent energy crisis, whether of limited duration or not, has raised the possibility of a future ceiling on indus-trial production.

Approaching it from another viewpoint, the Commission on Popu-lation Growth examined the question of whether population expansion is important for our economic health, as many believe: "We have looked for, and have not found, any convincing economic argument for con-tinued national population growth. The health of our economy does not depend on it. The vitality of business does not depend on it. The welfare of the average person certainly does not depend on it."[44] The thinking that underlies the concern with population growth is that rapid population growth brings about a more rapid growth in the economy as well, placing an inordinate strain on resources and the environment. In the United States the relationship between economic growth and our demand on world's resources is, of course, horrendous. In addition, the Commission finds that per capita income is higher when population growth is slower.

Although speculations over our economic future, especially the kind offered by Bell and by economist John K. Galbraith, do not

[42]Joseph Featherstone, "A Failure of Political Imagination, Part I: The Coming of Post-Industrial Society," *The New Republic*, September 15, 1973, pp. 24–25.

[43]For a broad overview of some of the problems involved with ecology and economic development, see Paul and Anna Ehrlich, *Population, Resources, and En-vironment* (San Francisco: W. H. Freeman and Company, Publishers, 1970); and John Culbertson, *Economic Development and Ecological Approach* (New York: Alfred A. Knopf, Inc., 1971).

[44]U.S. Commission on Population Growth, *Population and the American Future*, p. 41.

directly involve population growth, they do involve *economic* growth. In such theories of the probable changes in our economy—whether they come spontaneously or are planned for—the shift is seen or recommended to be toward services in the public sector of the economy. It is believed that the growth of public services allows for economic stability but curbs the kind of economic destruction that has been impairing our natural and psychological environments.

From an economic viewpoint, it is not merely the growth of population that poses both social and environmental problems, but the nature of a society and its guiding values and pervasive goals as well. It is as easy to imagine a smaller population than we now have ruining the environment, as it is to conceive of a greatly expanded population not doing so. As already noted for China, it is not the number of people that destroy a country—though we are often made to believe this—but the values of people and the kind of economic activity that predominates in a society. This is why simply focusing on growth or numbers of people, without also focusing on the predominance of various economic objectives, can be misleading. It is not merely that population affects the economy, but that economics so sorely affects the environment.

The best example of this in recreation and parks would be the White Mountain National Forest dilemma discussed earlier. It is not merely its proximity to 65 million people that makes this national park so vulnerable, but who these people are, as well as the industrial and social demands of that area. Backpacking, which is felt to be the second most destructive activity in the WMNF (after the loggers), is a fashionable and popular outdoor activity right now. According to the editors of *Wilderness Camping*, there are 10 million backpackers presently in North America:

> Servicing the wilderness is a big business, and club publications [of the Appalachian Mountain Club] often sound like a report to the stockholders. ... Altogether forty-six public and private agencies have an interest in the New England backpacker.... In the past ten years, backpacking has become a major industry. It supports not only the prestigious, old-line companies like Sierra Designs and The North Face, but also multiple-outlet chains like Eastern Mountain Sports. Even Sears, Roebuck & Co. has added a full line of lightweight packs, sleeping bags, tents and other backpacking accessories to its catalogue.[45]

The popularity of backpacking is not a simple phenomenon of population growth, or even population distribution. Although major population shifts in the past century have given rise to the multimillion megalopolis, such as the one that impinges on the White Mountains, changes in the economic and social life styles of people are also contributing factors. If only rural populations surrounded the White

45Ford, "The White Mountains," pp. 81, 83.

Mountains, how likely would they be to take up backpacking as a sport? As more Americans earn more money, usually at indoor sedentary jobs, and as they have more leisure time for vacations, the appeal of heretofore "elitists" outdoor vacations rises. A New York friend of mine recently told me that many of her friends earn more money than they know how to spend, so they take vacations, some expensive, some merely exotic or unusual, such as African safaris. As will be discussed in Chapter 5, the damage being done to parts of Africa and to that continent's stupendous wildlife are incalculable and for the most part irreversible.[46]

While backpacking may not be so exotic, for most Americans, especially those confined to urban areas, it offers great novelty along with the pleasures of the wilderness, and it can be inexpensive. The phenomenon is known as rising expectations, which directly emerge from an economy that rewards more and more people beyond the dreams of their parents and grandparents. That backpacking can also be expensive, let there be little doubt; otherwise it would not have attracted as many business firms as it has.

In addition to rising incomes, more leisure, higher levels of education, and more pervasive communications about what kind of vacations are available, another element, and an ironic one, brings about the dilemma of the White Mountains: In order to save the environment, ecologists and their supporters have called enormous attention to nature and its dying call. Rather than retreating and letting nature replenish itself if it can, we all crush into the remaining wilderness to get a "final" taste. True wilderness is soon to be a part of history; this is probably the saddest aspect of all.

The economy affects population in broader ways as well through the values and suppositions that underpin a society. For instance, national forests are a service provided through the public sector of our economy. Sounds good, but is it? If this service, and its many outdoor recreation activities, attracts not only tourists but business firms to "service" these tourists, then the theoretical benefits of a service-dominated economy seem to weaken. If we are ready to attack goods-producing industries for their unbelievable pollution and destruction of the environment, why are we confident that services won't also create and attract spin-off firms and industries that are equally damaging? Many corporations, in a desire to diversify, have entered the service industry; these services often reflect the values that we so readily associate with industrial blight and negligence.

Without a behavioral change in our social values and objectives, any so-called change in the economy, regardless of the population composition or distribution, is surely a false step toward solving our

46See, for instance, Norman Myers, *The Long African Day* (New York: The Macmillan Company, 1973); also Francise du Plessix Gray, "On Safari," *The New York Review of Books*, June 28, 1973, pp. 25–29.

environmental and social problems. In the past decade we have become increasingly aware of the negative side effects of economic growth:

> This is the stunning discovery that economic growth carries previously unsuspected side effects whose cumulative impact may be more deleterious than the undoubted benefits that growth also brings. In the last few years we have become aware of these side effects in a visible decline of the quality of air and water, in a series of manmade disasters of ecological imbalance, in a mounting general alarm over the environmental collapse that unrestricted growth could inflict. Thus, even more disturbing than the possibility of a serious deterioration in the quality of life if growth comes to an end is the awareness of a possibly disastrous decline in the conditions of existence if growth does not come to an end.[47]

Few of us need to question the enormous benefits to our society obtained from economic growth, especially during the past hundred years. It is the *risks* that further economic growth poses in an already prosperous society that need to be examined. Perhaps the best-known economist to raise the question of "Why grow at all?" is John Kenneth Galbraith. His message, and that of other economists who support this viewpoint, can be given very simply:

> the more-developed nations of the world have now reached a state where all reasonable and rational demands for economic goods have been or can be satisfied. As a result, the virtues of added economic growth may be an illusion because growth does not come free.... The developed countries may have reached a level at which the costs of additional growth in terms of labor and loss of environmental quality exceed the benefits....[48]

Barkley and Seckler stress that economic growth and ecology are part of the same general system. A change in the economy's growth rate affects the environment, for better or worse. An increase in population in an affluent economy thus has a disproportionately negative effect on its own and the world's resources and environments. Even though population, economic growth, and ecology are closely related, it is important to focus on rates of economic growth rather than on population growth alone. Even if our population continues its low growth rate, as more and more members of our society achieve greater wealth, the negative effect on the environment is bound to increase.

Many economists now feel that the longer economic growth continues, the more the environment will deteriorate. We cannot have it both ways no matter how scrupulous an environmental policy we enforce.

[47]Heilbroner, "The Human Prospect," p. 21: Heilbroner, a leader in the campaign to bring more ecological consideration into economics, renamed the Gross National Product (GNP) Gross National Cost to emphasize the price of growth and development.

[48]In Paul W. Barkley and David W. Seckler, *Economic Growth and Environmental Decay: The Solution Becomes the Problem* (New York: Harcourt Brace Jovanovich, Inc., 1972), p. 18.

Furthermore, if the affluent, who often are also pro-environment, agree that economic growth must be reduced or curtailed, they must not believe this will solve the problem. Without a concomitant redistribution of wealth, such a decision would further impoverish the poor and preclude their improving their economic status. Barkley and Seckler conclude that to bring about reduced rates of economic growth, and to begin to restore and maintain the quality of the environment, as well as to guarantee that all members of society benefit from such a no-growth decision, it will be necessary to provide a minimum income to all citizens.[49]

Even though our population has increased only about 45 percent since 1940, while environmental problems have increased by many hundreds of percent, we still should not relegate population growth to a minor role. Technology and population can be strongly interrelated in our ecological crisis. "Paul Ehrlich claims that only fifty million Americans, given our existing technology, could eventually destroy the planet. It is difficult to imagine any American life style which would prevent three or four hundred million people from accomplishing the same end in the long run."[50] Ehrlich also points out that each American has *fifty times* the negative impact on ecology as the average citizen of India.[51]

Every environmental issue invariably becomes an employment issue as well. If we assume that the production of certain products, e.g., plastics, is the underlying cause of pollution, then any curtailment in such production results in unemployment, unless industries have some plans for rapid diversification, an unlikely prospect. Interestingly enough, the plastics industry has been severely curtailed by the oil shortage, an essential ingredient in its manufacture. Some companies were even purchasing oil through a black market which, not surprisingly, sprang up in the United States as soon as the shortage manifested itself in late 1973. Since unemployment is not acceptable as a short-run solution, Thompson believes we then have to change the nature of what we produce or to concentrate on recycling. However, these would be regarded merely as interim solutions to the long-range problem of economic growth and social stability.

Some economists believe that a natural limitation in economic growth may be in sight, since the demand for certain goods will be at a declining rate (a fourth car?). Thompson notes that advanced economies grow in areas such as education, communication, and finance, to which we might also add recreational services. These services, for the most part, consume relatively small amounts of fuel and minerals.

[49]Barkley and Seckler, *Economic Growth*, p. 191; see also Moynihan, *The Politics of a Guaranteed Income.*

[50]Thompson, *Economics of Environmental Protection*, p. 3.

[51]Ehrlich, *The Population Bomb*, pp. 15–67.

I suppose most Americans, who are used to the benefits of our affluent and diverse economy, would wonder what an alternative to economic growth could conceivably be. Although he is talking about Great Britain, Mishan's description sums up our economic "religion" quite succinctly:

> If the country was ever uncertain of the ends it should pursue, that day has passed. There may be doubts among philosophers and heart-searchings among poets, but to the multitude the kingdom of God is to be realized here and now, on this earth; and it is to be realized via technological innovation, and at an exponential rate.[52]

Mishan's alternative to growth is equally succinct: don't grow.

But still we ask, are the people to blame for their material idolatry when corporations constantly bombard them with the necessity of luxuries? John Kenneth Galbraith has long focused on the role of giant corporations in stimulating this false demand:

> Consumers are riveted so firmly to the need for deodorants, flashy cars, crackly breakfast cereals, electric dishwashers, color TVs, and other symbols of affluence or conspicuous waste that some poorer families would rather go without food and medicine than resist the blandishments of Madison Avenue—and the Census Bureau reports they sometimes do. As Galbraith sees it, the giant corporations do not passively produce what consumers want... but instead get consumers to want what they produce.[53]

Galbraith's solution? That a substantial part of the private market be replaced by a comprehensive system of governmental economic planning, or in other words, by a "new socialism." Like Barkley and Seckler, he stresses a policy of guaranteed income to ease the transition, in addition to other governmental measures. The social services he recommends initially for government control would be housing, health services, and transportation. These are recommended because he believes the private market has failed miserably in their provision.

A concern with economic growth invariably leads to concern with the political structure and power of our society. As economics is interrelated with ecology, so too are these both interwoven into our political structure. Although we will not concern ourselves here with whether American government, as it is now run, could handle socialization of public services, we do not want to leave the impression that this isn't a *major* political question. The question we are more interested in now

[52]E. J. Mishan, *Technology and Growth: The Price We Pay* (New York: Praeger Publishers, Inc., 1970), p. 4. First published in Great Britain under the title: *Growth: The Price We Pay*. See especially, Part V, "Reflections on the Unmeasurable Consequences of Economic Growth," pp. 105–58.

[53]Melville J. Ulmer, "The Managerial Elite—Economics and the Public Purpose," *The New Republic*, October 13, 1973, p. 24; see also John Kenneth Galbraith, *Economics and the Public Purpose* (New York: Houghton Mifflin Company, 1973).

is what social attitudes would have to emerge before any attempts were undertaken to control economic growth through greater government intervention and planning. That is, how could the American people help alleviate the catastrophes of heedless economic growth?

Heilbroner foresees the need for an alteration in human behavior which might then lead to solutions for population growth, environmental damage, and economic growth. He is clear about one thing: unrestrained economic growth is not a problem inherent in capitalism. It is as much a problem in socialist and other political orders whenever growth is pursued as an end in itself. "More important yet, there is reason to believe that the pressures of the population explosion will come to bear increasingly on all industrial nations alike, socialist as well as capitalist."[54] Therefore, even though Galbraith recommends socialization of the services mentioned earlier, this does not suggest that socialist states have succeeded where capitalism has not. Population and economic growth are worldwide concerns.

Although there would be enormous difficulties in transforming American society into a more stationary capitalist state, if necessary, through *planned state capitalism* as inaugurated in Japan, Heilbroner does not think such a transformation impossible. In order to offset any tendency toward deflation, Heilbroner also suggests that the government get more involved in housing, education, recreation, and so forth.

The greatest problem in controlling or transforming economic growth would be handling the social tensions that would arise. The entire issue of a stationary economy raises the controversial issue of income distribution. Like other economists, Heilbroner feels an emphasis on services might save the day:

> One saving possibility must, however, be considered. Growth might be permitted to continue for an indefinite period, provided that it were confined to outputs that consumed few resources. . . . An expansion in the services of government, in the provision of better health and education, arts and entertainment, would not only rescue the system from a fatal encounter with the environment, but might produce enough "growth" to ease the income distribution problem.[55]

That is, rather than a post-industrial economy developing naturally, it would be purposefully planned. In any event, whether we are unable *to sustain* economic growth because of increased demands on world resources, or whether we are unable *to tolerate* such growth because of degradation to the environment, there is little doubt that our future will be quite different from now, though none of us is quite sure how different and in what ways.

[54]Heilbroner, "The Human Prospect," p. 28.
[55]Ibid.

POPULATION DISTRIBUTION AND OPEN SPACES

City and Country

If we define the ecological crisis realistically as a social crisis, of which population increase is a part, so too should we add the element of urbanization:

> If the ecological crisis exists, it is a social and political crisis, brought about in part by population increase and urbanization, and in great part, at least in this country, by the unfettered and selfish exploitation of natural resources by industry—aided and abetted by the government.[56]

Part of the natural resources of this nation are people, and the massive gathering of these into urban and metropolitan areas is one reflection of our nation's economic priorities. The massive and rapid urban growth in this century and during the latter part of the nineteenth century was not some inborn desire by rustics to leave their land and come to the big city. For the most part, the migrations into cities, as well as the immigrations from abroad, were largely motivated by economic necessity and the need for human survival. All of the moves— from the long migrations of the ex-slaves from the South, the immigrations of Asian and European peasants, to the amazing shift from rural to city life by farm families—have related directly to the economic, political, and social *values* of our age.

Even though Hollywood has done its best to show the glamour of city life, or the supremacy of the clever city man over the rural type, our roots remain deeply entwined with the farm or the village, with the joys and rusticalities of open space, earth, sky, sea foam, and the "beasties of the field." Even for those born and raised in cities, the appeal of the countryside and the less-complicated life style it represents persists. However inaccurate our images of life either in the country or in the city, these images nonetheless hold great sway over our dreams, plans, and forms of leisure and recreation.

As early as 1783 a poet could warn those dreaming of restful life in the country:

> Ye gentle souls, who dream of rural
> ease,
> Whom the smooth stream and smoother
> sonnet please;
> Go! if the peaceful cot your praises
> share,

---

[56]S. E. Luria, "What Can Biologists Solve?" *The New York Review of Books,* February 7, 1974, p. 27.

> Go look within, and ask if peace be
> there. . . .
>
> *George Crabbe*

Throughout our literature, and especially English and Russian literature, the images of town and country are constantly recorded. "The country, of course, has amassed the longer record, and—with its evocations of golden ages and latter-day Edens, its associations with virtue, peace, and independence—is subject to the greater correction."[57] In his book, Raymond Williams feels that the true choice is not between country life or the city; it is in recognizing that:

> we live in a world in which the dominant mode of production and social relationships teaches, impresses, offers to make normal and even rigid, modes of detached, separated, external perception and action: modes of using and consuming rather than accepting and enjoying people and things.[58]

These negative modes of life can triumph in city or in country, though most of us cling tenaciously to the belief that the country is purer, less poisoned by modern values. If the city both fascinates and repels, the country often simply attracts. Perhaps because we have been an urban folk for some while now we have forgotten that rural life has its Jekyll and Hyde quality as well.

Very few of us have gotten our impressions of urban or rural life directly, no matter where we have lived. These have come to us second hand, often dramatically through literature, poetry, music, painting, television, and most notoriously through the movies. If we go from the city to the country we bring a set of predetermined images which we "see" when we arrive. I have often asked people if they know the silence of New York City at dawn in the business districts, especially on Sunday. Their perception of the city is noise and hustle. Even the quiet Sunday dawn on Madison Avenue would remain second rate compared to their dream of what a rural or even suburban sunrise promises. And so urban dwellers continue to long for the country, while rustics taken in by Hollywood's glitter lean toward the city.

As professionals in recreation and parks, it is not our aim to get these images perfectly straight. Even if we could, I dread the thought of learning the final "truth" about the country and the city. Instead one of our aims should be to cater to the real needs of the populace, whether in town or field. We are a dream-filled profession, and that idea can serve as a perpetual rejuvenation of our ability to aid people in their leisure needs. However, to persist in favoring the country over the

[57]Robert Hatch, "Country Mice or City Mice—The Cat Doesn't Care," *The Nation*, December 3, 1973, p. 597. See also Raymond Williams, *The Country and the City* (New York: Oxford University Press, 1973), on which Hatch's review is based.

[58]Hatch, "Country Mice or City Mice," p. 598.

city is to forfeit a major responsibility to deal creatively with the urban setting.

Every time we take slum children to the country, we not only are showing them another way of life, we make sure they realize it is a better way of life. This is a questionable practice if we are in no position to better their life, either in town or in country. Remember, to the country poor, life in city slums appears affluent by comparison. The reason for harping on this point is to offset the rather mindless preference we recreationists often display for the open spaces. Even if open spaces are preferable, and I for one think they are, we cannot ignore that for the *majority* of our population these are virtually nonexistent or at a premium. Unless the future holds forced relocations to disperse our populace more evenly throughout the nation, then as recreationists we have to work within the urban milieu. If green belts such as the White Mountain National Forest are eventually closed, how prepared will our profession be for the inevitably increased demand for recreational experiences within or nearer to the confines of the city?

If we take a radical position we might strive for a relocation of this nation's population; if we take a more moderate position, we can begin to cope with the fact that we are an urban people. An ideal position would be to attempt both. To accept the urban situation as it now is would display a lack of imagination; not to cope with it would be irresponsible. A controversy among architectural professionals might highlight this point further.

A recent book on architectural theory has raised a great deal of controversy among professionals and laymen.[59] Briefly, Venturi, *et al.*, celebrate the commonplace in architecture, for instance, buildings with sculpted TV antennas included in the design, to accept the fact that we are a TV-watching society.

> The Venturis tells us that the garishness, variety, and symbolism of Main Street and the appointments of the superhighway are a genuine twentieth-century vernacular developed in answer to genuine contemporary preferences and needs. It is the expression of today's life style. This is our culture, and it is our architecture, like it or not, much more than the approved monuments of the tastemakers, who treat the rest of the built environment like a bastard child.[60]

While I do not in any sense accept the ugliness we see around us, architecturally or otherwise, as the reflection of any "genuine contemporary preference," I do agree that it is our architecture, like it or not. To come to terms with our environment is not the same as resigning

[59]Robert Venturi, Denise Scott Brown, and Steven Izenour, *Learning From Las Vegas* (Cambridge, Mass.: MIT Press, 1973); see also, Robert Venturi, *Complexity and Contradiction in Architecture* (New York: Museum of Modern Art, 1966).

[60]Ada Louise Huxtable, "In Love With Times Square," *The New York Review of Books*, October 18, 1973, p. 45.

ourselves to it. Nor is it to learn to like it, as the Venturis suggest. However, we will be immobilized if we continue to endure the present,
glorify the past, and mystify the future.

Because of improved transportation and communications, no place
in the world is safe from Americans or others seeking to get away. "Today, no country is more than a few hours away by plane, and the years
will see these few hours whittled down to minutes."[61] Our sense of space
and distance is diminished by these technologies, leading to what
McLuhan called "the global village." We can know more about what
happens in Europe on a given day than we often know about our neigh-
bor. As our *sense* of distance shrinks, our alienation expands—a strange
phenomenon, which often we carelessly attribute to there being too
many people.

Spatial concepts, of when we feel crowded or isolated, are thought
to vary by country. Americans are often disarmed by foreigners who
talk right into their face, very close, with an apparent disregard for
whether they might have that horror of all horrors, bad breath, or even
body odor. Certain national groups do not seem bothered by the intimate
proximity of their own specie. If you live in or have access to ethnic
neighborhoods, observe the distances between bodies when people talk;
do the same with Americans removed from ethnic ties. Other than at
affairs where liquor encourages us to cuddle up to all other drinkers,
note the distance Americans keep. We are far from a frigid people,
however; the one thing Englishmen and other Europeans have long
noted about Americans is our apparent love of strangers, our peculiar
propensity to tell a stranger, on an air flight for instance, things we
would never disclose to our friends.[62] No, we are not frigid, but we
believe in keeping our distance; as Robert Frost expressed in "Mending
Wall," "Good fences make good neighbors." We love and hate distance;
this is one of our true paradoxes.

> Not many people seem to be ready yet for complete abandonment
> of locale. And so long as locale means anything for many people, the
> concept of the local community has validity.... Unless everything we
> have learned so far about human relationships is dated—and the possi-
> bility of this contingency cannot be dismissed—communities will persist.[63]

It has long been the tenet of psychologists who do research with
rats and then make alarming inferences about people, that crowding is
debilitating to *Homo sapiens*, that we have none of the attributes of,
say, insects who can live piled on one another. A study in 1971 challenged this notion of our inability to live in spatially crowded environ-

[61]Mishan, *Technology and Growth*, p. 120.

[62]For a truly superlative discussion of this tendency, see Englishman John
Cowper Powys, *Autobiography* (Hamilton, N.Y.: Colgate University Press, 1958), about
his thirty years in this country.

[63]Jessie Bernard, *The Sociology of Community* (Glenview, Ill.: Scott, Foresman
and Company, 1973), pp. 185, 187.

ments.[64] Although this is the only study I know of on this question, it still makes one reconsider all that rat research; the more ratlike we are, perhaps, the less we like to be close to others. Nevertheless, along with the images of the great open spaces we all hold, we should ponder the facts about space, crowding, and population. We swallow too many concepts whole, making attempts to re-create or realign our society even more confusing.

This admonishment especially applies to professional recreationists who are faced with satisfying the leisure *dreams* of Americans. It is not our function to tell them they are fantasizing about places and life styles that have never existed. It is our task, however, to learn this for ourselves. In the process of assessing the recreation needs and possibilities for this society, there is not much purpose in squashing people's dreams outright. However, there is not much sense either in pretending all is well; it is not, perhaps it never was. Harping back to the great past is a favorite pastime, even though the past for most of humankind meant a short and brutish existence. It is, however, more than a pastime for some professionals, who see it as a deep need within most of mankind.

> The Great Nostalgia for the Impossible Dream . . . has exerted enormous influence on people's imagination. . . . Untold thousands dream of living in a small, congenial, cooperative community of loving, understanding, noncompetitive relationships; they long for togetherness and bemoan the lack of community spirit . . . undismayed by the fact that there probably never has existed the kind of community of which they dream.[65]

Daydreaming is probably very good for our mental health if we dream of Elysian Fields of supreme delight while living in the megalopolis. Along with the "nostalgia for the impossible dream" also comes the innate animosity people have against the modern city:

> People were, properly, on the land where, engaged in the most honorable of all occupations, the cultivation of the soil, they could be self-reliant, independent, and solid citizens. Urban communications were, at best, but secondary; at worst, destructive.[66]

For all the negative feelings we hold toward cities, they are the most exciting and stimulating places on earth for many people. "It is the city which uniquely gives the individual his chance for expression. It was not coincidence but consonance that individualism paralleled the trend toward urbanization."[67] Of course, this individualism has been gained at a very high price.

[64]Jonathan L. Freedman, "Positive View of Population Density," *Psychology Today*, September 1971.

[65]Bernard, *Sociology of Community*, p. 107.

[66]Ibid.

[67]Neil W. Chamberlain, *Beyond Malthus: Population and Power* (New York: Basic Books, Inc., Publishers, 1970), p. 92.

If as leisure planners we continue to confound the country and the city, we are sure to fail in our attempts to provide self-enhancing leisure and recreational pursuits. "We have to really look, in the country and city alike, at the real social processes of alienation, separation, externality, abstraction."[68] The division and opposition, in this notion between the city and country, between industry and agriculture, are the result of the division of labor stemming from our economy and, of course, from capitalism, though such a division is not peculiar to capitalist countries. How did we get this way?

The transition of this nation from rural society to city life has been very rapid. At the end of the nineteenth century almost two-thirds of the population lived on farms or in villages. Now two-thirds live in the city, and that percentage is increasing. The strains on our culture in this massive adaptation to city life have been enormous, perhaps incalculable, and the transformation is far from over. The U.S. Commission on Population has termed it a "demographic revolution in population distribution as well as in national population growth."[69]

And what we left behind, while not exactly a scorched earth, is far from some intact idyllic countryside that we might someday return to. "Between 1960 and 1970, the population of the United States grew 13 percent, while the metropolitan population grew 23 percent. Nearly all metropolitan growth took place through the growth of suburbs and territorial expansion into previously rural areas."[70] For many areas of this nation, the distinction between urban and rural is no longer an issue. The source of 74 percent of metropolitan growth between 1960 and 1970 was a natural increase of births over deaths, with the remaining 26 percent the result of in-migration.

The countryside is estimated to be disappearing at the rate of 1.1 million acres a year, or 3,000 acres each day that are being bulldozed. "It is not merely that the countryside is ever receding; in the great expansion of the metropolitan areas the subdivisions of one city are beginning to meet up with the subdivisions of another."[71] Here and there are patches of green, remnants of another age.

Rural populaton in 1900 was 46 million, in 1970 it had grown to only 54 million, even though the national population had nearly tripled. Today farm families represent only 5 percent of the population. In the past ten years nearly *half* of all U.S. rural counties experienced a drop in population. In addition to the decline in rural population, there has also been a decline in the proportion of the population which

68Hatch, "Country Mice or City Mice," p. 598.

69U.S. Commission on Population Growth and the American Future, *Population and the American Future*, p. 25.

70Ibid.

71William H. Whyte, Jr., "Urban Sprawl," in The Editors of *Fortune*, *The Exploding Metropolis* (New York: Doubleday & Company, Inc., 1957), p. 115.

live in towns of less than 50,000. These towns often suffer from high levels of unemployment and a shrinking economic base:

> Nor is it clear that population growth is good for all small towns or cities any more than for all metropolitan areas. For some types of activities, recreation for example, many rural areas may already have more people than desirable, even though density and population size are well below urban levels. The typical small college town, which has experienced rapid growth in the last decade, might well benefit from stabilization of its population as college enrollment levels off.[72]

Although we are often described as a nation of young people, the downward trend in the birth rate is actually making us an older population. The emphasis on youth seems more a political and marketing phenomenon than an actuality. With the exception of the baby boom in the 1940's, the proportion of the population made up of children is tending to be less. If the two-child family is the rate of growth for the remainder of this century, "the age structure would show a consistent pattern of becoming older; with the three-child rate, the age structure would become slightly younger."[73]

In 1970 there were 20 million men and women over 65; this number is expected to rise to 29 million by the end of the century, a 43 percent increase. In 1900 only 4 percent of our population was over 65, by 1970 it was almost 10 percent. If a two-child birth rate persists until the end of the century, the percentage of older people would rise about 16 percent. "A continuing problem of the aged in our society is finding socially valuable roles. . . . It remains to be seen whether patterns of compulsory retirement would be noticeably altered with slower population growth and smaller numbers of new entrants into the labor market."[74]

Much, of course, depends on attitudes toward work, especially where pension, health plans, and social security ease the burdens of unemployed old age. "If a 'leisure ethic' gains greater social acceptance, especially within the younger portion of the work force, people may come to look forward to retirement and the leisure it brings."[75] Much of the migration from rural to urban areas has left behind an older population who are disadvantaged in education and skills and so have limited ability to obtain employment if they so desire. The city has its share of elderly as well.

Urban growth reflects the supremacy of industry over agriculture, and, some argue, of services over industry and agriculture, though the latter is more debatable. The dominance of commerce over agriculture

[72]U.S. Commission on Population Growth and the American Future, *Population and the American Future*, p. 31.

[73]Ibid., p. 62.

[74]Ibid., pp. 66–67.

[75]Ibid., p. 67.

is a worldwide trend and has little to do with population size, density, or with the type of economic system. States with rapid growth, such as California and Arizona, have strong open-country images, yet most of their growth has been in metropolitan areas.

This growth in urban and metropolitan areas has been both bad and good. It has given economic opportunities to masses of people well above what they had ever known. On the other hand, it has confined racism to the inner city while it has given rural minorities better jobs. It has brought about widespread degradation of the environment, not only by the industries that employ all these millions but by the services and developments that have clustered around urban areas. Most of the growth is haphazard, ugly, and virtually all unplanned. Even planned communities leave much to be desired.

Some believe that the New Towns approach might solve the problems of overpopulation and chaotic development in our metropolitan areas.[76] Many New Towns have been built with or without federal support, from the well-known Columbia, Maryland, and Reston, Virginia, to others less well known in California, Minnesota, Illinois, Utah, Arizona, Texas, and Louisiana. The aim of New Towns is to offer a new, different, and better life for urban America:

> With few exceptions, the best of the developments now being promoted as innovative new towns, including many supported by federal or state programs, are no more than glorified suburbs. They may offer somewhat better public facilities and more attractive faces than the old tract subdivisions, but they are perpetuating rather than solving such nagging problems as wasteful land use, traffic congestion, environmental pollution, inefficient and unequal distribution of all public services, economic and racial segregation, and the shortage of decent, reasonably priced housing for low- and middle-income families.[77]

Probably the most predominant aspect of these New Towns in view of the fuel shortages, is their dependence on automobiles. "Cars are still essential for the simplest chores in most of the new towns. None of them is connected directly to the nearest city."[78] Even though these towns offer jobs in industrial parks, too often those who work at the jobs cannot afford to buy homes in the towns, thereby negating the goal of self-sufficient communities.

If New Towns and other planned communities are in actuality suburbs of urban areas, it is important to consider what is happening to some suburbs as they become increasingly more urbanized. Although the trend has not reached significant proportions, and probably won't

[76]Gurney Breckenfeld, *Columbia and the New Cities* (New York: David McKay Co., Inc., 1971).

[77]Leonard Downie, Jr., "Vision or Hoax? The 'New-Town' Mirage," *The Nation*, May 15, 1972, p. 618.

[78]Ibid., p. 619.

for some time, many suburbanites are returning to the city to live. "Big city officials are predicting that this trickle will enlarge as the fuel shortage makes commuting more difficult—encouraging people who have been planning an eventual move back to the cities to take the plunge now rather than waiting."[79] In New York City, the City Planning Commission reports that the exodus of whites from the city has finally slowed down.

Even though such people want to avoid the problems of the suburbs, where previously they had wanted to avoid the problems of the city, they are welcomed back into the city because they enhance the tax base. In terms of federal monies, and especially revenue-sharing funds, which are given on a per capita basis, people are important.

> Never mind if per capita aid remains the same—it is the aggregate total which must grow to give you the clout in the halls of Congress, and give you something to boast about at the next mayors' or governors' conference. So we saw the spectacle, when the census results were in, of outraged politicians everywhere crying that there must have been a miscount, that their fiefdom just *had* to have more inhabitants than the official tabulations showed.[80]

Politicians are usually happy to have more people live in cities.

As suburban problems of commuting, traffic congestion, rising taxes, uniformity and sterility, crime, and so forth begin to be outweighed by the attractions of city living, planners predict the present trend will accelerate. Many of the middle class, according to planners, are blacks who are taking advantage of the inexpensive homes now available in the cities. However, unless the social problems which give impetus to these criss-cross migrations are also confronted, our population relocations may only compound the problems of those who cannot afford to move when trouble comes too close.

Although metropolitan areas have burgeoned, most cities have had a drop in population. Fifteen of the 21 cities which had a population of half a million in 1960 had lost population by 1970. "In fact, declining central cities lost more people in the 1960's than were lost by declining rural counties. Over half the 1970 metropolitan population lived outside the central city...."[81] Almost all metropolitan growth during those ten years was in the suburbs.

We have been and continue to be a mobile people. For most of us, moving has held the promise of a better life. One in five Americans change their homes every year. "These rates have remained virtually

[79]"Crowds...Crime...Higher Taxes: City Problems Invade Suburbs," *U.S. News & World Report*, December 10, 1973, p. 66.

[80]Dolan, *TANSTAAFL*, p. 67; see also William E. Farrell, "Cities Ask Funds, Assailing Census," *The New York Times*, December 9, 1973, p. 37.

[81]U.S. Commission on Population Growth and the American Future, *Population and the American Future*, p. 31.

unchanged over the quarter century for which data are available. In part because of the decline in rural population, the majority of people moving long distances are now coming from urban areas."[82] Since World War II, especially, the bulk of migration to metropolitan areas has been black Americans; four-fifths of the metropolitan area black Americans live in the central cities. One can drive through great reaches of this country without once seeing a black person. Moynihan was correct when he perceived blacks as "living in a state almost of population seige." A great many black spokesmen in the past ten years have again and again returned to the vulnerability of black Americans in their urban slums.

The broad dimensions of population distribution are racial and economic, with black Americans and poor whites entrenched in the inner cities, while middle-class whites and those minority members who are better off live in the suburbs. The two societies envisioned and warned about in the Kerner Commission Report is well underway. If U.S. population grows at the two-child model rate of the U.S. Commission on Population Growth, by 2000 there will be 225 million people living in U.S. metropolitan areas; the three-child model's prediction would swell this figure to 273 million. Rather than our two racial societies becoming more removed from each other, they are becoming more and more concentrated, in adjacent areas.

The development of our urban society, evident from the turn of the century, has been from farm —→ to small town —→ to city —→ to metropolitan areas or mega-cities. These mega-cities are urban regions that spread in a continuous growth from the city, reaching farther and farther into the deserted rural areas. The city is devouring the countryside and threatening all open spaces regardless of their proximity to the city:

> There have been tremendous changes in the geographic scale at which we live. Transportation technology, particularly our extensive highway system, permits us to move great distances within a short period. ... Urban people in search of open space and recreation travel considerable distances to enjoy a weekend camping trip. A century ago, Central Park was the city park for New York. Now the "city" is the urban region along the Atlantic seaboard and its park is the Shenandoah National Park on Skyline Drive.[83]

The Commission predicts that by the year 2000, urban regions could take up one-sixth of U.S. land area and will house five-sixths of our population, if present urbanization trends continue. The Commission feels the best long-term strategy is to achieve a stabilization of population growth rather than working toward population redistribution, which would no doubt be a mind-boggling task.

[82]Ibid., p. 29.
[83]Ibid., p. 36.

Demand for Outdoor Recreation

Because of the diminishment of open space, most concern with recreation demand necessarily focuses on outdoor recreation. Over the past ten years visitors to our nation's national parks have more than doubled, while the amount of land given over to such parks increased by only about one-fifth. The rapid increase in the use of parks is attributed primarily to the increased leisure and incomes of Americans, or at least the increased desire to camp as a vacation. More and more people will have the desire "to get away" as remaining traces of natural life disappear from even the outer reaches of the megalopolis; then, one will drive great distances into the remaining countryside to be alone, or to hear birds singing and other one-time common sounds of daily life.

The U.S. Forest Service calculates that 3.1 million visitor days were recorded in 1970 in the White Mountain National Forest, a figure they expect to double by the end of the century. A visitor day equals one person using the national forest for a twelve-hour period. "Twenty-four Boy Scouts on a one-hour hike will generate two visitor days of use. So will a backpacker who enters the forest at noon today and leaves it at noon tomorrow."[84] By 2000 the Forest Service conjectures the WMNF will be used by campers, motorists, downhill skiers, sightseers, hikers, and "others," in that order. The "others" category is the disturbing one; it not only includes bird watchers and cross-country skiers, but "those gentlemen and ladies in Buck Rogers uniforms who roar through the wilderness on snowmobiles and motorcycles."[85] These "others," and it is not likely bird watching and cross-country skiing will grow at a fast clip, are expected to log 5,000 visitor days by the year 2000. Remember, twelve snowmobiles crashing through the wilderness for one hour equals only one visitor day!

Not only do more leisure and income lead Americans into the wilderness in greater numbers, but these vacationers take a bevy of motorized and electrical monstrosities with them. The U.S. Commission on Population Growth noted that the production of truck campers and camping trailers rose from 62,000 in 1961 to over half a million by 1971. Improved roads, roadside facilities, and camping areas encouraged the proliferation of such vehicles. The number of campers, vans, motor homes, house trailers, pickup truck shell covers, and camping trailers is expected to double by 1980.[86]

[84] Ford, "The White Mountains," p. 81.

[85] Ibid.

[86] Al Martinez, "Houses on Wheels: Clogging the Open Road," *The Nation*, August 21, 1972, pp. 114–16. See also, Greg Conderacci, "Motor-Home Makers, Hit by Fuel Crisis, Turn Their Vehicles Into 'People Movers,'" *The Wall Street Journal*, February 20, 1974, p. 38.

There has been some backlash to the growth of these vehicles and the noisy, polluting gadgets that accompany them, but not enough to much affect their presence on the summer highways. The problem with these vehicles, other than perhaps safety, is their intrusion into wilderness or near-wilderness settings. No one is quite sure what their ultimate effect will be, but many are skeptical. The U.S. Forest Service estimates that about half its campground visitors come in recreational vehicles. "Visual blots, status symbols, freedom wagons, polluters, home substitutes, low-cost vacations, nightmares in the summer dream, recreational vehicles are here to stay, and so is the growing debate surrounding their movement on the nation's highways."[87]

One possible means of "reducing" recreational demand is instituting the reduced work week. If, say, we adopt a three-and-a-half-day work week which is staggered over the entire seven-day week, this would drastically change our current peak-load weekends. Two benefits would result: (1) there would be fewer people in the metropolitan area at any one time; (2) there would likewise be fewer people in recreational areas at any one time, especially during the traditional two-day weekend. Also, of course, would be the accompanying benefits to traffic flow.

Attendance at national parks has been cited as increasing at a rate of 7 percent per year, increasing fourfold over the past twenty years. Again, the problem is not one of population growth as much as it is emergence of a more affluent and mobile population. On one weekend in 1970, Yosemite National Park had 50,000 people in it. "Since then, the number of·campsites has been reduced and traffic has been restricted in order to reduce noise and pollution. Still, visitors are put on notice that the water in the river is undrinkable."[88] Yosemite is only one of many public parks to suffer the same distressing fate. Lines and lines of recreational vehicles wait to enter, in contrast to the days when we were pleased to see an increase in the number of people using our parks.

Future estimates on national park use are predicted to be 240 million by 1980 (it was 63 million in 1959), and well over 400 million by 2000.[89] The Days believe that population increase alone would have brought about our present plight, but the increase in our standard of living at the same time aggravates the problem.

There has been some discussion about dividing the national parks into various management areas; for example, the White Mountains National Forest might have four areas: (1) for loggers, (2) for family campers, picnickers, etc., (3) for off-the road vehicles, and (4) for backpackers and cross-country skiers.[90] Biologist Garrett Hardin has sug-

[87]Ibid., p. 116.

[88]Steven Roberts, *The New York Times*, September 1, 1969, pp. 1, 15.

[89]Lincoln H. and Alice Taylor Day, "Excerpt from 'Too Many Americans,'" in U.S. Congress, House Committee on Government Operations, *Effects of Population Growth on Natural Resources and the Environment*, p. 166.

[90]Ford, "The White Mountains," p. 82.

ILLUSTRATION 3.1

Source: *The Nation*, August 21, 1972, p. 115.

gested the several uses for parks might be: (1) togetherness areas, (2) motor areas, (3) lively peopled areas, (4) quiet peopled areas, and (5) wilderness areas.[91] Hardin's notion is that one earns the right to use the wilderness, say, by having to walk ten or more miles before getting in: "It is clear that many of our present national parks and national forests and other recreation areas should be forever closed to people on crutches, to small children, to fat people, to people with heart conditions, and to old people in the usual state of disrepair. On the basis of their lack of merit, such people (and remember I am a member of this

[91]Statement in U.S. Congress, House Committee on Government Operations, *Effects of Population Growth on Natural Resources and the Environment*, p. 93.

deprived group) should give up all claim of right to the wilderness experience."[92]

Such schemes are usually prefaced by how we have to face facts, accept threats to democratic notions, and so on if we are to survive as a culture. What follows is usually a lot of nonsense that can be seen as such by even the oldest, fattest, childlike cripple with a heart condition.

Such a proposal as Hardin's would greatly reduce our park use, but it would make more sense if those who fall below Hardin's utopian concept of the meritorious citizen were to get into the wilderness and "shape up." He seems to be keeping out the wrong people. And what if one wandered into the wrong section? Would they be stoned? So much for Hardin; perhaps he's joking. In the White Mountains scheme there "is nothing to prevent a hiker from wandering through the other management areas, if he is willing to risk being struck by a snowmobile or a falling tree; but that is not wilderness travel."[93] As the demand for outdoor recreation rises, must our concept of solitude also change?

Much of the increased demand for outdoor recreation has been made possible by the automobile, the greatest mixed blessing of our age. The distribution of population, overwhelmingly concentrated in urban regions, has compounded the negative problems of automobiles. In addition to the automobile becoming a means of overburdening the national parks, highway construction also poses a distinct threat to the environment, with its increased noise levels and pollution, not to mention the loss of open space used up in highway construction. "Rail transit is potentially faster, less expensive, and far less damaging to the environment. . . . Yet today rail systems in the Northeast are bankrupt. . . ."[94]

American automobiles and trucks each year consume about 40 percent of all petroleum used in the United States. There is a great deal of attention being given to the waste left by automobile development, especially in view of the predicted serious shortages in energy supplies. The Office for Emergency Preparedness has said that in view of the need to conserve national fuel supplies, the predicted growth in automobile use would be unacceptable.[95] Even though we have reduced the pollutive emissions in 1973 cars, we now burn much more gas to go half the distance at a greater price per gallon. But it's good for the economy!

> Think of the economic progress involved in 12 million to 15 million of these newer cars being driven from 500 miles to 2,000 miles each to the great make-play enterprise of Disney World at Orlando, Fla., many of the powerful vehicles hauling campers and trailers behind their exhaust.

[92]Ibid., p. 96.

[93]Ford, "The White Mountains," p. 82.

[94]Ridgeway M. Hall, Jr., "Highway vs. Environment: The Long Island Fight," *The New Republic*, May 12, 1973, p. 17.

[95]Emma Rothschild, "Running Out of Gas," *The New York Review of Books*, November 1, 1973, p. 34.

Disney World expected 10 million vehicles at its parking lots during its opening year, and wound up with 12 million.[96]

The problem for urban transport planners, then, becomes one of how to:

> ... enhance urban life and at the same time to minimize the deleterious side effects. To achieve these objectives will involve new designs for urban settlement, the appropriate selection of transportation technologies, a desirable balance between public and private transport, and the use of transport facilities as a means of building better communities.[97]

How such a realignment of the dominant automobile culture is going to affect recreational demand is difficult to say. However, several possibilities emerge. If there is a greater reliance on public transportation, there may be a reduction in the number of recreational vehicles and all their gadgetry in public parks. If improved transportation facilities and reduced use of the automobile lead to the evolution of better communities, as Owen suggests, then attention can be given to developing outdoor recreational opportunities nearer to where people live, offering various options to the wilderness and near-wilderness areas we are struggling to preserve.

From some early evidence, this trend seems to be already emerging, at least in the private sector of campground development: "The gasoline shortage and tight money appear to have put the brakes on the feverish development of campground facilities across the United States. In addition, campground operations are cutting rates and stepping up promotional efforts to offset a drop in business."[98] The 1974 Rand McNally *Campground and Trailer Park Guide* lists only 110 additional facilities over its 1973 edition. During the years 1960 to 1973 this guide added approximately 1,000 new campgrounds, both private and public, each year.

SUMMARY

The emphasis throughout this chapter has been on the broader implications of population and economic growth; we must now review those implications from the viewpoint of the local community, more particularly with regard to leisure planning. Although the size of a community is an essential factor in planning for leisure needs, numbers of

[96]William Rodgers, "Nixon's Energy Policy: Exercise in Political Duplicity," *The Nation*, May 21, 1973, p. 647.

[97]Wilfred Owen, "Transport: Key to the Future of Cities," in Harvey S. Perloff, ed., *The Quality of the Urban Environment: Essays on "New Resources" in an Urban Age* (Baltimore: Johns Hopkins Press, 1969), p. 206.

[98]"Notes: Campgrounds Feel the Gas Pinch," *The New York Times*, Leisure Section, January 27, 1974, p. 4.

people alone are not the determinant, but who these people are and what they perceive and demand as their leisure rights. A community of, say, 30,000 in a depressed region of this country would raise very different demands than a community of comparable size in a more affluent setting. Furthermore, the growth and expansion of the former community, except for the spreading of poverty, would undoubtedly be less noticeable and make fewer social demands than the latter.

While we should concentrate on birth control efforts, if for no other reason than to deflate the disproportionate claim of each new American on the world's resources, we have to see planning as a need beyond population concerns. To fatigue ourselves over population problems, when many of these are highly debatable, would be gross shortsightedness and a waste of time. If our population growth were likely to get out of control, then there might be cause for hand-wringing. Nor should we facilely use population growth as the villain: don't use last year's explanations for this year's dilemma. Push population growth as the cause of our misery to its logical conclusion: If there are too many of us, or soon will be, don't we need clear-sighted planners more than ever? Planners who are not easily misled by fashionable solutions to complex problems?

Planning is a profession or a skill that can be greatly tempted by the facile solution, the fashionable thinking on what indeed is wrong. Last year it was population, this year ecology, then large oil cartels, next year who knows. As each key problem is circulated by the media and drenched in textbooks, we clutch at it as if it were the ultimate word. As I have argued, we are our own enemy not because there are too many of us—55 or so to the square mile—but because of the personal demands we make on our environment and the corporate ills we allow to continue.

Local planners rely on regional and national planners for ideas. Yet national planning is either nonexistent or notoriously poor. Whatever nonsense is practiced by national planners should not be watered down for local needs. There is a real necessity for fastidious appraisal of planning in larger systems before we appropriate these for leisure systems designs at the local level. Nowhere is this admonition more necessary than in the use of systems design for planning. To use an analogy:

> All the great social theories to date, including those of Marx, Weber, Durkheim, and behavioral social science, for example, are in fact false. They overextend categories appropriate only to a particular time and place; they offer us false predictions; they are deceived by the ideological structures of their own society; they formulate generalizations which they propose as laws where laws are inappropriate; they reify abstractions in misleading ways. But nonetheless all these great social theories have the power to incarnate and reincarnate themselves in social life, and by so doing give themselves a semblance of truth which they do not in the end

possess. In order not to be deceived by them we have to become fully conscious of what they are saying to us and of why what they are saying has the power over us that it has.[99]

If planning, as a technique, an art, or a social theory, fails, we still must come to understand why the desire to plan persists, why we long to plan for the future. Whether it is even possible to do good planning or not, our strong inclination toward social planning continues. In order not to botch our chances at planning, we must be aware of the failures and mystification that surround social planning, so as not to deify something that is imperfect. Therefore, we should become as fully conscious of its appeal and power over us as we can. Those who should be most critical of planning are the planners themselves. This book is not an attempt to say only glorious things about planning, and then leave the practitioners to discover the shortcomings themselves. That was precisely the drawback of systems analysis and systems planning in the federal government, most notably the Department of Defense—all praise from the implementers, hostility toward critics no matter how incisive. That rigid attitude tainted systems analysis for all other applications.

Planning for the future, whatever our intentions, is not a simple matter of following a model or a chart. It requires critical attention to be focused on every aspect of the process. Taking any social theory and accepting its implications without scrutiny, will bring chaos or at the least poor results. The space devoted in this chapter to population growth and its implications is the kind of scrutiny needed for all aspects of planning. We should accept nothing as gospel at the local level before giving a close and careful examination of all premises of planning, especially when we appropriate the style of national planning to a community.

The warning "THINK" which was posted to prevent industrial accidents rightly belongs before the planner's eyes. This is especially true for recreation and parks, where we often draw on the findings of other social sciences without a thorough appraisal of such inferences. For example, we use survey research methods without a good feel for the weaknesses of these methods. In local planning, where funds are limited and professional time scarce, we must be doubly sure we are not spinning our wheels and calling it planning.

The national and even international focus in this chapter is important because the local community draws on the beliefs and outcomes of the larger community—the nation or its cities. What is applicable to cities can often be of great value to towns, especially rapidly growing ones. But often it is not applicable. We need to discern the differences, which are not always evident if we allow others to do our

[99]Alasdair MacIntyre, "Durkheim's Call to Order," *The New York Review of Books*, March 7, 1974, p. 26.

thinking for us. If there is a need for provincialism it is in local planning, where we can resist the lure of sophisticated planning and take a closer look at the community, its idiosyncrasies and peculiarities, what differentiates it from whatever model we may have in mind. Planning guidelines, such as the model in this text, yes; lack of individual thinking, no.

If we are planning for a community that is losing its open space to industrial development, will we concentrate on that growth as the problem or will we scurry around trying to save the remaining green spaces? The decision, or even the capability, to go to the source of the problem is not an easy one. However, if we lament population growth while ignoring such industrial expansion, we have failed to accurately assess the local situation, even though our reasoning might be acceptable to most. The same goes for building developments and residential tracts; without recognition of the demands and threats these pose to a community's recreational capacity, we will praise our growing community at the risk of our own profession. I do not believe the function of leisure planning at the local level is to outsmart developers and other business interests. Unless we can work together or *demand* cooperative community planning, we shall be in an increasingly weaker position as the demand for resources continues and the judgment toward recreation as a social service harshens.

We too can become one of the many paradoxes of this nation: as the need for recreational services at the local level grew, the ability and capacity to provide those services diminished. The movie "Soylent Green" depicted a future society that places a high premium on one vestige of nature: a skimpy tree in a museum. Are we to be the keepers of that tree, to permit the resources essential to outdoor recreation and sports to be depleted? Will the skills of our profession be devoted to intensive planning, like intensive gardening, where one tries to obtain more and more out of less and less?

As planners, we too readily accept the premise of less resources without wondering where those resources are going and why the very planet itself seems to exist to serve those needs. How lamentable that we have been programmed for a future of less and less, while about us we see the open land being gobbled up. Reduced resources are not a fact, they are predictions of what is likely to occur unless we change our entire economic and social values, or at least seriously and actively reassess those values, as well as the manner in which resources are obtained and distributed.

Planners at the local level should not accept the status quo as it might be determined at the national level, but must examine and assess the broader implications for the community. If we decide to pool the transportation needs of several recreation centers, is this motivated by a control over fuel by a cartel-type industry, or by the logical appeal of communal transportation? If it were the former, it would be compliance with corporate dominance; if the latter, even if the idea sprang from the "energy crisis," presumably the decision would reflect a reversal of earlier values or their reassessment.

The great change in U.S. population has been not in its growth so much as its distribution, or as the U.S. Commission on Population Growth put it, "a demographic revolution in population distribution." We need to be familiar with the kinds of communities formed by such distribution patterns. The broadest shift has been, of course, from rural to metropolitan areas, which include both cities and suburbs. Thus, at first glance, we have basically three separate communities: cities and towns, suburbs, and rural or country areas. Naturally, there is overlap among these, especially at suburban fringes which grow directly out from the city or touch upon more rural areas. Although these basic communities may not be distinct in their leisure preferences, they are decidedly disparate in what they are likely to receive.

Ski areas are unavailable within the confines of the city, or often the suburbs for that matter, and have to be obtained outside the community. All a community planner can do if a community expresses a desire for skiing is to assess the likelihood of access to these areas. However, within the city limits, and with the resources available, the community planner can concentrate on leisure options that are possible to obtain or create. On the other hand, there wouldn't be much sense in designing mini-parks for rural areas, where outdoor activities requiring large amounts of open space are quite possible. With the widespread cultural activities in most cities, a fine arts or a cultural center might not make much sense in a city; yet it would in a suburb or rural village, where much less variety is available. On the other hand, mobile recreational vehicles make a lot of sense in cities, where impoverished families cannot afford to take their children to shows or other events; in a rural area such a service would not offer as much attraction. There is no need to look at animal puppets if one can see the real thing in the backyard, or to have someone turn on a hydrant on a hot day if there's a swimming hole nearby.

Planning leisure services requires the ideas of the community on what they would like, as well as the expertise of recreation and park specialists and other professionals on what it is possible to provide and what the probable future demands of a particular community will be. If a suburban community desires a golf course, and has a large area set aside, a landscape architect might quickly detect difficulties with that land: poor water drainage, for instance—a golf course under water most of the spring is hardly responsible leisure planning, no matter how appealing it looks on paper.

The age distribution of our population is also of interest for the local planner. Now that we have voluntary segregation of the elderly into special communities, e.g., Sun City, Arizona, there is a tendency to overlook the recreational and leisure needs of the older members of society: we seem to think that everyone past retirement is in a nursing home or in a sun-filled community of senior citizens. Not true; nor is it true that we are a country of young people. Not only are we all aging, but the elderly live longer, and are often left behind in rural areas or leading lonely and often impoverished lives in cities. One of the saddest marks of our culture is that the elderly receive services because they are considered "disadvantaged." We discard the aged, sometimes as early as the middle fifties, as if they were throw-away products we'd grown peevish with. They are our parents, our predecessors, and it little gains us to label them disadvantaged when it has been our own indifference that has earned them that dubious title.

Not only should older citizens be involved in local planning efforts, but leisure activities should be designed for them as well, preferably more than a perfunctory gesture for the old folks, or infantile arts and crafts to speed the jelling process of their brains. If older people have a say in the plan, you can be sure these kinds of misguided efforts will cease.

Because population distributions are largely political and economic, the local planner has to be alert to changes in the political and economic environment. A good example of this would be in segregated housing patterns. Now that the housing market is seriously deflated by interest rates, the "energy crisis," and related economic troubles, there is keen interest in stimulating purchases of homes. A good anxious market, ready to carry any kind of burden, is the black American family who desires to move to a better (i.e., white) neighborhood. Recently, the National Association of Realtors began negotiating with the U.S. Department of Housing and Urban Development to stimulate an industry-wide affirmative marketing agreement, wherein all realtors would follow uniform guidelines to ensure minorities free and open access to housing.[100]

One of the severest crises in leisure services has been attempts to meet, and to meet properly, the urgent demands of minority groups, especially black Americans, for recreational services and facilities. If we plan for all-white communities, or all-black central cities, we may face such a resurgent crisis in the not-too-distant future. Although there is widespread segregation in most communities, any changes in these broad patterns, no matter how minor, are immediately felt at the local level. The entire country does not have to be integrated before many communities face the demands of a changing population. Planners have to be aware of these changes, have foresight if possible, so future planning does match probable future needs and community composition as much as possible.

The one tendency in our society that recreation and parks seems

[100]"Realtors Trade Group, HUD Negotiating to Devise Industry-Wide Marketing Accord," *The Wall Street Journal*, March 4, 1974, p. 8.

neatly meshed with is that of a service economy, the post-industrial age. The creation or expansion of leisure services at the local level not only provides pleasure for community residents, these services also create jobs. However, as already mentioned, there is little reason to believe that a service-dominant economy, if and when we reach that stage, will be faultless. If the motivations and values that have spurred our massive industrial and financial enterprises still dominate, destructive growth and abuses to the environment will continue. We should not be smug about being a "social service" while ignoring the business aspects of our profession, as we see mammoth recreational enterprises undertaken by private individuals or corporations. An economy bolstered by Disney Worlds is not exactly an exhilarating prospect, even if such are labeled "services." We must be aware of the abuses inherent in services and not take refuge in post-industrial jargon. This consideration is especially crucial where communities seek to augment their leisure resources through cooperative efforts with private businesses. Beware of degradation to the environment in the name of fun and games; building a resort can be as much a mode of environmental destruction as strip-mining. The fact that the uses of the former appear more palatable than the latter should not detract from the physical and often psychological desecration done to a community and its environs by such undertakings. Remember that although our population has grown less than 50 percent since 1940, our environmental problems have increased by many hundreds of percent.

Perhaps the most difficult yet critical aspect of community leisure planning is the recognition of what is happening to the broader environment. For example, if you were designing a leisure plan for a community adjacent to or within traveling distance of the White Mountain National Forest, and were aware of the imminent changes in that park, how would this be reflected in your planning? First, it would make little sense to ignore the destruction of the park and continue to rely on it as a "bonus" over and above community resources. It would be wisest, for long-range planning to discount its availability no matter how improbable that eventuality might appear. Environmental destruction is occurring everywhere, not just in other states or areas, but in our own communities, counties, and regions. Local planners must integrate such awareness into their planning no matter how distasteful or pessimistic.

Communities set in lovely parts of this country have always relied on the surrounding countryside and wilderness as a free and seemingly endless source of recreational options. This reliance is changing rapidly. As a former resident of Aspen, Colorado, said, "Who would have thought twenty years ago that Aspen would have pollution, or that it would take ten minutes to cross a street because of heavy traffic." It would have been visionary twenty years ago to have suggested that such a community would experience unmet recreational demands within a generation. Consider formerly tourist-hungry states, such as Oregon, who now desire to stem the tide of tourism as well as in-migrations to that state. Their anti-tourist campaign complains about the despoilation and destruction of Oregon by the massive migrations it has absorbed, and warns of Oregon becoming another California, of the "Californi-cating" of Oregon. For communities in such tourist states that once offered recreation primarily for outsiders, how do they plan for their leisure needs now that they are purposefully altering the profile of their communities? Do those living in southwestern communities, for example, really relish a dude ranch?

While resort communities are somewhat atypical, their proximity to and reliance on natural sites is not so unusual a situation. If large and beautiful tracts of wilderness, forests, swamps, even deserts are destroyed, this destruction depletes the leisure options of all communities within traveling distance of that site. A planner cannot ignore the limitations these losses pose for leisure services, even if there is little one seems able to do to stop the destruction. The destruction of the environment, while usually examined in national terms, is a local reality, a catastrophe that touches almost every community in the nation. We can no longer rely on the bounty of nature to meet our outdoor leisure demands.

SELECTED REFERENCES

ALONSO, WILLIAM. *The System of Intermetropolitan Population Flows.* The Commission on Population Growth and the American Future, Washington, D.C., 1972.

BERNARD, JESSIE. *The Sociology of Community.* Glenview, Illinois: Scott, Foresman and Company, 1973.

BOGUE, D. J. *The Structure of the Metropolitan Community.* New York: Russell & Russell, 1950.

CHEN, KUAN-I. *World Population Growth and Living Standards.* New York: Bookman Assoc., 1960.

CLAWSON, M., AND KNETSCH, J. *Economics of Outdoor Recreation.* Baltimore: The John Hopkins Press, 1966.

EHRLICH, PAUL R., AND A. H. *Population, Resources, Environment. Issues in Human Ecology.* San Francisco, Calif.: W. H. Freeman and Company, Publishers, 1970.

FUGUITT, GLEN V. *Population Trends of Non-Metropolitan Cities & Villages in the United States.* The Commission on Population Growth and the American Future, Washington, D.C., 1972.

HAUSSER, P. M., ed. *The Population Dilemma.* Englewood Cliffs, N.J.: Prentice-Hall, Inc., 1963.

SPENGLER, JOSEPH J. "Declining Population Growth: Economic Effects." Commission on Population Growth and the American Future, Washington, D.C., 1972.

THOMLINSON, RALPH, *Population Dynamics*. New York: Random House, Inc., 1965.

U.S. Bureau of Census, Current Population Reports, Series P-23, No. 36, Fertility Indicators, 1970, 1971.

U.S. Bureau of Census, Current Population Report, Series P-25, No. 470, "Projections of the Population of the U. S. by Ages and Sex: 1970—2200," Washington, D.C., 1971.

U.S. Commission on Population Growth, *Population and the American Future*. The Report of the Commission on Population Growth and the American Future, Washington, D.C., 1969.

4

ATTITUDE, INTEREST, AND OPINION SURVEY OF THE COMMUNITY

A community survey is generally a twofold attempt to gather and analyze information from a constituency as well as to establish ongoing participatory relations with the respondents for the overall leisure plan.

INTRODUCTION

The need to solicit the attitude, interest and opinions of community residents on the comprehensive planning of leisure services might seem self-evident, but for many, justification is still needed for doing so. Many Americans at this point have been overpolled, interviewed, queried, and explored through surveys. In addition to the fatigue and disinterest, not to mention annoyance and hostility, that such an abundance of social surveying can cause, there is added the prevalence of poor and suspect survey techniques. A good example of the psuedo-scientific methods used in so-called "survey research" is discussed in an article on electoral polls, a form of opinion surveys familiar to most of us. In this article, Benson *et al.* note, among other problems, that:

> electoral polls suffer from severe theoretical and methodological defects which can severely distort reality and create Alice-in-Wonderland worlds of nonexistent "social groupings" and spurious correlations.[1]

[1]Lee Benson, Kevin Clancy, and John Kushma, "Pollsters and Pundits: The Tricks of the Trade," *The Nation*, November 30, 1974, p. 553.

128

At this juncture I am not so much concerned with the theoretical and methodological defects (themselves cause for concern), as with the implications of these defects on survey research in general and on community surveys in particular. *Any* work of poor quality done in a given field ultimately reflects on the entire field. Survey research, deservedly or otherwise, has always had a tint of charlatanism about it. With any social science tool, the barest tinge of trickery or misuse colors the entire use of that method. As with any method used for scientific or even quasi-scientific investigations, it is the failures and abuses that receive public attention and remain longest in the public's mind. Even within the academic community, where survey research has had its greatest and most reputable development, there is strong resistance to its use.

It may even be a truism at this point that Americans like to talk to strangers but resist being interviewed. The first exchange is more spontaneous, one decides what one will reveal; the latter *probes for information* (actual jargon in survey methodology). A great deal of the literature on survey methodology, some of which will be discussed in this chapter, deals with techniques of probing, a not so pleasant image for the paradoxical American who likes to offer opinions but resists anything that smacks of an invasion of privacy: remember the uproar caused in 1970 when the U.S. Bureau of the Census asked for the number of bathrooms in each household. One might readily brag to a stranger about having a home with two or three baths, but would bristle at being formally asked the same.

Such ambivalence toward revealing information must be kept in mind by a social agency about to undertake such a project. A project or agency director should *never* assume that people like to be asked their opinions, that they will be flattered to have been asked; anyone who has done even the slightest bit of interviewing can soon rid us of that notion. In informing a community why a survey needs to be conducted on various aspects of a comprehensive leisure plan, an agency director must be aware of, and not defensive about, the stigma attached to surveys of all kinds at all levels of this society. And as noted, the resistance to surveys is not merely from those who might misunderstand the methodology, but also by those quite knowledgeable about the technique and its varied applications. The response to this resistance, especially with community residents, should not be a public relations snow job, but a point-by-point description and explanation of survey methodology, the reasons for desiring specific information, and the uses to which such information will be put, i.e., its confidentiality.

It goes without saying that seemingly innocuous information for one purpose can be bothersome or harmful in another context. Consider the Welcome Wagon program in a community, a nice gesture no doubt. But who supports the program? Merchants and credit bureaus. They give but they also receive. In addition to receiving a family's possible patronage through the Welcome Wagon, they receive credit assessments (the representative's judgment of a family's "worth") and other seemingly innocent information that might affect a family's social situation. Any survey data collected for one purpose should be confined to that or comparable purposes, and released only in summary form to another agency or investigator. Under *no* circumstance should one agency give another agency access to the original questionnaires, no matter how simple the survey. Confidentiality of survey data extends to the life of that data, not merely to its usefulness to the original researcher. If we say all information will be treated in confidence we had better mean it, or we may not get another chance to collect much data in a community—or any future data we do collect might be riddled with distortions and lies, the great comeback of the once-betrayed respondent.

Before explaining (or convincing) community residents of the need for a survey, we should determine whether the need for specific data does indeed exist. There is a great deal of information available in or to a social service agency; it should not be freshly gathered merely because of research fussiness or laziness. If an agency has data, for instance, on the demand for recreation in an area, these data should be assessed before rushing to obtain comparable information from virtually the same respondents. There is nothing more tiresome than being asked several times, by the same agency, what our most pressing needs are if they asked it last year in another guise. Related to this is asking opinions on subjects about which we do nothing: do you think we should have more swings, fewer swings, same number, or no swings in the vest-pocket parks as in the regular parks? Then no mention is made again of vest-pocket parks, never mind the swings. Most of us can call to mind even more notorious examples of vital data never used. No wonder people do not respond or treat surveys as a sham. No wonder survey research suffers a decline. We must determine real need and purpose before we turn to the community to seek their cooperation and consent.

PURPOSES OF SURVEYS

Inextricably related to the need for conducting a survey are the purposes for which a survey is designed. The purpose of an attitude, interest, and opinion survey is basically to discover the leisure habits and interests of residents in the community, as well as their opinions and attitudes toward these.[2] Within this broader definition falls the

---

[2] A great deal of controversy and research centers on the difference between an attitude and an opinion, notably the difficulties of obtaining and measuring the validity of attitudes. For some discussion of this, see A. N. Oppenheim, *Questionnaire Design and Attitude Measurement* (New York: Basic Books, Inc., 1966), pp. 105–96. This will be discussed some more later.

concentration on conducting such a survey in a community. A community survey is generally a twofold attempt to gather and analyze information from a constituency as well as to establish ongoing participatory relations with the respondents for the overall leisure plan.[3] Since this book deals elsewhere with establishing and maintaining relationships with community participants and their representatives, this discussion concentrates more on the survey instrument itself. However, we must not forget that a community attitude, interest, and opinion survey is not isolated from the other activities of the ongoing leisure plan. That is, community residents should be aware of the survey before it is conducted, be it by mail, by telephone, or in person, and it should not come as a surprise to them. That is the task of a good public information program.

In relation to a comprehensive leisure plan for a community, there are basically four types of questions a survey instrument would utilize:

1. What are the scope and depth of opportunities available for the use of leisure?
2. In what activities do adults and youth say they participate?
3. What do adults and youth recommend for additional park facilities and recreation programs?
4. What do adults and youth believe is the present sufficiency of the agency in providing park facilities and recreation programs?

Although some of the information sought in these questions might be known intuitively by the agency director and staff, or even from attendance records, the purpose of the survey is to validate the views of adults and youth on these issues in light of the comprehensive leisure plan. These are not usually fact questions, but questions primarily of attitude. Fact questions may be simple demographics (age, sex, family composition). Questions of attitude, feeling, or opinion may inquire about an existing situation; other questions may deal with usual habits, behavior, preferences, or interests. The "nonfact" kinds of questions noted above are those most vital to community involvement in comprehensive planning. Any fact questions in an attitude, interest, and opinion survey are often subordinate to these sorts of attitudinal questions, and are usually simple demographic questions to identify a respondent statistically.

It may seem surprising that the first question above is even posed, for it might appear as an admission that an agency does not have the answer, which of course it does not. The agency is interested in obtaining their community respondents' *views* on leisure opportunities. An agency well knows the number of parks and facilities in its com-

---

[3]For further amplification of this point, see Roland L. Warren, *Studying Your Community* (New York: Russell Sage Foundation, 1955), pp. 306–47, a classic, comprehensive guide for community surveys.

munity, may even know of informal neighborhood "leisure centers," such as 24-hour restaurants, the off-track betting parlor, or what have you; but the planners are interested in the residents' perceptions of leisure, not outwardly accessible facts which may mean nothing in this context. Information must be sought on overall leisure opportunities, activities not governed or known of by the recreation agency, for this is a comprehensive leisure plan. Naturally, the researchers will not elicit information on all leisure activities, especially illegal or private ones, but the questionnaire should not be confined to agency offerings alone.

The second type of question becomes more specific, but still does not stress facts as much as perceptions of participation. An attitude, interest, and opinion survey is not out to prove something, though the answers may be compared with, say, records of facility or program use, in order to assess the validity of the data obtained. But this type of survey is not a theoretical or hypothetical tool; it is merely an attempt to gather attitudes and opinions on leisure activities. If youths or adults *say* they participate in specific activities, their answers stand as such unless we begin to suspect, based on comparisons with any independent data we may have, that their responses have been less than candid.

If answers to questions appear nonsensical, arbitrary, or in contradiction to other questions within the same survey instrument, questions purposefully included to cross-check with each other, then we can be concerned about the reliability and validity of the data. As to the statistical reliability of attitude/opinion surveys, that is another matter and one that is somewhat outside the purpose of this chapter, though we do touch upon it later. Countless research studies have been concerned with the reliability of data obtained in surveys. Primarily, personal fact data tend to be more accurately and consistently reported than nonfact material.[4]

As already mentioned, a community survey usually has ancillary purposes in addition to the collection of data. These are basically as follows:

1. To increase community involvement in decision making and planning
2. To provide the agency governing board, professional staff, and com-

---

[4]A vast literature exists on survey methodological issues such as that of reliability: see, for example, the *Journal of Marketing*, the *Journal of Marketing Research*, the *Journal of Advertising Research*, the *Public Opinion Quarterly*, the *Journal of the American Statistical Association*, the *Journal of the Royal Statistical Society*, the *American Sociological Review*, the *Journal of Applied Psychology*, and *Commentary* (a British survey publication). In addition, see Robert Ferber, *Market Research*, rev. paperback ed. (New York: McGraw-Hill Book Company, 1963); Robert Ferber, Donald F. Blankertz, and Sidney Hollander, Jr., *Marketing Research* (New York: Ronald Press, 1964); and Robert Ferber, ed., *Handbook of Marketing Research* (New York: McGraw-Hill Book Company, 1974).

munity residents with a better understanding of public parks and recreation

3. To provide supporting data for the governmental units making decisions relative to the planning process

That is, a community attitude, interest, and opinion survey seeks to obtain information, to offer information, and to develop relationships with community residents. In community surveys, "the process of defining the situation thus involves an interplay between analysis and action—between the gathering of information and the development of relationships."[5]

These auxiliary purposes are not hidden, but are definitive of a community survey. In fact, it is not likely a community survey would be worth very much if these intentions were not part of its overall design. This is one of the phases in planning in which the concept of participation comes into practice. The public information aspect of a community survey serves to give this technique a two-way role: information is obtained, information is given.

The information given is not to sway or induce respondents to answer one way or another. Rather, it is that the survey itself, the fact that it will be conducted, the press and other media coverage on its purposes, the explanatory cover letter that accompanies the questionnaire, all serve not only to justify its initial need to a lay board, but also to inform those who will participate in the survey or will use the data on the role of parks and recreation as a municipal service. Often researchers fail to properly motivate respondents to fill out questionnaires. Respondents frequently do not know the purpose of the survey or even the sponsoring agency. This certainly makes for a disinterested sample member.

INFORMATION TO BE OBTAINED

In any effective community survey the proper use of information is directly dependent on the purposes for which the information is wanted; that is, what kind of information is sought. In accordance with the purpose of the attitude, interest, and opinion survey, four distinct types of information are usually sought:

Demographic. From the Greek "demo," meaning of the people, and "graphic," meaning to describe, comes this term to denote information describing personal or community characteristics. Information in this classification includes age, sex, marital status, education, income, geographical location, occupation, place of work, and family size. For

[5]Robert Perlman and Arnold Gurin, *Community Organization and Social Planning* (New York: John Wiley & Sons, Inc., 1972), p. 118.

youth, it includes grade placement, allowance and earnings, etc. Both adults and youth are asked about the ownership of certain items which give insight into what they are like.

Time Use. To arrive at some idea of disposable time, it would be necessary to determine present time use in leisure activities. This classification includes questions on working hours, school hours for youth, attendance at required meetings, volunteer work or meetings, free periods during the week, vacation time, vacation period, and whether the vacation was spent in the local community.

Leisure Behavior. Leisure behavior is more difficult to assess, but for purposes of planning there is concern with what activities people participate in and approximately how often they participate. Determination of the facilities most used, both inside and outside the community, is also an important indicator of leisure behavior.

Attitudes and Opinions. Extremely long questionnaire schedules could be developed to appraise attitudes and opinions. It is necessary, however, to carefully define what information is most useful, and to direct the questioning to those points. In general, there is concern with people's attitudes toward the involvement of government at the local level in providing facilities and programs for broad recreation services. Consideration should also be given to finding out what types of facilities and programs people desire, and what improvements they feel are needed. Also of interest are the reasons why people *do not* participate in activities they consider desirable. Another purpose is to assess general attitudes toward the community and toward the recreation and parks department, and opinions on existing programs and facilities. In a youth survey, it is usually worthwhile to elicit several specific opinions concerning the planning and supervision of youth and teen programs. Before a questionnaire is drafted, we have to consider who will be receiving it.

Initially, answers to the following practical questions are needed: Who will receive the questionnaire? How large will the sample be? Shall we survey both adults and youth? What delivery method will be used to distribute the questionnaire? How will the data be processed? In addition it might be appropriate for the investigator to determine, what variables will be measured, what methods will be used, whether control groups will be needed, and what instruments are needed.[6]

Basically, five decisions have to be made before questionnaire construction begins: (1) the main and ancillary methods of data collection, such as interviews, mail questionnaires, observational techniques, and study of documents; (2) the method of approach to respondents, including sponsorship, stated purpose of the research, confidentiality, and anonymity; (3) the buildup of question sequences and the order

---

[6]Douglas R. Whitney, "The Questionnaire As a Data Source" (Iowa City: University Evaluation and Examination Service, University of Iowa, April 1972), p. 5.

of questions in the questionnaire; (4) if relevant, for each variable, the *order* of questions within each sequence; and (5) the use of precoded or open-response questions.[7] It is obvious that many of these decisions cannot be made by the nonprofessional, but require the advice of someone knowledgeable in survey research techniques.

SAMPLING THE POPULATION

It would be ideal if we could easily and economically examine every resident of the community (the survey universe), but such a procedure is prohibitive for many reasons. It is almost impossible to examine every resident because of the way they are distributed in the community and the time involved. It is also unnecessary from a practical point of view, since sufficiently accurate results may often be obtained much more quickly and inexpensively by examining only a small sample of the population concerned. In most situations, then, one must be content with looking at only a part of the whole. That part which is used for the purposes of the investigation is called a *sample*.

Samples may be selected in a variety of ways, but essentially they may be classed as *random* or *systematic*. A systematic sample, as the name implies, is one selected according to some system, such as selecting every fourth individual from a list of all persons living within the community. A random sample is defined as a sample selected in such a way that every pair of elements is statistically independent. This means that the selection of any element or individual for the sample in no way affects the probability or the likelihood of the selection of any other individual or element. Thus, a sample is random if every individual in the population has an equal and independent chance of being selected or included in the sample. To determine which sample size would provide a certain level of confidence in the results, a formula table developed by statisticians is used.[8] This formula table lists the number of individuals who must be included in the sample according to the number of occupied dwelling units in the community. Naturally, the sample size should be determined before the actual selection of the sample.

If there is any one aspect of survey research that is usually beyond the skill of the agency director or other laymen, it is sampling. It is the job of trained statisticians to plan and supervise sample design and selection. This warning cannot be stressed enough; sampling is not

[7]A. N. Oppenheim, *Questionnaire Design and Attitude Measurement* (New York: Basic Books, Inc., 1966), "Problems of Questionnaire Design," pp. 24–25.

[8]George A. Ferguson, *Statistical Analysis in Psychology and Education*, 2nd ed. (New York: McGraw-Hill Book Company, 1966).

merely picking a few apples from a barrel and calling that random, when in actuality it is purposeless. There are some very good books on sampling techniques, but these are generally to inform the reader about sampling. In planning a survey, one should always have a sampling specialist for guidance, even though the practical work of sampling can be done by the researcher.[9]

Many community groups find it difficult to understand simple sampling procedures and the need for validity and reliability in their selection. It is not unusual to have the mayor of the city or the head of the park board say, "You mean by collecting information from over 2,000 people, we are going to make decisions regarding the welfare of over 100,000 citizens in our city?" The answer to this question can be made only by someone skilled in sampling techniques.

Many universities and research centers have survey research laboratories as part of their community services. These units are often equipped to do broad-scale community surveys. If they do not conduct surveys themselves, they usually offer free or minimal-cost advice to groups undertaking or considering a survey. In addition, commercial survey organizations also conduct adequate community surveys; their expertise for the most part is confined to market research but we must remember that an enormous amount of experience in survey methodology has been obtained through marketing research.

Finally, it is more than likely, if a professional planning consultant is involved in a comprehensive plan, that he or she will have access to survey technicians, perhaps even on their staff. In any event, it must be remembered that survey research is not a laymen's undertaking, though it should not be viewed as some inner sanctum of abstruse skills either. There is much in survey design and conduct that a social service or any other agency can do themselves. Knowing the difference between what one can do oneself and what requires supervision of a technician is the key to effective data collection.

TYPES OF SURVEYS

A *self-administered questionnaire* is simply a printed form delivered or handed to a respondent, who answers a variety of questions and returns it to the sponsoring group. It is usually designed for a specific

[9]A good, brief overview of sampling can be found in Hubert M. Blalock, Jr., *An Introduction to Social Research* (Englewood Cliffs, N.J.: Prentice-Hall, Inc., 1970), pp. 46–58. More detailed treatments of sampling can be found in textbooks such as W. Edwards Deming, *Some Theory of Sampling* (New York: Dover Publications, 1966); W. Edwards Deming, *Sample Design in Business Research* (New York: John Wiley & Sons, Inc., 1960); Morris H. Hansen, W. N. Hurwitz, and W. G. Madow, *Sample Survey Methods and Theory* (2 vols.) (New York: John Wiley & Sons, Inc., 1953); Leslie Kish, *Survey Sampling* (New York: John Wiley & Sons, Inc.; 1965); and Mildred Parten, *Surveys, Polls, and Samples*, rev. ed. (New York: Cooper Square Publishers, 1966).

study, though a good survey is designed to be used for comparable purposes again and again. Thus, a community can often draw on questionnaires used in other communities. An interview schedule is a form used in *personal interviews* conducted by interviewers, though the term "questionnaire" is most often used to include both personal and self-administered surveys. Self-administered questionnaires are most often used when direct person-to-person contact with respondents is not possible or necessary. It is probably the most widely used data source in survey research. Some professionals in the field have estimated that as many as half the research studies conducted use a questionnaire as part of the data-collection process.[10]

There are a number of initial assumptions any investigator makes when he or she chooses to use a questionnaire. Typically, he assumes respondents are a competent source of information; that they will provide information willingly; that they understand the questions in the questionnaire; and that they will answer questions in the form intended and with candor. If at any point these assumptions do not hold true, one should immediately question the appropriateness of the questionnaire.

A mail questionnaire is the most common form of nonpersonal interview schedule, though questionnaire forms can also be hand delivered to sample members' homes, handed out and even completed at planning meetings, or picked up by or distributed to sample members in a variety of other ways. The choice between conducting a personal interview or a self-administered questionnaire is most often based on an examination of the advantages and limitations of each method in each particular setting. This brief summary in no way implies one method is clearly preferable over the other. Even a scanty perusal of the survey literature cited previously will quickly reveal the uncertainty as to which method is preferable and why. We concentrate on the *mail questionnaire* because this is by far the most prevalent method of self-administered questionnaire.

In most cases, the personal interview method is preferable to a mail questionnaire. Generally when the interviewer asks a question he or she will obtain a more reliable answer. One can clear up misconceptions of meaning or can supplement questions by others which will elicit more definite and precise answers. One of the chief objections to the personal interview, however, is the time, effort, and expense required for its successful administration. When an agency can afford these resources, they will be amply compensated by the usually greater validity and reliability of the information, the comparative ease with which the respondent is able to provide data, and the greater amount of time spent on the interview. Nonetheless, the interview technique is not always the best method for securing information. Exceptions are found where written answers are more reliable. For example, a

[10]Whitney, "The Questionnaire As a Data Source," p. 2.

respondent might find it much easier to state on a self-administered questionnaire that the park board is doing a poor job than to report this same criticism to an interviewer.

One practitioner of survey research, Erdos, believes there are ten major *advantages* of mail surveys over other methods of gathering data, notably over personal or telephone interviews:

1. Wider distribution
2. Less distribution bias in the neighborhood
3. Less distribution bias with the type of family
4. Less distribution bias with the individual
5. No interviewer bias
6. Better chance of truthful reply
7. Better chance of thoughtful reply
8. Time-saving (under some circumstances)
9. Central control
10. Saves money, with flexibility per dollar spent[11]

He also lists eleven *disadvantages* of mail surveys, which can apply to other data-gathering methods as well:

1. No mailing list available
2. Mailing list incomplete
3. Mailing list biased
4. Specially trained interviewers required for survey
5. Cannot be structured (for in-depth interviews)
6. Questionnaire too long
7. Questionnaire too difficult
8. Information confidential
9. Respondent not the addressee
10. Budget inadequate
11. Insufficient time available[12]

The advantages or disadvantages of time for community mail surveys are not critical factors. These are cited by Erdos for surveys that require responses anywhere from 48 hours to within two weeks. Such severe time constraints are not likely for the attitude, interest, and opinion survey we suggest, though there are, of course, deadlines and cut-off dates for all surveys.

A final word, about telephone interviewing:

> The phone interview is very similar to the personal interview, with the additional advantage of requiring less interviewer time. (It is not

[11]Paul L. Erdos, *Professional Mail Surveys* (New York: McGraw-Hill Book Company, 1970), "Advantages and Limitations in the Use of Mail Surveys," pp. 5–6.
[12]Ibid., pp. 10–11.

necessary to travel to conduct the interviews.) Using the phone also allows the respondent somewhat more anonymity than does face-to-face interviewing. Obviously, however, the costs of using this technique are prohibitive unless all respondents live in the same area or the interviewer has access to a toll-free telephone line.[13]

QUESTIONNAIRE DESIGN AND WORDING

As with sampling, questionnaire design cannot be adequately learned from books or classroom lectures. (See Appendix B and C for sample copies of questionnaires for youth and adults.) Every situation presents new and different problems. This is not to imply that the books and lectures will not help one avoid pitfalls, but it should be clear there is no substitute for professional and community involvement in the construction and development of questionnaires. As is evident, questionnaire construction is by no means the first stage in conducting a survey. A great deal of reading, design, community involvement, and testing is required before specifications for questionnaire design can be determined. When conducting a community attitude, interest, and opinion survey, meetings should be held with community leaders, public officials, school officials, planning officials, and youth and citizen groups, to determine the kinds of information necessary for reliable decision making. Too often questionnaires are cluttered with inappropriate and unimportant questions, quickly detected by the recipients.

When constructing the questionnaire, the researcher must be cautious that questions are not worded in such a way as to encourage either a positive or negative response. Failure to recognize this could bias the information and cause problems with later decision making. Ambiguous questions should be avoided: these are difficult to evaluate and it is impossible to secure valid information from them. One should also be cautious in the use of a lengthy questionnaire; a long, complicated form might affect the return rate adversely.

If all the problems of developing the questions could be traced to a single source, it would probably be taking too much for granted. Too often we assume that people know what we are talking about, that they have some bias for an accurate response, and that they understand our questions. Too often these assumptions are not warranted. Many people have never heard of a teen center, recreation commission, or certain sports or cultural facilities. Such respondents will have great difficulty in forming judgments and valid opinions.

What kinds of questions are used depend on the kind of information one is trying to collect. If the questionnaire will seek many

---

[13]Whitney, "The Questionnaire As a Data Source," p. 3.

kinds of information, it will require different types of questions. There are basically three types of questions: the *open-ended*, the *close-ended*, and the *multiple choice*. An open-ended question is one to which the respondent supplies the answers. A close-ended question is one where the respondent selects an answer from or marks a list supplied by the investigator. The multiple-choice question is framed so the respondent must choose one or more of several possible answers that comes closest to his opinion.

Example of Open-Ended Question

What park and recreation facilities would you like to see constructed in Elk Grove Village? _____

_____

_____

Example of Close-Ended Question

To which outdoor organizations do you belong? (Check all that apply)

_____Audubon Society   _____Sportsman's Club

_____Izaak Walton League   _____Garden Club

_____Outdoor Motor Club   _____None

_____Other (List) _____

Example of Multiple-Choice Question

Which words best describe La Salle County? (Please check in the square according to the best description.)

1	2	3	4	5
☐	☐	☐	☐	☐
Clean River				Heavy Pollution

Obviously there are a number of advantages and disadvantages to each of these kinds of questions. Some advantages of the open-ended questions are:

1. They are subject to little influence from the investigator.
2. They elicit a wide variety of responses.
3. They will assist in interpreting the results of the questionnaire.
4. They give the respondents a chance to have their say.
5. They are less threatening and do not appear to be too investigatory.
6. They lend more credibility to the final report.

In a recent study conducted in a community in Illinois the following open-ended question was asked: "What improvements would you recommend for existing park and recreation facilities and programs?" This kind of question encourages a free flow of ideas. The respondent was not given a predetermined list of responses, but was able to reply unrestrainedly. Some of the replies to this question included: there should be supervision at all parks; we need a community recreation center; the parks are great but not enough activities; we need a swimming pool in the area; extend the hours of the day camp program. Obviously, there is a wide variety of responses, but replies such as these assist recreation agencies in interpreting the meaningfulness of questionnaire results.

Open-ended questions often yield such a variety of responses that the task of classification and analysis is both time-consuming and difficult to handle statistically. Some survey experts recommend the use of open-ended questions for small surveys and pilot studies. Techniques for analyzing narrative data systematically are gradually being developed, so it is hoped that in the future this kind of questioning can be more readily used.

The close-ended question also has advantages:

1. They are more uniformly interpreted by respondents.
2. They are easier to categorize and classify for data processing.
3. They are unaffected by respondent bias.
4. They tend to eliminate some problems of vocabulary and definitions.
5. They permit more questions to be asked.
6. They keep the questionnaire simple and clear (a significant factor in increasing the response rate).

The multiple-choice question is particularly useful when the issue is not clear and cannot be represented accurately by a dichotomous question. With multiple choices, many degrees of opinion can be given an opportunity for expression. The difficulty lies in framing questions that represent the entire range of opinion. It is important that the list of alternatives or categories be complete enough to cover all possible answers. If the list is incomplete, there is a likelihood the respondent will think one of the alternatives covers his response and will read something into it which belongs in a different category. Even when the alternatives are understood, the multiple-choice question might still give misleading results because of people's known tendency to choose the middle ground, thus giving too much weight to the intermediate categories in the scale.

In wording the questionnaire, one must consider whether facts or opinions are sought, and what degree of latitude the respondent is given in interpreting the questions. Much care is required in formulating the questions so that reliable and meaningful responses are assured.

While certain precautions in the phrasing of questions are necessary when factual information is to be secured, even greater care must be exercised when opinions and attitudes are sought. Researchers in public opinion have shown how seemingly neutral words may influence the reply of the respondents.

Payne's *The Art of Asking Questions* was for a long time a great favorite for survey questionnaire construction, for the good reason that it concentrated on the prime problem of questionnaires: formulating the questions.[14] Once the researcher or investigator, along with community representatives and survey professionals (if available), decides what information is to be solicited, writing the specific questions becomes the next far-from-easy task. If you have ever taken part in designing a questionnaire, you are aware of the inordinate amount of time spent, even by professional survey researchers, in formulating and wording questions. How each question is worded, how it is related to every other question in the schedule, and how it relates to the overall intention of the survey are vital matters for scrutiny.

The survey method used to some extent affects the wording of questions. If it is to be a personal or telephone interview, the emphasis or tone of the interviewer's voice may enhance the clarity of the question. If it is a self-administered questionnaire, on the other hand, then the question wording must be absolutely without the slightest ambiguity, for there will be no interviewer to clarify matters. Of course, whatever the method used, all questions must be clear, but in schedules filled out solely by the respondent, clarity and intent of a question are the foundations on which the entire survey rests. Many beautifully laid out, costly questionnaires that were badly constructed and irritating to complete have too often found their way to the garbage can or the bottom of a pile, never to be completed. While visual design is important, the content is more essential than the form.

The reason for stressing the clear and meaningful wording of questions is not simply to increase the response rate, but to ensure that reliable and meaningful responses are received. A high response rate to misinterpreted questions is a meaningless achievement. The questions that pose the greatest challenge are not fact questions (though these can be botched), but questions dealing with attitude, interest, or opinion. As with the other areas of survey methodology already discussed, the entire field of attitude and opinion measurements, their reliability and, less often, their validity, have been major issues in most social science research. There has been major controversy regarding the solicitation, measurement, and analysis of opinion, and particularly of attitudes.

Simply stated, reliability is "usually defined as the accuracy or consistency with which measurements are taken. Validity . . . refers to

[14]Stanley L. Payne, *The Art of Asking Questions* (Princeton, N.J.: Princeton University Press, 1951).

the degree to which an instrument measures what it is *supposed* to measure."[15] Fact questions, except those that ask for recall of past information, are more readily assessed for reliability. The simplest method for checking reliability on factual questions is to ask the same question, or a related question, in different parts of the same questionnaire, *viz.*: the date and place of birth in one question, your age in another. Validity of factual data can be checked against whatever independent sources of factual information may exist. If attendance records show low use of a particular program, and respondents claim high use, we have reason to suspect the validity either of the questionnaire responses or our record-keeping.

Wording attitude and opinion questions to ensure reliable responses is not so simple, and in some cases is not even possible:

> The pilot work should play a crucial role in determining groupings of attitude items, as well as in eliminating items which do not correlate with others in the same logical groupings. When items are treated in this way, standard procedures for quantifying the internal consistency of the scales can be applied—often with pleasantly higher coefficients. . . . Generally speaking [for validity], there is no criterion available against which attitude responses can be compared.[16]

The more information sample members have about the subject of the survey beforehand the better the likelihood of their understanding the overall intent of the questions:

> If the informant knows very little about the survey topic he is more likely to be influenced by the specific words or phrases used than would be the case if he were thoroughly familiar wtih the topic. He will grasp at such clues as familiar words and phrases and will react to them rather than to the question as a whole.[17]

This shortcoming is, of course, the fault of a poor public relations program and not the wording of the questions themselves. The bulk of neutral answers to attitude/opinion questions is not due to respondents being neutral about the issue, but to their not being informed enough about the subject to express clear preferences.

For specific wording of questions, we draw on Parten's suggestions for questionnaire word construction, along with examples for recreation and parks surveys:

1. *Use simple words which are familiar to all potential respondents.* Phrases such as assessed valuation, *ad valorem*, tax levy, tax rate, comprehensive planning, or park standards are often used in seeking information about recreation and park programs. To the profes-

---

[15]Whitney, "The Questionnaire As a Data Source," p. 22.

[16]Ibid., p. 24.

[17]Mildred B. Parten, *Surveys, Polls, and Samples*, 1950 ed., p. 200.

sional recreator this is everyday language. To most laymen these are meaningless terms to which they are unable to apply judgments. How much better it would be to use phrases such as, the value of your house, the city tax rate, or long-range planning for the community. These phrases would be understandable, and as a result respondents could offer more reliable information.

2. *Make the question as concise as possible.* A question that contains long dependent or conditional clauses may confuse the respondent, even though he understands the words. In trying to comprehend the question as a whole, he may overlook or forget a clause, hence his answers may be wrong. Concise wording and clear arrangement of columns and column headings make it possible to condense a wide range of information in a very short space.

3. *Formulate the questions to yield exactly the information desired* and use terms that lend themselves to tabulation and statistical treatment; make them self-explanatory as far as possible. For example, an item calling for date of birth will also reveal a person's age. When a person gives his address, he will also reveal his neighborhood and the park and recreation facilities closest to him. Before the final wording for the questionnaire is adopted, the investigator should see how the answers can be coded and whether they are suitable for machine tabulation.

4. *Avoid "double-barreled" or multiple-meaning questions.* Unless each question covers only one point, there will be confusion as to which one the answer applies to. Such items should be formulated as two or more questions so separate answers can be obtained. An example of a double-barreled question is, "List the activities you would participate in at the recreation center and how far you would travel to participate in these activities?"

5. *Avoid ambiguous questions.* If the question does not direct the respondent to answer the question the investigator has in mind, it is unsatisfactory. Ambiguity may arise if the vocabulary is beyond the comprehension of the respondent. For example, a question may ask for the respondent to reveal the assessed valuation of his home. If the respondent does not understand the term "assessed valuation," he may give the fair market value of the house, or he may report its worth as calculated by the county tax assessor.

6. *Avoid leading questions.* These are questions worded in such a way as to suggest the answers. "Do you always attend park board meetings?" Many respondents would mark "yes." However, they probably do not attend when they are away or on vacation. The question more simply stated would be, "When you are available, do you attend park board meetings?" Another example of a leading question is, "Did you read the park and recreation department summer program

brochure?" Research has shown that this kind of question will usually elicit a positive response.

7. *Decide on your use of names and personalities.* Answers to questions in which personalities are injected will be conditioned by the respondent's personal feeling toward the person mentioned. One questionnaire asked citizens if they approved of the way an administrator was operating a recreation department. Obviously, this question relates to an individual and not the services provided. It would have been much better to ask the respondents how they felt about certain services provided by the recreation department. If opinions are not carefully structured or if names carry a great deal of weight, the influence of names on a response may be very great.

8. *Avoid "danger" words, catch words, stereotypes, or words with emotional connotation.* A suggestive word is one that so qualifies a statement that the response will differ when the word is omitted. For example, tests show the word "reasonable" to be in this class. The question, "Are you willing to have 'reasonable' increases in prices with the hope that it will bring back prosperity?" resulted in 11 percent more affirmative votes than when the word "reasonable" was omitted. Words whose meaning is vague are danger words because they elicit meaningless or noncomparable responses. The word *why* is one of these. People often give a great variety of answers to the question of *why* and most of them are unclassifiable.

9. *Decide whether to include indirect questions.* Some experts suggest the occasional use of "slant-side questions." A good illustration of the slant question is in a study in which homeless men were asked, "Are you married?" Most replied in the negative; but when the question was posed, "Where is your wife?" a much higher percentage revealed they were married. When there is a danger of reflecting on deficiencies of respondents, the investigator might get the true situation through indirect rather than direct question. For example, if you were attempting to determine whether an individual paid his taxes, a question phrased, "On what date did you pay your local real estate tax?" would be better than asking, "Did you pay your real estate tax this year?"

10. *Be cautious in the use of phrases that may reflect upon the prestige of the respondent.* Most people like to think they are reasonable, intelligent, generous, understanding, and respected members of the community. People tend to answer questions in terms of what they "ought" to think or feel about a situation. For example, the question, "Do you favor a well-planned community recreation program?" brought out a number of favorable replies which subsequent questioning indicated were untrue.

11. *Decide on whether to personalize some of the questions.* Such ques-

tions require the respondent to state whether he would follow a specific course of action if the decision were his. These kinds of questions elicit a different response than do general or impersonal questions. For example, "Would you be willing to pay additional tax for the sports area?" or "Would you vote in favor of the park and recreation bond issue?" make a respondent more critical of his response.

12. *Allow for all possible responses.* If a respondent is to underline or check his answer, provision should be made for all possible replies. Generally the most usual responses are listed and there is additional space for "other," as illustrated below:

How do you most often spend your weekend? (Check one)
- [ ] Traveling
- [ ] Visiting friends and relatives
- [ ] At home
- [ ] Outdoor water sports
- [ ] Resort area
- [ ] Camping
- [ ] Other (Please list) _____
  _____
  _____

13. *Make the alternatives in multiple-choice questions realistic.* They should conform more or less to the way people really think and feel about the issues involved.

14. *Keep to a minimum the amount of writing required on the questionnaire.* Most handwriting is so poor that there is a danger of misinterpretation and errors. When feasible, use symbols for the replies. The symbols should be explained either at the bottom of the page or on the reverse side of the questionnaire. If the possible response can be foreseen or discovered by pretesting, the question can be formulated so that the respondent does one of the following:

A. Writes *yes* or *no*. Example: Do you usually have weekends free?

B. Write a number. Example: What is your age?

C. Put a cross (X) after the correct answer or in a box. Example: How often do you ice skate per year? (Please check.) [ ] [ ] [ ] [ ] [ ] [ ]
                                           1   2   3   4   5 More

D. Indicate the appropriate answers. Example: Circle the number of times you participated in touch-football this past year. 1 2 3 4 5 More

15. *Plan to include a few questions that will serve as checks on the accuracy and consistency of the questions as a whole.* Two questions that bring out the same fact but are worded differently and placed in different sections of the schedule serve to check the internal consistency of replies.

16. *Avoid questions that call for responses toward socially accepted norms or values.* Such questions often fail to indicate a person's real opinion unless they are followed by others which make the issues concrete or place them on a behavioral level. Research has shown that questions that bluntly state a deviation from an established norm or value are less likely to be answered favorably than those which express the same deviation but state it more by implication. (Example: The smoking of marihuana should be legalized. _____ Yes _____ No) People are reluctant to favor a statement of policy that suggests that a law must be changed to carry it out.

17. *Opinion questions on mail surveys should be listed for best placement to increase chance of a response.* It is particularly important to group questions under headings that emphasize the principal topics upon which information is being sought.[18] Studies undertaken at the Office of Recreation and Park Resources at the University of Illinois often use the following headings: Community Characteristics, Time Use, Leisure Behavior Patterns, Leisure Behavior Attitudes, and Attitudes Toward Community. Grouping makes the page appear interesting as well as easy to fill out, and it helps the respondent become aware of shifts in the subject matter.

Parten also offers suggestions on physically arranging items to give variety to divisions; this facilitates filling out questionnaires correctly and efficiently:

1. Number each item consecutively. Never repeat a number on the questionnaire, so there will be no confusion in reference to items when instructions and definitions are prepared. It is also important to have each item clearly distinguished for tabulation purposes.

2. When material is to be written in, allow enough space for clear and legible entries. Completeness of response is frequently related to the amount of space provided. Avoid crowding the items unduly, for this leads to confusion and errors.

3. Set off the questions by dotted lines, solid lines, bold face type, or spacing.

4. Vary the type within the question to emphasize the most important parts.

[18]Ibid., pp. 200–213 *passim.*

5. Arrange the items in columns or rows so that those not filled in can be seen at a glance.

6. Allow space on the back of the form for notes, coding, and checking.

7. Place answer boxes, circles, x's, numbers in parentheses, or brackets after questions so all the respondent has to do is encircle or check the correct answers. If the questionnaire has been pretested, relatively few answers should fall in the "other" category.[19]

PRETESTING

Pretests or pilot studies of an attitude, interest, and opinion survey (or any survey for that matter) are essential to the ultimate success of the full-scale survey. A pretest is merely a miniature survey to uncover and eliminate any difficulties that may exist in the entire procedure planned for the survey as well as in the instrument itself. It can also be used for experimental purposes, and often is by survey researchers, for a wide variety of theories they may have about the multiple aspects of conducting a survey. While there is discussion in the literature about how to run a pilot study, there is little or no controversy about the necessity for doing so. Conducting a full-scale survey without a well-planned and executed pretest is like going to sea with a leaky boat: most of the holes may be hidden from view, but still you sink.

Although the necessity for pretesting is accepted by most survey researchers, invariably their clients are impatient to get the full study underway, are unwilling to pay the costs of a pretest, or feel it may ruin the "purity" of the survey itself to have a sort of sneak preview. Any project administrator, be he a survey technician or not, must insist on a pretest from the start of survey planning and must never treat it as a frill. A pretest is comparable to preventive maintenance; it will ultimately cost less to spend the initial resources on determining if any problems exist in the survey design, from the licking of stamps to the procedures for coding, editing, and storing the returned instruments.

Every aspect of the survey procedure should be decided on and tested: How are the questionnaires to be folded (does the paper cut a person's fingers when it's handled)? Will automatic folding machines be used? How much postage is needed? Take a mock sample of whatever will be mailed out and returned to the post office, well before any material is printed or distributed, to be weighed on their scales; a fraction of an ounce may affect costs: lighter paper might be used, or window envelopes might be more efficient for mailing. All these minor aspects are readily incorporated into a simple and painless pretest if

19Ibid. Abridged and adapted from pp. 200–216. Copyright 1950 by Harper & Row, Publishers, Inc. By permission of Harper & Row, Publishers, Inc.

one knows what a pretest is meant to achieve. Many surveys have been fouled up by odd-sized envelopes, or too little postage put on envelopes weighed on a faulty scale (and back come thousands of letters from the post office, grubby envelopes, cover letter out of date, additional postage to be added on to perhaps metered mail, etc.). And these are only minor procedural problems that a little forethought and pretesting would invariably reveal. The major problem of a poor instrument may dim in importance if the envelope won't fit in the postal meter!

Pretests can be very simple, depending on the type of survey, its extent, and its importance. If a student is incorporating a survey into a term paper, then he or she can easily pretest with friends and relatives. However, if the survey is of any magnitude, a pilot study is designed with the seriousness and thoroughness of a full-scale survey. A pilot test requires a sampling technician to select a meaningful subsample from the original mailing or sample list. A number is not simply picked out of the air: a subsample has to be representative of the larger sample as much as that sample is representative of the entire population of the survey universe. A researcher can even include the pretest sample members in with the final data if the full-scale survey follows fairly soon (say within a month).

There are, of course, rules of thumb for subsample composition and selection, as there are for samples, but these rules are the purview of the sampling technician and are unrealistic to apply without a good knowledge of sampling. A great fault of amateur surveyors is knowing just the rules of thumb of survey research, applying these without knowledge of the formidable research and controversy from which these rules emanate, then wondering why they have worthless data on their hands. A lot of first-time researchers find themselves with boxes of completed questionnaires which for a wide variety of methodological reasons are useless. A little modesty and patience in response to this seemingly simple task of "finding out what people think" is a solid piece of advice to anyone considering a survey. It is *not* a simple technique; it is an *effective* technique, and that makes the difference between professionalism and charlatanry in survey research. A variation on the old adage, "If it's worth doing at all, it's worth doing well": "It has to be done, and it must be done well."

Erdos sums up six purposes for pilot tests with mail surveys, although these can apply to other data-collection methods as well:

1. To test the quality of the mailing list
2. To check the percentage of returns
3. To check the effectiveness of data gathering (postcards, advance letters, incentives, and any follow-up procedures)
4. To check the occurrence of bias in wording of the questionnaire, cards, letters, etc.

5. To check how well questions are understood and answered

6. To check or determine the overall cost estimate for the survey[20]

Whitney suggests some further points that might be considered for a pretest:

- Do the tabulating and coding procedures work efficiently?
- Are the computer programs or computational aids ready?
- How long did it take to get the data ready for analysis?
- Did this fit in with the overall timetable for the survey?
- Was the response rate high enough?
- Did any rating scales used yield a satisfactory spread of responses?
- Can some questions be eliminated?
- Is the questionnaire too long? What parts did the respondents dislike or have difficulty responding to?
- Did you try to contact nonrespondents?
- Do you need a bigger sample?
- Are there any strange or peculiar results?
- For a final report, have you asked all the questions you need to ask?[21]

Finally, Whitney suggests that the pretest questionnaire not be mimeographed but printed or attractively reproduced. The pretest should be designed to encourage response and not be a slapdash, quickie test. A public information campaign on the survey should clearly note the existence of a pretest, so some sample members will not be confused when they receive a pilot mailing, or later sample members feel they were overlooked.

DISTRIBUTION AND RETURN OF THE QUESTIONNAIRE

There are three basic ways of delivering and retrieving a questionnaire: (1) mail out and mail return, (2) hand deliver and return by mail, or (3) hand deliver and hand pickup. There are a number of conditions that determine the appropriate delivery and retrieval methods for a particular survey. In a large city it might be impossible to use the hand delivered/hand pickup method, because it might not be possible to secure the services of a large number of people to carry this method out; therefore, the mail out/mail back method would be the next most appropriate method. In a small community where the sample size is small and community interest and awareness are more intense, the hand delivered/hand pickup method might be considered. I have found the hand delivered/hand pickup the most productive for securing the greatest return. The table below illustrates this point in greater clarity:

[20]Erdos, *Professional Mail Surveys*, "Pilot Studies," p. 84.

[21]Whitney, "The Questionnaire As a Data Source," pp. 28–30 *passim*.

Study	Method of Delivery and Retrieval	Percentage of Return
Study of problems of ill and disabled, State of Ill.	Mail out/mail back	40
Community survey, Lawrence Township, Ill.	Mail out/mail back	31
Community survey, LaSalle County, Ill.	Hand delivered/mail back	64
Community survey, Homewood-Flossmoor, Ill.	Hand delivered/hand pickup	73
Community survey, Glencoe, Ill.	Hand delivered/hand pickup	72
Community survey, Elk Grove, Ill.	Hand delivered/mail back	56

The reasons for the higher response rates are undoubtedly the assurance of delivery, the personal treatment afforded the survey, and the stimulation to encourage response by informing sample members that the questionnaire will be personally picked up within a certain period. These all lend an air of importance and value to the entire survey.

Many survey administrators seek the assistance of neighborhood block captains or the like to deliver and retrieve questionnaires. The block captains often have questions about the information being sought or the purpose of the survey. After doing numerous attitude, interest, and opinion surveys, the Office of Recreation and Park Resources at the University of Illinois recorded the questions most frequently asked by block captains. These questions and the answers are given below:

1. *Question:* What if the person refuses to fill out the questionnaire?
   Answer: The block captain should always be courteous. He cannot demand the questionnaire be filled out. The questionnaire should be returned to headquarters.

2. *Question:* Must the name be signed to the questionnaire?
   Answer: The block captains should emphasize the fact that no names are required on the questionnaires.

3. *Question:* How long will it take to fill out the questionnaire?
   Answer: This will depend on the length. Each questionnaire should be pilot tested and the time determined. The block captain should know this information and be prepared to discuss it with various respondents.

4. **Question:**   Who should fill out the questionnaire at a household—male or female?

   Answer: The questionnaire is delivered to the household. Either the husband or the wife may fill it out. It has been our experience that the distribution of males and females is about the same.

5. **Question:**   What if people are on vacation or away?

   Answer: An effort should be made to determine when they will return. If it is within the time of the survey delivery period, the block captain should return and attempt to get the questionnaire filled out.

6. **Question:**   Will the results of the questionnaire be made available?

   Answer: A public review meeting will be held, and all respondents to the survey will be invited to hear the results and discuss the recommendations of the report.

7. **Question:**   When will public results of the questionnaire be available?

   Answer: The results should be available approximately three to four months after the questionnaire has been completed.

8. **Question:**   Should the block captain stay with the person while he fills out the questionnaire?

   Answer: No; however, on the return to pick up the questionnaire, respondents sometimes do have specific questions. These should be politely answered so that an intelligent response can be made.

9. **Question:**   Should you leave the questionnaire in the mailbox?

   Answer: No. This is against postal regulations. If it is found, you can be charged the first-class mail rate for the questionnaire.

10. **Question:**   How can call-backs be made if the phone is an unlisted number?

    Answer: Usually there is no way of getting information concerning the phone number; therefore, the block captain will have to return in person to follow up.

11. **Question:**   Will the recreation and park office be open on the day of delivery and pick up of the questionnaire?

    Answer: Someone will be in the office at all times during the delivery, pick-up, and follow-up. So when you have the questionnaires, bring them to the office as soon as possible.

12. **Question:**   Can our children help us deliver the questionnaire?

Answer: This is not advisable. Those receiving the questionnaires will be more receptive if they receive it from an adult.

13. *Question:* What do we do if we lose the questionnaire?

    Answer: An ample supply of questionnaires will be at the recreation and park office. Pick up additional copies as needed.

14. *Question:* What has been the return rate in other surveys that have been conducted?

    Answer: When personal delivery by block captains is used, the return rate has been between 50 and 72 percent. However, when the questionnaire is mailed to the respondent and returned by mail to the park and recreation office, the return rate has been as low at 25 to 29 percent.

Many considerations need to be taken into account when trying to increase the return rate of mailed questionnaires. For example, those who reply after much urging are different from those who do not reply and from those who reply without a reminder. The following are among the reported variables influencing questionnaire response:

1. Resident interest in the subject correlates positively with degree of response.
2. Late returns are somewhat prognostic of nonreturners.
3. A rural resident background of respondents is associated with positive tendencies to return questionnaires, as is increased education.
4. Stamped, addressed envelopes generate increased response. (Note: first-class mailing produces more returns than third class.) Young found that when the envelope is addressed to Mr. & Mrs. and the cover letter is directed to the family, the wife takes an active part in completing and returning the questionnaire and thus improves the response.
5. Placing small-denomination stamps of various colors on the envelopes will enhance the return—presumably, because respondents attach a sense of personal interest to the idea.[22]
6. Personally typed letters on letterhead paper and follow-up phone calls prove very effective.

[22]S. Reid, "Respondents and Non-Respondents to Mail Questionnaires," *Educational Research Bulletin*, XXI (1942), 87–96; C. R. Pace, "Factors Influencing Questionnaire Returns from Former University Students," *Journal of Applied Psychology*, XXIII (1939), 388; A. L. Ferris, "A Note on Stimulating Response to Questionnaires," *American Sociological Review*, XVI (1951), 247; J. E. and J. T. Gullahorn, "An Investigation of the Effects of Three Factors Response to Mail Questionnaires," *Public Opinion Quarterly*, XXVII (1963), 294–96; D. S. Longworth, "Use of a Mail Questionnaire," *American Sociological Review*, XVIII (1953), 310; Parten, *Surveys, Polls, and Samples*, p. 602; and G. A. Roeher, "Effective Techniques in Increasing Response to Mailed Questionnaires," *Public Opinion Quarterly*, XXVII (1966), 307.

7. Establishing a deadline for the return of the questionnaire is effective.

8. The cover letter should be made as personal as possible and not appear as a form letter. Nothing will receive as little attention as a mimeographed form letter with a stamped or mimeographed signature. An official title below the name on the cover letter also improves the return rate. The letter should be written on official stationery of the sponsoring survey agency. When the letter conveys the impression of scientific competence, the response rate will increase. A suggested cover letter is on the following page.

9. The physical appearance of the questionnaire often affects the response rate. Studies have shown that artwork such as those illustrated on page 156 can greatly improve the appearance of the questionnaire.

10. It is also desirable to have the questionnaire look easy to fill out. This can be done by requiring very little writing and arranging the items so the questionnaire does not appear crowded. Whenever possible, a simple and convenient response system such as checklists, fill-ins, and multiple-choice questions should be used.[23] Following are some examples:

I consider my spending money (other than meals and housing):
- ☐ 1. subsistence
- ☐ 2. minimal
- ☐ 3. adequate
- ☐ 4. more than adequate

I usually travel to campus by:
- ☐ 1. car   ☐ 4. walking
- ☐ 2. bicycle   ☐ 5. bus
- ☐ 3. motorcycle   ☐ 6. other

The main reason for leaving my previous housing was:
- ☐ 1. the cost of housing   ☐ 7. noise and disturbance
- ☐ 2. the food quality   ☐ 8. to be with friends
- ☐ 3. the food cost   ☐ 9. security problems
- ☐ 4. the rules   ☐ 10. distance from campus
- ☐ 5. privacy   ☐ 11. size of bedroom
- ☐ 6. other residents   ☐ 12. other_____
     (roommate, etc.)   _____

11. Before the final questionnaire is adopted, the proposed question-

[23]Young et al., "Getting Better Returns from Mailed Questionnaires," p. 724.

AC PLANNING ASSOCIATES
1203 W. Oregon
Centerville, New York 14029

October 29, 1975

Dear Citizen of Bondville:

The Bondville Recreation and Park Board has requested the AC Planning
Associates of Centerville, New York, to conduct a survey of leisure
attitudes, interests and behavior of Bondville youth and adults. It is
hoped that the information collected in this survey will assist the
recreation and park board in designing activities and programs as well
as providing facilities and areas that will meet the need for the present
population as well as future citizens of our city. In order to assist
us, we would appreciate it if you would have an adult male or female
answer the attached questionnaire.

The questionnaire has been designed so as to be completed in a short
time. In this questionnaire, there are no correct answers, so please
answer all questions as best you can. Your replies will be kept strictly
confidential, as we are interested only in group results; therefore,
questionnaires will be available only to research personnel at AC Planning
Associates. Please complete the questionnaire and return it to your
block captain within the next two or three days.

Your cooperation will be greatly appreciated.

Sincerely,

John J. Storf
Survey Director
AC Planning Associates

Michael H. Sims
Chairman
Bondville Recreation and Park
Board

JJS,MHS:cjs

Enc.

155

| FACE NO. 1 | FACE NO. 2 | FACE NO. 3 | FACE NO. 4 | FACE NO. 5 | FACE NO. 6 |

6. PLEASE RESPOND TO (a)–(i) BELOW BY WRITING IN THE NUMBER OF THE FACE THAT BEST EXPRESSES YOUR SATISFACTION WITH THE FOLLOWING:

(a) the way this park is maintained. Face No. _____.

(b) the attractiveness of this park's natural environment. Face No. _____.

(c) the amount of time you had available to spend here this trip. Face No. _____.

(d) the weather you experienced during your visit to this park. Face No. _____.

(e) the number of other people who were visiting the park at the time you were here. Face No. _____.

(f) the behavior of the other people who were visiting this park at the time you were here. Face No. _____.

(g) the recreational activity (or activities) you participated in during your visit this trip. Face No. _____.

(h) the opportunities this park offered you to participate in the recreation activities in which you wanted to participate. Face No. _____.

(i) your overall evaluation of your visit to this park. Face No. _____.

I usually eat dinner in:
- ☐ 1. University residence hall
- ☐ 2. Private residence hall
- ☐ 3. University Center
- ☐ 4. Off-campus restaurant
- ☐ 5. My own apartment/room
- ☐ 6. Other _____

I share a room with :
- ☐ 1. no one
- ☐ 2. one person
- ☐ 3. two persons
- ☐ 4. three or more persons

Source: School of Architecture, University of Illinois, Urbana-Champaign.

naire should be pilot tested on a sample population. Testing, revising, and retesting questionnaires yield not only high returns but also more reliable, accurate, and complete information.

12. A series of logically interdependent questions should be put on one page of the questionnaire. The respondent can conveniently see the flow of logic and thus tends to avoid listing internally inconsistent or nonsense answers.

13. It is a usual practice to send a reminder postcard to nonrespondents in mail surveys. In a study by Nichols and Meyers they found a three-day postcard follow-up was the single most effective way to increase the number of respondents. They further found the best response rate was obtained from a combination of an early and later follow-up—that is, a card sent three days after the delivery of the questionnaire and another after a sixteen-day interval. This

technique produced a substantial advantage (77 versus 51 percent) over a group that received no postcard follow-up.[24]

14. The accompanying letter plays an important role as to whether people will respond, and in a truthful and candid way. A letter should explain the purpose of the survey clearly and persuasively. The sponsors of the survey should be clear and apparent. Approval and endorsement from someone whom the respondents see as prestigious will be of great help. Other useful techniques include convincing the respondents of the importance of the study and assuring them of confidentiality. In a study by the University of Illinois Student Housing Division, the following statement was made: "The results of this survey will be made available to you and other students through the off-campus housing office. We will also use the results to make specific recommendations to the University concerning its housing program." This statement not only indicated the purpose of the survey but assured the respondents of some information concerning the results of the study. It is also important to stress to the respondents that they are part of a carefully selected sample and that their response is vital to the study.

15. Directions or instructions are an important factor in determining the return rate and the validity and reliability of the information received. Attempt to inform the respondents as clearly as possible how and where to answer each question. Often those who construct the questionnaire mistakenly assume that it is self-explanatory. Give sufficient definitions of possibly unfamiliar terms to ensure that all individuals interpret your language in the same way. Insofar as possible, personalize the directions: phrase them as if you were conducting an interview, and use boldface, capitals, and italics to draw attention to the directions. Giving the directions in a different kind of type set and in colored ink also helps. Providing clear directions is especially important when using questions that sequence to other questions. See the following example:

7a. Do you work with any youth programs?

  39 1☐ No (If no, continue to 8)
     2☐ Yes

 b. If **yes,** which ones? (check all that apply)

  40 ☐ Scouting for boys   44-7☐ Other (List)_____
  41 ☐ Scouting for girls   _____
  42 ☐ 4-H   _____
  43 ☐ Y Indian Guides   _____

[24]R. C. Nichols and M. A. Meyer, "Timing Post Card Follow-Ups in Mail Questionnaire Surveys," *Public Opinion Quarterly*, XXX (1966), 306.

8. Which of the following items of recreational equipment do you own? (Check all that apply)

48 ☐	Power boat	54 ☐	Golf clubs
49 ☐	Sailboat	55 ☐	Tennis racket
50 ☐	Canoe	56 ☐	Tent and other camping gear
51 ☐	Outboard motor	57 ☐	Camera
52 ☐	Shotgun or rifle	58 ☐	Toboggan or sled
53 ☐	Bow and arrow	59 ☐	None
60	Other _____	62	_____
61	_____	63	_____

CRITICAL PATH METHOD (CPM)

As indicated in Illustration 4.1, the Critical Path Method is a diagrammatic method for scheduling a survey or any comparable project. CPM graphically depicts in advance all the steps necessary to a particular operation, regardless of the complexity or length of that operation. The Critical Path Method is suitable for survey procedures, since these are not too complicated and do not take place over a lengthy period of time. For more complex surveys, such as panel studies over several years, more elaborate diagrams on systems are more useful. For purposes of a community survey, the Critical Path Method of visualizing the work involved seems ideal.

A prime advantage of the Critical Path Method, or any method of formal diagrammatic scheduling, is that it requires a great deal of forethought and decisions to be made on aspects of a project that one would be happy to put off or to treat vaguely until later. As can be seen from Illustration 4.1, the period encompassed for a community survey is about eight months. Most administrators might be too involved with the activities of signing a contract (in December) to concern themselves with the following summer, when the final report should be ready.

The Critical Path Method requires an administrator to plan ahead, to do so realistically, and to know before a project begins where the points of pressure are likely to be, how these might be anticipated or relieved, and whether realistic deadlines are being made. It is easy enough in December to agree to a remote August deadline for a final report. But soon enough the details of a survey pile up, the data are in, and all staff are vacationing in August, so who will do the final report? The earlier and the more detailed the concern with all aspects of a project, the more smoothly the project will run.

There are, of course, snags and frustrations in any project, but the greater the number of these that can be anticipated and reflected in a time schedule, the better for everyone. It is much easier to tell a client in

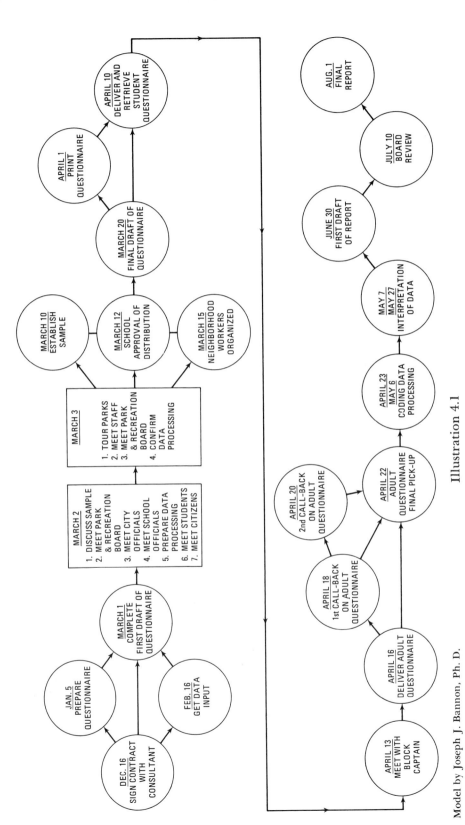

Illustration 4.1

Critical Path Attitude, Interest, Opinion Survey

Model by Joseph J. Bannon, Ph. D.

January that a final report cannot be available by August, than to tell them two weeks before it is due, or two weeks after! Most delays are tolerable if they are expected in advance, but are irritating or harmful when they come late in a project. Most time schedules are underestimated; everyone thinks they can complete various phases in record time. The Critical Path Method, while not assuring that such optimism won't be reflected in time schedules, can at least draw attention to the multiplicity of details that have to be completed before a project is finished.

Preparing a Critical Path Method diagram is comparable to preparing an outline for a book. In fact, the diagram makes a very logical draft outline for the final report, which can be easily translated into a table of contents for the enterprising writer. Although some writers can write well without an outline, most projects require some guidelines. Simply using the table of contents of any survey research textbook is a good beginning for compiling a Critical Path Method diagram. It can be supplemented with phases appropriate to the particular project.

In preparing a time schedule, do not become overly enamored of two-week or four-week time periods. If a phase of a survey is going to take longer, or an odd number of weeks, please note that. Do not seek to achieve some even balance in the schedule. Also make sure that ten-day and two-week slots take into account weekends and holidays. Prepare the schedule with a good calendar that records all holidays and projected staff vacations, with some indication of sick leaves or other absences from agency records. The diagram is not for the purpose of impressing anyone with the efficiency of the agency or with the artwork of the director. It should accurately and realistically reflect what the agency is prepared to do. If CPM is to be useful, it must be realistic, not aesthetic.

The dates selected for the sample illustration of CPM are merely conjectural dates. If we begin with the signing of contract in, say, mid-December, we then forecast the completion date, or at least the submission of the final report, by the beginning of August. If there is to be any leeway in the time schedule it should not be presumed, but recorded on the diagram. If desired, there may be two sets of dates—those preferred, and absolute deadlines—though these have a way of downplaying the importance of CPM. It is better to record two dates than to have the administrator alone know that a later date is all right. You might as well dump the diagram, for once staff and others find out that the diagram is a mere formality its usefulness is ended.

The Critical Path diagram must be updated and corrected as each phase is completed or delayed. If the diagram is not in a central, visible location in the project, but instead is kept in the administrator's drawer, then its purposes are severely limited. It should be maintained by one staff member (everyone should not be permitted to come in and jot down dates), it should be available at all project meetings (or a copy of it), and any changes of importance should be given to everyone immediately.

For those who are resistant to formal project planning, the importance of CPM will soon become evident as a result of the primacy given it by the project administrator. However, if CPM or another planning method is foisted on a project administrator by some terms in the contract, then there is little to do but treat it seriously or ignore it. There is no middle ground with these diagrams.

Early Phases of Survey Planning. Based on discussions elsewhere in this book, we assume the comprehensive plan for the delivery of leisure services will involve the services of a professional planning consultant. The contract that is agreed to is the absolute first formal stage in survey design. Nothing should be done without a contract. Surveys are too costly for gentlemen's agreements. Since the contract with a planning consultant involves a variety of other aspects of the over-all plan, the section or discussion on surveys need not be as detailed as a separate contract with a survey research firm might be. Most of these firms have their own contracts or sample contracts which can be reviewed by the park agency's legal advisor. The contract is also reviewed by the park board, by citizen representatives, and by any others involved in the plan.

If a separate survey research technician or firm is contracted, then the contract should be reviewed by the planning consultant as well. Unlike professional planners, survey researchers as yet have no professional association (though many of them are members of the American Marketing Association), so a code of ethics on survey practices does not exist. However, the American Marketing Association does have a general code of ethics on market research, though this is not of much use for assessing the skills of a particular survey researcher.

As noted on the CPM diagram, within two weeks of signing the contract, preparations for drafting the questionnaire should begin. At least two months have been allotted for this task, a period that is far from unrealistic. Designing a satisfactory questionnaire, even for the roughest of drafts, is far from easy—especially if the survey is to be detailed or complex, involving more than one survey instrument. While one staff member can be assigned responsibility for questionnaire composition, he or she will work with various other members of the project, with any consultants, and with community representatives. It is not unusual to have a dozen drafts of a questionnaire go through various stages of review and revision well before pretesting. This is often the case even with professional survey organizations.

The material for questions to be included in a community survey comes from several sources: The first and most logical source are questionnaires used in other communities for the same purpose. It is foolish to create a questionnaire from scratch when others designed for the same purpose exist. Survey research organizations usually maintain files of every questionnaire they have ever used, or every questionnaire they can get their hands on. A copy of another community's questionnaire is an excellent stimulator for obtaining information from those who are to contribute to the project. Of course, if the park agency has undertaken previous community surveys, those questionnaires could be used for drafting another questionnaire.

To obtain the correct information for questions or scales, the person in charge of questionnaire construction must know *what kind of information* is wanted from the survey. This information will come from the planning consultant, the agency director and staff, the lay board, and the community representatives. As noted on the diagram, by March 2 a series of meetings begin to discuss the first draft of the questionnaire. If the first draft has been compiled from other sources, then at these meetings the various groups noted on the diagram would have an opportunity to look over the questionnaire and respond to it by March 20, when a decision on the final questionnaire must be made.

It is important to distinguish at the very start of questionnaire construction what information is wanted, what information is desirable, what information may be part of research undertaken as part of the survey (some research organizations often like to conduct small research projects as part of surveys), and what information is already available or not needed. It might be nice to know the height and weight of respondents, but for this survey it is totally useless, unless one is contemplating lowering ceilings and narrowing doors to the recreation center! Some researchers (at least beginners) think a questionnaire is a catch-all for all the questions they had about a community but were afraid to ask. . . . The questionnaire must be thematic, confine itself to the purposes for which the survey is being conducted, and not ramble or stray from that intention.

Once a first draft of the questionnaire is in the hands of the lay board, agency staff, consultants, and citizen representatives, the project director begins to concentrate on sample design and selection. As mentioned earlier, this part of survey research is not a layman's task; the agency director or project director should have arranged to have a sampling consultant, or someone skilled in sampling techniques, available at this time. In addition to selecting the survey sample, the technician would also select the pretest subsample at the same time.

In addition to preparation of the sample, the project director would begin to decide on the data-processing techniques and procedures. If a survey research organization is used, these services are usually part of the contract, though contracts can be made for discrete parts of surveys. The data processing involves the receipt of the returned questionnaires, how they will be edited and coded (or precoded on the questionnaire itself), what computations will be involved, what computer program is best suited for data computations, what form the data will be converted to for report analysis, how the original questionnaires, computer cards, tapes and worksheets will be stored, for how long, and how confidentiality of the data will be ensured.

Survey research organizations offer data analysis as well, though most clients naturally wish to undertake this themselves. Initial analysis of the data can be done by such organizations, thus saving the project report-writer time, but ultimately the analysis and, of course, the interpretations or recommendations from the data rest squarely with the project director. Experience has shown that clients who have their entire survey conducted by a research organization—from drafting the questionnaire to the final report—are in one way or another dissatisfied. It is not that the client needed to be so familiar with the data as to edit the questionnaires himself, but that analysis and interpretation of the data, when done by another, somehow leave an unsettling feeling with the client. They are simply not confident that the data indeed show what is shown, even if the results are flattering or satisfactory. Having a consultant write the final report brings up that problem of the spiral-bound report mentioned in Chapter 1. No matter how beautifully laid out and well written these reports are, some intimacy with the project on the part of agency staff can ensure a report and data interpretation that somehow strike home more closely.

In addition to meeting with the various groups on the draft of the questionnaire on March 2, the consultant or project administrator meets the following day with agency staff involved in the project. The consultant and his staff would also tour the parks to familiarize themselves with the public recreation facilities. If possible, they would also confirm the plans made the previous day for data-processing procedures. These procedures are usually fairly standardized based on the form in which the data are desired, with canned computer programs already available, and editing and coding procedures available for these kinds of survey instruments.

Since it is a bit more complicated, a decision on the sample design and selection procedures will be delayed until March 10. With this sampling information on hand, the project administrator or consultant can seek approval from the school board for distribution of any youth questionnaires that are part of the leisure survey. This approval must be in writing and fairly detailed as to how the questionnaires will be distributed, completed, and collected, as well as the confidentiality of the data, the time involved in conducting the survey, and an information program to inform the sample members what is expected of them. Knowledge of how to obtain school board approval on such matters should, of course, be known in advance so that the survey is not held up for a school board meeting or any other redtape. The purpose of CPM is not to appoach the school on March 12 to secure approval, but to *have* approval by that date, knowing well in advance what is required to obtain it.

Since we suggest using community volunteers for surveys such as these, by March 15 these groups should be organized. The field director of a survey organization is the person in charge of all interviewers and other field personnel. Someone in the agency, or from the consultant's staff, would have this responsibility and work with organizing cadres of local volunteers. Presumably this staff member would be someone fully aware of how to contact volunteer groups, how to work with them, and how to obtain their ongoing support and participation in the survey and the comprehensive plan itself.

By March 20 the final draft of the questionnaire should be approved by the park and recreation board and prepared for the printer. This draft must be *officially approved* by the city officials and acceptable to all groups involved in the survey. Once the questionnaire is in print, it is too late to make any changes or additions. The final questionnaire and other materials associated with the survey should be ready by April 1. This is three and a half months after signing the contract.

The questionnaire need not be printed but can be reproduced by any of the very suitable and attractive reproduction methods available, such as ITEK or Multilith. If printing estimates are too high, it makes sense to check other forms of reproducing questionnaires. Also questionnaires need not be confined to white paper: colored paper, especially if these are color-coded for data processing or for distribution, are very useful and attractive. The youth questionnaire might be one color, the adult another. This is not only attractive but easy to handle in the processing and storing of questionnaires.

The delivery of the youth and adult questionnaires are about a week apart. Make sure the youth date does not conflict with any activities at the school (they should not be distracted by an imminent dance or a vacation). The reason for distributing these questionnaires a week apart is twofold: so the project staff will not be rushed, and so the data processing of one set of questionnaires can begin before the second set arrives. Data processing is much more effective if questionnaires of one type are done together. Mixing both youth and adult questionnaires is confusing and might lead to errors if different coding and editing procedures are involved. Between the delivery and retrieval of the youth questionnaire and the distribution of the adult questionnaire, the project administrator would meet with the block captains to prepare for the community-wide distribution of the adult questionnaire. The volunteers used in the schools may be teachers in each classroom or in assemblies, whatever is better.

Since the youth questionnaire will be delivered and picked up on the same day, there will be no call-back for retrieval. However, the community questionnaire for households will be left at the sample houses and picked up within two days. For those questionnaires that are not picked up then, another callback will be made four days after distribution, and a final callback six days after distribution. Beyond this the sample member should not be bothered about returning the questionnaire: he or she is obviously a nonrespondent and will be treated as such.

The purpose of a community survey is to get willing respondents, not to harass sample members into participating. It is terrible public relations to attempt to get a high response rate at the cost of good relations with a community. The block captains should be trained to relate properly to sample members, as well as be familiar with the kinds of information required for hand-delivered surveys.

Between April 23 and May 6 the data processing would be undertaken in earnest, since the 22nd is the last date for the receipt of adult questionnaires. Beyond this date questionnaires should not be accepted. In survey methodology a questionnaire that comes in that late should be treated as a nonrespondent, even though the analyst may be tempted to include it. Whatever the reason for the delay, the delay itself indicates that it should not be included in the analysis.

Most of May would be spent in analysis and interpretation of the data and in drafting the final report. Almost two months are scheduled for this, not only because it is the most difficult part of survey research, but because everyone involved in the project will be a bit tired of the survey and may not approach the data freshly. Printouts of the data and perusals of the information may give ideas of the findings of the survey, but these should not be released in any form until the final report is seen and accepted by the park and recreation board, and presented to and approved by city officials. Once their approval and acceptance are obtained, then full-scale public distribution of survey findings and recommendations can begin.

SELECTED REFERENCES

DEMING, W. EDWARDS. *Some Theory of Sampling.* New York: Dover Publications, Inc., 1966.

FRANKEL, L. R. "How Incentives and Subsamples Affect the Precision of Mail Surveys." *Journal of Advertising Research,* I, No. 1, September 1960.

HANSEN, M. H., AND WILLIAM N. HURWITY. "The Problem of Nonresponse in Sample Surveys." *Journal of the American Statistical Association,* XLI, No. 236, December 1946.

HEATON, EUGENE. "Increasing Mail Questionnaire Returns with a Preliminary Letter." *Journal of Advertising Research,* V, No. 4, December 1965.

"An Introduction to IBM Punched Card Data Processing." White Plains, N.Y.: IBM Technical Publications Department, n.d.

LAZARSFELD, PAUL F., AND RAYMOND FRANZEN. "The Validity of Mail Questionnaires in Upper Income Groups," Part II. *Time Research Report* No. 950, May 1946.

ROBINSON, R. A. "How to Boost Returns from Mail Surveys." *Printers Ink,* CCXXXVII, No. 6, June 1952.

SIMON, RAYMOND. "Responses to Personal and Form Letters in Mail Surveys." *Journal of Advertising Research,* VII, No. 1, March 1967.

SUCHMAN, E. A., AND BOYD McCANDLESS. "Who Answers Questionnaires?" *Journal of Applied Psychology,* XXIV, No. 6, December 1940.

WALDO, WILLIS H. *Better Report Writing.* New York: Reinhold Publishing Co., 1965.

5

OPEN SPACE, LAND DEVELOPMENT, AND FACILITY ANALYSIS

The disappearance of recreation lands is part of the problem of environmental decay in the United States. The question of the seventies is: Shall we succumb to the fast-buck housing developer, the shopping center magnate, or the highway sprawl? Be sure, future generations will judge our decisions.

INTRODUCTION

The same nation that can readily estimate distances in celestial space in billions of light-years is only beginning to comprehend the importance of terrestrial space in planning recreation and park programs. In many of our large metropolitan areas, open space amounts to nearly one-third of the total space available in the city. Its use is decisive in offering adequate recreational areas for an increasingly numerous, affluent, leisured, and mobile people to ensure the fullest possible personal development of all inhabitants of a city. Although for generations we have taken for granted the open farms and woodlands around our cities, the city parks and public spaces are virtually priceless assets.

Today, we are running out of open space, and recreation areas are rapidly disappearing. Those who are concerned with the preservation of our natural resources, the retention of our open spaces, and the sound planning so necessary for developing conservation programs must be constantly alert to the ever-threatening bulldozer, the land developer, and

167

the shopping-center advocate. It isn't very practical to acquire new parks while at the same time destroying those we already have. Because of the insufficiency of park acreage and the tremendous competition of land for other uses, public officials and laymen should resist any proposed encroachment on parkland. Since parks are not being created at a rate to keep pace with population growth, the violation of a park should simply be impermissible.

There are times (although rare) when a purpose of overwhelming regional or national importance requires appropriation of all or part of a park. However vital such an action, the consequences should first be carefully reviewed. In such situations, regardless of the cost, the encroaching agency should provide another park to serve the same population, equivalent in size, natural quality, and recreational potential to the one appropriated. Park encroachment should never be allowed merely as a device to save money. Parks are not land reserves to facilitate land "bargains" for public projects, nor are they designed as potential rights of way for highways, or as development sites. Parks are to make life more livable. The loss of a park is more costly to a community, especially an urban community, than any savings that might possibly be derived from its use for another purpose.

A good example of recent efforts to gobble up parkland is in San Antonio, Texas: A four-to-six-lane highway has been proposed to run through the entire city, which would require condemnation of a large portion of one of the city's major parks. An internationally known planner, the late Sam Zisman, summarized the route:

> The proposed expressway curves and winds through this open space system crossing an Audubon bird sanctuary and Almos Creek, a [San Antonio River] tributary in its natural state; it moves along a picnic ground and recreation area, obliterating a Girl Scout Camp and nature trail; it stretches across the Almos Flood Basin and rises to enormous height to go over Almos Dam; it severs the campus of Incarnate Word College; it cuts through the lands of the San Antonio Zoo; it blocks off a half-built public school gymnasium; it slides along the rim of the sunken garden; it hovers over the edge of the outdoor theater, squeezing itself between the latter and the school stadium and blocking a major entrance; and it slashes through residential areas along the golf course and across a wooden portion of the San Antonio River's natural course.[1]

As in many communities, residents are unaware of the threat of creeping urbanization until the rumble of the automobile is there, until the towering apartment building rises across the street, or they discover that a planned expressway cuts through their backyard.

There is little doubt that where good land-use planning exists, and where there is an appreciation of nature, cities can remain open and livable. This approach to planning is evident in England where develop-

[1]Sam Zisman, "Open Space and Urban Growth," *AIA Journal*, December 1965, p. 51.

ments are kept compact and maximum open space is preserved for recreation, education, and scenic purposes. London has a greenbelt 5 to 10 miles wide surrounding the city, which yields several benefits: It limits growth because building regulations are very strict in the greenbelt; it provides unspoiled countryside for over 8 million people; and it provides a degree of biochemical and physical cleansing for air flow in and out of London. Beyond the London greenbelt, the government supervises the planning of various self-contained towns.

Staten Island, one of the five boroughs of metropolitan New York and the last to be developed, is another example where land-use planning and a respect for nature have been reflected in an urban area. At a designated point on the island, in the community of Annadale-Huguenot, 1,080 acres have been saved from being developed in the archaic pattern of gridiron housing subdivisions. These acres are rich in woods, ponds, and other natural attributes which are rare in an age of tacky houses and other monotonous residential developments. Viewing the community from an aerial photograph, one can see the line of demarcation—an avenue that cuts across part of the island clearly separating the 1,080 acres preserved from rows of tightly compacted residential subdivisions. "Given such a tract of land, most U.S. cities today wouldn't know what to do with it, except perhaps to turn it over lock, stock, and barrel to a bevy of ticky-tack operations. Not New York."[2]

After nearly ten years of indecision, in 1969 New York City decided to establish Annadale-Huguenot as a model community by acquiring these 1,080 acres itself. Through this action, considered radical in concept, Annadale-Huguenot became the first open-space community in the United States sponsored by a municipality. Few states or cities want to do any direct planning themselves, but a revolution in state and city planning is potentially nascent in the action undertaken by New York in Annadale-Huguenot.

Before this decision, the entire community seemed destined to resemble most urban areas, especially those on the East Coast, overdeveloped by unimaginative private developers. As early as 1920 this tract of land was threatened by a rumored plan for an underground tunnel connecting Staten Island to Brooklyn. Such a rumor received much credence, and set off widespread land speculation in the area. After the tunnel idea failed to materialize, and with the onset of the 1929 Depression, most of this land eventually found its way into the hands of the city via tax foreclosures; in fact, one-third of Staten Island was owned by the city by that time.

In 1950 Mayor Wagner, wishing to get as much land into private ownership as possible to enhance tax returns, sold over $250 million worth of land to speculators and developers. While Annadale-Huguenot wasn't greatly affected by this land grab, it became evident that it too

---

2"Where the Cookie Cutter Stops: Annadale-Huguenot," *Open-Space Action*, I, No. 3 (March-April 1969), 24.

would go the way of rampant, unimaginative development unless it were properly protected. Therefore, in 1963 the New York City Planning Commission designated the tract as an urban renewal area, drawing a line of demarcation beyond which traditional private developments could not go. However, the choice of the term "urban renewal" was unfortunate for to most Islanders this meant clearance for public housing, relocation of the poor, and so forth. Rather than explaining to citizens what this nomenclature actually meant for Staten Island, local politicians instead prevailed on Mayor Wagner to start selling the city-owned land in the community to private developers to avoid the terrors of urban renewal.

Fortunately, there was some resistance to merely selling off this land. In 1965 an *ad hoc* citizens' committee on Open Lands on Staten Island brought suit in Supreme Court to prevent New York City from dropping the "urban renewal" project; once an area is designated for renewal, they argued, the law requires preparation of a plan before a decision can be made whether or not to proceed. In 1969, after four years of legal and political haggling, a plan was prepared for Annadale-Huguenot which left undisturbed most of the occupied homes in the area at the time; the gridiron street system which would have paved over a third of the remaining acreage, was replaced by a curvilinear system involving less than 20 percent of the tract.

A brochure describing the plan highlights the community's open-space values:

> Each home in a cluster has its own private patio or yard and shares in the use of a larger open space held in common and maintained by a homeowners association. A pedestrian path connects this open space with the neighborhood shopping area ... [and] continues through a park containing a fenway. This fenway is part of the system of natural streams and lakes which have been preserved and utilized as a component of the new storm water drainage system.... The park is reached by another greenway system extending the full width of the community....[3]

The plan also includes a lagoon and marina, waterfront boardwalks, and public access to the beaches.

Since urban renewal funds at the time were constrained, the city decided to finance land acquisition and the installation of public improvments in Annadale-Huguenot through a capital budget appropriation. Most officials and laymen concerned with the renewal project believe the city will get this money back "twofold" through resale of the land to private developers. The Annadale-Huguenot project faced several hurdles: approval of the capital expenditure, assurance that a certain number of housing units would be available for moderate-income families, and the problems of dealing with hundreds of private owners. "You have to use the power of eminent domain, acquire the land, then integrate the previ-

3Ibid., p. 25.

ous development with the new one. More cities should exercise this power to assemble land for redesigning the infrastructure of development."[4]

The benefits of advance acquisition of land by municipal and public agencies have been recommended by others as well. The advantages of advance purchase as an instrument of land-use policy and control have been amply documented by the Institute of Public Administration in a report prepared for HUD.[5] In this report, the IPA notes that the government obtains the benefits of gains in land values; that advance acquisition enables the provision of public services at a lower cost; and that advance acquisition can also ensure that planning decisions will be implemented before any other vested interests are served.

Although there is a tendency to simply blame private concerns for all the bad development experiences, we must recognize that the tremendous demand for housing, and a startling lack of imagination in planning by many local officials, are strong components leading to developer abuse of land design. There is no denying the nation's need for more and improved housing in response to population expansion and rising incomes, as well as the economic advantages of a healthy housing industry. In 1969, it was estimated that one million acres of open space were converted annually for housing developments; it may even be more.[6]

Since the 1950's, American cities have begun to deteriorate at an accelerating rate. In fact, the history of the city in the West has been one of steady deterioration.[7] In addition to crime, traffic jams, and high rents, are problems of air and water pollution, spreading black ghettos, and an immense migration to the suburbs, all of which help bankrupt the central cities. In most metropolitan areas throughout the nation, the flow of people moving into suburbs from the cities and into cities from rural areas caught local planners unaware. Most planners and city officials quickly realized that zoning alone was not the answer to rapid planning pressures. In fact, as will be discussed, in some cases zoning actually entrapped the developer into wasteful uses of land, such as rectangular lots, wide streets, and single-family dwellings. Even though one acknowledges the impact of housing demand, and the reluctance of many cities and other municipalities to get involved in planning, the private developer, too often the "private wrecker," still remains the primary offender of open space:

> In the process of scalping the land, the . . . developer ignores the most basic of ecological considerations. Without the slightest hesitation,

[4] Ibid.

[5] See John G. Mitchell and Linda A. Murray, "On the Track of the Cat," *Open Space Action*, I, No. 3 (March-April 1969), 21–22.

[6] Ibid., p. 16.

[7] See Lewis Mumford, *The Culture of Cities*, rev. ed. (New York: Harcourt Brace Jovanovich, Inc., 1970).

he will bulldoze trees, flatten topography, fill in streams. And when the subdivision becomes a natural disaster area, he is already over the next hill, doing his thing all over again. Occasionally, some fine old tree will be spared, possibly because it is too large to knock over with a bulldozer. But in the grading, the roots are smothered; and what the bulldozer couldn't handle directly is soon enough accomplished by nature.[8]

Although housing subdivisions are often built in places that are dangerous—e.g., on the steep eroding slopes of Southern California—most criticism of private developments is that they are offensive to the eye, their monotonous sterility banishing all hope of joy and pleasure in such surroundings, not to mention outdoor private or communal recreation. Many developers who build repetitive, monotonous tracts, with little or inadequate open space provided, argue they are simply providing what the public demands. This is too facile an answer, since most home-owners are more concerned with the number of rooms or closets in a house, and the attractiveness of the kitchen, and leave the broader environmental and recreational aspects, if they even think of these, to other professionals. Yet some subdivision developers have allocated even less land than the long deficient formula of 10 acres per thousand population to be set aside for common open space, including school grounds.

In response to complaints about inadequate open space and the needs for improved development planning, a growing number of builders and developers are involved in so-called "New Towns" or New Town type developments. One approach that has been used is Planned Unit Development (PUD), which is a slight refinement of cluster development. The main difference is that PUD encourages a diversity of housing types, as well as nonresidential land uses. New York City's Planning Commission adopted this method in 1967. PUD provides the buyer, builder, and the community with the following benefits:

- Conventional zoning regulations may be modified to permit a reduction of lot size and a waiving of yard and height regulations within the development.
- Larger houses can be sold for less money—because of the lot-size reduction.
- By abandoning the tradition of unusable sideyards and regulation-width streets, PUD permits as much as 30 percent of the land to remain as open space in its natural state.
- PUD's common open spaces can be used not only for recreation but to create pedestrian "greenways" connecting houses with schools and shopping areas.
- By requiring fewer and shorter streets, more efficient utility runs, and better drainage (through the elimination of street patterns that work against the natural contours of the land), PUD saves the builder-developer money.[9]

[8]Ibid., p. 17.
[9]Mumford, *The Culture of Cities*, p. 19.

Murray Barbash, a builder involved in a PUD project in New York City wanted to have his land rezoned for multiple-family dwellings so he could offer the remaining acreage to the Audubon Society, thus preserving some of the wetland intact by not building more numerous single-family dwellings. Through rezoning, and actually using less land for building, Barbash argues that good land conservation indeed can be profitable for the builder. "If the property is rezoned as we want it, it will make more money than if we built on the total acreage."[10] Conservation can pay off for the private developer. Thus, New Town development has required many local governments to rethink their zoning regulations:

> New Towns as now conceived differ from conventional bedroom communities in several ways. Perhaps most important, the minimal economic size of 30,000 inhabitants and 5,000 acres offers an important scale difference from the normal 500-home subdivision; and from the large-scale operation sufficient profits can hopefully be generated to provide, in time, for a better communal environment of parks, recreation facilities of all types, and for that fine-grained diversity of land use and human activity that characterizes superior traditional urban centers.[11]

Although the New Town program has not received the financial backing from the federal government that was anticipated, as a concept it has caught on and has much merit. Breckenfeld feels that without substantial federal backing of the New Towns concept, private financing in the United States is inadequate to handle the horrendous task of creating imaginative new urban environments. Columbia (Maryland), which is predicted to cost $2 billion, will have homes for 110,000 people in seven villages spread over 18,000 acres, 3,200 acres of which will be open space:

> The focus of the Columbia suburb—for it retains the seemingly inevitable suburban look—is learning. Each neighborhood of 900–1,200 families is built around an elementary school. Each village of 3,000–5,000 is focused on a shopping center which is adjacent to the facilities of the junior and secondary high schools. All the villages are tied into an urban downtown representing the usual urban nexus and containing three colleges. Also included in Columbia is a satellite hospital of Johns Hopkins University, a comprehensive prepaid health care plan, the Interfaith Housing Corporation (which provides low-rent apartments) and church buildings shared by Catholic, Jew and Protestant.[12]

---

[10]Ibid., p. 20.

[11]Gary Gappert, "A Benign Boosterism: Columbia and the New Cities," *The New Republic*, September 4, 1971, p. 32, a review of Gurney Breckenfeld's, *Columbia and the New Cities* (New York: David McKay Co. Inc., 1971). See also Percival and Paul Goodman, *Communitas—Means of Livelihood and Ways of Life*, 2nd rev. ed. (New York: Vintage Books, 1960), for a discussion of the design of more livable cities and the political context in which city planners operate. This book operates from the premise that human needs should determine the planning of cities, not the needs of real estate developers or industry.

[12]Gappert, "A Benign Boosterism," p. 32.

Problems of bad planning and development are not limited to this country. Gabriel Marcel, a French philosopher, was horrified on a visit to South America, to see the massive abuse of land design and ecology manifested there:

> ...I had the feeling that what had been a landscape was being turned into a builder's yard. There you may witness the kind of planned sectioning and cutting up which I would venture to call sacrilegious. I had this feeling most strongly in Rio de Janeiro, where the hills were going to be levelled without the slightest consideration for the reality of the original site. This is something very significant; whereas in the past a city moulded itself on the natural structure of pre-structure, as if it were fulfilling it, we are likely to see larger and larger agglomerations piling up without the slightest regard for the natural preformation. There is not the least hesitation in doing violence to nature to carry out an abstract plan.[13]

Open space is a fundamental element in any decent, desirable living environment, no matter where it is. We have already entered an era in this country when parks and open space are assuming vital importance for Americans. Surely the test of the future is not only how well we do in outer space or in international affairs; we are also challenged to create healthful and imaginative communities for all Americans. To implement this task, citizens in all communities, as well as their elected representatives at all governmental levels, have a tremendous responsibility to act swiftly and boldly. Both time *and* space are at a premium.

Acquiring land and developing open space make good fiscal sense in the short run as well as the long run. From a short-term standpoint, it can be less costly for a municipality to purchase and maintain a park than to provide municipal services for residential development. In the long run, parks enhance the taxable value of surrounding property, sometimes so much so that additional taxes attributable to the park pay for its acquisition, development, and maintenance. If a community has some available vacant land which it is considering purchasing as a park, it should not assume that the alternative to a park is retaining the land as privately owned vacant land on the tax rolls. It is much safer to assume the land will be developed. Since residential development is by far the largest consumer of land, it is also fair to assume the site will be used for residences. The following two cases seem to support these assumptions:

Case 1:
It was found that in a community in Westchester County, New York, each dwelling pays $100 less in real estate taxes than it receives in municipal services. It was calculated that the acquisition of a public park at the current cost of the land in the community, including the loss of the tax revenue from the vacant land and the cost of maintaining the

[13]Gabriel Marcel, "The Limitations of Industrial Civilization," in *The Decline of Wisdom* (New York: Philosophical Library, 1955), p. 14.

park, would result in a 15 percent lower annual cost to the community than if the land were developed with houses.

Case 2:

A similar computation was made in a community in Massachusetts. It was concluded that if the community purchased 2,000 acres of its total area of 10,000 acres as a park, the cost would be about $75,000 annually, whereas the cost of servicing new homes on the same 2,000 acres would far exceed the $75,000 cost.

It is a well-established fact that land adjacent to parks is the most sought after. As early as 1939 a study completed by Union County, New Jersey, indicated that parkland easily paid for itself. This study revealed that the value of properties adjacent to county parks increased during 1922–1939 much faster than the average rise in adjoining municipalities. The extra values produced more than enough taxes to pay the annual operating costs of the park as well as the interest and amortization of the park bonds. In five years, the incremental tax revenues equaled the $1.2 million outlay for acquisition and development of the parks.[14]

The Essex County (New Jersey) Park Commission also found, in 1916, that four parks caused three times the increase in adjacent real estate values than was the case for the rest of the city. These gains in property values are reported as sufficient to have covered acquisition, development, and most of the annual operating cost.[15] Undoubtedly, the most interesting study would be to assess the present-day value of this land as it relates to other land values in the county.

Recently, dozens of books and hundreds of magazines and newspaper articles have been written that emphasize the gloom and doom awaiting if we do not do this, that, or the other about our environment. Shock tactics may shake some people out of disinterest in their own environment; however, creating a crisis attitude may do more harm than good by leading one to believe there is little hope for today's, much less tomorrow's, environment. This is simply not true. The following quote indicates the scope of action that can be undertaken to improve the quality of our environment:

> What is the value of a tree? A view? Birdlife? The Tacoma Audubon Society, Tacoma, Washington, has prepared a report on the destruction values of various components of a particular landscape. The site is 4,150 acres, the delta of the Nisqually River where it flows into the southern part of Puget Sound.
>
> Members of the Tacoma Audubon Society, under the guidance of Robert W. Ramsey, a Tacoma landscape architect, carefully established the dollar values of most components of the Nisqually Delta's landscape. The point

[14] Based on the *Twenty-five Year Report of the Union County Park Commission in New Jersey, 1921–1946.*

[15] Based on *Essex County Park Commission Annual Report for 1916.*

of this effort was to awaken Tacoma area people to the values of the landscape that would be destroyed if a proposed port is built on the delta. The authors estimated at $4,000 per lot the value of views that would be lost if the port is built. The total view loss for 530 lots would be $2,120,000.

Using the National Shade Tree Conference values of trees as $9 per square inch of the tree's diameter at 4½ feet above the ground, together with an assumption of ten trees of 6-inch diameter for every 1,000 square feet on a 300-acre reforested portion of the proposed port site, the tree destruction value was estimated as $6,657,000.

Valuation of birdlife was $115,000 for the hunting that would be lost and $18,750,000 for an estimated loss of 75,000 new birds per year, computed at $5 per bird over the expected 50-year life of the port.

Loss of grass, soil, and other landscape components were included. The total values that would be destroyed were put at $40,617,000.

The Landscape Destruction Value Doctrine propounded by the Tacoma Audubon Society states that developers "should pay to a public body of jurisdiction a destruction penalty equal to the appraised ecological loss incurred." It further recommends that such funds be used only to administer programs for land acquisition, and for protection, management, and maintenance of greenbelts, wetlands, shorelands, etc.[16]

CONSERVATION AND PRESERVATION

Although the terms are often used interchangeably, and at times at odds with each other, recreation, conservation, and preservation are specific and distinct terms which relate to the leisure services movement. In simple terms, recreation refers to land and water facilities that are used by people, sometimes quite intensively. Conservation, on the other hand, depicts land and water areas that receive limited development, such as trails and nature sanctuaries; these are usually open for public enjoyment and pleasure. (Even within the conservationist group there is a split between recreationists and protectionists.) Preservation is more stringent than conservation, wherein a natural setting is left in its original state as much as possible, with only safeguards added to prevent negligence or plundering by humans.[17]

There is a regrettable tendency—with the concern surrounding the dissipation of natural resources—for adherents of these three gradients often to be polarized one against the other. This polarization is especially

[16]U.S. Department of Agriculture, *Landscape for Living*, Yearbook of Agriculture, 92nd Congress, House Document No. 229 (Washington, D.C.: Government Printing Office, 1961), pp. 355–56.

[17]It is interesting in this context to read about Africa, where the difficulties of preservation of wildlife are most acute. In some instances, wildlife preserves no longer even permit visitors to view the animals, for the simple reason that their presence (most times in noisy vehicles) disturbs the animals enough to affect instinctual activities of preying and mating. See, for instance, "African Safari," *The New York Review of Books*, June 28, 1973, p. 25.

acute in urban areas where there is so little "surplus" water and land in the first place. Throughout this country there are powerful organizations and lobby groups representing the clearly delineated concerns of recreation and parks, conservation, and preservation. While it is valuable to have associations or groups representing each of these seemingly disparate attitudes toward the natural environment, it is unforunate that the logical connection and analogous philosophies of these groups are not more clearly appreciated. The challenges to parks and recreation, conservation, and preservation are virtually identical, no matter that the potential use of the land and water they crave varies.

In urban areas especially, it is quite understandable that there is often great controversy not only between land developers and conservationists, but between recreationists and those who wish the few remaining natural resources of these areas to remain protected by severe restrictions on public or private use. For instance, one can readily understand a preservationist desiring to preserve the few coastal wetlands or farmlands remaining in urban areas. These are so rare, especially on the East Coast, that the idea of saving them at any cost has great appeal:

> . . . the coastal wetlands [are] one of the most fertile parts of the environment, essential to life in the ocean. Wetlands require some 10,000 years to build their delicate mechanisms; once destroyed, they are permanently gone. Although coastal lands are only 12 percent of the U.S., a third of our population lives there and is increasing at almost double the rate of the rest of the country.[18]

These are irreplaceable; their supply is quite finite. But on the other hand looms an almost infinite demand, both real and anticipated, for leisure outlets and facilities in urban areas with anywhere from 3 to 14 million people.

> National, state, and county parks are rarely accessible to the minority groups and the poor who live in the central city. The provision of usable parks and open space is vital in renewing old neighborhoods.[19]

Recreationists are not rabid in their attempts to convert open space into parks and recreation centers, nor are they insensitive to the position taken by conservationists and preservationists. For instance, they are quite amenable to conserving areas for nature trails and bird and wildlife sanctuaries where this is even remotely feasible. However, recreationists in compacted urban areas are under enormous pressure to meet the demand for more recreational spaces. Since their task as a municipal service is to meet these demands, they are in real difficulty when they try to mitigate such demands in favor of "saving the land" in its purer form.

---

[18]Anne W. Simon, "Saving the Land," *The New Republic*, January 6 and 13, 1973, p. 16.

[19]"The Neighborhood," *From Sea to Shining Sea*, A Report of the President's Commission on Recreation and Natural Beauty (Washington, D.C.: Government Printing Office, 1968), p. 31.

It is essential, therefore, that these three groups seek, first, to understand and appreciate the others' viewpoints and pressures and, second, to enter into cooperative planning arrangements where at all possible, especially in the acquisition of open space and land-use legislation. There are many places which are amenable to sharing as wildlife and recreation areas, as well as issues that directly affect all groups, such as encroachment on open land by highways.[20]

It is up to recreationists, as well as conservation and preservation groups, to *educate* the public about the value of environmental protection and the cultural and physical aspects to be gained from various degrees of ecological sanctuary.

The maintenance of the environment is critical at this time, as the population increases and technology expands. Chief among the issues which must be dealt with is that of public awareness of the environment and its many facets. In certain cities, recognition of local environmental problems is not difficult. Smog, water pollution, lack of public open space, poor housing, solid and sanitary waste disposal problems, and public disorder have become virtually accepted as daily nuisances and inconveniences. Surely, this is not the relationship humans desire with their surroundings, if they have a choice. We must be made aware that there is a choice, and unless the choice is made for an environment that is truly "livable," then the long-range implications for human activity are rather gloomy.

Through the ongoing efforts of well-devised urban and regional planning, we are making progress in securing vital environmental improvements and facilities. The school-park concept, the acquisition of more natural parkland in urban areas, and river cleanups are accepted as necessary environmental ameliorations. However, environmental education must develop along with these community improvement projects. Not only will education of this type point out the benefits of such projects to the community, but it will also bring about a realization of proper maintenance of a community's natural environment. When the concept of environmental maintenance is accepted as a part of a community's goals, we are well on our way to establishing the proper ecological relationships in an environment.

"Saving the Land," whether for intensive use as recreational areas or for the more subtle touches of the conservationist and preservationist, can be a slogan for all groups interested in saving the environment. It wasn't until the seventeenth and eighteenth centuries that mankind began to develop an interest in the natural environment at all, praising it in poetry

[20]Roy Bongartz, "Dredging the Atchafalaya," *The Nation*, April 30, 1973, pp. 560–62, discusses an effort by fishermen, outdoorsmen, bird watchers, hunters, and conservationists to save the threatened Atchafalaya River as a recreation *and* wildlife area; and Ridgway M. Hall, Jr., "Highway vs. Environment: The Long Island Fight," *The New Republic*, May 12, 1973, pp. 17–18, discusses the menace of urban sprawl into semirural areas.

and paintings. This might be surprising to those of us who consider man's love of nature as instinctive. It is not, or at least it wasn't until the past few centuries. In most instances, love for private gain is far more instinctual. We have *learned* to love our environment. To many cultures, love of nature and one's environment is antithetical to the life they lead, the dangers they perceive and endure in that environment. In Africa, the sharp contrast between whites paying a high price to view animals in the wild, and the Africans who perceive these same wildlife as a real threat, is an excellent example of love of nature versus fear of nature. Many Africans, especially those who farm, are incredulous that whites would want to drive around in buses and landrovers to view animals in a natural state. These Africans are more familiar with "Nature red in tooth and claw," than visiting whites who see nature as awesome, yet benign.

There is a direct correlation between industrialization and a concern with saving the environment; yet our prescriptions rarely concentrate on controlling industrialization as much as they do on saving what one can. Until we come to grips with the ambivalence we have toward earning money via industrialization, and preserving our environment, it seems futile to simply concentrate on saving the land. Such concern is merely one-half of an integrated equation:

> America is the archetype of what happens when democracy, technology, urbanization, capitalistic mission, and antagonism (or apathy) toward natural environment are blended together. The present situation is characterized by three dominant features that mediate against quick solution to this impending crisis: (i) an absence of personal moral direction concerning our treatment of our natural resources, (ii) an inability on the part of our social institutions to make adjustments to this stress, and (iii) an abiding faith in technology.[21]

It is ironic that many visitors to Africa who can afford the exorbitant fee of a safari probably earned that money through industry or its spinoffs. Visitors praise the sagacity of the Africans and of the earlier colonialists in Africa for foresight in preserving much of the splendor of that continent. At the same time, they bemoan the paucity of vision in highly developed countries, without for a moment recognizing the impact of their own apathy on such poverty of vision! We are all complicit in the destruction of the environment; the few who had foresight to resist pervasive and irresponsible ecological destruction for a long time were derided as fanatics.

Now that concern for the environment has become fashionable, we should avoid the complacent belief that fashion alone will solve the problem. The mere discussion of a pressing topic can become an end in itself, making us feel concerned and aware, while obligating us to do

[21]Lewis W. Moncrief, "The Cultural Basis of Our Environmental Crisis," in Robert and Nancy S. Dorfman, eds., *Economics of the Environment* (New York: W. W. Norton & Company, Inc., 1972), p. 290.

nothing. For too many of us, environment and ecology are just words that we tack on the litany of social ills. How often we hear, and ourselves reiterate, that what is wrong with this country are poverty, racism, urban blight, unemployment, classism, *and* pollution, population, etc. And how little we see the relation between these ills and our own potential role in them. One can see a car rolling along the highway, its occupants descrying the ruin of the environment, while a soda can or other refuse comes flying out the window. Or a radio tuned to a high pitch, broadcasting about air pollution while it contributes to noise pollution. Complicity ranges from the ridiculous to the more serious:

> It might be bad in China with 700 million poor people, but 700 million rich Chinese would wreck China in no time.... It's the rich who wreck the environment... occupy much more space, consume more of each natural resource, disturb ecology more, litter the landscape... and create more pollution.[22]

The stakes are quite high in the ongoing controversy over land use, but through environmental education, and hopefully through a conjointed effort among recreationists, protectionists, conservationists, and preservationists, as well as all levels of government, Americans can gain a deeper and more urgent understanding of their relationship to their immediate and peripheral natural surroundings. Recreation planners and administrators must comprehend their function not only in terms of meeting the demand for parks and recreation, but as visionaries of a sort, who went beyond mere lip service to the ecological tragedy of our age.

METHODS OF ACQUIRING PARKLAND

A wide variety of methods can be used for acquiring and preserving recreation and open-space land, ranging from full-title negotiation to acquisition on only scenic and conservation easements. The following discussion, while not exhaustive, describes the most popular means presently used by local government in obtaining land for open space.

1. *Full-Title Negotiation*
   The outright purchase of full title to land is, and probably will remain, the most popular method of acquiring park and open-space land. This method virtually assures permanent public ownership because land bought with public funds is not readily discarded. Cost is the primary disadvantage to full-title purchase of parkland.
2. *Eminent Domain*
   Under the powers of eminent domain, a governmental unit has the

---

[22]Jean Mayer and Granger T. Harris, "Affluence: The Fifth Horseman of the Apocalypse," *Psychology Today*, III (January 1970), p. 46.

right to condemnation of land under the assumption that public interest is to be served by such an acquisition. Cost of the land acquired through condemnation and the overhead cost involved render it one of the most expensive methods for acquiring open-space land. For this reason, condemnation is recommended *only* when other less expensive methods have failed.

3. *Excess Condemnation*

   Excess condemnation is the exercise of eminent domain for land acquisition in addition to the primary objectives for which it is being used. In general, additional land is acquired for park purposes in conjunction with other acquisition programs such as highways, schools, or public utility facilities. Through the use of excess condemnation, entire tracts of land have frequently been acquired, resulting in reduced per-acre costs. To maximize the effectiveness of this approach, the land acquisition programs of all agencies should be thoroughly coordinated.

4. *Advanced Acquisition*

   Acquisition of land in advanced need, while desirable because of savings which can result in lower land costs, is practiced by few government agencies. In the past, the availability of funds for recreation and open space has often followed rather than preceded the need. It is anticipated that this method, because of rising land costs and competing land uses, will be used more frequently.

5. *Installment Buying*

   Installment buying of open-space land spreads costs over a number of years, rather than spending all acquisition funds in one year. This method also benefits the property owner since capital gains are reduced by spreading them over a number of years.

6. *Tax-Delinquent Land*

   The acquiring of tax-delinquent land by governmental units can often be an effective and inexpensive way of obtaining needed open space. The land is frequently located in older sections of urban areas where the need for such open space may be greatest. Such properties are often unkempt and can be turned into small playgrounds or vest-pocket parks in areas of high residential density.

7. *Transfer*

   Vacant available land suitable for recreational activities is often owned by other governmental units such as the Army Corps of Engineers, state highway departments, or school districts. This land may no longer serve the purpose for which it was originally purchased, and title to it can be transferred to a recreation agency for little or no cost.

8. *Donations*

   Donations of land are excellent for acquiring recreational sites, because little or no expense is incurred by the government agency. One serious drawback to land received as a gift is that it may be unsuitable for park purposes because of location, size, or development cost. If unsuitable land is donated to a recreation agency, it may be possible to sell it and use the money to purchase more suitable open-space land.

9. *Easements*
The purchase of development rights through the acquisition of scenic or conservation easements is an additional means of preserving needed open space. Although this method has not been used to a great extent, it appears to be gaining popularity with recreational agencies across the nation. Easements are purchased for selected areas, the landowner being paid to retain the land in an undeveloped state. The payments represent the differential between the market value of the property, with the easement restrictions, and the value if developed for more intensive uses. With this approach, land will be kept open without displacing present property owners and at less public cost. In addition, the property remains on the public tax rolls. Easements can also be purchased to allow access to recreation areas and for trails and other similar facilities.

10. *Leases*
Leasing land from persons or corporations is another method for providing recreation sites. If this approach is used, the lease should be long enough to ensure extensive enjoyment of capital improvements developed by public agency on the leased land.

11. *Official Mapping*
Official mapping has been used to preserve open space and recreation land, but has limited application because of its questionable legality. The official city map is an indication of local government's intention to acquire specific sites for public purposes. Building is usually prohibited in those areas mapped for later public acquisition.

12. *Taxation*
Taxation is another proposed means to help maintain low-density development and hence increase the recreation and open-space character of the land. Taxation is believed to be a factor in influencing development decisions, as well as providing incentive for the retention of open land in undeveloped uses. Since many think that high taxes force open space into development, local governments are using tax exemption, preferential assessment, deferral, and differential rates through a system of classification of land uses to try to keep land open.[23]

13. *Time-Development Zoning*
By controlling the timing and location of development by zoning, it may be possible to use temporary open space and recreation land for

[23]William I. Goodman and E. C. Freund, *Principles and Practices of Urban Planning* (Washington, D.C.: International City Manager's Association, 1968), p. 204.

public use. Such zoning would allow development in specified districts and prohibit development elsewhere until all available land in the development district has been used. In those districts not slated for immediate development, it would be possible to preserve the open space and recreation land temporarily. Aside from the obvious merits of time-developed zoning for much broader development control, this type of zoning does offer one means for providing temporary open space, which should not be overlooked when assembling a program of techniques for increasing open space and recreation land.[24]

14. *Large-Scale Development Zoning*
   This is cluster or density zoning expanded to the scale of a neighborhood or town, including all uses usually found in a town. Such zoning permits development of New Towns which offer the promise of planning for community life with well-integrated open space, among other things. This type of zoning depends on long-range plans for future comprehensive development for the area. With such zoning, it is possible to plan open spaces as an integral part of the community.[25]

15. *Compensable Regulation*
   This is a means of strengthening zoning and providing compensation for controlled land.[26] Compensable regulations severely restrict the uses which may be made of land, yet compensate the property owner for any decrease in land value caused by the regulations. Under these regulations, permanent open space, as well as open-space reserves for future development, can be provided. Land would remain in private ownership under these regulations, thereby producing taxes and not introducing any new public maintenance costs.

16. *Land-Dedication Requirement* (See Appendix D)
   Many states are presently creating enabling legislation which requires land developers to dedicate land, or the payment of fees, or a combination of both for park and recreation purposes as a condition of final subdivision approval. The enabling legislation usually provides that:
   A. An ordinance has been in effect for a period of thirty days prior to the filing of the tentative map of the subdivision.
   B. The ordinance includes definite standards for determining the proportion of the subdivision to be dedicated and the amount of any fee to be paid in lieu thereof.
   C. The land, fees, or combination are to be used only for the purpose of providing park and/or recreation facilities to serve the subdivision.

[24]Ibid.

[25]Ibid., p. 206.

[26]Jan Krasnowiecki and A. L. Strong, "Compensable Regulations for Open Space: A Means of Controlling Urban Growth," *Journal of the American Institute of Planners*, XXIX (May 1963), 87.

D. The legislative body has adopted a general plan containing a recreation element, and the park and recreation facilities are in accordance with definite principles and standards.

E. The amount and location of land to be dedicated or the fees to be paid shall bear a reasonable relationship to the use of the park and recreation facilities by the future inhabitants of the subdivision.

F. The city, county, or agency creating the ordinance must specify when development of the park and recreation facilities will begin.

G. Only the payment of fees may be required in subdivisions containing fifty parcels or less.

The 1971 case of *Associated Home Builders of the Greater East Bay, Inc.* v. *City of Walnut Creek* (California) is a prime example of the land-dedication ordinance being upheld, thus serving as a precedent for other municipalities to preserve open space in their communities. In 1967 the Associated Home Builders, a nonprofit organization formed to promote the home-building industry, filed suit to challenge the validity of land dedication in Walnut Creek, California. Section 11546, which was eventually upheld by the California Supreme Court, permits local governments to require that real estate developers dedicate land *or* pay fees for parks and recreation facilities as a precondition of subdivision approval.[27] This legislation was originally enacted in 1965 to ensure land for California's critical need for open space, which had been under continual pressure from expanding subdivision developments throughout the past few decades. A report by the California Assembly Interim Committee on Municipal and County Government recommended that such legislation be established, stating:

> Concern is being expressed statewide in California that we may be in danger of "... building ourselves into a cement-lumber jungle." Land pressures have been building steadily and the rising market price of each available scrap of urban land has made land the focus of competitive interests and ... values. Recreation experts, planning commissions, and conservationists have long insisted that the provision of recreation areas in subdivisions is a necessity.... Population congestion magnifies the need for urban open space. It is perhaps the visual impact of thousands upon thousands of houses built row on row without relief of open space which has been most responsible for stimulating burgeoning citizen interest in the problem of providing for recreation areas in subdivision developments.[28]

[27]Daniel J. Curtin, Jr., "Preservation of Open Space in California: *Associated Home Builders* v. *City of Walnut Creek*," *Los Angeles Bar Bulletin*, XLVII, 3 (January 1972), 108–13.

[28]State of California, *Final Report of the Assembly Interim Committee on Municipal and County Government*, 1963–65, VI, No. 21, 31–45.

In addition to the land-dedication requirement for developers, this legislation also delineates what procedures are to be followed by local governments, especially the requirement that land, fees, or both are to be used for the sole purpose of providing recreation and park facilities for the subdivision under development. Walnut Creek was one of the first in California to adopt legislation to implement Section 11546. Their ordinance required that two and a half acres of land be provided for each 1,000 new residents (based on a ratio of an acre for each 1,100 dwellings in a single-family zone), or a fee equal to the "fair market value" of the land, or a combination of land and fee. The fee would be used to purchase or develop a park or recreation facility within three-quarters of a mile of the planned subdivision.

In their suit, the Associated Home Builders argued that Section 11546 was a violation of their constitutional rights under the Fifth and Fourteenth Amendments because it denied subdivision developers equal protection by permitting confiscation of property without due process. The Home Builders felt all residents of a city should be required to bear the costs of such public facilities, which could be used by people living outside of the subdivision as well. In upholding this Section, the Supreme Court based its decision on the broader need to promote open space in urban areas of California:

> ...We would have no doubt that Section 11546 can be justified on the basis of a general public need for recreational facilities caused by present and future subdivisions. The elimination of open space in California is a melancholy aspect of the unprecedented population increase which has characterized our state in the last few decades. Manifestly governmental entities have the responsibility to provide park and recreation land to accommodate this human expansion despite the inexorable decrease of open space available to fulfill such need.[29]

Since the test case in California, similar statutes have been upheld in New York, Montana, Wisconsin, and Connecticut, but have been denied in Illinois, Oregon, and Rhode Island. In addition, the Supreme Court of California noted that Section 11546 "did not require cities and counties to reduce the dedication or fee requirement whenever subdividers voluntarily provided recreational areas, but held that such an omission was of no consequence. . . . 'While the city is not required to give credit for recreational facilities contributed by the subdivider, if it chooses to do so it must be given broad discretion to assure that the proposed facilities are in keeping with the master plan.' "[30] The court also approved the use of fees for improvements such as drainage or landscaping and other purposes related to the acquisition and improvement of the dedicated land.

In response to an argument from the Home Builders that such dedi-

[29]Curtin, "Preservation of Open Space," p. 111.
[30]Ibid., p. 112.

cations force developers to set unreasonably high costs, which might prevent low-income families from entering the community, the court replied: "The desirability of encouraging subdividers to build low-cost housing cannot be denied and unreasonable exactions could defeat this object, but these considerations must be balanced against the phenomenon of the appallingly rapid disappearance of open areas in and around our cities."[31]

It is easy to point out deficiencies of public recreation and parks in many American cities, as well as the general apathy and complacency of municipal governments concerning the conservation of open space and recreation land. It is often difficult to explain this complacency and apathy because most citizens believe public officials would be opposed to a system that did not provide maximum opportunity for recreation experiences. However, one also knows that the public expresses itself in voting for representatives who often weigh priorities and make decisions under pressures from special-interest groups and with limited budgets. The deterioration of public parks and the encroachment of highways on public lands during the past decade illustrate the enormous effort which must be made if later generations are to have the open space and recreation land so important for providing basic human services. It is hoped the above mechanisms for land acquisition and retention will provide ideas as to how this task might be accomplished.

CONSIDERATIONS FOR DESIGN
OF OPEN SPACE AND RECREATION LAND

Action to preserve open space and recreation land in American communities has been justified on several grounds: open space provides recreation opportunities, conserves valuable scenic and natural resources, and gives form and aesthetic value to a community. Tantamount to all these reasons is a belief that open space serves very basic human needs and values. Senator Harrison A. Williams, Jr. (D., New Jersey) best summarized this belief:

> There is a certain psychic relief in open space that cannot be underestimated. It gives us visual relief from the tangled, jarring, and often monotonous sight of urban development and a sense of orientation and community identity. Very few can picture the location of every street in town, but most of us can immediately place the location of an attractive park or open space in our mind's eye.[32]

The primacy of serving human needs is accepted by most recreation and park planners. However, little has been done to define *what* these

[31]Ibid., p. 111.

[32]U.S. Senate Subcommittee on Banking and Currency, *Housing Legislation of 1961,* 87th Cong., 1st sess., 1961, p. 997.

needs are or *how* recreation lands can best be designed to meet them. Too often recreation and park design is determined by profit-conscious land developers or by simply "waving a magic wand over the city map." In many cases a park design is accepted because it looks good on a multi-color map, or political interests deem it expedient to accept the plan. What research has been done usually concentrates on how to measure and project the acreage requirements for broad types of open space. While this work has been useful in obtaining general land requirements for standard recreation activities, all too often it has produced stereotypic plans. Traditional concepts about the development of parks and open space ignore such questions as:

- What impact will the park design have on human values and preferences?
- How can citizens' groups become involved in open-space planning?
- To what extent should citizens be involved in planning decisions?

A recreation and parks open-space plan should be premised on the concept of "openness": open to choice, open to active use and manipulation, open to view and understanding, open to access, open to new perceptions of experiences. It should be a system intimately connected with the overall environment and a community's daily life—not a specialized antithesis to the city, but a functional part of it. It should be designed in the context of the whole—the pattern of other city uses and circulations, the regional setting, the constellations of living systems.

A set of drawings and text should show the pattern of use, form, and character of all open spaces as a complete subsystem in relation to the pattern of the city as a whole. All have to be taken into account, not simply the publicly owned spaces specifically designed for recreation. The design would necessarily be based on a comprehensive visual analysis of the community. It is fundamental that open spaces are meaningless except in relation to their use and to the characteristics and aspirations of their users. The design should show who would use the recreation areas, how they would reach them, and how these uses relate to present or future desires, or to ways in which hoped-for changes in those desires could be brought about. Along with the design for the form of open spaces would be a program for use, training, and administration.

The design of individual open space should emphasize variety and avoid park stereotypes. The spread of user requirements and technical possibilities should evoke an equally wide spread of types of open space in a city. There is need for design for movement. This has a potential for enjoyment in itself, an ability to communicate the meaning of large environments, and an obvious relation to access and to the fundamental nature of the city. This requires linear open spaces, specialized routes, and general organizing networks.

The above comments have stressed the need for flexibility—the nature of spaces which can be actively used or manipulated, and which are amenable to change of function. There are tremendous technical possibilities for shaping open space, as well as many unexploited dimensions and materials, such as underwater and underground artifical light and three-dimensional sequence.

All of these are general statements which become more specific when applied to real situations, to a particular city with its idiosyncrasies of form, setting, function, climate, social pattern, and cultural aspirations. As in any good design, an open-space plan should be undertaken with a sense of special place so it appears as if it could never have arisen except in that particular location.[33]

GUIDELINES FOR PLANNING
RECREATION AREAS

The next thirty years will bring about tremendous competition for the use of open space. To assure that present and future generations will have recreation and open-space land, it is essential to have more effective planning and management of such areas. Effective supply can be expanded through more efficient use of existing resources, as well as through private and public acquisition and development of additional recreation lands. Both approaches will have to be used if needs are to be met.

Recreation requires the use of a broad range of resources, from highly developed sites to undisturbed primitive areas providing enjoyment for small and large groups. Between these extremes are areas of various types that have been or may be modified. Some are developed solely for recreation, and others are managed for recreation in conjunction with other resource uses. While the physical and situational aspects of resources strongly influence the kind of activities that can be carried out, it is really management in its broadest sense that determines use. Whether a particular piece of open space remains undeveloped, and thus appropriate for limited kinds of recreation, or whether it is modified to sustain a wide range of opportunities for large numbers, depends on management criteria and decisions.

In 1962 the Outdoor Recreation Resources Review Commission (ORRRC) recommended a system for classifying recreation areas. The Commission's approach was recreation zoning based on the relationship between physical resource characteristics and public recreation needs. With this concept, particular resources would be managed for definite recreation uses, sometimes in combination with other uses. Because of a wide variety of possible recreation activities in many areas, the purpose for which each area is particularly suited must be carefully determined to

[33]The ideas and concepts in this discussion were taken from Marcus O'Leary & Associates, "Open Space for Human Need," unpublished report, part of master plan for open space, no date.

assure a desirable variety of opportunities and values. The classification system is as follows:[34]

1. Class I   High-Density Recreation Areas
2. Class II   General Outdoor Recreation Areas
3. Class III   Natural Environment Areas
4. Class IV   Outstanding Natural Areas
5. Class V   Primitive Areas
6. Class VI   Historic and Cultural Sites
7. Class VII   Open-Space Areas

Class I.   High-Density Recreation Areas

1. *Physical Requirements.* Physiographic features such as topography, soil type, drainage, etc., should be adaptable to special types of intensive recreation use and development. An attractive natural setting is desirable; however, man-made settings are acceptable. There are no specific size criteria and there is great variation in size from one area to another.

2. *Location.*   Usually within or near major centers of urban population, but may occur within such units as national parks and forests remote from population concentrations.

3. *Activities.*   Intensive day or weekend type, such as picnicking, water sports, winter sports, group field games, and other activities for many people. Although high-density areas are subject to high peakload pressure at certain times, they often sustain moderate use throughout the year.

4. *Developments.*   High degree of facility development which often requires heavy investment. They are usually managed exclusively for recreation purposes. Development may include a road network, parking areas, bathing beaches and marinas, bath houses, artificial lakes, playfields, and sanitary and eating facilities.

5. *Responsibility.*   Commonly held under municipal, county, regional, or state ownership. Many commercial resorts have similar characteristics and collectively provide a significant portion of recreation opportunities for urban population centers.

Class II.   General Outdoor Recreation Areas

1. *Physical Requirements.*   May have varied topography, interesting flora and fauna within a generally attractive natural or man-made setting adaptable to providing a wide range of opportunities. These areas range in size from several acres to large tracts of land.

---

[34]Outdoor Recreation Resources Review Commission, *Outdoor Recreation for America* (Washington, D.C.: Government Printing Office, 1962), p. 97.

2. *Location.* Usually more remote than Class I areas; however, relatively accessible to centers of urban populations and accommodate a major share of all outdoor recreation. Included are portions of public parks and forests, public and commercial camping sites, picnic grounds, trail parks, ski areas, resorts, streams, lakes, and hunting preserves.

3. *Activities.* Extensive day, weekend, and vacation types such as camping, picnicking, fishing, hunting, water sports, winter sports, nature walks, and outdoor games.

4. *Developments.* Generally less intensive than Class I areas. Includes, but not limited to, access roads, parking areas, picnicking areas, campgrounds, bathing beaches, marinas, streams, natural and/or artificial lakes. Areas are equipped with some man-made facilities, which may vary from simple to elaborate. Thus, campgrounds may have only the barest necessities for sanitation and fire control or they may have ample and carefully planned facilities such as cabins, hot and cold running water, laundry equipment, stores, museums, small libraries, entertainment, juvenile and adult playfields. Other features may include permanent tows for ski areas, fully equipped marinas, lodges, dude ranches, and luxury hotels.

5. *Responsibility.* Federal, state, or local governments, including regional park and recreation authorities, and private clubs and other forms of private ownership assisted by public agencies on problems of access and development of basic facilities.

Class III. Natural Environment Areas

1. *Physical Requirements.* Varied and interesting land forms, lakes, streams, flora and fauna within attractive natural settings.

2. *Location.* Usually more remote from population centers than Class I and II areas. Occur throughout the country on an acreage basis; are the largest class in both public and private ownership.

3. *Activities.* Extensive weekend and vacation types dependent on quality of the natural environment such as sightseeing, hiking, nature study, picnicking, camping, swimming, boating, canoeing, fishing, and hunting. The primary objective is to provide for traditional recreation experience in the out-of-doors, commonly in conjunction with other resource users. Users are encouraged to enjoy the resource "as is," in natural environment.

4. *Developments.* Access roads, trails, picnic and campsite facilities, and minimum sanitary facilities. There may be other compatible uses of the area such as watershed protection, water supply, grazing, lumbering, and mining, provided such activities are managed to retain the attractiveness of the natural setting.

5. *Responsibility.* Federal, state, or local governments, including regional park and recreation authorities, and private ownerships.

Class IV. Outstanding Natural Areas

1. *Physical Requirements.* Outstanding natural features associated with an outdoor environment that merit special attention and care in management to ensure preservation in their natural condition. Includes individual areas of remarkable natural wonder, high scenic splendor, or features of scientific importance. One or more such areas may be part of a larger administrative unit.

2. *Location.* Anyplace where such features are found.

3. *Activities.* Sightseeing, enjoyment, and study of the natural features. Kinds and intensity of use limited to the enjoyment and study of the natural attractions so as to preserve the quality of the natural features and maintain an appropriate setting. May be visited on a day, weekend, or vacation trip.

4. *Developments.* Limited to minimum development required for public enjoyment, health, safety, and protection of the features. Wherever possible, access roads and facilities other than trails and sanitary facilities should be kept outside the immediate vicinity of the natural features. Visitors encouraged to walk to the feature or into the area when feasible. Improvements should harmonize with and not detract from the natural setting.

5. *Responsibility.* Public agencies, (federal, state, and local), and private landowners, with assistance from public agencies, who may identify, set aside, and manage natural features. (Generally the federal government assumes responsibility for the protection and management of natural areas of national significance, the states for areas of regional or state significance, and local government and private owners for areas of primarily local significance.)

Class V. Primitive Areas

1. *Physical Requirements.* Extensive natural, wild, and undeveloped area and setting removed from the sights, sounds, and smells of civilization. Essential characteristics are that the natural environment has not been disturbed by commercial use and that the areas are without mechanized transportation. The area must be large enough and so located as to give the user the feeling that he is enjoying a "wilderness experience." The site may vary with different physical and biological conditions and may be determined in part by the characteristics of adjacent land. Size may vary in different parts of the country. These areas are inspirational, aesthetic, scientific, and cultural assets of the highest value.

2. *Location.* Usually remote from population centers.

3. *Activities.* Camping out on one's own without mechanized transportation or permanent shelter or other conveniences.

4. *Developments.* No development of public roads, permanent habitations, or recreation facilities except trails. No mechanized equip-

ment allowed except that needed to control fire, insects, and disease. Commercial use of the area that may exist at the time of establishment should be discontinued as soon as practical.

5. *Responsibility.* Usually federal but may also be state agencies or private landowners (such as the high mountain country held by large timber and mining companies).

Class VI. Historic and Cultural Sites

1. *Physical Requirements.* These are sites associated with the history, tradition, or cultural heritage of national, state, or local interest and are of enough significance to merit preservation or restoration.

2. *Location.* The location of the feature establishes the site.

3. *Activities.* Sightseeing, enjoyment, and study of the historic or cultural features. Kinds and intensity of use limited to this type of study and enjoyment.

4. *Developments.* Management should be limited to activities that would affect such preservation and restoration as may be necessary to protect the features from deterioration and to interpret their significance to the public. Access to the area should be adequate but on-site development limited to prevent overuse. Development should not detract from the historic or cultural values of the site.

5. *Responsibility.* Public agencies (federal, state, and local), and private landowners who identify, set aside, and manage historic and cultural areas.

Class VII. Open-Space Areas

1. *Physical Requirements.* Varied and interesting undeveloped lands that provide relief and contrast to the majority of surrounding land uses.

2. *Location.* Wherever it is found and it is deemed desirable to preserve it in relationsip to surrounding uses or developments.

3. *Activities.* May vary, from uses suggested in Class IV to simply preservation of the space for visual contrast and relief, buffer, historic, or conservation reasons.

4. *Developments.* Limited to minimum development required for public enjoyment and preservation of the area.

5. *Responsibility.* Local governmental agencies should recognize need, identify areas, preserve, develop, and manage such areas.

One of the strengths of this classification system is that it allows for the logical relation of the entire range of recreation activities to the range of available resources. When physical conditions permit the classification of a given area in more than one class, the classification that promises the optimum combination of values in the long run should be selected.

As noted, desirable open space in or near urban areas is quickly diminishing, while the urban population and the demand for open space are rapidly increasing. There is an urgent need for states, metropolitan areas, and municipalities to develop and implement comprehensive open-space programs. In planning such programs, decisions must be made on desirable patterns of development. Open space is one of the major determinants guiding the profile of a community. When the open character of the land is preserved, development pressures are channeled elsewhere. Therefore, a decision on open space now is a decision influencing the future pattern of development.

An open-space program for a community should be an integral part of its total planning process. Intelligent choices for the land development pattern of an area can be made *only* with a balanced survey of the type and scale of demand for all types of land uses. Open-space choices must be weighed against other choices.in terms of cost, priority, and allocation of land.

Coordination of open-space planning and acquisition is needed. Open-space planning and acquisition are often performed by separate agencies. Frequently, many agencies are responsible for various aspects of the same plan. Lack of communication between planners and those who acquire or regulate land can deprive planners of sound, practical information which might be used to change planning proposals; such poor communication can also deny to enforcement officials an understanding of the premises underlying the plans.

An understanding of the effect of community growth upon recreation resources is a vital prerequisite to an adequate open-space program. Since community open space is quickly diminishing, it is vital that every community readily determine how much and what kind of open space is needed to assure a healthy balance between man and nature, between community development and open space. Acquisition programs alone are not enough—a broad range of measures needs to be used to keep land opened. State enabling legislation and city ordinances should be reviewed carefully for their adequacy for open-space preservation.

SUGGESTED DEFINITIONS FOR RECREATION AREAS

Open-space and recreation areas are classified by service area, size, type, and degree of facility development and primary function. This section offers suggested definitions for open-space and recreation areas, with emphasis on resources usually provided by public recreation and park systems. The open space provided for public recreation and conservation should be designed to fit into one of ten categories which relate to community development:

Mini-Parks   Wayside Parks
Neighborhood Parks   Greenways
Community Parks   Ornamental Areas
Metropolitan Parks   Special-Activity Areas
Nature Preserves   New Developments

Mini-Parks

Mini-parks are small parks where children can play or adults can relax in a pleasant setting. The parks are not designed for organized programs, but simply provide a common ground "just down the street" where neighbors can meet on a casual, day-to-day basis. As local play areas, mini-parks are intended to serve any residential area where a need exists for play apparatus. Mini-parks in high-density areas help compensate for the lack of private yards to play in and help break the monotony of asphalt and buildings.

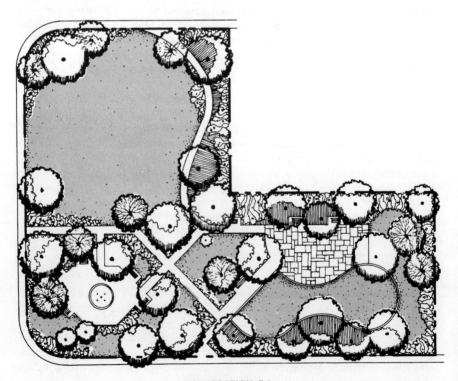

ILLUSTRATION 5.1

Mini-Park Design

Courtesy of Dade County, Florida, Department of Parks and Recreation

Neighborhood Parks

A neighborhood park is a "walk-to" park primarily serving the neighborhood, the smallest planning unit of the area. Neighborhood planning units generally are bordered by heavily traveled streets, but not transversed by them. Within the neighborhood, children can usually walk or ride bicycles without competing with thoroughfare traffic. Because of this, neighborhood parks are designed primarily for children's activities with organized recreation programs primarily for 6- to 12-year-olds. Where there is a preponderance of older citizens, facilities and programs at neighborhood parks should also be structured to meet these needs.

The park service area often coincides with the service area for an elementary school; the population required to support a neighborhood park closely coincides with that needed to justify an elementary school. Because elementary schools and neighborhood parks serve the same age group, they should be located adjacent to each other. They have compatible land uses and, because of a common need for recreation facilities, can be mutually beneficial.[35]

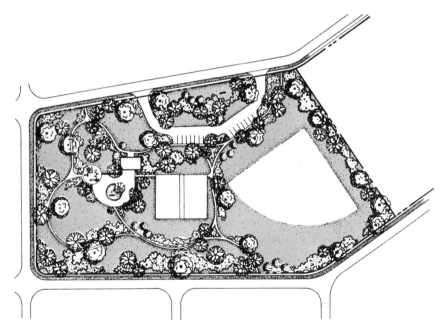

ILLUSTRATION 5.2

Neighborhood Park

Courtesy of Dade County, Florida, Department of Parks and Recreation

[35]For further discussion of this concept, see the section on trends in intergovernmental relations in this chapter.

Because the recreation needs vary from one neighborhood to another, depending on the income, age, and social background of its residents, the facilities and the programs of a neighborhood park should not be rigidly standardized but designed to meet the particular needs of a neighborhood. They should include such basic facilities as a recreation building, multi-purpose courts, open fields for play, and a play apparatus area. It is essential that a neighborhood park include a "parklike" setting and a well-shaded, quiet area where adults can gather to chat and watch their children.

Community Parks

A community park is a "ride-to" park designed to serve the residents of a group of neighborhoods, usually four to six, constituting a community. A community park is larger and contains more facilities than a mini-park or neighborhood parks and is primarily intended to meet the programmed recreation needs not met by these smaller parks. At the community park, activities for teenagers and adults are introduced. Essentially, these are family recreation centers with programs and facilities for all age groups.

Typical community park facilities include athletic fields, tennis courts, a swimming pool, play apparatus area, and a recreation building designed for arts and crafts, games and meetings. In addition to facilities for active play, pleasantly landscaped acreage for passive relaxation

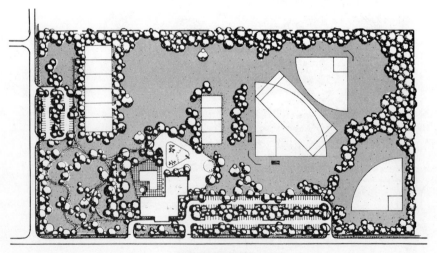

ILLUSTRATION 5.3

Community Park

Courtesy of Dade County, Florida, Department of Parks and Recreation

should be provided at a ratio of one acre for passive use to two acres for active. Without adequate passive area, a park has little more parklike atmosphere than a school athletic field. As with neighborhood parks, programs and facilities should be adapted to the particular needs of the community being served.

The service area for a community park generally coincides with the service area for a junior or senior high school. The park and school should be located adjacent to each other because both require similar recreation facilities and a larger percentage of park users are school students. Community parks also should be located near major streets and arterials to provide better access. Because community parks attract fairly large numbers of people, they should be well buffered from adjacent residences.

Metropolitan Parks

Metropolitan parks are intended to serve county residents. They are developed primarily to make available special natural resources for recreation use. Since they are generally designed for resource-oriented activities, such as boating, swimming and fishing, location is dependent on the availability of the resources desired. Sites chosen for metropolitan parks should be areas of outstanding natural beauty or have particularly good potential for improvement, such as abandoned rockpits, where many sought-after variations in topography are present.

Metropolitan parks should be readily accessible to the urban population, ideally within a 30-minute drive from the area served. Metropolitan parks are the primary areas where the much-demanded access to water can be provided. Marinas, boat ramps, beaches, picnic grounds, campgrounds, nature study trails, and hiking trails are generally provided. Some metropolitan parks where the natural environment is not outstanding can be suitably developed as major athletic and sports centers, and for other activities which do not require particular natural resources.

As urban development rapidly expands and destroys natural areas, metropolitan parks are among the few places where the public can go within a single day to enjoy outdoor recreation in a natural environment. The facilities provided must, above all, be designed and related to each other so they do not destroy the beauty and serenity the metropolitan park is intended to provide. The need for a place to retreat from the noise and congestion of the urban area and to "return to nature" cannot be overemphasized.

Nature Preserves

Nature preserves are areas vital to the maintenance of natural function such as wildlife reproduction and feeding. The primary purpose

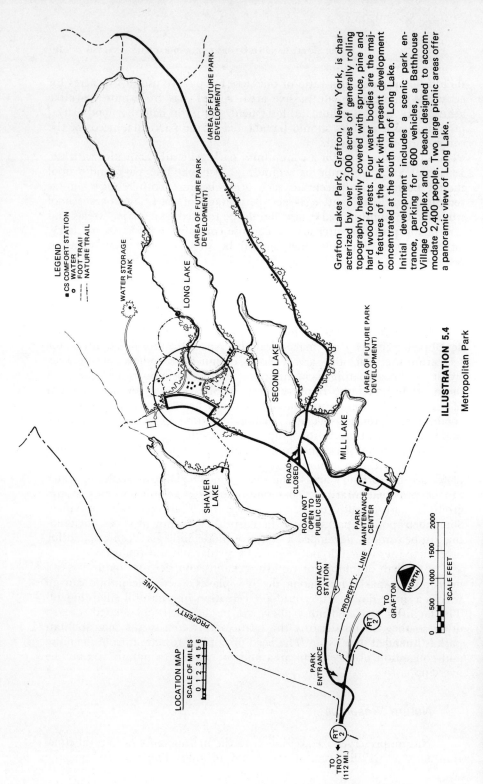

LEGEND
- ■ CS COMFORT STATION
- ○ WATER
- —— FOOT TRAIL
- – – – NATURE TRAIL

Grafton Lakes Park, Grafton, New York, is characterized by over 2,000 acres of generally rolling topography heavily covered with spruce, pine and hard wood forests. Four water bodies are the major features of the Park with present development concentrated at the south end of Long Lake.

Initial development includes a scenic park entrance, parking for 600 vehicles, a Bathhouse Village Complex and a beach designed to accommodate 2,400 people. Two large picnic areas offer a panoramic view of Long Lake.

ILLUSTRATION 5.4

Metropolitan Park

Courtesy of New York State Parks and Recreation

is to preserve nature in its untouched form for public enjoyment. Because these are intended for the study and enjoyment of nature, development should be primarily directed toward providing access and nature study facilities. Compatible recreational facilities for nature preserves may include, in addition to nature study facilities, campsites, boat launching facilities, beaches, and bridle paths. Nature preserves of immense proportions, such as the Everglades National Park and Water Control Conservation Area, could support a larger variety of recreational facilities without destroying the overall natural character. Nature preserves are of countrywide and, in some instances, nationwide significance.

Wayside Parks

Wayside parks primarily serve as resting places for the automobile traveler and as small picnic grounds. A wayside park is an enroute stopping place and not ordinarily the primary destination of an auto-

ILLUSTRATION 5.5

Nature Preserve

Courtesy of Dade County, Florida, Department of Parks and Recreation

mobile trip. These areas should be conducive to relaxation and rest. Areas of scenic beauty are preferable locations. Wayside parks are especially suitable and desirable for inclusion in the proposed greenway system.

Greenways

Greenways are linear open spaces that can follow canals, rivers, the bay shoreline, electric power transmission line rights-of-way, streets and highways, or even bicycle paths. Names frequently given to greenways

ILLUSTRATION 5.6

Wayside Park. One of more than 250 rest areas along New York State highways, this area is located on the Adirondack Northway (Interstate Route 87) near Clifton Park in Saratoga County.

Courtesy of New York State Department of Transportation

serving a particular function include parkways, boulevards, and green-belts. Whatever form they take, greenways are intended to make movements from one part of the country to another more pleasant. Because of linear form, they are particularly conducive to such recreation activities as hiking, bicycling, horseback riding, or driving for pleasure.

Ornamental Areas

Ornamental areas are green spaces designed for visual enjoyment. Most frequently they are provided to enhance the rights-of-way of streets and highways. Examples of ornamental areas are median green strips, triangles, and malls.

Special-Activity Areas

Special-activity areas are designed and used for one predominating activity. Examples of such areas are golf courses, swimming pools, munici-

ILLUSTRATION 5:7

Greenways

Courtesy of Dade County, Florida, Department of Parks and Recreation

ILLUSTRATION 5.8

Ornamental Park

Courtesy of Dade County, Florida, Department of Parks and Recreation

pal stadiums, and recreation centers. They usually exist where large parcels of land are not available for development of a multi-facility area, or when a facility can fulfill a function without the aid of complementary facilities.

New Developments

Vest-pocket parks. These tiny parks located in the midst of urban areas do not conform to the usual pattern of either city or county parks, since they rarely add much acreage to the park system, and are usually placed in areas that give parks a very high profile in the neighborhood. Such a profile invariably leads to high maintenance costs because of heavy use. At one time, Departments of Parks were opposed to any park smaller than three acres, since smaller parks were considered difficult to build and maintain. They strongly believed their funds should go toward maintaining existing larger parks that were not receiving proper main-

ILLUSTRATION 5.9

Special-Activity Area

Courtesy of Saratoga Performing Arts Center, Inc., Saratoga Spa, New York

tenance, rather than toward creating additional vest-pocket parks which would drain a disproportionate amount of maintenance funds.

Since small vacant lots in urban areas are ideally suited to vest-pocket parks, it is ironic that there seems to be a coordinated effort by many cities "to turn all available pieces of vacant land into junkyards, for the city of [New York] owns most of the existing vacant lots, which remain empty because small lots are not practical for building new homes or as yards. . . . Therefore, as soon as a lot comes under city ownership, it is fenced in with corrugated metal panels with the specific purpose of keeping children outside."[36] Thus, instead of playing in vacant lots, such a policy forces children to play in crowded, dangerous streets.

Previous research as to vest-pocket parks in New York City had shown there were a number of vacant lots throughout the city, but atten-

[36]Julian R. Peterson, "Vest-Pocket Parks in Harlem," in Whitney N. Seymour, Jr., ed., *Small Urban Spaces: The Philosophy, Design, Sociology, and Politics of Vest-Pocket Parks and Other Small Urban Open Spaces* (New York: New York University Press, 1969), pp. 123–24.

tion was focused in the late sixties on central Harlem, which has sub-stantiated a need for more recreational facilities. Since the city was not interested in undertaking a project to build vest-pocket parks itself, the J. J. Kaplan Fund, in conjunction with the Park Association of New York City, purchased several garbage-filled lots from the city. This group decided to build three vest-pocket parks at a cost of $5,000 each: (1) a tot lot for children under 10; (2) a teenager lot for social and athletic activities of older children; and (3) a sitting park for neighborhood adults. Inter-estingly enough, the tot park which was fenced in and closed at night received more damage than the other two parks. Thus, fencing is not considered necessary or even appropriate for vest-pocket parks, which should be open 24 hours a day.

Although play equipment in a tot park could be very durable ma-terial such as concrete or steel, children especially like playing with wooden logs, poles, old boats, etc.; through use they would have to be changed often, but their popularity and success seem to justify their frequent replacement. Parks can be easily refurbished with old wooden objects, avoiding the widespread use of unimaginative concrete play equipment: "A good park need really be little more than a level, clean area with a few simple wooden play devices."[37]

The teen park was the most successful, with elaborate wall decora-tions by youngsters from the neighborhood where it was located. The main visual appeal of the park was in the brightly painted walls of the adjacent buildings. However, the intensive use of this little park soon damaged most of the equipment—tables, chairs, basketball net, a canopy, and the like—all of which were replaced. Most important, this experience in Harlem pointed up the necessity of organized activities and supervision in a park designed exclusively for teenagers.

The adult park, on the other hand, did not experience any vandal-ism or much wear and tear. It is a lovely little park, consisting "essentially of closely spaced trees, which present a bright patch of green to those viewing it from the outside and a verdant ceiling for those sitting on the benches inside the park. The overall effect is that of a cool green wood-land, a small-scale version of many Parisian parks."[38] Maintenance has not been difficult, and this project in particular has shown that a small sitting park, well designed and built, is possible even in low-income neighborhoods. Although repairs and replacements have not been a problem for the adult sitting park, it has been for the tot and teen parks, both of which in addition to the daily cleaning often require immediate repair of damages. For most low-income neighborhoods, especially when such parks are sponsored by private citizens, maintenance costs can pre-sent somewhat of a hardship. Since cleaning and maintenance are the biggest costs, it is wise to limit the initial purchase of equipment if there are limited funds.

[37]Ibid., p. 130.
[38]Ibid., p. 132.

These vest-pocket parks in Harlem, one of the most densely populated areas in the world, proved successful for two reasons: first, it helped persuade the city to give vest-pocket parks a try; second, it indicated that private parks are practical if some organization is willing to spend time and money to maintain them. Soon after these three parks were constructed, both the city and the federal government, as well as other private organizations, expressed interest in and approval of the concept. Many urban areas are like New York—low on recreational space and facilities and high on garbage-filled vacant lots. Such vest-pocket parks, for all age groups, can meet the park needs of inner-city residents which are largely unmet.

Illustration 5.10 is an example of an imaginative vest-pocket park in Sunnyvale, California. Eleven such parks were built in Kansas City, Missouri, at a budgeted cost of $440,000 with 50 percent financial funding from HUD.[39] "On the whole, vest-pocket parks have proved themselves to be a relatively quick and cheap method of graphically demonstrating the efforts of government action at the neighborhood level."[40] An interesting sidenote on inner-city parks: Although old pieces of wooden objects and other articles have been hailed as useful in such parks (such as the Harlem tot park discussed), the Kansas City group felt that to slum people junk is junk; therefore, they spent a sizable amount of their funds on appropriate and creative play equipment.

Adventure playgrounds. Even if junk is junk to community residents, to most kids it's exciting stuff. "Children prefer dirt to concrete, and show strong interest in imaginative and varied playthings."[41] As Iona and Peter Opie stress in their book on childhood play, children love "wastelands," where their imagination has freedom to explore, manipulate, fantasize, and create.[42] In urban areas, where space of any kind is at a premium, some attempt had to be made to reunite children with some aspects of the "lost landscape of spontaneity" so evident in the youthful memories of their predecessors.[43] Although not the wilderness and mystery of unexplored places, adventure playgrounds are the closest we have come in recreation and parks to emulating some of the mysterious and exciting pleasures of childhood.

An adventure playground is a recreation area where children are allowed *and* encouraged to create their own play environment under nonrestrictive adult supervision. The land is left in its original state,

[39]William L. Landahl, "Vest-Pocket Parks and a County," *Parks and Recreation*, Vol. 7 (August 1972), 20–21.

[40]Ibid., pp. 21ff.

[41]Peterson, "Vest-Pocket Parks," p. 41.

[42]*Children's Games in Street and Playground* (New York: Oxford University Press, 1969).

[43]Clare Cooper, *The Adventure Playground: Creative Play in an Urban Setting and a Potential Focus for Community Involvement* (Berkeley: University of California, Center for Planning and Development Research, April 1970), p. 1.

ILLUSTRATION 5.10

Vest-Pocket Park

Courtesy of Sunnyvale Parks and Recreation Department, Sunnyvale, California

with building materials (such as wood, cardboad boxes, logs, planks, bricks, and so forth) provided for the children to build almost anything they desire. Although there are no fixed programs or activities, there is endless opportunity to participate in creative play and adventure. The atmosphere is one of open encouragement, with minimum guidance to assure a degree of safety. Building a house, planting a garden, digging a tunnel, cooking a meal, swinging on ropes from the trees, creating a mysterious artifact, anything children enjoy which does not endanger them or others is permitted. The only limitation of the adventure playground is potential danger. If children require dangerous activities to excite them, there will be plenty of opportunity to obtain this outside of parks! For city kids who have not had the pleasures of country life, plants and animals are integral parts of the playgrounds. (Illustration 5.11 is an example of an adventure playground in a rural setting.)

The demand for adventure parks grew out of a protest against the unimaginative playgrounds of asphalt and mechancial equipment which most city children have been offered for their play activities. In England, adventure playgrounds were located in bombsites; these spaces were appropriated for creative purposes, rather than simply being converted into parking lots or being allowed to become rubbish dumps. The Opies also mention that British children, other European children, and more recently the children of North Vietnam were quite happy to play in bombed-out buildings, using pieces of planes and other equipment for playthings.

Some researchers believe that adventure playgrounds can help prevent juvenile delinquency, "especially if they [children] have little to do during the dark evenings and long school holidays. Providing these children with playgrounds has greatly helped to reduce the incidence of local juvenile crime, insofar as this stems from boredom and broken homes."[44] Although it is not argued that juvenile delinquency is prevented by involvement in any single activity, such a suggestion has merit; so much of the time of city kids is spent in trying to find something to do.

ILLUSTRATION 5.11

Adventure Playground

Courtesy of the Champaign Park District, Champaign, Illinois

44Lady Allen of Hurtwood, "Adventure Playgrounds," in Seymour, *Small Urban Spaces*, p. 91.

Adventure playgrounds, using the discarded materials and artifacts of city life, offer children something challenging and beneficial to do.

Experience has shown that it is not practical to set up an adventure playground on less than one-third of an acre. Anything smaller limits the number of children who can participate at a given time. To avoid wasting land, especially in urban areas, maximum use of an adventure playground has to be sought. For instance, while older children are in school, preschool children can be encouraged to use the playground, with the school-age children coming in about 4 P.M. until 8 P.M., and all day on school holidays. Teenagers can then use the playground for more adult activities from about 8 to 10 P.M., or later. "In this way the comparatively small sites are fully used, something which cannot be said of many orthodox playgrounds."[45]

Fear of accidents and lawsuits is the argument most often used against adventure playgrounds. After ten years of experience in England with adventure playgrounds, Lady Allen assures us that she has never received a claim from one parent about injuries received while at the playground. "There are, of course, burns, cuts, perhaps even a broken arm, but these are accidents that are never deliberate injuries."[46] Children work with real tools, take expected risks, all without fear of criticism or rebuke.

One key to the success of adventure playgrounds is the adult supervisors. However, few professionals in recreation and parks are presently suited by training or experience to handle the job, nor are park departments willing to pay substantial salaries to attract people who are. In fact, park departments seem more willing to build orthodox parks, which don't run the risk of offending adjacent property owners, than to create these "unsightly" playgrounds for the overall pleasure and enjoyment of children. Since most playgrounds and playground equipment are built for adults—the taxpayers—children are the ones to lose. Adventure playgrounds can be an adventure for everyone: adults can experience the "adventure" of an unorthodox park in their midst; children can show them how to use it.

STANDARDS

Undoubtedly, there is no one factor that has a greater impact on urban recreation than recreation standards. An exhaustive search has been made to determine if there are tested standards which could be considered effective. Unfortunately, many of the standards used in most of our metropolitan areas are adaptations of standards from as far back as the early 1900's. For example, the traditional standard formula of one

45Ibid., p. 93.
46Ibid., p. 94.

acre of parkland per 100 persons, or 10 acres per 1,000 persons, can no longer be considered realistic; however, such a formula is still offered as a rule-of-thumb measurement in parks and open-space planning.

There is a great deal of disparity between using such a formula for Hoboken, New Jersey, with 45,000 people living in two square miles, and a small town in Nebraska which might have the same number of people spread over 50 square miles. Also there is something wrong with having one standard apply to both rich and poor communities, regardless of the goals or the abilities of a community to achieve such standards, not to mention their social priorities and resources. While such a traditional formula might have the appeal of being simple to apply, it is virtually useless for modern planning in recreation and parks. No two communities are alike, and standards must reflect the particular resources and needs of each area. In addition, standards are often a reflection of what a *minimum* recreation system should involve.

Although there is a real need for practical and definitive standards in recreation and parks, such standards should not be overly restrictive. A standard should be a guideline, not an inflexible straitjacket.

Since its existence, the National Recreation and Park Association (NRPA) has been a leader in the movement to establish standards for parks and recreation. As early as 1906, the NRPA issued a report delineating the need and space requirements for certain recreation facilities. In 1934 the Association published a report offering detailed recommendations on space standards for playgrounds in neighborhoods of different sizes. To meet the need to update and revise traditional standards, NRPA established a National Committee on Recreation Standards in 1960 to appraise all recreation standards which had been recommended.

From this committee came the suggested *Standards for Municipal Recreation Areas,* published by NRPA in 1962.[47] This publication was a comprehensive compilation of area standards and a list of sources. The standards were slightly revised by NRPA in 1967.[48] Then in 1969 the NRPA held a national forum in Kansas City on park and recreation standards, attended by more than 150 planners, administrators, educators, private consultants, and researchers. There it was decided that NRPA should continue to develop, evaluate, coordinate, and review standards for application to parks and recreation planning.[49]

Although the NRPA has always emphasized that standards were to be used only as guides, there was a tendency for those "guidelines" to be applied without any revision, undoubtedly because of the paucity of

[47]George D. Butler, *Standards for Municipal Recreation Areas* (New York: National Recreation and Park Association, 1962).

[48]U.S. Department of the Interior, Bureau of Outdoor Recreation, *Outdoor Recreation Space Standards* (Washington, D.C.: Government Printing Office, 1967).

[49]Robert D. Buechner, ed., *National Park, Recreation and Open-Space Standards* (Washington, D.C.: National Recreation and Park Association, 1971), p. 7.

alternatives. "This had a compounding effect which increased the authority of the original standards and encouraged still more communities to accept them without revision or question."[50]

Since recreation and parks standards will determine to a great extent the allocation and use of recreational resources, the "creation and use of reliable park and recreation standards—whether it be in the central city or in our wilderness areas—is the creation and use of recreational environmental quality controls."[51] Therefore, the quality of recreation standards will be reflected in the quality of our recreational and leisure environment. Although there are no definitive studies on the quality of standards, there are several factors which are indicative of the present status of standards research.

The first is the wide variety of numerical values used for space standards. Although we recommend flexibility in the application of standards, it is somewhat disconcerting that such a wide range exists among, for instance, the number of canoes or boats to have per mile of stream. "Admittedly, definitions and conditions vary and standards should not be considered absolute values, but there does appear to be a larger range than one would expect if these standards were really reliable."[52] A second difficulty with standards is that too many of them are simply replicated and are not really tested for reliability. Although experience and personal judgment are not to be negated, well-designed research projects to develop valid standards are essential as well to improve the quality of recreation and parks planning.

As mentioned, the basic compilation and comparison of various standards have been done periodically by the National Recreation and Park Association. A good example of this type of descriptive research is evident in *Outdoor Recreation Space Standards*.[53] However, these publications usually do not include any evaluation of the numerical values based on field experience with standards. Another investigative method used by many federal and state agencies is to put design-capacity standards into practice on a trial-and-error basis, after some prior discussion with area managers. This method was used often by the U.S. Army Corps of Engineers. Needless to say, such a method usually does not yield much information about factors that affect standards and design. For standards to have any validity, a good deal of rigorous research needs to be done. The National Academy of Sciences also emphasized this point:

[50]Seymour M. Gold, *Urban Recreation Planning* (Philadelphia: Lea & Febiger, 1973).

[51]Michael Chubb and Peter Ashton, *Park & Recreation Standards Research: The Creation of Environmental Quality Controls for Recreation,* a Report to the National Recreation and Park Association (East Lansing, Mich.: Department of Park and Recreation Resources, January 1969), p. ix.

[52]Ibid., p. x.

[53]U.S. Department of the Interior, Bureau of Outdoor Recreation.

. . . vigorous research is needed to develop models of the economic demand for outdoor recreation that will make possible inclusion of sociological and demographic aspects by analyzing the dependence of the number, quality and distribution of recreational experiences sought on the location, size, social characteristics, and psychological needs of the user population. . . .[54]

The U.S. Forest Service has undertaken scientific studies on various aspects of recreation sites which are related to carrying capacity, but these studies do not "attempt to determine the desirable magnitude of any particular standard."[55] Several universities and private consultants have also done some studies on the psychological aspects of standards, but what is really needed is research that investigates *all* the quantitative and qualitative circumstances involved in determining numerical values. The Army Corps of Engineers has done some research to produce more reliable standards than the trial-and-error method produces. Chubb and Ashton report on a project they conducted at Michigan State University "to develop improved boating standards by creating new field techniques involving an integrated system of aerial photography, user preference interviews, and inventories of related resources and cultural phenomena."[56] Although all these studies have merit, the overall scope of standards research has to be greatly expanded to meet the demand for valid and reliable standards in recreation and parks today.

One research proposal to develop a park location theory to determine the optimal location of city parks in terms of distance traveled has interesting possibilities.[57] This proposal concerns two larger research problems as well: the adequacy of parks, and the development of a general theory of public facility location. "If the problem of isolation from public parks [in urban areas] is viewed as one of spatial distribution, perhaps the techniques and tools of location theory can provide the beginning of a solution by helping the researcher (1) determine the effectiveness of the current size and spacing of urban parks and (2) determine an optimal pattern for future expansion and relocation of the park system."[58]

In this optimality proposal, elements of location theory are "modified and synthesized to develop a model to test the spatial efficiency of an urban park system in terms of the distribution of the park service."[59] The model concentrates on a single recreation system, and within that

[54]National Academy of Sciences, *A Program for Outdoor Recreation Research* (Washington, D.C.: NAS, 1969), p. 5.

[55]Chubb and Ashton, *Park and Recreation Standards Research*, p. xii.

[56]Ibid., p. xiii.

[57]Steven Smith, "The Location of Urban Parks: An Optimality Approach," unpublished proposal, mimeo, n.d.

[58]Ibid., p. 3.

[59]Ibid., p. 16.

system on an investigation of neighborhood playgrounds. The model takes into consideration variable demand—based on population density and willingness to travel—as well as barriers to travel and urban land uses. An examination of the park system is done by determining a threshold population through empirical observations; by applying this figure to a map of the population distribution of a city, the lower limit for such a threshold can be determined.

Using these limits, it will be possible to section off a city into various regions and to locate the parks within these regions based on minimum travel cost and spatial efficiency. Such a location pattern can be used to "consider the physical, racial and social barriers, by supplying separate parks to mutually antagonistic neighborhoods or to neighborhoods otherwise separated, if one or both have a threshold population."[60] The author of this proposal concludes that if the model "predicts park locations that are highly correlated with observed locations, it can be safely assumed that there are economic laws or tendencies operating on the distribution of parks. . . ."[61]

Gold—in a review of recreation plans involving space standards, at all levels of government—found that about 60 to 80 percent of the plans "reflect the same standards, even though each planning area has a wide range of demographic, recreation resource, fiscal and climatic variables."[62] He also found a similarity in standards for most urban facilities, where the differences among sites would not seem to warrant such similarity. From this Gold concludes that (1) NRPA standards have been widely accepted and used; (2) there was no evidence of a relationship between geographic and demographic variables in the use of standards; and (3) most plans "regard the standard as a goal or objective and make superficial goal statements which do not relate to stated policies, objectives, and often the standards themselves."[63]

The argument is given that the difficulty of applying standards in the inner city is that there is often a serious disparity between the amount of recreation and park space available and the amount of acreage suggested in nationwide standards. Gold discovered, when applying the more traditional formula of one acre per 100 persons, that in many inner-city areas there was a difference of at least 100 percent between recommended standards and actual practice; he further feels that this difference—if one accounted for other variables such as environmental conditions, density, mobility, and demand and need—would be as high as *1000 percent!*[64] However, in a 1961 survey of the 51 largest county

60Ibid., p. 17.

61Ibid., pp. 20–21.

62Gold, *Urban Recreation Planning*, p. 161.

63Ibid., p. 163.

64Ibid., p. 166.

park systems in the suburbs and "exurbs," NRPA found that only 20 counties had more than 10 acres per 1,000 population, and that the average for these counties was only 8.7 acres, or about half of the 15 acres per 1,000 population that is the common standard for county parks.[65]

Even when more traditional formulas seem to have wide acceptance, they do not necessarily have wide use. It is not clear from these data whether the nonattainment of universal space standards is a reflection of their poor applicability to a wide variety of needs, or simply of not enough land being available or allocated for recreational purposes in the first place. As Clawson notes for New York City, to meet the traditional standard of one acre per 100 persons for the population of Manhattan would exceed the area of the island itself. He further emphasizes that by the year 2000 approximately 5 million acres of city parks would be required throughout the nation, and it is "most improbable that any such area can be provided."[66] This prediction reflects both constraints on available land and costs of attaining and developing inner-city land, presently estimated at almost $50 billion.[67]

Another rationale given for the nonattainment of suggested standards is the loss of so much potential recreational space to the demands of builders for other purposes; yet the standard could be used as an argument *against* the unprecedented encroachment on recreational land. On the other hand, the use of ideal or even so-called "minimum" standards for public recreation may be at the loss of other social needs. Recreation planners must not simply seek the ideal ratio or formula, but a formula or alternative means of planning for recreation needs that reflect the overall social situation of a particular community. Without such a perspective, standards "presume judgment about the recreation experience, residential environment and public goals or objectives which have no empirical basis."[68]

Furthermore, recreation standards ignore the possibilities for investing funds in other forms of leisure activity, such as educational television, museums, public theaters, or the private development of various urban leisure activities. Many of these could offer recreational experiences which are equal to or better than the more traditional parks and playgrounds. "There is no evidence to indicate that the problems of the inner city are primarily environmental, nor is there any reason to

[65]U.S. Department of the Interior, *Outdoor Recreation Space Standards.*

[66]Marion Clawson, *Land and Water for Recreation* (Chicago: Rand McNally and Company 1963), p. 21. One must remember that Manhattan Island is only 22.6 square miles with a population of about 1,540,000, as of the 1970 census.

[67]Herbert Gans, "Recreation Planning for Leisure Behavior: A Goal-Oriented Approach," unpublished Ph.D. dissertation, University of Pennsylvania, 1957, pp. 457–67; and Gold, *Urban Recreation Planning*, pp. 174–75.

[68]Gold, *Urban Recreation Planning*, p. 173.

assume that 10 acres per 1,000 population is any better or worse than 5 or 15 acres."[69]

Existing standards cannot be systematically applied, especially to the inner city, without some recognition of the economic and environmental changes which occur in these areas. Parks built for middle-class neighborhoods and later occupied by lower-class or ethnic minorities may no longer by sufficient or useful. Furthermore, the growing importance of self-determination and citizen advocacy in all kinds of planning is belied by the existence of traditional standards, which smacks more of top-down administration. Standards can thus serve to weaken the recreation movement they were intended to enhance if they negate or discourage citizen involvement. The indiscriminate use of rigid standards can readily lead

BY CLASSIFICATION AND POPULATION RATIO

CLASSIFICATION	ACRES/ 1000 PEOPLE	SIZE RANGE	POPULATION SERVED	SERVICE AREA
Playlets	*	2,500 sq. ft. to 1 acre	500–2,500	Sub–neighborhood
Vest pocket parks	*	2,500 sq. ft. to 1 acre	500–2,500	Sub–neighborhood
Neighborhood parks	2.5	Min. 5 acres up to 20 acres	2,000–10,000	¼–½ mile
District parks	2.5	20–100 acres	10,000–50,000	½–3 miles
Large urban parks	5.0	100+ acres	One for each 50,000	Within ½ hour driving time
Regional parks	20.0	250+ acres	Serves entire population in smaller communities; should be distributed throughout larger metro areas	Within 1 hour driving time
Special areas and facilities	*	Includes parkways, beaches, plazas, historical sites, flood plains, downtown malls, and small parks, tree lawns, etc. *No standard is applicable.*		

*Not applicable

By Percentage of Area

The National Recreation and Park Association recommends that a minimum of 25% of new towns, planned unit developments, and large subdivisions be devoted to park and recreation lands and open space.

ILLUSTRATION 5.12

Source: Robert D. Buechner, ed., *National Park, Recreation and Open Space Standards* (Washington, D.C.: NRPA, 1971).

[69]Ibid., p. 176.

STANDARDS FOR SPECIAL FACILITIES

The following standards are recommended for individual recreation facilities:

FACILITY (OUTDOOR)	STANDARD/1000 PEOPLE	COMMENT
Baseball diamonds	1 per 6,000	Regulation 90 ft.
Softball diamonds (and/or youth diamonds)	1 per 3,000	
Tennis courts	1 per 2,000	(Best in battery of 4)
Basketball courts	1 per 500	
Swimming pools—25 meter	1 per 10,000	Based on 15 sq. ft. of
Swimming pools—50 meter	1 per 20,000	water for each 3% of population
Skating rinks (artificial)	1 per 30,000	
Neighborhood centers	1 per 10,000	
Community centers	1 per 25,000	
Outdoor theaters (noncommercial)	1 per 20,000	
Shooting ranges	1 per 50,000	Complete complex including high power, small-bore, trap and skeet, field archery, etc.
Golf courses (18 hole)	1 per 25,000	

Note: All of the above mentioned facilities are desirable in small communities, even though their population may actually be less than the standard. Every effort should be made to light all facilities for night use, thus extending their utility.

ILLUSTRATION 5.13

Source: Robert D. Buechner, ed., *National Park, Recreation and Open Space Standards* (Washington, D.C.: NRPA, 1971).

to creating inappropriate recreational facilities for many inner-city populations.

In 1971 the National Recreation and Park Association published an updated list of open-space and facility standards, which developed from its 1969 Kansas City Forum mentioned earlier. Again the NRPA stressed the warning that standards "have all too often been represented as a maximum or ideal rather than minimum requirements. We well recognize that intrinsic values derived from open space are difficult to measure, but that moral, social, and physical deterioration may result from the absence of such guidelines."[70] With the permission of NRPA, four tables are reproduced from the *National Park, Recreation and Open Space Standards* report (Illustrations 5.12 through 5.15). In using these standards, NRPA emphasizes that these are for the *ultimate* population of a given service area, not the present population, and that these

[70]Buechner, *National Park, Recreation and Open Space Standards*, p. 4.

SPACE STANDARDS FOR NEIGHBORHOOD PARKS

Suggested space standards for various units within the park. The *minimum* size is 5 acres.

FACILITY OF UNIT	AREA IN ACRES	
	PARK ADJOINING SCHOOL	SEPARATE PARK
Play apparatus area—preschool	.25	.25
Play apparatus area—older children	.25	.25
Paved multi-purpose courts	.50	.50
Recreation center building	*	.25
Sports fields	*	5.00
Senior citizens' area	.50	.50
Quiet areas & outdoor classroom	1.00	1.00
Open or "free play" area	.50	.50
Family picnic area	1.00	1.00
Off-street parking	*	2.30**
Subtotal	4.00	11.55
Landscaping (buffer & special areas)	2.50	3.00
Undesignated space (10%)	.65	1.45
Total	7.15 acres	16.00 acres

*Provided by elementary school
**Based on 25 cars @ 400 sq. ft. per car

ILLUSTRATION   5.14

Source: Robert D. Buechner, ed., *National Park, Recreation and Open Space Standards* (Washington, D.C.: NRPA, 1971).

standards should be applied in concert with the planning guides, standards of methodology, and the classification of park and recreation areas contained in other sections of their report.

In addition to the special facilities listed in these four tables, the NRPA recommends the following facilities as also desirable for every community whenever feasible.

Aquariums	Casting pools
Arboretums	Coasting and tobogganing
Arenas and coliseums	areas
Beaches	Culture centers
Bike rights-of-way	Day camps
Boccie courts	Drag strips
Botanical gardens	Fishing piers
Bowling greens	Football fields
Campgrounds	Handball courts

SPACE STANDARDS FOR DISTRICT PARKS

Suggested space requirements for various units within the park. The *minimum* size is 20 acres.

	AREA IN ACRES	
FACILITY OF UNIT	PARK ADJOINING SCHOOL	SEPARATE PARK
Play apparatus area—preschool	.35	.35
Play apparatus—older children	.35	.35
Paved multi-purpose courts	1.25	1.75
Tennis complex	1.00	1.00
Recreation center building	*	1.00
Sports fields	1.00	10.00
Senior citizens' complex	1.90	1.90
Open or "free play" area	2.00	2.00
Archery range	.75	.75
Swimming pool	1.00	1.00
Outdoor theater	.50	.50
Ice rink (artificial)	1.00	1.00
Family picnic area	2.00	2.00
Outdoor classroom area	1.00	1.00
Golf practice hole	*	.75
Off-street parking	1.50	3.00 **
Subtotal	15.60	28.35
Landscaping (buffer & special areas)	3.00	6.00
Undesignated space (10%)	1.86	3.43
Total	20.46 acres	37.78 acres

*Provided by Junior or Senior High School
**Based on 330 cars @ 400 sq. ft. per car

ILLUSTRATION   5.15

Source: Robert D. Buechner, ed., *National Park, Recreation and Open Space Standards* (Washington, D.C.: NRPA, 1971).

Hiking and riding trails
Horseshoe courts
Ice curling rinks
Ice rinks, natural
Jogging paths
Lakes and water sports
Libraries

Marinas and boating centers
(for powered and nonpowered boats)
Miniature golf
Model airplane areas
Model boating ponds
Motorized vehicle areas

Museums	Spray pools
Natural areas	Stables
Nature centers	Stadiums
Nature trails	Surfaced play areas
Picnic areas	Teen centers
Running tracks	Volleyball courts
Scenic overlooks	Wading pools
Shuffleboard courts	Wildlife preserves
Ski centers	Zoological parks
Soccer fields	

In order to determine what standards were being used to acquire open space for recreation in urban areas, a mail inquiry was sent to a selected number of metropolitan areas. The following discussion includes the standards information which was obtained from this survey.

PHILADELPHIA, PENNSYLVANIA*

Space Standards for Playgrounds and Playfields

	Area in Acres	Population Served	Service Area
Playground—Type A	3–8	11,000– 12,000	¼ mile radius
Playground—Type B	4–8	11,000– 12,000	⅜ mile radius
Playground—Type C	6–8	11,000– 12,000	½ mile radius
Playfield	8–20	————	Serves 5 or 6 playground service areas

*Source: Philadelphia Master Plan, Department of Recreation, Tables 1 and 2, City of Philadelphia Master Plan, 1960.

Development

Intensively developed to accommodate maximum users on limited space Type A:

1. Apparatus areas for preschool and elementary school children.
2. Spray pool.

3. Hard-surfaced area for informal games: dodgeball, kickball.
4. Building for year-round activities with game and clubrooms, meeting rooms, restrooms, office and storage space.
5. Quiet recreation area, landscaped with benches.
6. Hard-surfaced area for a number of organized court games: basketball, volleyball, handball.
7. Turf area for softball.

Less intensively developed Type B: Same elements as in Type A play ground, but in different proportions. Fewer hard-surfaced areas for court games might be provided, but larger turf area.

Extensively developed Type C: Same elements as in Type B playground, with larger turf areas for baseball or football. Other facilities might be added according to space available and community interest:

1. Turf areas for softball, baseball, football.
2. Hard-surfaced areas for court games.
3. Park area for quiet recreation, with picnic area where feasible.
4. Recreation building containing auditorium, gym, swimming pool, kitchen, plus features of playground recreation building.
5. Ice and/or roller rink.
6. Automobile parking area.
7. Lighting for evening use.
8. May include playground.

Space Standards for Parks

Type	Area in Acres	Service Area
Local Park	1–5	$\frac{1}{4}$ to $\frac{1}{2}$ mile radius
District Park	20–100	Serves a major portion of the city
Regional Park	300–2,500	At least one regional park within 40 minutes' travel time of majority of homes in metropolitan region

Development

Landscaped with ornamental pool or fountain and/or other facilities as space allows.

Developed according to the characteristics of the area. Provisions should be included for outdoor sports and enjoyment of natural beauty.

Automobile parking.

May include playfield.

1. Facilities for swimming, boating, ball playing, golf, tennis, day camping, bicycling, hiking, picnicking, outdoor concerts.

220   OPEN SPACE, LAND DEVELOPMENT, AND FACILITY ANALYSIS

2. Automobile parking areas.
3. Cabin or tent camping area.

KANSAS CITY, MISSOURI*

The Mid America Regional Council (MARC), along with the
Kansas City Parks and Recreation Department, have adopted standard
nomenclature for park classification and standards for acreage-use relationship.

Type	Acres/1000 People	Size in Acres	Population Served	Service Area
Playground	1.5	0–4	2,500; 1.5 acres for each 1,000	One neighborhood
Neighborhood	2.0	5–14	7,000	One neighborhood
Sub-Community	2.5	15–49	20,000; 2.5 acres for each 1,000	Several neighborhoods
Community	5.0	50–99	70,000; 7 acres for each 1,000	Several neighborhoods
Metropolitan	7.0	100–499	_____	Several communities
Regional	12.0	500 up		Entire metro area
Linkages	____	_____	_____	Varied
Special Use Areas	____	_____	_____	_____

The MARC Public Park Standard of 30 acres per 1,000 people is
one of the highest ratios of acres per 1,000 population of the nation.
Kansas City Parks and Recreation does not feel it is responsible for providing regional parks. It endeavors to provide 18 acres per 1,000 population. This city now has a combined park-boulevard-parkway-greenway
average of about 16 acres per 1,000 population. The park portion is 12.46
acres per 1,000 people. While this is one of the largest existing park-
people ratios in the country, it does not accurately reflect the needs of
the people for neighborhood and sub-community facilities.

Kansas City residents have available to them within the Kansas City
corporate limits today 8,274 acres of parks, playgrounds, and parkways.
They also have available 9,721 acres of state and county parks in Clay
and Jackson Counties. If this plan is realized, by 1990 Parks and Recrea-

*Source: Kansas City, Missouri, Parks and Recreation Department, 1973.

tion will consist of 19,218 acres of parks, playgrounds, open space and parkways. And, if known plans for federal, state, and county projects in Clay and Jackson Counties (27,068 acres) are realized, a total of 56,008 acres of open space should be available. This amounts to 106 acres per 1,000 Kansas Citizens based on 1990 population projections.

Our objective of providing a recreational opportunity within a half mile of every resident can be achieved. High-density population concentrations can seriously affect the quality of the recreational experience if the 1½ acre per 1,000 population ratio is not maintained. We do not believe it is financially feasible or physically possible to arrange an adequate acreage-people ratio at this time in 43 of the 350 residential sections (existing and proposed) into which the city was divided for this study.

DALLAS, TEXAS*

Park Area and Service Standards

The following standards are proposed for the various categories of park areas required in a complete park system (Illustration 5.16).

The recommended standards of park area would provide a total of 20 acres of park and reservation land for each 1,000 persons in the urban area. The 20 acres would be apportioned as follows:

Playgrounds	1 to 2 acres per 1,000 persons
Playfields	1 to 2 acres per 1,000 persons
Large parks	5 acres per 1,000 persons
Special parks and parkways	2 acres per 1,000 persons
Total within urban development	10 acres per 1,000 persons
Reservations, preserves in outlying areas	10 acres per 1,000 persons
Total all park areas	20 acres per 1,000 persons

DETROIT, MICHIGAN†

Community Services Criteria

Major community Recreation Facilities should be provided in the form of component playfields of 10 to 15 acres located at all junior and senior high schools, and at other locations where the number of

*Source: Dallas, Texas, Department of City Planning and Department of Parks and Recreation, *Parks and Open Spaces: Dallas Metropolitan Area*, April 1959, pp. 57 and 62.
†Source: *Detroit Master Plan: 1972 Urban Areas Sections*, Amended July 1972 pp. 19–21.

TYPE OF PARK AREA	SIZE	RECOMMENDED AREA PER 1000 PERSONS	SERVICE AREA	LOCATION	USUAL FACILITIES & REMARKS
Playlot	Less than 1 acre	Special facility	Usually limited to single block or project.	High density neighborhood where usual private yards do not exist.	Paved areas, sitting area and play equipment for small children usually private responsibility.
Playground	6 acre minimum additional for parking & natural scenic areas desirable.	1 to 2 acres per 1000 persons depending upon shape & intensity of development.	Approximately ½ mile or a 1 sq. mi. neighborhood, same as elementary school.	Preferably adjoining the elementary school near center of neighborhood unit.	Softball & other games, play equipment, multiple-use paved areas, turf areas & planting, some rustic & passive areas desirable, minimum of automobile parking.
Playfield (includes athletic field)	10 to 25 acres. May be part of larger scenic area if location provides convenient service.	1 to 2 acres per 1000 persons with at least 1 acre active play area per 1000 people.	Approximately 1 mi. or 4 or 5 neighborhood units. Similar service area to high school.	At or near the intersection of major or secondary thoroughfares near center of 4 or 5 square mile service area.	Baseball, football, softball, tennis and other active athletic areas, possible field house community center & swimming pool. Some facilities may be lighted for night use, substantial automobile parking required, may include playground type area.
Large park	Minimum of 100 acres, preferably several hundred acres.	Approximately 5 acres per 1000 persons.	3 miles or more with good accessibility by auto.	Where appropriate sites can be obtained incorporating natural features, one area for each 50,000 to 100,000 persons desirable within urbanized area or on the periphery.	Active athletic areas similar to playfield but at least ½ area should be rustic & provide picnicking, hiking, archery, etc., golf courses, fishing, boating, & water sports may be included. Much off-street parking required, shelters, swimming pools & quiet passive areas desirable.
Parkways ornamental areas special parks	Size varies depending on conditions & nature of area.	Approximately 2 acres per 1000 persons.	No specific service areas as most facilities serve entire urban area.	Along waterways, as esthetic treatment for civic buildings, subdivision, etc. Zoos, botanical museums, & gardens. Exhibitions should be near center of urban area.	Largely scenic areas but may include picnicking & play facilities. Special parks may include golf courses, hobby centers, zoo, monuments, fairgrounds, & a variety of special functions.
Reservations & preserves	Several hundred to a thousand or more acres.	10 acres per 1000 persons. May include some close-in regional recreation areas.	Entire urban area.	Usually on fringe of urban development at appropriate sites.	Rustic & wild areas, camping, nature & hiking trails, bridle paths, bird sanctuary, boating, fishing, & similar uses not requiring intensive development.
Regional recreation areas	Several thousand acres.	No specific standard. May be partially included in area of reservations & preserves.	Entire region.	Within 1 to 3 hours driving time of urban center.	Lake, river or reservoir providing fishing, boating, water sports, picnicking, hunting, camping & similar facilities.

ILLUSTRATION 5.16

residents requires additional facilities. In addition, a series of small parks should be located along the Riverfront, south of and connected to the Model Neighborhood area by pedestrian paths and bicycle paths, to more fully capture the Riverfront's recreation potential.

Community Services Facility Standards

To increase the amount of local and community services to levels which will adequately serve the residents of the Model Neighborhood, facilities should be improved to the minimum standards indicated below:

Facilities	*Standards*
Recreation	
1. Elementary school playfield	2.7 acres
2. Junior high school playfield	7.8 acres
3. Senior high school playfield	10.0–15.0 acres
4. Component playfield	1.5 acres per 1,000 residents
	10–15 acres per facility
5. Playground	1.0 acre per 1,000 residents

*MINNEAPOLIS, MINNESOTA**

STANDARDS FOR RECREATION SHELTERS AND NEIGHBORHOOD AND COMMUNITY RECREATION CENTERS

Minneapolis has a population of approximately 450,000 to 500,000. In carrying out planning concepts on a citywide basis, the Minneapolis Planning Commission has created ten communities. These community units are large enough to provide for shopping and business districts, educational, recreational, and other types of land uses. These communities normally have a population of approximately 50,000 and are subdivided into neighborhood units, each the size of an elementary school district with a population of 6,000 to 12,000 people. These population figures vary and are influenced by such items as highways, rivers, railroads, and other types of physical and social barriers which affect the size and shapes of the communities. For purposes of park planning these basic concepts have been used to develop standards.

Purpose

In developing a comprehensive park and recreation system, a basic requirement is a decentralized system of recreation buildings designed to provide services for the land unit being planned. The building types include the recreation shelter and neighborhood and community recreation centers. The service function is devoted to two major purposes:

1. To provide a facility for conducting a year-round recreation program under leadership for the ages which the building is designed to serve.

*Source: City Plan of Minneapolis.

2. To provide facilities for neighborhood or community organizations to use on a self-directed basis. The park system exercises control only over the use of the building and does not participate in shaping policies of these organizations. Such groups include women's clubs, civic groups, religious organizations, political, philanthropic, service, and recreation groups—any and all types of organizations. The type of uses encouraged are meetings, banquets, lecturers, forums, card parties, scouting, bazaars, in short, uses to satisfy all forms of local needs.

Classification of Buildings

The size of building facilities will determine the quantity of use and frequency of occupancy. The aforementioned purposes are intended for all buildings; however, size will normally determine the recreation program be directed to the following age group:

Recreation Shelters: through 5th or 6th grade
Neighborhood Recreation Center: generally through junior high school age and adults
Community Recreation Center: all ages, i.e., preschool through adult.

Recreation Shelter

The recreation shelter is normally a facility which supplements the neighborhood recreation center and is constructed in a playground or neighborhood park. It usually is limited to seasonal operation with part-time recreation staff or building attendants. The building serves as a focal point for the seasonal programs of wintersports and in summer, spring, and fall to part-time leadership services such as supervised playgrounds, nurseries, after-school programs, etc.

Such a facility is available to community organizations to use also as outlined, but limited size makes the neighborhood or community recreation centers more attractive for such use. The shelter is designed to serve an area smaller than a neighborhood and generally is substantially less than 5,000 square feet in size. Facilities may include warming or meeting room, small kitchen, storage area, office, restrooms, and craft room.

Neighborhood Recreation Centers

The neighborhood recreation center is the basic recreation service facility in the neighborhood and is normally located in a neighborhood park. Its purpose is to serve the neighborhood in which it is located, 6,000 to 12,000 people. The residential service area is approximately the same as an elementary school and can be planned in conjunction with or apart from a school and/or a private agency. Staffing is normally intended to be year round, full-time.

The building is approximately 5,000 to 7,000 square feet in size depending upon neighborhood characteristics. Typical center facilities include one or two meeting rooms, office, and warming facilities. It is designed to avoid duplicating neighborhood facilities unless such are overtaxed, and conceptually the intent is to encourage use of existing neighborhood facilities.

Community Recreation Centers

The community recreation center is as centrally located as possible and serves as the focal point of a community.

It is designed to serve the total community, normally, 30,000 to 50,000 people, depending on such conditions as traffic barriers, railroads, rivers, lakes, and other features which may influence accessibility. As a general rule, a community recreation center should be available in each residential community of Minneapolis.

These centers provide a full complement of indoor facilities, and typically are located in a community park. The facilities may vary from building to building due to different community conditions.

The community center ranges in size from approximately 12,000 to 20,000 square feet, and normally includes an auditorium-gymnasium, multipurpose room, game room, arts and crafts room, kitchens, lounge, offices, meeting rooms, ice skating shelter, storage, and patio.

Community recreation centers are open on a year-round basis with full-time personnel.

General Comments

Planning for recreation shelters and neighborhood and community recreation centers will allow such facilities to be separate and autonomous park operations or a part of a coordinated plan of community facilities. Such determinations are dependent on indigenous factors appropriate to sound planning concepts rather than decisions based solely on popular modern techniques.

ESTIMATING DEMAND FOR RECREATION

In estimating the demand for recreation purposes, too many standards or guides use only precise predictions. For these standards or formulas to be realistic, they need to reflect other variables, such as space or the attitudes and interests of citizens. The following are examples of formulas that use a multivariate approach for estimating demand for parks and recreation.

SAN DIEGO, CALIFORNIA*

The day of the computer is here, and as a result, there is a strong movement to reduce as many managerial decisions as possible to mathematical models. Not that mathematical models have been entirely neglected in the past; our city has used several, two of which I will mention here. The relative priority of installation of traffic signals is always open to violent pressures of subjective judgment. In an effort to induce some

---

*This entire section is reproduced with permission from Joel D. Parks, former administrative assistant, Recreation Department, San Diego, California.

objectivity into this controversy, our city has devised a system of "warrants," which are values determined by the number of accidents at the designated intersection, volume of traffic flow, and other considerations. This system may not work perfectly, but it settles a lot of arguments.

Similarly, eligibility of elementary schools for professional city recreation staffing is determined by a system of "points" derived from factors dependent on the number of pupils in the school and population of the service area.

Priority in the acquisition and development of parks was, however, not covered by such a formula. We had standards for population-based parks, based on population of the service area and distance from other developed recreation areas, but selection of parks for acquisition and development was based on "seat of the pants" judgment, taking into account the established standards. This system worked moderately well, but there was no method of comparing the relative need of park service areas on a discrete basis.

About two years ago, our mayor, the Honorable Frank Curran, caught up in a crossfire of opposing views in selection of a park site, asked, "Why can't we devise a system similar to our warrant system in traffic, to settle these arguments?" The answer to this question was obvious, and we set to work to devise such a system.

The Development of the Need Index for Neighborhood Parks

To arrive at an index of need for a service area without a developed park, it is necessary to compare qualifications of the service area to those of a standard area. Standards for a neighborhood park developed by a Citizens' Advisory Committee in 1963, and accepted by the Council, include the following:

Population served: 3,500 to 5,000
Area served: Within a radius of ½ mile

(Community park and recreation centers also serve as the neighborhood parks for a ½ mile radius around the center.)

Thus, it can be seen that the need for a neighborhood park depends principally on population density and distance from a developed park or recreation area. Lot size has some bearing in comparing two areas of single-family dwellings. Moreover, to a large extent, population is a function of lot size. This does not eliminate lot size as an element in decision making in applicable cases, but does eliminate it in the general formula.

The first step in the development of a formula was the division of the city into park service areas. Ideally, these service areas for neighborhood parks would be roughly ½ mile in radius from the park site as a center, and include a population of from 3,500 to 5,000 people. In actual practice, due to geographical and highway barriers, the park service areas are irregular in shape and vary widely in population.

Illustration 5.17, an excerpt from our study plan, shows a number of our neighborhood park service areas.

If we assume that the need index will be composed of two elements, a population element and a distance element, then the most feasible method of combining these two elements is to compare each element

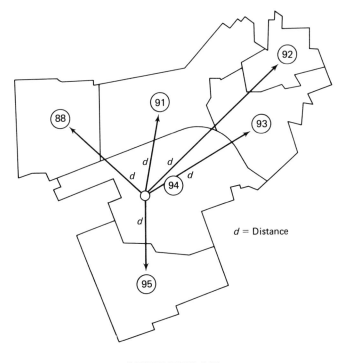

ILLUSTRATION 5.17

separately with a standard and add the two ratios. In other words, the need index is expressed as follows:

$$N = E_p + E_d$$

where N = need index
E_p = population element
E_d = distance element

Next, it is necessary to decide the weight to be given each element. We decided, on a basis of experience, that the population element should have roughly double the weight of the distance element. How we arrived at the element values is explained below.

In arriving at the population element of the formula for neighborhood parks, the population of the service area has been compared to the minimum population recommended by the Citizens' Advisory Committee for a neighborhood park, i.e., 3,500. This element then becomes $\dfrac{P}{3500}$, (where p = population of the service area) or the ratio of p to the minimum standard. It will readily be seen that for a park service area with a population of 3,500, the value of E_p is 1.000.

In arriving at the distance element of the formula, the airline distance from the center of the service area was measured to the nearest developed park. This distance was measured in feet on a large-scale map and reduced to miles, the answer carried to three decimal places.

In Illustration 5.17, if we assume that site 94 possesses a developed park available for use, and sites 88, 91, 92, 93, and 95 do not possess a developed park, then the distance (d) for each service area other than 94 is the distance from the center of each service area to the developed park at site 94.

If we use the same logic in arriving at the distance element as we used in arriving at the population element, and weight the value of the distance element by one-half:

> Given: Standard radius of service area = ½ mile
> Then: Standard distance between parks should be
>   ½ + ½ = 1 mile and E_d = ½ = ½ d

In actual practice, we used a formula which comes to the same answer when used for a standard distance, but which varies with the value of d in less than direct proportion. This formula is:

$$E_d = \frac{d - \frac{1}{2}}{d}$$

Note that when d = 1 mile (standard distance) under this formula:

$$E_d = \frac{1 - \frac{1}{2}}{1} = .5,$$

which is ½ the value of d in this case, as it is when we use the formula

$$E_d = \frac{1}{2}\frac{d}{1}.$$

But let d = 1.5 and

$$E_d = \frac{1.5 - .5}{1.5} = \frac{1}{1.5} = .666,$$

compared with a value of ½ d, equal to .750. This formula has the effect of dampening the variation of the distance element as d varies from the standard.

In support of this approach, it is assumed that a distance of ½ mile or less is within walking distance, and that access to a park from greater distances would require vehicular transportation. The inconvenience of using vehicular transportation increases with the distance traveled *but not in direct proportion*; that is, it is more inconvenient to drive two miles than one, but not twice as inconvenient.

Expressed algebraically, the formula becomes:

$$N = \left(\frac{p}{3500} + \frac{d - \frac{1}{2}}{d} \right) \times 1000$$

where N = need index
  p = population of the service area
  d = distance to a developed park or beach recreation area.

(The ratios are carried out to three decimal places and multiplied by 1000 to eliminate decimal fractions.)

The Development of the Need Index
in Community Park and Recreation Centers

The approved standards for a community park and recreation center include (in addition to the park) a community building and various indoor and outdoor recreation facilities to serve a community of 18,000 to 25,000 people within a radius of 1½ miles. Computing our raw need index in the same manner as for neighborhood parks,

$$N_1 = \left(\frac{p}{18,000} + \frac{d - 1\frac{1}{2}}{d} \right) \times 1000$$

where p = population of the service area
d = distance in miles from the nearest developed recreation center (standard distance is $1\frac{1}{2} + 1\frac{1}{2} = 3$ miles)
N_1 = raw need index

This raw need index, N_1, needs to be weighted for use by various segments of the public. Our experience has been that attendance at park and recreation centers is composed of approximately 68% youths (aged 18 and below) and 32% adults. Variations in youth population density in park and recreation center service areas spread from 18.3% to 50.7% of total population, with an average of 32.8%. Our object was to weight the raw need index (based on distance and total population) by a factor using the percentage of youth population in the service area as compared with the city average.

Given: Need index computed on distance and population for a service area = N_1
Youth attendance at recreation centers is 68% of total attendance.
Average youth population of city is 32.8%.
Let: Y = youth population in a service area (%)
N = adjusted need index for service area (adjusted for youth population)
Then: $\dfrac{Y}{32.8}$ = ratio of youth in service area to city average.

The simplest approach would be to adjust the raw need index in direct proportion to the youth ratio, thus:

$$N = \frac{Y}{32.8} \, N_1.$$

For our purposes, this appeared to weight the need index too heavily for the youth factor, and this approach was discarded.

Next we broke the raw need index down into adult and youth components:

$.68N_1$ = Youth component of N_1
$.32N_1$ = Adult component of N_1

And since:

Y = Youth population in the service area (%)
and

32.8 = Youth population of the city (%)

Then:

100 − Y = Adult population of service area (%)
and

67.2 = Adult population of city (%)

Adjusting the components of the raw need index proportionally, we have:

$$N = \left(\frac{100 - Y}{67.2}\right) .32N_1 + \left(\frac{Y}{32.8}\right) .68N_1$$

This is a pretty complicated formula, and is, in fact, more complicated than is necessary. In practice, we found that to obtain meaningful differentiations in need indices of the centers, it was necessary only to adjust the second term of the right side of the equation thus:

$$N = .32N_1 + \frac{Y}{32.8}(.68N_1).$$

Use of the Need Index in Determining Priority
of Projects in Partially Developed Areas

The need index has considerable potential use in this respect, particularly in park and recreation centers, which are ordinarily developed in increments. In order to use the need index in this respect, it is only necessary to *divide the index by the percentage of adequacy*. By comparing the site with a *standard* we can arrive at a uniform measure of adequacy. The Citizens' Advisory Committee recommended the following standard elements for park and recreation centers:

	Assigned Value
1. Playlot	5
2. Play apparatus	10
3. Multi-purpose courts	10
4. Sportsfield (4–7 acres)	10
5. Tennis courts (6)	5
6. Shuffleboard courts (5)	5
7. Pavilion	5
8. Picnic area (2–2½ acres)	10
9. Lawn area for passive recreation (2–4 acres)	5
10. Parking (½–1 acre)	5
11. Community center building	25
12. Landscaping (2–2½ acres)	5
Total	100

If we assign values as listed above to the standard requirements, we can arrive at 100 points of adequacy. (The weighting of the values might be subject to some correction; the values assumed here are only for purposes of discussion.)

Then a center 50% adequate would have an urgency factor (U) of $\dfrac{N}{.50}$ or 2.00 N. A center 90% adequate would have a factor of 1.11 N. A center only 10% adequate would have a factor of 10.00 N. For example, if we assume that Center A is 90% adequate and Center B is 75% adequate, and compute the need index (N) of the two centers:

Center A	$N = 2162$
Center B	$N = 1939$

For Center A, the urgency factor then becomes: $U = \dfrac{N}{.90} = 2402$

For Center B $\qquad\qquad\qquad\qquad\qquad\qquad\qquad U = \dfrac{N}{.75} = 2585$

This approach is deceptively simple. In actual application of this procedure, we found that so much subjective judgment entered into the computation of the percentage of adequacy as to destroy objectivity of the result. At the very start, subjectivity enters this picture in the assignment of values to the various elements of the standard. Then, in computing the percentage of adequacy of each element, quality (for example, comparison of a good lawn with a poor lawn) must be considered. Also, some doubt exists as to whether adequacy of, say, tennis courts is directly proportionate to the number of courts.

Obviously, the problem of computing an objective percentage of adequacy requires more study. It appears that the solution may be facilitated by more precise standards. To obtain an objective evaluation of adequacy, standards would have to be written with this problem in mind, and should be as precise and definitive as a contract specification.

A Caveat

In this, as in all formulas of this type, answers obtained must not produce too wide a variance from evaluations based on experience and judgment. The old "seat of the pants" values cannot lightly be discarded. They are like the "hunches" used in problem solving, which are intuitions based on experience. Similarly, in the application of scientific inventory control formulas, buyers' business judgments are sometimes more reliable than a mechanically computed economic order quantity "buy." *The task here is not to produce formulas that will result in revolutionary changes in values, but to more precisely define and compare existing values. Revolutionary changes in values have little chance of acceptance, whereas precise values which are not too far out of line with "judgment" values are generally accepted without opposition.*

Limitations of the Need Index

In dealing with such matters as park and recreation facilities which have such a personal impact on the public, it is impossible to reduce everything to a mathematical formula. The need index and its derivations can only be considered as *guides to decision making*. Other factors will be influential in making decisions in this area. I have mentioned lot size as one; others might include the ethnic composition of the service area, federal funds available for "disadvantaged" areas, and others. The need index formula does, however, provide a firm basis for comparison on the basic criteria.

In addition to the above limitations noted by Joel Parks, there is now the question of the validity of this or any other mathematical formulas used for the acquisition and development of park sites. Such a formula is based on experience, supplemented by judgment and intuition. While it is not my desire to negate these inputs, such a formula also requires a validity check to ensure its purposeful applicability for recreation and park needs.

Determining Recreation Needs

Maricopa County, Arizona[71]

Methods used to determine recreation needs for Maricopa County in 1980 are new and somewhat revolutionary. They are also extremely complex and difficult to explain. The following is an attempt to illustrate, in simple and concise terms, how the 1980 demand for one type of facility (picnicking) was predicted and how it was related to one regional park (McDowell). The identical procedure was used for twelve leading outdoor activities for all the regional and semi-regional parks.

1. Population distribution maps were made for 1960 and 1980. Data for 1958 (adjusted to 1960) and 1980 were adapted from the reports of the Advance Planning Task Force of the city of Phoenix and Maricopa County. The figures 664,000 for 1960 and 1,440,000 for 1980 were used consistently.

2. Regions of use were plotted. Points equidistant both in time and distance between the five proposed regional parks were located on a Maricopa County map. Time/distance lines, at 15-minute intervals, were plotted from McDowell Regional Park outward to a time/distance interval of one hour's driving time. The geographic area thus created was called the "region of use." Although not the only recreation "choice" factor, it was concrete and measurable.

3. Population socio-economic characteristics were correlated with density of population. The socio-economic characteristics of median age, median family income, median number of years of education, and

---

[71]Buechner, *National Park, Recreation and Open-Space Standards*, section on "Selected Standards Proposed by Other Agencies." "The standards presented in this section have been developed by the agencies indicated. Most were predicated on previous standards of the National Recreation and Park Association. They represent a range of geographical areas, both city and county systems, and reflect the variance in classification of parks and recommended standards. They should be useful for comparison purposes. All are based on the acres/population method." (p. 30.)

occupation were graphically plotted on maps of the Phoenix urban area to determine the dominant 1960 characteristics of three density groups: low (0—4.9 persons per acre), medium (5—19.9 persons per acre), and high (20 persons per acre up).

4. The 1980 population 12 years of age and over was computed according to low, medium, and high density. For the McDowell region of use the results were: low density, 39,420; medium density, 185,420; county rural, 16,790. (Throughout the report, county rural areas were equated as to socio-economic characteristics with high-density urban areas.) The total population for 1980 of 242,000 was not by itself significant.

5. The effect on participation rates of the socio-economic characteristics of each density group was derived from studies of the Outdoor Recreation Resources Review Commission (ORRRC). This was accomplished by a complicated computer analysis which "weighted" the effect on recreation participation of each of the four socio-economic characteristics of age, income, education, and occupation. The result was in the form of "percent participating" in each of the three density groups.

6. The "percent participating" figures for picnicking were then multiplied by the population in each McDowell density group, set forth in 4 above. The products of these three multiplications were then totaled to give the total number of participants in picnicking for the McDowell region of use in 1980. This total number was of persons 12 years of age and over—one of the limitations of the ORRRC studies. This figure was 130,000.

7. The number of user days per participant for a three-month peak period was multiplied by the number of participants. According to ORRRC, each participant will spend 3.8 days picnicking during a three-month peak period. Thus the total number of participants, 130,000, was multiplied by 3.8 to give 494,000 user days for a three-month peak period of picnicking.

8. The number of user days in a three-month peak was divided by 3 to give a one-month peak of 164,502.

9. From this figure a peak weekend day was derived, or 10,281. To arrive at this figure, 164,502 was multiplied by 25% to give total user days for a one-week peak. This result was again multiplied by 25% to give a peak weekend day, since 50% of the use during a week is on the weekend.

10. The number of users on a peak weekend day was reduced to the number of "picnicking units." The average size of a family (excluding those under 12) in the McDowell region of use was found to be 2.5 persons. Thus the users on a peak weekend day, 10,281, was divided by 2.5 to give the number of family units who need picnicking facilities—4,112.

11. The total amount of acres for picnicking was then calculated. Using the "standard" of ten family units per acre—or 1/10 acre per unit—it was calculated, by multiplying by 4,112, that 411.2 acres should be planned for picnicking for the McDowell region of use.

12. The number of picnicking facilities existing or planned in the

McDowell region of use was deducted from the number of facilities required to get the net number needed. An analysis of the McDowell region of use showed that no significant picnicking facilities existed or were planned. Therefore, the net need was the same as the gross need—411.2 acres.

13. Since it must be assumed that McDowell Regional Park will fulfill the outdoor recreation needs of the people living within the McDowell region of use, the facilities needed by the region of use are the same as those which must be provided in the regional park.

*Chicago, Illinois**

In a number of past urban park and recreation studies, priority of need has been expressed by a needs index system. Mathematical measures of various factors having a demonstrated or assumed relationship to recreation need are utilized. The numerical indices of these factors are summed, with some arbitrary weighting, to produce a single index number. This number alone usually forms the basis for decision making.

A serious weakness of this evaluation system involves the assignment weights to the various factors under consideration. Since the system relies on a single summary index number, only one of many possible combinations of weighting can be considered in the final evaluation. In a case where three factors are being considered, for example, seven possible combinations of rank-order weights (1, 2, and 3) could be utilized in calculating a summary index number. Each combination would result in a slightly different summary index number, but according to the usual needs index method, only one summary index number can be utilized. No matter how thoughtfully or how scientifically that one particular combination of weights is selected, the weighting could nearly always be challenged as being arbitrary.

Another weakness of the needs index method, as it has sometimes been applied in the past, is that the decision-maker must rely solely on numbers in utilizing and interpreting the results of the evaluation. There may be no clear way to reconcile conflicts between the index number and the subjective judgments of knowledgeable park planners and administrators.

Rank-Sensitivity Analysis

Rank-sensitivity analysis is an evaluation technique that utilizes needs index numbers, but avoids the problems of arbitrary weighting and offers the decision-maker the opportunity to inject a degree of subjective judgment under controlled circumstances. The technique has the desirable quality of providing a systematic basis for evaluating a variety of pertinent factors, given all possible combinations of relative weighting or ranking. The procedure for assigning priorities discussed here combines the needs index method with rank-sensitivity analysis, both to evaluate need in unserved areas and to assign priorities for acquisition activity. Rank-

*This section is taken from the Chicago Park District, *Planning Guidelines for Recreational Services and Facilities*, April 1970, pp. 9–16.

sensitivity analysis also is employed to evaluate alternative park sites and to designate the site best suited for acquisition.

When assigning priorities to areas of need, the rank-sensitive analysis technique provides a means whereby a number of factors having a demonstrated or assumed relationship to recreation need can be analyzed simultaneously. The analysis will determine the probability of each unserved area's having the greatest need for recreation facilities—or second greatest, third greatest, etc.—when each of the factors is in turn assigned highest importance. Separate calculations are performed for each factor. The unserved area that consistently ranks first would be assigned highest priority; second priority would go to the area that consistently ranks second, and so on.

The application of the rank-sensitivity technique for evaluating relative need entails the following activities:

The factors relating to the need for a particular type of park are identified, together with a statistical means for measuring their impact. Thus, if youth population, income, distance, and density are the factors to be given consideration for playgrounds, they would be stated as:

Factor	*Statistical Measure*
Youth population	Number of children aged 0 to 19
Income	Number of households with incomes under $3,000
Distance	Airline distance measured in feet from the center of the unserved area to the nearest park
Density	Number of persons per square mile

Index numbers are calculated for each factor, based on the numerical values of their statistical measures. The index numbers for each factor are derived by simply placing these numerical values along a range from 0 to 1. (This statistical process is known as normalization.) The index number 1.00 is assigned to either the highest or lowest numerical value, depending on whether the factor has a positive or negative relationship to recreation need. In a case where four unserved areas are under consideration, and the size of the youth population is assumed to have a positive effect on recreation need, index numbers for the youth factor would be calculated in the following manner:

Numerical Value (number of children aged 0 to 19)		*Index Number*
Area I:	10,000	1.00
Area II:	7,500	0.75
Area III:	5,500	0.55
Area IV:	3,700	0.37

Each factor is weighted most important. A distinguishing feature of rank-sensitivity analysis is the capability of making an objective evaluation without arbitrary weighting. This is accomplished simply by giving each factor the opportunity of being weighted most important, with a random combination of weights assigned to the other factors. In the playground example cited before, when the youth factor is given first importance, a possible combination of weights for the other three factors would be:

Factor	Possible Combinations of Weights		
Youth	First	First	First
Income	Second	Third	Fourth
Distance	Third	Fourth	Second
Density	Fourth	Second	Third

Similar random combinations of weights are developed when income, distance, and density are assigned first importance. In addition, a complete random combination of weights can be considered. The rank-sensitivity analysis technique therefore is actually a series of separate analyses—analysis when income is weighted most important, and so forth, for each factor under consideration.

For each separate analysis, each index number is multiplied by its weight and the weighted index numbers are summed. The highest weight is set equal to the total number of factors being considered. If four factors are being considered, the multiplication would be:

		Multiplication	
Factor	Weight	Area I	Area II
Youth	First	Index No. × 4	Index No. × 4
Income	Second	Index No. × 3	Index No. × 3
Distance	Third	Index No. × 2	Index No. × 2
Density	Fourth	Index No. × 1	Index No. × 1
		Summation	Summation

Second, third, and fourth weights are assigned randomly. The summations for each unserved area are compared, and the area with the highest total is considered to have the greatest need, given that particular combination of weights. These calculations for each factor are then repeated many times to assure a complete random distribution of weights to the other factors. After all calculations are completed, the percentage of the time that each area totals highest, second highest, etc., represents the probability of that area's having the greatest need, second greatest need etc., when one particular factor is given the heaviest weight.

Because of the many individual calculations that are required, the only practical means of doing the analysis is with the aid of a computer. In an actual application, when six factors were considered, anywhere from 1,000 to 2,000 iterations or sets of calculations were completed for each factor. This meant that between 6,000 and 12,000 sets of calculations were required for the analysis.

The results of the analysis are expressed in a probability matrix for each factor considered. In the playground example, the probability matrix for the youth factor might resemble this:

	Greatest Need	Second Greatest Need	Third Greatest Need	Fourth Greatest Need
Area I	73.7%	23.5%	2.2%	0.6%
Area II	0.2	3.8	10.9	70.9
Area III	0.9	5.2	81.6	13.2
Area IV	26.1	67.7	4.4	1.6

In this example, unserved Area I would have the greatest need for recreation facilities 73.7 percent of the time when youth is considered most important. Area IV would have the greatest need 26.1 percent of the time. A similar matrix would be produced for each factor.

A choice is made based on the probability matrices. When the rank-sensitivity analysis technique is used, one or two areas almost invariably rank consistently high—as Area I did above—no matter which factor is assigned the greatest importance. If the probability of one area is always high, the decision-maker has a strong basis for justifying a selection. If two or more areas rank high, he knows that these areas are almost equally in need of improved recreation facilities. At this point, the decision-maker can inject some subjective judgment and consider other factors such as public reaction, administrative problems, probable delays, and so forth. In the case where two or more areas rank high, the probability matrix for a random assignment of weights among factors can be consulted for further guidance. This matrix, essentially the same as an average of the other probability matrices, will provide a summary comparison of all recreation need factors.

In the playground example, a partial summary of the four probability matrices may resemble this:

	Area Exhibiting Greatest Need			
Factor Assigned Greatest Importance	Area I	Area II	Area III	Area IV
Youth	73.7%	0.2%	0.0%	26.1%
Income	73.7	0.0	0.0	26.3
Distance	52.0	0.0	0.0	48.0
Density	73.7	0.2	0.0	26.1

In this case, unserved Area I would receive highest priority; Area IV would receive second priority, and Areas II and III would receive least priority.

Los Angeles, California

In Los Angeles, a "recreation needs instrument" was designed for a "Study of Recreation Needs and Services—South Central Los Angeles" following the 1965 Watts riots.[72] The analysis and instrument discussed here were used only for the City Department of Recreation and Parks and did not include any other city or county regional resources. The instrument was developed to determine the comparative priority of the need for recreation and youth services in an urban setting.

The assumptions underlying the instrument are that: (1) there are measurable social characteristics and neighborhood recreation resources which indicate comparative need for recreation and youth services by areas, communities, or neighborhoods in an urban setting; (2) all citizens have basic needs for recreation services, but because of different socio-economic characteristics and interests, they have different needs for recreation services; (3) priorities in community-subsidized recreation services should be for those with maximum social presssures from population density, number of youth, low income, and signs of social disorganization.[73]

As a complement to the needs index, it was necessary to compile a neighborhood recreation "resources index," which included full- and part-time professional staff hours per 1,000 population per year in a neighborhood; acreage of neighborhood recreation centers per 1,000 population, and the number of recreation centers per 10,000 population. Additional items, such as other institutions and agencies, or developed indoor and outdoor space, might be included if such resources would be used for recreation.

The recreation needs index uses four basic factors which reflect social as well as recreation needs: (1) youth population (5–19 years), (2) population density, (3) median family income, and (4) juvenile delinquency rate. By contrasting the resources and need indices, a comparative priority of need was determined, as shown in Illustration 5.18.

To make such a comparison between indices, the raw scores for each component are rank-ordered and converted to C-Scores. "Needs" and "resources" are then compared area by area to see where the greatest gaps or priority exist. The C-Scale relates a group of unrelated quantitative raw scores or measurements to comparable scales, which can be added, divided, or subtracted.

For instance, merely knowing that a community has 0.84 acres per 1,000 inhabitants does not indicate whether this ratio is good, poor, or average. By assigning each of the measurements a corresponding position in the C-Scale, one achieves this relation. The C-Scale ranges from 0 to 100 points in intervals of 10, the median at 50. Thus, if 0.84 acres per

[72]Reported in Edwin J. Staley, "Determining Neighborhood Recreation Priorities: An Instrument," *Journal of Leisure Research*, I, 1 (Winter 1969), 69–74.

[73]Ibid., p. 69.

AN INSTRUMENT FOR DETERMINING COMPARATIVE PRIORITY OF NEED FOR NEIGHBORHOOD RECREATION SERVICES

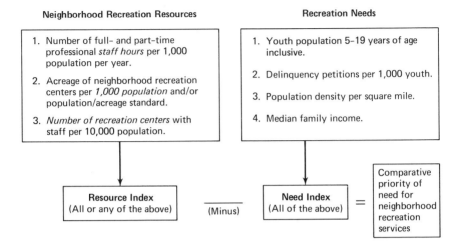

Neighborhood Recreation Resources

1. Number of full- and part-time professional *staff hours* per 1,000 population per year.
2. Acreage of neighborhood recreation centers per *1,000 population* and/or population/acreage standard.
3. *Number of recreation centers* with staff per 10,000 population.

Recreation Needs

1. Youth population 5-19 years of age inclusive.
2. Delinquency petitions per 1,000 youth.
3. Population density per square mile.
4. Median family income.

Resource Index (All or any of the above) ___(Minus)___ Need Index (All of the above) = Comparative priority of need for neighborhood recreation services

ILLUSTRATION 5.18

Source: Edwin J. Staley, "Social Dimensions of Recreation Demand," unpublished paper, p. 2, Anaheim, Calif.

1,000 inhabitants is assigned the C-Score 60, this particular community ranks slightly above average for the communities under study.

Two limitations of the C-Scale are that the results are quantitative, and the scores are rank positions and do not represent equal units of individual differences. Also, slight errors in the data are neutralized because of the relatively large intervals of 10 on the scale.

> Generally, the C-Scale has proved to be quite valid as a descriptive and comparative tool.... It would be best to keep these data current by revising them every year or two. It would be still better to develop a program for the city's data processing equipment by which data can be kept current! This would enable the department to determine at any time its current priorities of need for neighborhood recreation services, and make the necessary planning, budgeting, and administrative adjustments necessary.[74]

Computer Mapping of Recreation Facilities[75]

In 1966 the Parks and Recreation Department of the city of Dallas was faced with a need for additional recreational facilities. A basic

[74]Ibid., p. 79.

[75]This section is based on Louis Hodges and Carlton S. Van Doren, "Synagraphic Mapping as a Tool in Locating and Evaluating the Spatial Distribution of Municipal Recreation Facilities," *Journal of Leisure Research*, IV, 4 (Fall 1972), 341–53.

decision to be made was where to locate these new facilities. The department conducted a survey of users of existing centers. From these data a sample of every tenth address was plotted by a symbol representing each recreation center on a large 23′ x 23′ street map of the city.

This dot map illustrated the use patterns of municipal recreation centers and the distance each user traveled to a city recreation program. Along with other variables—population growth, socio-economic characteristics, age distribution, traffic flow, school locations, comprehensive plans, land availability, and the judgment of the department staff—this map was the basis for the spatial analysis used to locate new centers. The map took about 480 man-hours to complete by the Dallas staff. The Department of Recreation and Parks at Texas A & M University, utilizing synagraphic mapping, estimated that the original map could have been developed in half the time and expense.[76]

Synagraphic mapping is a character-printed map which uses the ordinary computer line printer. Three types of maps can be produced: (1) contour or isoline; (2) conformant (based on conformance to zone boundaries); and (3) proximal (based on nearness to a data point). The most time-consuming aspect is outlining the coordinates of the area. Features such as interstate highways (letter I), rivers (R), airports (A), parks (P), lakes (L), and political boundaries (*) may also be indicated on the outline. Visitation data were recorded by census tracts, with each tract denoting a data point on the computer map.

A composite contour map slotting all 13 of Dallas's recreation centers is shown in Illustration 5.19. Three centers—Harry Stone, Jaycee, and North Hampton—have high use (6,000 to 9,500 visitors from a census tract during a one-week period). Two of these centers, Harry Stone and Jaycee, have a large service radius, attracting 90 percent of their visitors from a zone of 5.0 miles, while North Hampton's radius is only 1.5 miles. Additional centers can be located at or near peaks of visitation such as Beckley-Saner in the south, and Oakcliff, Exline, and Pleasant Oaks in the southeast, whose centers have visitor concentrations of 3,000 to 6,000 per census tract. The proposed six new recreation centers are also shown in Illustration 5.19: Redbird, Cummings, Fireside, Opportunity, Skyline, and Fretz.

Illustration 5.20 shows the proximal SYMAP which supports the spatial logic used in locating the new centers. On the proximal map, each location is assigned the value of the data point nearest it. Since all the Dallas data were aggregated by census tract, the shaded areas of Illustration 5.20 approximate the census tract outlines and indicate total population by tract. The six new centers, for the most part, are located near a tract with above-average population.

Since transportation to recreation centers may be a barrier for some

[76]The basic SYMAP program can be purchased from the Harvard University Laboratory for Computer Graphics. The program was originally written in 1963 by Howard T. Fisher, Northwestern University.

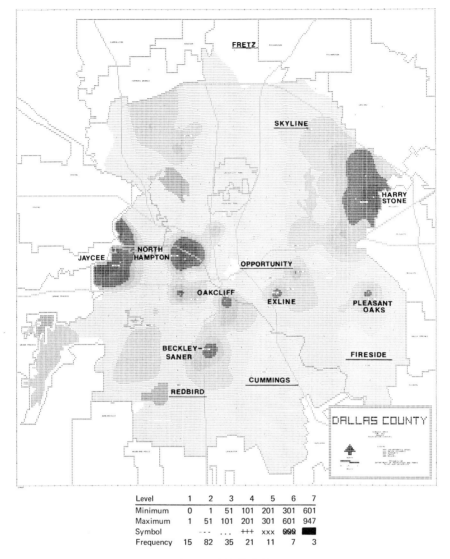

Level	1	2	3	4	5	6	7
Minimum	0	1	51	101	201	301	601
Maximum	1	51	101	201	301	601	947
Symbol		- -	...	+++	xxx	ɑɑɑ	■■■
Frequency	15	82	35	21	11	7	3

ILLUSTRATION 5.19

Service Areas for All Dallas Recreation Centers

Source: Louis Hodges and Carlton S. Van Doren, "Synagraphic Mapping As a Tool in Locating and Evaluating the Spatial Distribution of Municipal Recreation Facilities," *Journal of Leisure Research*, IV, 4 (Fall 1972), p. 348.

users, a map of potential mobility was also constructed (see Illustration 5.21). This map is based on an index constructed from the percentage of automobile ownership by census tracts, with the darker area indicating tracts with few automobiles.

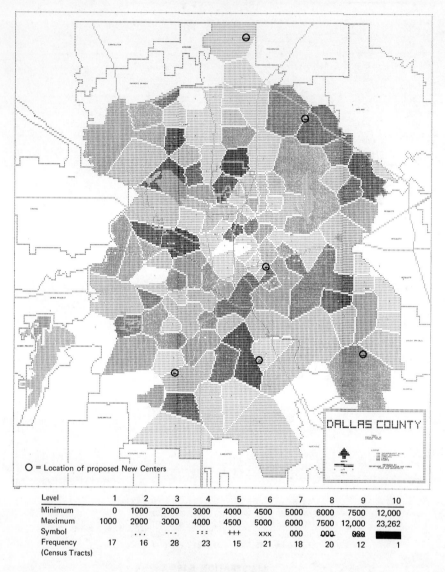

O = Location of proposed New Centers

Level	1	2	3	4	5	6	7	8	9	10
Minimum	0	1000	2000	3000	4000	4500	5000	6000	7500	12,000
Maximum	1000	2000	3000	4000	4500	5000	6000	7500	12,000	23,262
Symbol		. . .	- - -	:::	+++	xxx	000	000	000	▇
Frequency (Census Tracts)	17	16	28	23	15	21	18	20	12	1

ILLUSTRATION 5.20

Population by Census Tract

Source: Louis Hodges and Carlton S. Van Doren, "Synagraphic Mapping As a Tool in Locating and Evaluating the Spatial Distribution of Municipal Recreation Facilities," *Journal of Leisure Research*, IV, 4 (Fall 1972), p. 349.

In Dallas, these maps were analyzed using specific criteria of priority; the criteria for a new recreation center were as follows:

• *High Priority:* An area with a relatively large population and a high

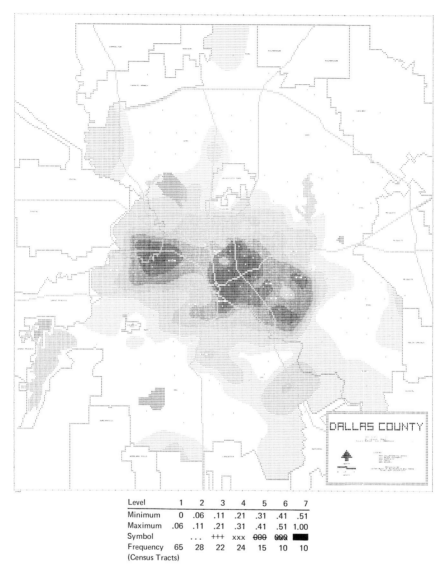

Level	1	2	3	4	5	6	7
Minimum	0	.06	.11	.21	.31	.41	.51
Maximum	.06	.11	.21	.31	.41	.51	1.00
Symbol		...	+++	xxx	000	000	■■■
Frequency (Census Tracts)	65	28	22	24	15	10	10

ILLUSTRATION 5.21

Mobility-Immobility Index

Source: Louis Hodges and Carlton S. Van Doren, "Synagraphic Mapping As a Tool in Locating and Evaluating the Spatial Distribution of Municipal Recreation Facilities," *Journal of Leisure Research*, IV, 4 (Fall 1972), p. 349.

percentage of school-age children located at a distance of three miles or more from an existing center. Other factors included the relative mobility of the population, trends (apparent or inferred) in population expansion and movement, and existing visitation patterns.

- *Intermediate Priority:* An area with intermediate population and an intermediate percentage of school-age children located at a distance of less than three miles from the nearest existing center. Again, mobility and population trends were considered.
- *Low priority:* An area with low population, a low to intermediate level of school-age children, and/or located fairly close to another recreation center (within one to two miles). Low mobility and anticipated population changes were also considered.[77]

Although the SYMAP technique is less expensive and time-consuming compared with other methods, it does have some drawbacks. For example, two maps were produced from the same data—contour and proximal. The proximal map is obviously better for identifying census tracts, particularly those with no visitation. The contour map is more reflective of the situation, although certain data were hidden. If extreme detail is required the major drawback is the loss of such detail because of "the interpolation necessary between data levels, especially when non-continuous or discrete data are mapped. In some cases, this drawback may also be the feature that makes such maps most useful."[78]

Park and Recreation Information System (PARIS)[79]

Several variables are needed to obtain sound estimates of the demand for recreation: the number of people in each county; the socio-economic characteristics of each county's population; the per capita demand in "participation days" for each recreation activity stimulated by each socio-economic group; the distribution of demand for each recreation activity by travel time zones from the metropolitan areas; the seasonal distribution of participation in each recreation activity; the distribution of daily demand for each activity within its peak season; and the average group size expected to use a recreation facility. Illustration 5.22 depicts such a demand subsystem used in California. This subsystem estimates the total potential demand for each recreation activity, allocates the total potential demand for each activity among the travel time zones of each metropolitan area, determines the peak period demands within each zone, and estimates the facilities needed to meet such demands.

The method used in PARIS is based on a hypothesis that people have certain needs or desires for outdoor recreation, regardless of the supply, and that a choice exists in the selection of leisure activities. These needs can be translated into a potential demand for specific recreation, either active or passive.

[77]Hodges and Van Doren, "Synagraphic Mapping," p. 352.
[78]Ibid.
[79]This section draws on material from *PARIS: Park and Recreation Information System; Supply-Demand Analysis for California Outdoor Recreation Facilities* (State of California, Department of Parks and Recreation, November 1966).

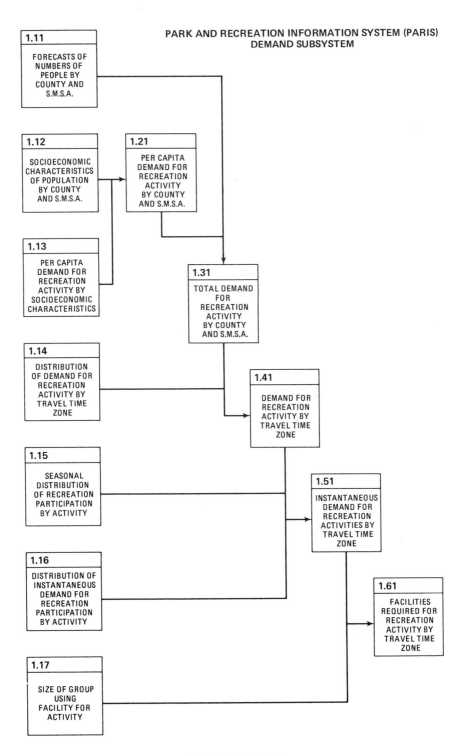

PARK AND RECREATION INFORMATION SYSTEM (PARIS)
DEMAND SUBSYSTEM

1.11
FORECASTS OF NUMBERS OF PEOPLE BY COUNTY AND S.M.S.A.

1.12
SOCIOECONOMIC CHARACTERISTICS OF POPULATION BY COUNTY AND S.M.S.A.

1.21
PER CAPITA DEMAND FOR RECREATION ACTIVITY BY COUNTY AND S.M.S.A.

1.13
PER CAPITA DEMAND FOR RECREATION ACTIVITY BY SOCIOECONOMIC CHARACTERISTICS

1.31
TOTAL DEMAND FOR RECREATION ACTIVITY BY COUNTY AND S.M.S.A.

1.14
DISTRIBUTION OF DEMAND FOR RECREATION ACTIVITY BY TRAVEL TIME ZONE

1.41
DEMAND FOR RECREATION ACTIVITY BY TRAVEL TIME ZONE

1.15
SEASONAL DISTRIBUTION OF RECREATION PARTICIPATION BY ACTIVITY

1.51
INSTANTANEOUS DEMAND FOR RECREATION ACTIVITIES BY TRAVEL TIME ZONE

1.16
DISTRIBUTION OF INSTANTANEOUS DEMAND FOR RECREATION PARTICIPATION BY ACTIVITY

1.61
FACILITIES REQUIRED FOR RECREATION ACTIVITY BY TRAVEL TIME ZONE

1.17
SIZE OF GROUP USING FACILITY FOR ACTIVITY

ILLUSTRATION 5.22

Source: PARIS: *Park and Recreation Information System; Supply-Demand Analysis for California Outdoor Recreation Facilities* (State of California, Department of Parks and Recreation, November, 1966), p. 135.

Potential demand in this system is measured in "participation days," the days or portions of days when a participant engages in a specific activity. It has been shown that type, intensity, location, and other characteristics of participation are related to the socio-economic characteristics of the participants. Illustration 5.23 shows the relationship of various socio-economic characteristics to recreation participation.

PARIS uses the *National Recreation Survey* data for the Western states to estimate average annual, per capita participation in various recreation activities for each of the Standard Metropolitan Statistical Areas (SMSA's).[80] These estimates are an average of the per-capita participation days of each socio-economic group, weighted by the number of people in each group in the SMSA.[81] The total demand is estimated by multiplying the number of residents in the county or SMSA by the average per capita demand.

To gain a *geographical distribution* of recreation demand, PARIS allots the total potential demand for each activity, measured in participation days, to each of the travel time zones. This allocation is based on observed travel patterns of recreationists. The relationship between travel time and participation is estimated as follows:

One-Way Travel Time in Hours	Percent Total Participation
0 to 1	40.7
1 to 2	14.2
2 to 3	8.1
3 to 4	5.5
4 to 5	4.2
5 to 6	3.4
More than 6	4.1
Subtotal	80.2
To out-of-state recreation areas	19.8
Total	100.0

The geographic distribution for camping participation was determined by analysis of data from the Bureau of the Census and various department records, which showed the following relationship between the percentage of camping participation and the amount of one-way travel time:

[80]U.S. Bureau of the Census, Outdoor Recreation Resources Review Commission, *National Recreation Survey, ORRRC Study Report 19*, 1962.

[81]Systematic and regularized projections of socio-economic characteristics are essential for PARIS or other state planning programs.

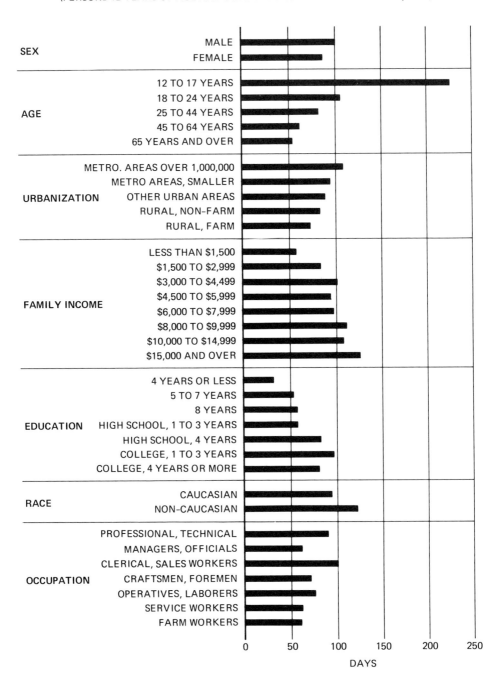

ANNUAL PER CAPITA PARTICIPATION DAYS IN OUTDOOR RECREATION
(PERSONS 12 YEARS OF AGE AND OLDER IN WESTERN UNITED STATES, 1960)

ILLUSTRATION 5.23

Source: Stanford Research Institute, based on data obtained from the Outdoor Recreation Resources Review Commission.

Travel Time Zones in Hours	Percent Camping Participation
0 to 1	11.6
1 to 2	27.5
2 to 4	30.8
More than 4	14.1
Subtotal	84.0
To out-of-state recreation areas	16.0
Total	100.0

In PARIS, a metropolitan area's total potential demand for each activity is multiplied by the percentage of demand expected within a travel time zone to estimate the potential demand within the travel zone. To estimate the peak demand at any one time, demand in each travel time zone is multiplied by the percent of total participation in recreation activities during the summer months and then by the percent of total peak season use.

To determine the number of facilities needed at any one time, it is necessary to know what percentage of the total demand occurs on peak days. Some attendance records of selected recreation areas throughout California were examined. The use patterns for day use and overnight activities are shown in Illustrations 5.24 and 5.25.

Assuming that the turnover rate in the use of these facilities is two to two and one-half times per day, *it is reasonable that the provision of facilities to accommodate one percent of the total summer demand for a day-use activity at any one moment* will result in satisfying 2 to 2.5 percent of the total summer demand on any one day with overcrowded conditions on only about three to eight days per summer... providing camping facilities for one percent of the total summer demand for camping will result in overcrowding about 50 out of 92 summer days. Each additional development of facilities to accommodate an additional .01 percent of total summer camping demand will reduce the number of overcrowded days by about three days. Therefore, *a reasonable first objective from the standpoint of economics is to provide camping facilities to satisfy 1.5 percent of the total summer camping demand on any one night which will result in about nineteen overcrowded days.* In both cases, daily use is expressed as a percentage of the total summer demand. Better data could be obtained by making the same type of analysis for each individual recreational activity.

The number of facilities needed for each recreation activity within a travel time zone is determined by dividing the total demand for that activity by the average size of the group using one facility. The use standards used in the PARIS calculations are based on accepted standards

DISTRIBUTION OF DAILY RECREATION USE

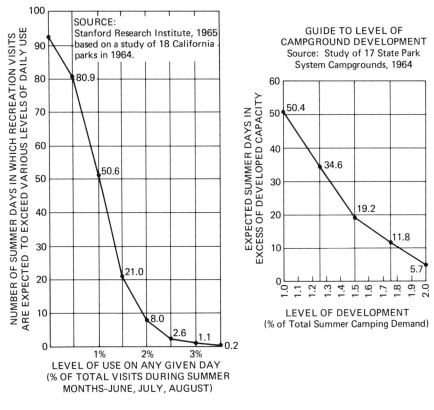

SOURCE:
Stanford Research Institute, 1965 based on a study of 18 California parks in 1964.

NUMBER OF SUMMER DAYS IN WHICH RECREATION VISITS ARE EXPECTED TO EXCEED VARIOUS LEVELS OF DAILY USE

80.9
50.6
21.0
8.0
2.6
1.1
0.2

LEVEL OF USE ON ANY GIVEN DAY
(% OF TOTAL VISITS DURING SUMMER MONTHS–JUNE, JULY, AUGUST)

ILLUSTRATION 5.24

GUIDE TO LEVEL OF CAMPGROUND DEVELOPMENT
Source: Study of 17 State Park System Campgrounds, 1964

EXPECTED SUMMER DAYS IN EXCESS OF DEVELOPED CAPACITY

50.4
34.6
19.2
11.8
5.7

LEVEL OF DEVELOPMENT
(% of Total Summer Camping Demand)

ILLUSTRATION 5.25

and analysis of on-site visitor interviews, as summarized in Illustration 5.26.

LEISURE INFORMATION RETRIEVAL SYSTEM

A project in Seattle, Washington, was undertaken to develop a system for "identifying, gathering, storing, and retrieving recreation program and facility data on a city-wide basis. . . ."[82] The need to prepare and maintain an inventory of leisure services is important not only at the local level, but at the state and federal levels, including public and private agencies, as well. A comprehensive leisure services inventory is

[82]*Leisure Information Retrieval System City-Wide Recreation Project.* Prepared for the Seattle Model City Program and the Seattle Department of Parks and Recreation (Seattle, Wash.: Leisure Services, Inc., 1972).

USE STANDARDS FOR SELECTED RECREATION FACILITIES

ACTIVITIES	AVERAGE OR STANDARD SIZE OF GROUP
Picnicking	4 persons per table
Horseback riding	20 persons per mile of riding trail
Swimming	.05 persons per square foot of swimming pool or 580 persons per acre of bathing beach
Water–skiing	4 persons per boat (1 boat per acre of water surface)
Sailing and canoeing	9.72 persons per boat access parking space[a]
Other boating	4.21 persons per slip or mooring[a]
Hiking	40 persons per mile of riding and hiking trail
Camping	4 persons per camping unit

[a] These figures used for computational purposes only since not every boater requires these facilities. Figures derived from data in *California Small Craft Harbors and Facilities Plan*, March, 1964.

ILLUSTRATION 5.26

Source: PARIS: *Park and Recreation Information System*; *Supply-Demand Analysis for California Outdoor Recreation Facilities* (State of California, Department of Parks and Recreation, November 1966), p. 23.

the *desideratum* and optional outcome of comprehensive planning in recreation and parks. As we move potentially toward a 24-hour culture, with a demand for leisure and other social services rapidly expanding, a comprehensive tally of facilities and programs of value for leisure activities seems not only logical but imperative.

We often forget that planning presupposes a recognition of the value of foresight. This is not to wave the doomsday flag at nonplanners, but rather to stress the illogicality of ignoring, for example, the value of sharing complementary facilities with schools and other agencies for recreation purposes. If we plan well now, we can enjoy the rewards of such foresight later. There is nothing onerous or even socialistic about an overall evaluation of the programs, facilities, and plans for leisure activities in the private and public agencies of a community. There is an understandable prejudice against master plans: too many of these are more impressive in concept than in action. Nonetheless, the Seattle approach offers a keen possibility of undertaking a rather straightforward, yet comprehensive, quantitative assessment of the recreational and cultural resources of U.S. cities. Such an assessment is a necessary prelude to the channeling and coordinating of these resources.

With the assumption that other cities in the United States might have developed a leisure resources retrieval system, the first phase of the Seattle project was to survey other cities with populations of 250,000 or more, to determine their involvement in such an activity. Of the replies to this mail-questionnaire survey, 84 percent indicated they had no such system, while only eight cities indicated that they did have; these eight, however, were quite different from the system proposed for Seattle.

Michigan has a system which offers consultation to all public, commercial, private, or volunteer agencies that seek help in developing, operating, or promoting leisure services. This consultation includes aid in program and facility development, staff training, and program promotion.

New York was the only city at the time of this survey in July 1972 with a computerized inventory system, but it included data on facilities only. New York does not provide computerized information about available activities or programs, but has a summer telephone service with information on all programs in the city's parks instead. New York indicated this information service handled between 800 and 1,200 calls a day, but noted that "the need for a more elaborate system which would include all public and privately sponsored programs, is apparent."[83] Their program information basically reflects city-sponsored or scheduled programs, and does not include private, voluntary, or commercial programs.

Rochester [New York] in its system tries to coordinate all federal and state funds for the city. For instance, all applications for grants are reviewed by their Office of Planned Variations before being sent to funding agencies. Through a review of the parks and recreation applications, the Office of Planned Variations coordinates the activities of various municipal departments. However, their system needs to include all leisure activities and be offered as a public service.

Indianapolis uses a "notebook directory" system drawn from an annual questionnaire sent to public, private, and voluntary agencies, which is supplemented by personal contact by a community services council. However, the Indianapolis Park and Recreation Department says that these data will be soon computerized for program planning and coodination. The system in Monroe County [New York], which has existed since 1949, is used more for in-department planning and evaluation. St. Louis County and Sacramento use their systems for planning, evaluating, and coordinating, but seem to use more variables for describing the programs tallied and the client and groups served.

Three of these last four systems used a questionnaire to obtain program information, whereas two used brochure analysis. All four stressed that ongoing personal contact with other agencies in their area was of great importance. Three of them systematically update their data annually to supplement ongoing information which is being collected. These four systems were all financed by departmental funds and did not charge users. All systems are manually filed, in notebook directories or

83Ibid., p. 16.

standard files, but none of them was evaluating program quality. All of the systems are located in a park and recreation office or center, and three of the four systems use personal contacts for obtaining data.

However, when asked about satisfaction with their particular system, three of the four indicated that they were *not* satisfied, while the fourth did not respond. The reasons given for dissatisfaction were:

1. System is not as complete and finished a product as we would like.
2. System is not a full-time operation. Program is picked up by existing staff who are currently overloaded with other duties.
3. System needs continual revision and must find better system of matching available programs and facilities to client needs.
4. The time element/availability of personnel to retrieve, research, and gather material is insufficient.[84]

TRENDS IN INTERGOVERNMENTAL RELATIONS

In recent years, intergovernmental relations at the local, state, and national levels have captured the attention of many political scientists and practitioners. This interest developed as a result of various social, economic, and technological changes—urbanization, personal mobility, affluence, as well as the growth in governmental functions. Developments in governance have long since eliminated the possibility of any level of government operating independently from other levels for any length of time.

Intergovernmental cooperation—that is, two or more units voluntarily working together for a public goal—can involve a variety of procedures and methods, including establishing a joint agency to perform a service, constructing a joint public facility, contracting by one unit for a service provided by another, coordinating the activities of two or more governmental units for a mutual objective, and similar arrangements. It may be horizontal cooperation involving only local governments, say, among various cities; or it may be vertical cooperation among various levels of government, such as counties and a state. Cooperative arrangements vary from the simple exchange of ideas and information to creation of a complex organization to provide a public service.

There are three essential criteria for intergovernmental cooperation:

1. It must be voluntary. A truly cooperative program cannot be otherwise.
2. The basic control must be in the elected governing bodies of the agencies. While joint boards or commissions may be necessary in some instances, the membership of such agencies should be accountable directly to the governing bodies of the affected units.

84Ibid., p. 15.

3. It must preserve the separate identities of the existing units of government.

With all levels of governments competing for a limited tax base, intergovernmental cooperation may not be good business, but it is mandatory business. E. A. Mosher, Executive Director of the Kansas League of Municipalities, cites the reasons why such cooperation is a must:

1. Cooperation is advisable when a governmental problem does not recognize political boundaries—when an area or regional approach is advisable. For example, water supply and flood protection are being recognized as regional problems.

2. Cooperation is often necessary simply for economic reasons. Many small units simply can't afford to provide certain services or own certain equipment; collectively, they can.

3. Cooperation is often necessary to provide an adequate level of service. To illustrate, the future demand for competent administrative, professional, and technical personnel necessary for the performance of many services may well exceed the supply unless local governments get together.

4. Cooperation is often desirable for reasons of efficiency. For example, even if all the units in an area could afford to own separately an item of equipment or a facility for special, seldom-used purposes, it could be more efficient to provide for its joint use.

5. Cooperation may promote the more equitable distribution of the cost of providing certain services. For example, when one unit provides a service substantially used by the residents of a nearby unit, cooperation may provide a means of fairly sharing the cost.

6. Cooperation is advisable in some instances to prevent state or federal assumption of a function or activity which should be kept on a local government basis.

7. Cooperation is advisable in some instances to prevent the growth of those special-purpose districts which are not directly responsible to the public they serve.

8. Cooperative programs may well be a prerequisite in the future, for various federal grants and aids, or a larger share of federal participation. This is already a requirement for certain federal programs.[85]

Communities need local officials who are concerned about local government and who are willing to work for legislation which facilitates intergovernmental cooperation. Local officials should have and exercise the authority to cooperate when:

- It is mutually advantageous to the affected units, where the public benefits.

85E. A. Mosher, "Trends and Practices in Governmental Cooperation," First Annual Seminar on Intergovernmental Relations (Lawrence: University of Kansas, Governmental Research Center, 1966), pp. 37–38.

- Cooperation provides a means of obtaining a more adequate or effective level of public service.
- It provides an opportunity for the more economical or efficient performance of service.
- It is a practical alternative to state, federal, or special-district encroachment on an activity which should be continued on a local government basis.[86]

School-Community Cooperation

Authorities responsible for school development must recognize that school facilities not only serve for educational purposes, but also must be social, civic, recreational, and cultural centers for the community. Each anticipated building must reflect the unique features of a community, as well as its social organization and the existence of other public facilities.

In the last decade some communities have made appreciable growth in the cooperative development of land acquisition, planning, and maintenance of areas and facilities designed for school and community recreational use. This cooperation has been necessary because of the tremendous demand for increased services at public expense. It is always essential that public services be at a cost compatible with good service. Hence, duplication of facilities must be reduced to a minimum if taxpayers are to receive effective service for every tax dollar.

Improved community conditions are a goal of all units of local government; therefore, planning by school and recreation officials should reflect analogous objectives. A cursory examination of the services provided by both institutions suggests that cooperative activity is not only desirable but essential. In too many instances the taxpayer carries the burden for facilities and programs which could be more properly administered through joint development and operation of these two agencies. On the other hand, some communities have made great strides in coordinating basic programs and facilities for expanded and additional services.

A survey of several school and park developments indicates that several methods of achieving cooperative planning are essential. Two of the most important procedures for setting up endeavors are:

1. Establishing a joint committee with members from the school board, city council, and recreation and park authority, the superintendent of schools, the director of parks and recreation, the city manager, and the planning director
2. Periodic conferences between city and school officials at both the policy and administrative levels

[86]Ibid., p. 42.

Topeka, Kansas

Topeka, Kansas, is a community that made an all-out effort to achieve cooperative efforts in planning and development. In 1964 a joint committee was appointed with representatives from the school board, recreation commission, and city park department. The superintendent of schools, the superintendent of recreation, and the superintendent of parks served as ex-officio members of this commitee. Though this committee was not empowered to take official action, it provided an opportunity for the discussion of mutual projects. Representatives could then report these discussions to their respective boards. As a result of numerous meetings with department staffs and board members, the resolution below was adopted by the three agencies, thus officially setting the stage for future cooperative developments:

> This joint resolution is an effort among three public boards to increase the services provided by each, to heighten the efficiency or operation of each, and to fulfill their specific obligations to the citizens of the community with the lowest cost to the taxpayer.
>
> The following statements of this resolution shall constitute a basis for actions of the Board of Education, the Park Department, and Recreation Commission in the execution of their plan of cooperation for joint acquisition, planning, and respective use of school-park sites in the City of Topeka.
>
> The Board of Education, the Park Department, and the Recreation Commission mutually agree that, in the acquisition and planning of school-park sites, whether acquired jointly or independently, each will inform the other, as far in advance as is practicable, of its plans for acquisition and development of sites which may become mutual resources.

Coordinated School-Park Site
Planning and Development

Theory of School-Park Planning

With a mutual desire to better serve the citizens of Topeka, the Park Department, Recreation Commission, and Board of Education support and encourage the development of school-park sites within the community. By combining a school and a park in one area, portions of the school building can serve community needs and indoor recreation requirements; on the other hand, portions of the park can provide facilities for the school recreation and educational program, as well as for community needs.

It is recognized that cooperation in acquisition, planning, and constructing of school-park properties results in certain economies in capital expenditures, as well as reduces the cost of maintenance and increases the effectiveness of maintenance and use.

In subsequent months, an elementary school was jointly developed which is presently used by the Topeka Recreation Commission as a neighborhood recreation center. As a result of this development, a more detailed contract was required to define the responsibility for each of the agencies. Again, the contract was developed through meetings between the agency staffs and the joint planning committee:

TOPEKA RECREATION COMMISSION
TOPEKA BOARD OF EDUCATION

CONTRACT FOR JOINT USE OF FACILITIES

THIS AGREEMENT, made and entered into, in triplicate, this day of _____, 1965, by and between the Board of Education of the City of Topeka of the State of Kansas, a quasi-municipal corporation, hereinafter called the "Board," and the Topeka Recreation Commission, a corporation, hereinafter called the "Recreation Commission."

RECITALS:

A. Board is the owner of public school grounds and facilities located within the City of Topeka, Kansas, school district; and the Recreation Commission has recreation grounds and facilities under its operation and control located within the City of Topeka, Kansas.

B. The Board of Recreation Commissioners desires to provide opportunities for recreational and/or physical fitness programs and to offer the Topeka community the maximum benefits from joint and mutual use of the respective grounds and facilities for such purposes, upon the terms and conditions hereinafter set forth.

NOW, THEREFORE, it is mutually agreed as follows:

1. The school grounds and facilities, including buildings located at the public elementary and junior high schools in the City of Topeka, Kansas, shall be made available to the Recreation Commission so long as it does not interfere with the public school program.

2. For each school building used in its recreational program, the Recreation Commission shall pay to the Board the sum of one dollar ($1.00) per hour of such use for heat, light, and other utility services, except that such charge shall not apply to the use by the Recreation Commission of school buildings on the cooperative and planned sites or during the Recreation Commission's summer program. The term "cooperative and planned sites" as used herein means the jointly planned and developed school and recreation sites and facilities such as the one located at 31st and Arnold, Topeka, Kansas.

3. Any facilities at the cooperative and planned sites under the control of the Recreation Commission shall be available to the Board so long as it does not interfere with the Recreation Commission's planned programs.

4. There shall be no charge to the Board when using any facilities of the Recreation Commission.

5. At least annually, the representatives of the Board and the Recreation Commission will inspect the facilities of the Board which are to be used

by the Recreation Commission; and the Recreation Commission will be liable to and reimburse the Board for any damage, beyond normal wear and tear, resulting to the Board's facilities during the use of such facilities by the Recreation Commission during the regular school year.

6. The Recreation Commission will be liable to and reimburse the Board for any damage, beyond "normal wear and tear," resulting to the Board's facilities during the use thereof in the Recreation Commission's summer recreation program except in case of window breakage; and in such case, the Recreation Commission will pay sixty percent (60%) of replacement costs and the Board will pay forty percent (40%) of replacement costs.

7. The policy of the Board is to require a custodian to be in attendance at its school buildings when in use during the school year and otherwise; and for the services of the custodian in excess of the normal 40-hour week at any school facility for the purposes of the Recreation Commission during the school year, the Recreation Commission shall reimburse the Board for such services, sixty percent (60%) of the excess costs incurred by the Board to provide the services of the custodian, it being understood that the normal week of the custodian is from Monday to Friday, inclusive, of each week, and between the hours of 8 a.m. and 4 p.m., inclusive of each day. The services of a custodian on holidays, as specified by the Board, shall be construed as services in excess of his normal work week.

8. There shall be no charge to the Recreation Commission for custodial service at all cooperative and planned sites. During its summer recreation program, the Recreation Commission will provide and pay for the custodial service which is reasonably necessary and proper to keep and maintain in clean condition the portion of any school facility used by the Recreation Commission in such programs.

9. The Recreation Commission and the Board shall each appoint personnel to meet with designated representatives of the other to discuss, clarify, and establish all details concerning the operation and maintenance of the use of the facilities owned by the Board and under the control of the Recreation Commission.

10. The Board will submit periodic itemized statements, as the Board may determine, to the Recreation Commission covering such items as may be payable to the Board hereunder.

11. This Agreement is a continuing one but it may be terminated by either of the parties hereto by serving written notice of termination upon the other party at least 90 days prior to the effective date of termination as specified in the notice.

12. No assignment of this Agreement or any rights hereunder by either party shall be valid without the written consent of the other party.

Mount Prospect, Illinois

Other communities have also been successful in developing joint facilities. The Mount Prospect Park District, Mount Prospect, Illinois, approved an agreement with Consolidated School District 59 for joint use of facilities. In June 1966 the park district opened a swimming pool next to a junior high school. It was reported by the director of parks and recreation that physical education classes were scheduled soon after the pool was filled in the spring and again in the fall until October. The Board of Education agreed to share in the cost of maintaining the swimming pool on a 50-50 basis, up to a maximum cost of $10,000 per year.

The contract between the Park Board and Board of Education provides for the following conditions for facilities in joint use:

1. The School Board agrees to:
   A. Grade and provide drainage of all areas included in this agreement.
   B. Not restrict public use of the properties after school hours.
   C. Provide space within the school buildings, including classrooms, kitchen, and lavatory facilities for after-school program activities.
   D. Provide permanent outdoor facilities such as drives, parking lots, and surfaced play areas as required for normal school use.
   E. Pay for all water and electricity used for the maintenance of the facilities with the exception of water and electricity required for the swimming pool and ball fields.
   F. Provide the facilities listed in the contract for a fee of $1 per year.

2. The Park Board agrees to:
   A. Provide and plant all trees and shrubs on sites.
   B. Plan, purchase, and install outdoor play equipment including apparatus, ball fields, goals, outdoor cooking grills, etc.
   C. Maintain grounds owned by the Board of Education at sites included in the agreement. This maintenance is to include mowing, trimming, and pruning, but is not to include snow removal.
   D. Provide trained, qualified leadership for Park District-sponsored programs in school building and grounds.
   E. Provide outdoor facilities needed for normal community use.

Austin, Texas

Austin, Texas, is another community that has done an outstanding job in school-community development. The policy adopted by the city administration and the Board of Education recognizes the need for recreation as a contribution for a more wholesome life. The policy further recognizes the responsibility of these two governmental units to offer the community the greatest possible benefits from their investment in public expenditures.

It is acknowledged that the Board of Education must acquire land that primarily will meet the educational needs of the district. However, park and recreation needs receive high priority in land acquisition. After sites have been tentatively selected, the superintendent of schools notifies the city manager, the planning director, and the director of recreation and parks. After they have had a chance to review the project, a meeting of all concerned is held to determine a course of action. The cost of jointly acquired and developed areas is based on the length of time it is used by each agency. Under the present plan this time ratio is nine months for school use and three months for recreation and park use; Austin reimburses the School District 25 percent of the cost of acquiring and developing the outdoor area.

The Austin authorities have done an excellent job in working out agreements for joint use of facilities. Working out details of joint use is often difficult. Such questions as whether a custodian is used and who shall pay for heat and lights would seem to be easily resolved, but they often create major problems in reaching agreements. The Austin authorities have agreed on the following policies:

1. A school custodian shall attend all buildings used by the Recreation and Park Department when more than a specific part of the school building is open. A school custodian will not be required when only a specific part of the building is being used.
2. When the recreation program is in progress and the custodian is still on school time, there shall be no charge to the Recreation and Park Department.
3. The maintenance and repair of the school building shall be assumed by the school authorities except when damage to the facility is unusual and is a result of the recreation program.
4. The heat for the building is furnished by the Board of Education.
5. To compensate the school district for electricity and water consumed by the Recreation and Park Department, the City assumes the responsibility for the district's utility bills during the months of July and August.
6. Watering and mowing of areas used for recreation purposes by both agencies are done by the City. However, the trimming, watering, and hand-mowing of areas immediately adjacent to the school facility are done by the district.
7. Time of custodial services begins at the opening of the building and extends a sufficient period of time beyond the closing of the activity to allow for proper cleanup.

Elk Grove, Illinois

The Elk Grove Park District in Elk Grove, Illinois, is in the beginning stages of school-community development. Already in operation as a youth center is the Grant Wood Elementary School. This facility is jointly developed and paid for by the Village of Elk Grove and School District 59. When one sees this facility, one can readily identify the building as truly a community facility by its name: Grant Wood Elementary School and Youth Center. At the present time park district offices are also housed here. After-school and weekend programs are conducted at this location. During the day, the youth center portion of the building is used for physical education classes and as a lunchroom.

Presently under study is a swimming pool addition to the Thomas Livey Junior High School. As in Mount Prospect, Illinois, this facility would serve not only as an education facility but as a community facility as well.

Grand Rapids, Michigan

The desire to construct school buildings that would also serve as recreation centers for community groups presented financial and administrative difficulties to the school and city authorities in Grand Rapids, as elsewhere. These difficulties have been overcome, however, and a valid set of agreements have been reached which are yielding beneficial results. They are described by the superintendent of parks as follows:

> A specific plan of development is being prepared by the city for each school-recreation area, showing the exact layout and design of the area, clearly defining the "school area" and "city area." "School area" is the site where the school building is placed, and such developed areas as will principally be used for school purposes. Its extent is determined by negotiations between the representatives of the city and the schools and is decided upon for each school. The "school area" generally contains the school building itself, the main approaches to the building, the hard-surfaced wet-weather play areas, the kindergarten play and apparatus area, a portion of the play and apparatus area for the older children, some playfield sections, and landscape features.
>
> The balance of the grounds is the "city area" and contains all the facilities and playfields which are principally used by children and adults during off-school hours and vacation. A clear and concise definition of these areas is important, since it involves the expenditures incurred by the board and the city. These dividing lines are on paper only and do not under any circumstances influence the overall design of the grounds, nor are they visible in any way.
>
> The park-school agreement of the City of Grand Rapids states that the cost of development of the "school area" shall be the responsibility of the Board of Education and the cost of the development of the "city area" shall be borne by the city. It is evident from this arrangement that the Board of Education is paying for facilities which are beneficial mainly to the school itself, while the city pays for installations which mainly benefit the general public.
>
> The ownership of land to be used for the park-school plan is divided into three categories:
>
> 1. The board owns all the land.
> 2. The city owns the land directly adjacent to land owned by the board, and the land owned by the board contains the "minimum area" at a

suitable location. (A minimum area is 5 acres for an elementary school.)

3. The land upon which the program is to be conducted is owned by the city, or the board owns adjacent land which does not contain the "minimum area."

Where category 1 exists, the school board leases to the city for a consideration of $1.00 per annum the amount of acreage over and above the 5 acres "minimum area." The reason for this is to prevent the criticism that the city is spending capital money on land to which it has no legal rights. Under category 2, both parties retain ownership rights to their respective parcels.

Under category 3, the city sells to the board sufficient land so it may obtain the "minimum area," the value of the land to be determined by an appraiser mutually agreed upon. These types of ownership seem to be fair and equitable and have so far not resulted in any disagreement. The boundary lines of these parcels, whether leased or owned, are not visible on the grounds, and the previously mentioned "school area" and "city area" are not the same as the leased or owned lands.

Under the agreement the city repairs and maintains all areas outside of the building line with the exception of snow removal from school walks. The Board of Education compensates the city for the repair and upkeep of the areas and facilities located within the "school area." The amount is a predetermined sum paid annually and is based upon the estimated amount mutually agreed upon; it may be changed from year to year.

The "school area" is under the control of the Board of Education during the hours the school is in session. During all other hours, control of the area is under the city.

This agreement, including the leases, is to endure for a twenty-year period unless changes in the city charter make it impossible, either for the board or the city, to incur obligations over so long a period, in which case it is to endure over such a period as is legally permissible.

Seattle, Washington

A coordinating cooperative program of site acquisition and facility development has been worked out in Seattle between the board of park commissioners and the city's school authorities. The Laurelhurst Community Center illustrates how the idea has worked out: A city planning commission survey showed that the district badly needed enlarged facilities. The Laurelhurst Community Club agreed with the finding and put its weight behind a request for more space. A joint park-school staff committee meeting each week ironed out details of financing, constructing, administrating, and maintaining, and developed a plan which received official approval. Under this cooperative scheme, the Laurelhurst school gym was enlarged, apparatus added, and social rooms provided. The statement of intention drawn up by the park-school board joint committee makes clear the basis for the new cooperation.

Spokane, Washington

Cooperation in the acquisition, improvement, and operation of school and city recreation properties in Spokane is achieved through an advisory coordinating committee. The committee consists of two members from the park board and two members from the school board, plus the superintendent of schools and the recreation director of the park department. Board representatives on the committee are appointed by the two board presidents. Area and facility plans are usually initiated by the department executives, but all such plans and projects are submitted to the coordinating committee for review and approval. Their recommendations are then referred to the two official boards for action.

The advisory committee meets on call of the chairman, and the proceedings of the meetings are reviewed at the regular meetings of the two boards by designated members of this joint committee. The superintendent of schools, the city planning engineers, the parks superintendent, and the recreation superintendent work closely in developing plans for the acquisition and the improvement of new areas and facilities.

School properties are designed with the cooperation of the park department to provide adequate centers for community recreation outside of school hours. Park playground areas, so far as possible, are located adjacent to schools and are equipped to serve the schools as well. Each department purchases the area needed for its specific use. The park board purchases the area intended for recreation purposes adjoining the school site and equips it at its own expense. The school board fully equips the units on its own property, but school areas are usually confined mainly to the building site.

School facilities are assigned to the recreation division of the park department for use outside of school hours under the supervision of the recreation director. Park facilities are assigned to the schools, as needed for school activities, under the direction of the superintendent of schools or his designated assistants.

The cost of this joint operation is distributed as follows: The park department pays for the recreation leadership and janitorial services during the hours such facilities are used by the park department. The schools furnish light, water, heat, and other items that pertain to the maintenance and upkeep of the buildings. The equipment used in the conduct of the program for the most part is furnished by the park department, except as the recreation director and the superintendent of schools find it advisable to use school equipment.

Richmond, Virginia

In all new school buildings the department requests that the following be provided:

1. Outside entrances to washrooms, cafeteria, auditorium, gymnasium, library, shops, or any other special facilities. Also an arrangement whereby inside doors can be locked securely when outside entrances are in use and access through building is not desired. Separate buildings for auditorium and gymnasium are desired.

2. "Cutoffs" (fire doors or folding gates) so that cafeteria, gymnasium, auditorium, and six classrooms (more or less as needed), preferably on first floor, can be heated and used separately.

3. Folding gates or suitable arrangements that will prevent access to the entire building when only a portion is needed.

4. Movable tables and chairs in cafeteria and classrooms that are used for community purposes.

5. Storage space for recreation supplies, games, and equipment—in the form of extra closets in classroom or a separate storage room, conveniently located.

6. Softwood floors on auditorium stages; dressing rooms and storage space arranged in a practical manner for drama presentations.

7. Arts and crafts rooms with running water, work tables, good lighting, and storage closets or cabinets.

8. Entrance lounge and checkroom.

9. Office space for the staff of large centers.

Plans for new recreation areas and outdoor facilities are developed by the department of recreation and parks. Just as school indoor facilities are made as useful as possible for joint recreation use, it is the policy for municipal recreation areas, where possible, to be adjacent to public schools and made adaptable for school uses. School officials, therefore, review plans for the development of play areas and make suggestions, which are incorporated as much as possible.

Although there is joint planning and use of areas and facilities, action of the city council assigns jurisdiction of the areas, including maintenance. Except for damages directly related to a special activity, both school and recreation departments maintain the areas directly under their jurisdiction, including costs of electricity, heat, water, gas. Program costs, including leadership staff, overtime for custodians, maids, and firemen, are assumed by the respective using agency. There is no charge for rent and no charge for custodial help when activities are conducted during their regularly assigned working hours. The using agency pays extra costs only for special services or overtime. The director of recreation and parks states:

> In our situation, there are instances where both schools and recreation have outdoor space adjoining each other, complementary to each other, and each has the jurisdiction including maintenance of its own space. Responsibility is clearly defined. In instances where one agency either constructs or maintains a facility or area under the jurisdiction of another agency, the agency under whose jurisdiction the area comes reimburses the one performing the service. We have no joint ownership of indoor facilities.

It is my feeling that before long we will be constructing community centers with gymnasiums near schools (particularly the old school buildings which are not very adaptable for recreation purposes) which will also be used for school purposes. There is growing community interest for such an arrangement which appears to be of mutual advantage to all concerned.

Muskegon, Michigan

Cooperation in Muskegon is facilitated through the joint employment of a landscape architect by the Board of Education and the department of parks and recreation. The landscape architect does the planning for new areas and for improvements on present properties of both the department of parks and recreation and the Board of Education. It is reportedly a bigger job than one person can handle, and joint employment of a draftsman is anticipated. According to the director of the department of parks and recreation, the department's taking over the entire maintenance of school facilities is being considered, regardless of whether they are used for recreation purposes, on the assumption that public property which has any area at all should be considered as a park and beautified and made useful accordingly.

The drawing board and files of the landscape architect are located in the office of the department of parks and recreation and he participates regularly in department staff meetings. He also meets frequently with the business manager of the public schools and discusses mutual problems with him and with the park and recreation director. He is a civil service employee, is paid from the department, and has pension rights as a city employee. At the end of each year, the department of parks and recreation bills the Board of Education for half of his salary plus extras such as the use of a car and office material. The director states:

> The business manager has asked us for a written outline of the things we think important in planning these new school buildings and I believe every attempt will be made to see that they are fulfilled. He has even suggested that they take out of the general contract the landscape and building of the outdoor playfield facilities and give us that responsibility.

A community is responsible for the proper provision of facilities for education and recreation. Schools and parks not only affect the life of each person, but in themselves form a vital portion of the physical structure of a community. In addition to providing educational facilities, modern schools are becoming focal points in the community for both young and old. Parks are a major asset, a necessary and essential part of a city; they provide areas for recreation and preserve natural scenic beauty in a community. The adequate provision of schools and parks makes a community a satisfying place to live. The taxpayer has the right to expect that local officials will cooperate when feasible to bring the best possible service at the lowest possible cost.

SELECTED REFERENCES

BLAKE, PETER. *God's Own Junkyard: The Planned Deterioration of America's Landscape.* New York: Holt, Rinehart and Winston, Inc., 1964.

BOYLE, ROBERT H. "How to Stop the Pillage of America." *Sports Illustrated,* December 11, 1967.

ECKBO, GARRETT. *The Landscape We See.* New York: McGraw-Hill Book Company, 1969.

HUNTER, MOSS, *et al. Land: Recreation and Leisure.* Washington D.C.: The Urban Land Institute, 1970.

LEDERMANN, ALFRED, AND ALFRED TRACHSEL. *Creative Playgrounds and Recreation Centers.* New York: Praeger Publishers, Inc., 1968.

MACK, RUTH P., *et al. Urban Transportation and Recreation, Summary and Import.* Washington D.C.: U.S. Department of Commerce, 1970.

National Facilities Conference. *College and University Facilities Guide—For Health, Physical Education, Recreation.* Chicago: The Athletic Institute, 1968.

RIPLEY, T. H. *Tree and Shrub Response to Recreation Use.* Asheville, N. C.: U.S. Forest Service, Southeastern Forest Experimentation Station, Research Note 171, 1962.

SHOMON, JOSEPH J. *Open Land for Urban-American Acquisition, Safekeeping & Use.* Baltimore: The Johns Hopkins Press, 1971.

UDALL, STEWART L. *The Quiet Crisis.* New York: Holt, Rinehart and Winston, Inc., 1963.

U.S. Department of the Interior, Bureau of Outdoor Recreation. *Outdoor Recreation Space Standards,* 1967.

6

EVALUATION
OF THE DELIVERY
OF LEISURE SYSTEMS

Evaluation and appraisal provide the primary method of quality control in leisure services. They reveal discrepancies, which once corrected, can result in better services to the public. As a planning tool, evaluation enhances the likelihood of making accurate decisions regarding continuation, expansion, or limitation of services.

INTRODUCTION

A review of the literature suggests that evaluation has been defined differently by different people at different times. Similar studies have revealed a number of evaluative research designs. From the world of business and industry one sees the "maximizing" model where effectiveness is based on the relationship of input to output, where evaluation has been traditionally based on the notion of goal achievement consistent with classical organization theory. Evaluation in the public domain has been largely concerned with the measurement of change as indicated on specific criteria and the assessment of the extent to which various objectives are met.[1]

The purpose of evaluation has been shown to be varied. Some theo-

---

[1]The author wishes to recognize the research assistance of Ernest Olsen, graduate student in the Department of Leisure Studies at the University of Illinois, for his help in retrieving information for this chapter.

rists have suggested that evaluation may be used to examine and modify a program in the formative stages or to look at the terminal effects of a program development. Others have pointed out that evaluation is primarily used as control, i.e., evaluation may be viewed as a monitoring process. Implicit in each of these notions is the idea that evaluation has for its major purpose the provision of information to assist the decision-maker.

An early definition of evaluation tended to identify evaluation with *measurement*. Evaluation was held to involve the development of an instrument to collect performance data which could be compared with some objective criterion which typically was of a normative nature. A major disadvantage with this approach was its instrumental focus. Value judgments were ignored, and if something couldn't be measured it couldn't be evaluated.

Of more contemporary origin is the notion that evaluation is the statement of *congruence between performance and objectives*. Evaluation theorists suggest that this definition has expanded the utility of evaluation by no longer focusing on the participant but including content by providing feedback to assist in the decision process.

A third definition equates evaluation with *professional judgment of the merits* of some program.

None of these definitions by itself is sufficient to provide all the necessary information or to include the multiplicity of activities now regarded as evaluation. A definition of evaluation should be based on the assumption that the function of evaluation is to assist in the decision process in a specific context. Consequently, Alkin defines evaluation as:

> ... the process of ascertaining the decision areas of concern, selecting appropriate information, and collecting and analyzing information in order to report summary data useful to decision makers in selecting among alternatives.[2]

Other authors have assumed that evaluation is always undertaken with reference to some intentional action designed to influence persons or change, that it is the measurement of desirable and undesirable consequences of an action intended to forward some goal that has value.

Some indicate that evaluation is concerned with finding out how well action programs work.

Hjelte and Shivers define evaluation as the process of assessing how nearly a program or activity achieves an accepted standard or criterion.[3]

In each of the above definitions is implicit the notion of judgment, assessment, or appraisal. Evaluation attempts to assess something's worth;

[2]M. C. Alkin, *Toward an Evaluation Model: A Systems Approach,* Working Paper No. 4, Center for the Study of Instructional Programs (Los Angeles: University of California, 1967).

[3]G. Hjelte and J. S. Shivers, *Public Administration of Recreational Services* (Philadelphia: Lea & Febiger, 1972), p. 492.

that much seems to be agreed upon. The disagreement seems to stem from the attempt to define evaluation in terms of its *process* and *purpose*. Stake and Denny succinctly summarize this idea and in so doing present a useful concept of evaluation as it relates to education.

> Considered broadly, evaluation is the discovery of the nature of worth of something. In relation to education, we may evaluate students, teachers, curriculums, administrators, systems, programs, and notions. The purposes for our evaluation may be many, but always evaluation attempts to describe something and to indicate its perceived merits and shortcomings.[4]

APPROACHES TO EVALUATION

Compliance With Standards Approach. If one approach can be said to typify evaluations of leisure service programs, it would most likely be this approach. This method provides for a program or institution to be examined in terms of a list of standard criteria, i.e., number of participants per camp supervisor, number of clients per case worker, presence or absence of specified services, and adequacy of buildings or equipment.

Recreation programs and systems have been frequently evaluated on precisely these kinds of criteria. The rationale underlying the compliance approach is summarized by van der Smissen:

> A standard is a statement of desirable practice, a level of performance for a given situation. Standards direct measurements of effectiveness using the cause and effect approach so that if stated desirable practices are followed, the program should be effective.[5]

Advocates of this approach suggest that the checklists employed require few of the research skills typically associated with evaluative research. The checklist approach is relatively inexpensive. The standards approach permits some comparison across programs. This approach also provides the administrator with a chance to look closely at his program; in fact the greatest strength of this approach may be not the evaluation itself, but the process of self-appraisal. Although the compliance to standards approach is viewed as essential, there appears a general consensus that such standards are not absolute and should be modified for the differences inherent in different systems. Van der Smissen prefaces her schedule of standards and criteria:

> The standards and evaluative criteria apply to *all* public recreation and park departments inasmuch as they are considered to be fundamental aspects of an effective operation. But it is recognized that communities differ and must adapt the standards to the conditions of their situations.[6]

[4]R. Stake and T. Denny, "Educational Evaluation: New Roles, New Means," Sixty-Eighth Yearbook, National Society for the Study of Education (Chicago, Ill., 1969), p. 370.

[5]Betty van der Smissen, *Evaluation and Self-Study of Public Recreation and Park Agencies* (Washington, D.C.: National Recreation and Park Association, 1972), p. 4.

[6]Ibid., p. 5.

The very tentative nature of standards causes one to question their utility. Of greater concern is the implied linkage between the criteria (standards) and effectiveness. There is very little evidence to support the notion that adherence to program standards predicts some ultimate criterion of program success, as further discussion in this chapter will suggest. In addition to these problems, several others should be considered.

It is conceivable that reliance on the standards approach could result in the displacement of otherwise important goals. The standards and criteria suggested by the checklists and schedules could in fact become the ends to which the organization strives, displacing the goals which the standards are supposed to predict.

Reliance on national standards or guidelines may mask the necessity to identify the needs and desires of the population to be served. Furthermore, evaluating through checklists and schedules seldom requires the description of the impact of program activity on the community or participant. The judgment of program effectiveness is often limited to one person. Collective judgments are seldom tapped, and the self-appraisal nature of the approach is clearly subject to bias.

Many checklists are of a global nature, examining all aspects of a program, but failing to weight program constitutents differently. Thus, the evaluator can be duped into thinking that all aspects of a program bear equal attention.

Professional or Expert Judgments Approach. In some instances programs are evaluated by having expert observers make judgments as to program effectiveness. Often these observations include diagnoses and prescriptions.

This form of evaluation has a certain utility in that it is devoid of "messy" measurements and affords instant feedback to assist in decision making. Also the judgments of prestigious observers may lend credibility to a program. On the debit side, however, are a number of significant limitations. Observers see only a slice of the program. Their judgments are subjective and not subject to checks on reliability or validity. A Hawthorne Effect may alter the performance of significant actors, thus modifying the program and presenting a biased program representation.[7]

Surveys of Interest and Need Approach. Although not usually as-

---

[7]The Hawthorne Effect is a phenomenon first noted in a classic study during the 1930's Depression at the Hawthorne Electric Company. In this study the productivity of several girls set apart from other workers began to increase whatever changes occurred in their surroundings—changes for the better or the worse. "Each time a change was made their productivity increased, leaving the impression that each change was one for the better.... The obvious explanation was that the motivation of the girls had been improving all along, not because of the specific changes but because they were flattered at having been singled out and given extra attention by management...." Herbert M. Blalock, Jr., *An Introduction to Social Research* (Englewood Cliffs, N.J.: Prentice-Hall, Inc., 1970, p. 27). See also, F.J. Roethlisberger and W.J. Dickson, *Management and the Worker* (Cambridge, Mass.: Harvard University Press, 1939), for a more detailed discussion of the Hawthorne Effect and other similar studies.

sociated with evaluation, surveys of interest and need are implicitly associated with program assessment. A popular tool in recreation is the Leisure Attitude, Interest, and Opinion Survey (see Chapter 4). The data from these surveys are used primarily in program design and afford one form of evaluative criteria.

Journalistic Investigations Approach. In essence this approach involves the combined judgments of a number of experts commissioned to evaluate a given program. The conclusions of such a panel are generally of a subjective nature and are presented in a narrative fashion. As with the expert judgment approach, a basic limitation in this approach is the reliance on subjective judgments from a narrow reference frame.

Case Studies or Historical Approach. The case study approach to evaluation involves essentially a step-by-step portrayal of a program. The approach attempts to describe and explain the many interactions which typify a program. One obvious limitation is the time associated with making pertinent observations and, of course, the problem of observer bias.

Correlational Approach. This method uses a correlational design wherein people subjected to a specific treatment are contrasted with those who have not been treated, most often within the same group. The design of correlational research is simple, involving little more than collecting two or more scores from the same subjects and then computing correlation coefficients. It is felt that when massive effects are expected or desired, less precise techniques are. almost as good as precise ones. Thus this correlational approach is a useful substitute for more precise experimental designs, even though it has clear limitations. Such designs are particularly useful in the investigation of effects which are believed to be the result of long-lasting treatment.

The Eclectic-Synthesis Approach. This type of nonexperimental model is a combination of the best of other approaches, and in fact may utilize experimental methodology when such an approach is deemed suitable by the evaluator. The approach is typified by the collection of process-oriented qualitative research—the emphasis on the development of events through time, and use of a small number of case studies to generalize to the larger population. The central thrust of this approach is to develop a coherent and appropriately near to complete description of the relevant community systems prior to the intervention of a program, of the nature of the intervention, and of the new system which develops when the intervention is a dynamic constituent.

The Countenance Model Approach. The Countenance Model, developed for educational program evaluation by Dr. Robert Stake at the University of Illinois, represents another approach incorporating several types of methodology and viewing programs from a systems perspective. Essentially, Stake's model uses three types of data: antecedent, transactional, and outcome data. Evaluation using these data involve identifying *intents* (goals), making observations of each of the intents, and finally assessing the extent to which intents and outcomes are judged congruent or the extent to which outcomes meet acceptable standards.

VAN DER SMISSEN AND DUNN-HATRY EVALUATION MODELS

As society becomes more complex, as lesiure becomes more abundant, and as the role of the public recreation becomes proportionately complex, the role of program evaluation becomes increasingly crucial. Program evaluation is now frequently required by funded programs. A concerned public has prompted administrators to be increasingly concerned about the merits of the programs they offer. Planners are concerned with seeking evaluative information from current and past programs as a basis for future planning. The notion was recently borne out in a study of recreation superintendents in Illinois: 80 percent of the 30 surveyed indicated that program evaluation was one of their major concerns.

There can be no question that evaluation is important. What we need to question, however, is just how successful are we in evaluating recreation programs. In the survey above, none of the administrators felt that they were doing an adequate job of program evaluation. For the most part, they did not have adequate training, they felt, to evaluate effectively and they viewed the guides and systems available to them as generally of little value. For the most part, the respondents were unaware of participant outcomes, maintained no formal evaluation system, and relied primarily on attendance records and intuition.

Little has been done to develop a systematic approach to evaluation. The current emphasis appears to be toward refining checklists and standards, which are unfortunately lacking in empirical theory. When one examines the approaches touted as useful in recreational program evaluation, it becomes evident that the following criticism of program evaluation is appropriate today:

> Well, there is the N.R.A. Schedule for Appraisal of Community Recreation—but it is just a quantitative guide—nothing more than an inventory, although one might start with such. And the standards quoted, although revised, are not based on basic research. . . .
>
> In short and bluntly speaking, we just do not have adequate qualitative and evaluative tools.[8]

Unfortunately, the evaluation picture for recreation programs appears to have changed little since van der Smissen's 1972 description. The current emphasis is still toward the development of standards and checklists.

There is a profound need to devise something better than *a priori* checklists. There currently exists no conceptual model which clearly describes a meaningful alternative to typical recreation evaluative approaches. An attempt will be made to do this in this chapter. It is obvious that if recreation program evaluation is to achieve some legitimacy, to meet the exigencies of today and the demands of a leisure-oriented future,

[8]Van der Smissen, *Evaluation and Self-Study.*

the best thinking concerning evaluation has to be examined, synthesized, and adapted to the evaluation of recreation programs.

An example of the application of *a priori* standards in the evaluation of recreational programs, as mentioned previously, is the current work of van der Smissen. She presents 35 standards that, "if followed," will result in an effective program. They cover six areas: (1) philosophy and goals, (2) administration, (3) programming, (4) personnel, (5) areas, facilities, and equipment, and (6) evaluation.[9] For each standard presented a number of criteria are described to denote whether a standard is met. The point is to provide general standards and criteria that apply to *all* public recreation and park departments since they are fundamental aspects of an effective organization.

The strength of van der Smissen's approach primarily lies in its pedagogical value. She recognizes this function when she states that this approach is not a "quick checklist," nor a "self-evaluation questionnaire" but rather a "study manual." The "study manual" contains a broad range of statements describing functions and activities of park and recreation systems. Such information may help the administrator clarify his role and the role of the agency and may possibly stimulate further thinking and investigation. As a pedagogical device, the van der Smissen approach may have some legitimacy. However, for the purpose of evaluation, this guide appears to have a number of limitations.

As indicated earlier, the fundamental assumption of an evaluation procedure employing standards and criteria is that success can be predicted by such indicators. The standards employed in this guide are vague and ambiguous, and many show little logical relationship to effectiveness. For example, one standard proposed is:

> The department's structure should reflect its purposes, its methods of operation in relation to its resources, and its relationship to the community.[10]

That really doesn't tell one very much. It is perfectly reasonable to assume that the structure of an ineffective organization can reflect the organization's purpose, its methods of operation in relation to its resources, and its relationship to the community. The checklist approach fails to tell explicitly what relationships are indicative of success. Van der Smissen claims that if her standards are met, the organization should be effective, but she presents standards that are difficult to operationalize and frequently lack substance.

Considerable research has been done concerning organizational effectiveness. Some research indicates strong relationships between effectiveness and such variables as division of labor, legitimacy, communication, centralization, leadership styles, and decision making. For example, it has been suggested that organizations that have a high degree of communica-

9Ibid., p. 6.
10Ibid., p. 13.

tion are more likely to have a high degree of effectiveness than organizations that have a low degree of communication. Van der Smissen's approach entirely fails to consider the question of organizational communication. Nor does it include standards relating to organizational structure, leadership styles, decision making, efficiency, and legitimacy.

Another problem with the van der Smissen approach is that of the relative value of the standards. Each standard is assigned a weight which is based upon the best opinions of professionals serving on the initial review committee. Do such opinions accurately reflect the extent to which the standard contributes toward effectiveness? For example, according to van der Smissen's weighting scheme, it is five times more important to have a systematic planning program than to provide opportunities for all levels of skill, ages, and sexes. From the participants' point of view it may be more important to have a broad scope of opportunities than a systematic planning program for areas and facilities.

Until we know more about what constitutes effectiveness in leisure service delivery systems, it may be premature to assign weights to a *priori* criteria in such fashion. The weighting of criteria also may create problems in administrative behavior. Studies in goal displacement suggest that the administrator may place more emphasis on heavily weighted goals than is desirable. In fact, heavily weighted goals may entirely displace seemingly less important objectives.

Another current approach to evaluation in the recreation field is that proposed by Dunn and Hatry. In the publication entitled *Measuring the Effectiveness of Local Government Services—Recreation,* Dunn and Hatry outline a scheme that is concerned with assessing the *value* of the recreation program.[11] The Dunn-Hatry approach is patterned after what might be called the goal-achievement approach to evaluation, whereas the van der Smissen scheme evaluates an entire system against a *priori* standards. Like the van der Smissen approach, the Dunn-Hatry approach has several apparent weaknesses that need to be considered.

The Dunn-Hatry measures of program effectiveness essentially deal with participation rates, accessibility of facilities or activities, the crowdedness of facilities, the variety of activities and facilities offered, "safety indices," physical appearance of facilities, perceived "overall satisfactoriness," delinquency and crime indices, incidence of illnesses affected by recreation, and economic impact.

Throughout their discussion is the implicit theme that the "suggested measures" are causally linked to the program objectives. That is to say, it is implied that recreation may be related to reduction in crime and antisocial behavior, that recreation is a positive force in maintaining sound community mental health, and that recreation has a significant influence on the economic status of a community. Unfortunately, the extent to which recreation yields such outcomes is not really known. This is readily admitted, for throughout the paper the reader is repeatedly

[11]Diana Dunn and Harry P. Hatry, *Measuring the Effectiveness of Local Government Services—Recreation* (Washington D.C.: The Urban Institute, 1971).

reminded of the tentative nature of the relationships implied. For example:

> The documented linkages between illness and recreation service availability are considerably weaker than those between juvenile delinquency and recreation services.[12]

And what of the recreation services and juvenile delinquency? Dunn and Hatry have this to say:

> The adequacy of recreation activities can affect crime rates, particularly juvenile delinquency. It is usually assumed that improved recreation opportunities will reduce crime and delinquency. However, there is the possibility that they can increase crime and delinquency—at least in the short run—because of the congregation of people.
>
> Data on how current recreation services are affecting crime and delinquency rates do not generally exist, nor do standard data collection techniques appear very promising. . . .[13]

So in essence this approach says that we don't know very much about the relationships between recreation and delinquency, and we know even less about "linkages between illness and recreation," but nevertheless these are two measures by which we can assess the effectiveness of a recreation program.

It is conceivable that the information collected by one using the Dunn-Hatry approach would be useful in describing the scope of the program. However, until the implied relationships have been more closely examined by recreation and leisure researchers, it is doubtful that this is a viable format for program evaluation.

Both the Dunn-Hatry and van der Smissen approaches, and this appears typical of most recreational evaluative designs, view recreation systems primarily from the theoretical frame of "Classical Organizational Theory," with the characteristic emphasis on overtly declared professional and organizational goals as primary effectiveness criteria.

In recent years the trend in organizational theory has been away from the classical model of evaluation. Contemporary theorists tend to view organizations as systems in an environment of systems, each interrelated and having multiple as opposed to unitary goals. Although concepts concerning organizational effectiveness fail to achieve consensus among systems theorists, there appears a tenuous thread that suggests that an organization can be viewed as effective only if it is capable of meeting its own survival and maintenance needs as well as related needs of the environment in which it functions. From this frame of reference, the ultimate criterion of organizational success rests not with the degree to which an organization achieves *a priori* standards or meets organizational goals, but the degree to which it meets the needs and demands of its

12Ibid.
13Ibid.

environment as well as its own internal demands for maintenance, growth, and adaptation. *In other words, an organization is effective to the extent that it meets a wide range of expectations held by a multiplicity of societal and organizational parties of interest.*

EVALUATING THE RECREATION AND PARKS EXECUTIVE

The appraisal of executives is a difficult task which can be lightened somewhat by the clarity of managerial terminology we use as guidelines. As we turn to viewing managers as managers, it is with an eye toward scrutiny, for now we do not wish to describe the quality of managerial traits, but to assess the performance of managers on the job. Some researchers feel that one of the "weakest links in management has been the evaluation of managers."[14] Outside the realm of objective evaluation has been the even more troublesome difficulty of managers trying to assess their own effectiveness in a sort of personal vacuum. A more formal, periodic approach to the evaluation of managers will not only aid those who seek to formally appraise managerial performance, but will also aid managers in a more objective and sure way to assess themselves.

There are many executives who would ignore the need for evaluation, because they are too busy or too skeptical; more power to them if they are good executives. There is no point in taking on evaluation as some sort of mania, for there are clearly unappraised and unexamined executives who perform highly creditable jobs, whose effectiveness might be stymied by the too-careful eye of evaluation. Since the desire to evaluate performance as a separate area of inquiry is relatively new, with it come all the pitfalls and warnings against fashionable "theories" we have repeatedly stressed throughout this book.

One should remain sensitive about the use of *any* appraisal instrument for humans, no matter how highly recommended it comes, no matter how painless it appears. If someone performs well in any capacity, the need for evaluating him should be reexamined: If we wish to learn *how* he performs well, that is not evaluation but examination. If we wish him to describe *why* he performs well, again that is not evaluation but description. Both are analytical investigations of a task or career. Evaluation, to be useful, should focus instead on tasks where the value of performance is uncertain or ambiguous, or where the executive desires to be evaluated. The reappraisal of tasks already performed well is useful only for reemphasizing the value of the skills involved, but this may not be necessary with astute executives. To foster evaluation as a good in itself can be harmful, useless, and frustrating, unless those involved in appraisal see its clear value.

Evaluation of executives concentrates on weaknesses *and* strengths;

[14]Harold Koontz, *Appraising Managers as Managers* (New York: McGraw-Hill Book Company, 1971), p. ix.

it is not merely a method for highlighting error, though its prime value lies, of course, in that direction. The main rationale for evaluation is not to appraise what is already known, but to describe and judge what is not known about an executive's performance. Executive evaluation is different from job evaluation in that it appraises the *person* in the job, not the job itself. For this reason, it is a highly personal, though not necessarily subjective mode of appraisal. However, there can be no evaluation without some verifiable objectives toward which the recreation and parks executives and the agency are striving.

Before evaluation can be used in an agency setting, that agency's leadership must have stated its goals clearly and realistically, not in such vague terms as "to offer recreational opportunities to the community." That is not a verifiable goal, it's an aspiration, good in itself but poor for evaluation. The recreation and parks executive may indeed offer a wide array of programs for the community, but if other qualities of his or her management are poor, an evaluation using such broadly stated goals will be weak and misleading. An overheard comment from a program director at a community center: "I wonder why no one comes to our programs? I thought perhaps I was the problem, so I stopped coming, then no one came!" Clearly, this is a situation and a leader in dire need of appraisal and encouragement. The programs exist, the community desists from participating: broad goals are not the way to appraise the executive in charge of such a situation; it will require some degree of dissection to discern the root of the problem. A detailed critical analysis of an executive's performance presupposes clarity and specificity of agency goals and objectives. The overall goals of the immediate or broader environments they operate in also cannot be ignored. If executives are admonished to set managerial goals with an eye to the overall milieu in which the organization operates, then the executive must be appraised within that broader context as well.

Executives, while judged in view of the broader milieu in which they operate, should also be more specifically evaluated in terms of the goals for which they themselves are responsible. Even though an executive may take on nonexecutive duties, and handle them spendidly, evaluation should concentrate on the duties and responsibilities of the the executive tasks, though nonmanagerial tasks can be included. In establishing any method for managerial appraisal, Koontz suggests the evaluation system at least meet the following criteria:

1. The program should measure the right things.
2. The program should be operational.
3. The program should be objective.
4. The program should be acceptable.
5. The program should be constructive.[15]

15Ibid., pp. 12–15.

The initial criterion is basically determining what verifiable organization objectives will be used to assess the executive.[16] As for an evaluation system being operational, the method of appraisal should assess an executive in terms of what he is doing, what can be seen and verified, not relying on traditional assessments of personality, work habits, or conviviality. Objectivity in evaluation can be obtained to some extent by using verifiable objectives. Even qualitative goals can be assessed if these are properly stated and if they avoid the vagueness discussed earlier. In addition, any effective evaluation program must be acceptable to those who will be using it *and* those whom it will evaluate. If a program is not acceptable and valued by those who participate in it, and if no discernible results are seen as the outcome, then the evaluation system very quickly becomes a joke. Not only does this harm an evaluation method, it almost destroys the possibility of any other evaluation system, no matter how worthwhile, being taken seriously.

Therefore, acceptability is a key criterion for any evaluation system introduced into an organization. The outcome of evaluation may be in the form of promotion (or demotion), a raise, bonus, or lack of these; such a connection with an appraisal program aids its chance of being taken seriously. Lastly, an effective appraisal program will aid an executive in self-assessment in terms of his job performance and will give him an opportunity for improvement and further development, in addition to leading directly to promotion and other rewards or incentives for excellence.

The executive has to be appraised both in terms of verifiable goals, which he or she had a say in determining and is responsible for, and in terms of performance as a manager. Thus, in addition to an evaluation system which relies on management by verifiable objectives, is added the attempt to assess an executive as an executive, or a manager as a manager. It is this less specific area which is the more compelling to evaluations; not only because of its lack of specificity in comparison to verifiable objectives, but because the manager-as-manager concept adds a completeness to evaluation that was not present before, or at least it reflects the desire to make evaluation systems more realistically complete:

> As all kinds of enterprises have awakened to the importance of managing and the appropriate use in practice of sound principles and the crude, but helpful and important, science of management, one should expect that the most alert ones would add an appraisal of managers as managers to the already valuable appraisal against verifiable objectives.[17]

As with objectives, the fundamentals of management used to appraise managers should not be vague or broad, such as "the manager

---

[16]For a discussion on setting objectives in recreation and parks, see Joseph J. Bannon, *Problem Solving in Recreation and Parks* (Englewood Cliffs, N.J.: Prentice-Hall, Inc., 1972), Chapter 7, "Defining Objectives."

[17]Koontz, *Appraising Managers*, pp. 109–10.

plans, organizes, staffs, directs, and controls" an agency or division. Such statements are useful for broad definitions of managerial functions, but not for evaluation purposes. To be more specific, the method should rely on the more basic principles of management. These principles, although still crude as measurements, do concentrate more closely and objectively on what is expected of an executive as an executive and avoid tangents of evaluation as to whether the executive has charisma, is loyal, intelligent, and so forth (the traditional evaluation system of management by traits). Koontz suggests breaking down the broad functions of management—those of planning, organizing, staffing, directing, and controlling—into the more specific principles of management.[18] Some authoritative source for descriptions of management principles is essential: "Even in a small, closely knit company, managers will ordinarily vary considerably in their understanding of concepts and principles."[19]

Below are some of the questions Koontz includes in his suggested evaluation system:

Planning

1. Does he set for his departmental unit both short-term and long-term goals in verifiable terms (either quantitative or qualitative) that are related in a positive way to those of his superior and his company?
2. Does he understand the role of company policies in his decision making and assure that his subordinates do likewise?
3. When he submits problems to his superior, or when a superior seeks help from him in solving problems, does he submit considered analyses of alternatives (with advantages and disadvantages) and recommend definite suggestions for solution?

Organizing

1. Does the organization structure under his control reflect major result areas?
2. Does he exact commensurate responsibility when he delegates authority?
3. Does he maintain unity of command or disregard it only when the advantages of doing so clearly offset the disadvantages?

Staffing

1. Does he take full responsibility for the staffing of his department, even though he obtains needed assistance from the personnel department?
2. Does he take steps to make certain that his subordinates are given the opportunity for training for better positions, both in his operations and elsewhere in the company?
3. Does he select or recommend promotion of his subordinates on the

---

[18]To avoid any ambiguity when first designing such a system, Koontz suggests that managerial functions be broken down in accordance with Harold Koontz and C. O'Donnell, *Principles of Management*, 4th ed. (New York: McGraw-Hill Book Company, 1968).

[19]Koontz, *Appraising Managers*, p. 113.

basis of his objective appraisal of their performance and in the light of their potential growth in the company?

Directing

1. Does he understand what motivates his subordinates and attempt to build into their position and position environment a situation to which these motivations will respond?

2. Does he so lead and guide his subordinates and interpret company and departmental objectives as to make them see that their own self-interest is in harmony with, although not necessarily the same as, the company's or department's goals?

3. Does he expect his subordinates to suggest changes or express objectives to what they may regard as the wrong objectives, policies, and programs, or does he expect blind compliance with company policies and programs and his own decisions?

Controlling

1. How effectively does he tailor his control techniques and standards to reflect his plans?

2. Does he keep abreast of and utilize newer techniques of planning and control?

3. Does he help his subordinates develop control techniques and information that will show them how well they are doing in order to assist in "control by self-control"?[20]

In the original evaluation form used by Koontz—"Performance as a Manager"—he includes 14 questions under Planning, 19 under Organizing, 12 under Staffing, 12 under Directing, and 16 under Controlling. In response to the above types of questions, Koontz suggests eight ratings or evaluations: Superior, Excellent, Good, Average, Fair, Inadequate, Not applicable to position, or Do not know accurately enough for rating.

Evaluation, to be effective, should be done formally and at least twice a year, or a minimum of once a year if every six months seems unnecessary for a particular agency setting. An executive should be rated by his immediate superior; in the case of a recreation and parks executive this would most likely be the lay board. The executive in turn rates any others in managerial positions who are subordinate to himself. The executive can also evaluate himself with such a system. Whatever evaluations are undertaken are then reviewed with the person evaluated, so a clear understanding can be gained of how the executive or manager is perceived, their strengths and weaknesses, areas for improvement, and so forth. Such an evaluation system, where many questions are included on a variety of managerial tasks, also helps executives obtain a better grasp of what management itself entails.

Finally, it should not be forgotten that whatever the extent of use of the manager-as-manager appraisal method suggested here, it must be

[20]Ibid., pp. 113–46 *passim.*

accompanied with an appraisal of managers by verifiable objectives as well:

> What basically is desired from all managers is performance in the attainment of enterprise objectives.... managers do not operate in a vacuum. They manage to assure that group effort accomplishes desired objectives. Therefore, appraisal should be tied to both aspects of performance.[21]

This appraisal system, to be effective, requires time, especially in an organization such as recreation and parks where norms of production and profit do not exist. Because of the nature of recreation and parks, the management fundamentals used for evaluation may be reduced or rewritten to more directly reflect the tasks of an executive in the agency. The time needed to streamline and convert such an evaluation system would not be excessive, nor would the time needed for each evaluation be that lengthy. If the human services desire to be more effective, then one source for greater effectiveness is an in-house evaluation of its executives. It can be a step in the right direction.

EVALUATION SYSTEM FOR THE DELIVERY OF LEISURE SERVICES

An important component of the model on comprehensive planning for the delivery of leisure services is an appraisal or evaluation not only of existing leisure services in a community, but of any comprehensive leisure services plan that is approved and implemented for a community. The evaluation of an ongoing leisure system is so vital, and potentially so complex, that we have devised a conceptual model of "An Evaluation System for the Delivery of Leisure Services," shown in Illustration 6.1.

We use the term "conceptual" quite precisely to intellectually represent what we believe is essential to evaluation in the leisure services. The model anticipates the steps and procedures necessary for designing and carrying out an objective evaluation system. The components that comprise this evaluation model, however, represent not only what is conceived as essential to achieving meaningful evaluation of leisure programs, but what procedures have been used, to one degree or another, for such evaluations. Nonetheless, there is a long way to go in human services evaluation research before we can feel completely confident not only with our conceptualizing but with our methods as well.

At the beginning of this book we strongly recommended the hiring of a planning consultant to guide and aid in leisure planning. In addition to the various duties for a consultant discussed in Chapter 2 can now be added that of initial evaluator or designer of an evaluation system.

Whoever directs the evaluation procedure must be not only knowledgeable about evaluation techniques, but also effective in working with

---

[21]Ibid, pp 161–62.

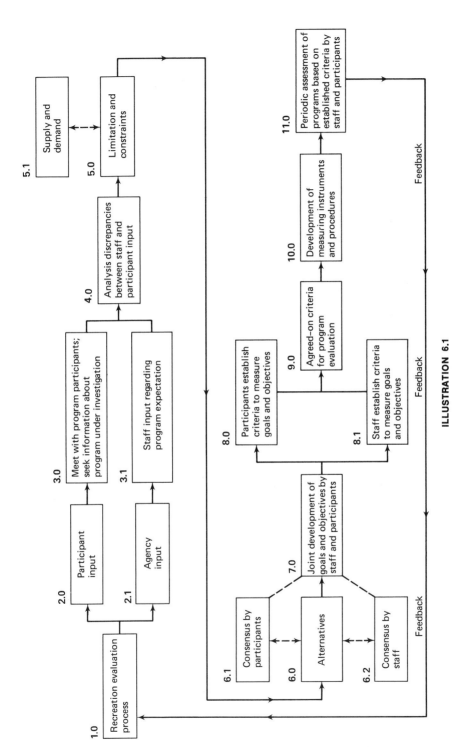

ILLUSTRATION 6.1

An Evaluation System for the Delivery of Leisure Services

Model by Joseph Bannon, Ph.D.

281

two groups of people—agency personnel and citizen participants; these often have diverse views, interests, and aspirations. Some knowledge or skill gained from group-process techniques might be useful, but a sensitive grasp of community organization, and of the desires of all involved in the plan, should prove even more valuable. The advantages of having an outside consultant handle evaluation are the same as those cited for having a professional planner in the first place: the perspective from an outsider is more likely to be objective, a key quality for an evaluation. Since the consultant is not immediately responsible for the daily operation of the agency, he or she is not as emotionally linked with its programs and has more time to concentrate on evaluation. Furthermore, because the consultant is responsible for evaluating specific activities in an agency, his work is more selectively and more clearly defined:

> the practitioner in the individual organization employs monitoring and feedback mechanisms to deal with *all* the work of that organization, but [the consultant] . . . is concerned primarily with the aspects of the organization's work that are germane to the central planning enterprise as defined at a given time.[22]

The consultant, or evaluator from within the agency, has to concentrate in two areas in terms of the comprehensive plan discussed in this text. First, as mentioned, is an assessment of what present leisure services exist in the community. This assessment is not a judgment made with a plan for correction of poor services, but is rather more an inventory of what services exist, who is served by these programs, who is not, who they were intended to serve, their cost, scope, value, the amount of community and agency staff involvement, and so forth. These services are then evaluated to the extent of judging their efficacy and part in any comprehensive leisure services program suggested for the community.

The second area of evaluation the consultant or staff member concentrates on, and this is the more difficult and critical of the two, is an appraisal of any new leisure plan that is implemented in a community. The model included in Illustration 6.1 is a guideline of what such follow-up evaluation entails, as well as the scope of those involved in determining evaluations. The purpose of this second area of evaluation can be easily seen if one follows planning or decision making to its intended conclusion, which is implementation of a community leisure services plan. Evaluation concentrates in this second area on the outcome or final action of the planners. That is why evaluation is often used interchangeably with monitoring and feedback in most models or systems of problem solving and decision making. Evaluation, ideally, monitors and feeds back information to the evaluators about the outcome of a plan or program on a continuous predetermined basis.

The purpose of such evaluation is to judge the success or failure of a

---

22Robert Perlman and Arnold Gurin, *Community Organization and Social Planning* (New York: John Wiley & Sons, Inc., 1972), pp. 226–27.

community plan, as well as to offer guidance for future action. The evaluation model here is not merely the accumulation of data on what is happening with the various leisure services implemented in the community, but the involvement of those most concerned with leisure services, to gain direction, as needed, for improving the plan once it is in force. Any plan that is implemented for a community, and especially if that plan intends to be comprehensive, should never be judged in its totality as a success or failure. It can only be finally judged as an expensive failure or a tolerable success if any intensive, serious, and well-designed evaluation program is unable to guide the agency and the community through implementation. A plan can also fail, of course, if evaluation is not attempted at all. We might say that before a ny plan proves hopeless in a community, other failures and inadequacies have preceded it, a notable one being ineffective efforts at ongoing plan evaluation.

Evaluation, though necessary, is not a breathing down the neck of enacted programs to see if they are effective. Thoreau's comment on evaluating personal experiences might philosophically apply to our more pragmatic evaluation:

> Do not tread on the heels of your experience. Be impressed without making a minute of it. Poetry puts an interval between the impression and the expression—waits till the seed germinates naturally.[23]

If one designs and inaugurates an evaluation program that "follows hard upon" the implementation of a program, it will encourage distrust and discomfiture, and most likely serve to stifle the very actions it only meant to judge. Here is an excellent place where suspended judgment can be used. Suspended judgment does not mean delayed reaction or sloppy thinking; it is purposeful delay or suspension of critical faculties to allow full life to whatever will eventually be judged and appraised in its own right.[24]

Spontaneous evaluation, that is, judgments that are not part of some prescribed evaluation system, are made throughout the planning process. But the evaluation that follows implementation of a plan is necessarily more formal and didactic. Even though it is not inaugurated immediately after the plan is implemented, an evaluation system is designed and decided upon well beforehand. Evaluation should never be an afterthought; it is weakest when its need is first seen because of difficulties or dilemmas in implementation. It should be a natural and necessary component of any decision-making effort and action. Evaluation is, therefore, useful not only to modify and appraise the quality of actions and

23Henry David Thoreau, *Journal* (Boston: Houghton Mifflin, 1949), Vol. II, p. 341.

24For discussion of suspended judgment in creative thinking and problem solving, see Alex F. Osborn's *Applied Imagination* (New York: Charles Scribner's Sons, 1957). This is also discussed in Bannon, "Research and Experimentation in Problem Solving," in *Problem Solving in Recreation and Parks*, pp. 13–34.

decisions made throughout planning (for which the model here can also be useful), but to determine whether the definition of a problem has changed, or whether people in the community or in the related agencies and institutions have changed in their perceptions of community needs and aspirations, after the plan has been in action.

The most well-known conception of evaluation, and that most formally applied, is the monitoring of an action, plan, or program once it has been implemented, when the initial planning has virtually been completed:

> Data are obtained on outcome and effectiveness and are used to make decisions on continuing, discontinuing, or modifying the policy or program under scrutiny. . . . When evaluation takes place after a policy has been in effect for some time, the judgments that are made concerning its effectiveness—of the unanticipated consequences that followed its implementation —provide material for a new round of problem-formulation and planning.[25]

Although comprehensive planning is essentially completed at the implementation point, we can see that community planning is ongoing, almost cyclical; this is why, in the model given here, the completion of the steps in evaluation lead back to the beginning of evaluation. The very essence of a systemic approach to evaluation, or any part of problem solving for that matter, is this circular movement, hopefully not repetitious, but each return bringing greater insights and improved modifications in any *unanticipated consequences.*

Since evaluation must be continual, taking place at specific periods and in a predetermined manner, it can be expensive, and if not well designed, time-consuming as well. In addition to its probable expense, to undertake a meaningful evaluation program and to persist in it, require some resolve on the part of an agency's leadership. If only lip service is given to the need for evaluation, which we can see in so many evaluation efforts that quickly become a joke, then it is not worth the effort to begin, unless you are in the business of deception. An evaluation system such as the model suggested here is too critical to be appended merely as a flourish to completed planning, without any serious intention of heeding its implications and the inevitable repercussions of following these implications. Without a doubt, the casual or deceptive use of evaluation programs has blemished the whole field of technical and informal evaluation more than any inherent weakness in evaluation itself. It takes wits and guts to run an effective evaluation program.

A broader concern with evaluation, which is raised here primarily for speculative purposes, is why evaluate in the first place? What is the ultimate aim of evaluation? Since this book is concerned with human services, our speculation is confined to those services. Evaluation is used

[25]Perlman and Gurin, *Community Organization and Social Planning,* pp. 74–75.

first of all to appraise a situation, to reward excellent performance if it is part of an incentive program, but more importantly to improve or correct, or at least to point out those aspects of a program or community plan which may require modification or reanalysis. Modification can mean firing people, dismantling an entire program, or it can mean simple adjustments, revisions, exchanges or viewpoints. Whatever the degree of reform, evaluation ultimately seeks to improve the condition of both the people in the service agency and those in the community it serves. In the social services, some of us have begun to ask whether it is legitimate (i.e., possible) goal to both seek high morale within the agency and achieve a high level of services to the community. It is not merely resources, and the constraints put upon them by such broad demands, but whether there is a basic error in attempting, through various managerial techniques, to raise the status of employees while also attempting to improve the situation of the community residents.

Of course, this may be a moot question, since in most instances there is little choice: employees demand and the community demands, often with recognizable and justifiable aims. Nor are these aims always in conflict, for much employee unrest, especially in social welfare, is advocacy for clients. In such cases, the internal aims of the agency and the external aims of the community interact and mesh. When their aims are compatible, the human service agencies and their constituents can be very forceful indeed. Too often, even in the absence of clear hostilities, they do not mesh. Employees are, of course, interested in an evaluation system that reflects and enhances their concerns, which may rest far from any comprehensive leisure plan. Community residents, on the other hand, will only respect an evaluation system that actively benefits them or protects them from incompetency or outrage and is not some in-house device to placate them.

The model presented here is collaborative, in that it tries to recognize the *equal weight* of both agency staff and citizens in evaluation. But when the heat is on, either from budget cuts, scandal, employee strikes, or what have you, how much do we really adhere to these precepts of equal weight? Even without pressure, it is easy to seek joint collaboration and still be superficial in applying its implications. Any evaluation system, no matter how sophisticated or rudimentary, is part of a larger power system. Evaluation can easily become a tool of that power structure, which allows the natives to think they can improve their own lives (in this case the "natives" are agency personnel and the community), while in actuality it is merely another bone given to silence the growl. As said earlier, this misgiving is speculative, because "why evaluate" in this broader context has no clear-cut answer. We evaluate because we trust it will mean improvement for all involved in leisure services, and because it presents one logical method for bringing about such improvements. One might say it is sort of faith in the potentialities of evaluation.

The Evaluation Model

Although this evaluation model is more valuable for evaluating a program that has been implemented as the result of comprehensive planning, where such an evaluation system is part of the original plan and where the major participants have been involved all along, it can also be used to appraise existing programs. The overall model for comprehensive leisure planning naturally requires an appraisal of what leisure services presently exist, their effectiveness, scope, cost, and so forth. The following discussion implies evaluation at that point of current appraisal, but most notably it concentrates on evaluation after an agreed-upon new plan has been put into effect.

The essential purpose of an evaluation system is to determine to what extent the objectives of the implemented plan (or the existing program) are being achieved, why they are not being met if such is the case, and what needs to be changed to bring about a closer relation between performance and objectives. It is not simply a matter of the evaluator collecting performance data and comparing these data against predetermined objectives, noting compliance or deviation, then exploring methods to achieve more perfect alignment between efforts and goals. The basic intention of evaluation is that simple, but the process of evaluation in the human services is far more complicated and demanding. Objectives that were once agreeable to those involved in the the planning of the community's leisure service have a remarkable tendency to begin to shift once a program is enacted. The only way the evaluator can determine if the objectives used to appraise a plan's effectiveness have changed is to go to the source of the original objectives, the community citizens and the agency personnel.

For this reason, the model presented here is a two-track model that seeks ongoing information for evaluation purposes from the same groups that were involved in planning from the very start. Once a program has been approved and implemented in a community, the agency personnel do not shake hands with the citizen representatives, thank them for their participation in planning, and send them on their way so the "professionals" can get down to work. The citizen groups are aware of their ongoing involvement in implementing the program, supporting the aims of the plan, and objectively appraising the efficacy of the program.

If neighborhood groups are aware of their continual involvement from the start, and if they understand the critical importance of evaluation in planning, they are less likely to see the end of planning as the end of an agency's interest in their participation. The two-track approach is an attempt to give equal weight to both agency personnel—staff, management, and the board—and to neighborhood participants. Therefore, the first step in this conceptual model is to seek information on the program from the agency and from the community. Even if the community were left out of an evaluation effort, any citizens' group worth its power would demand such involvement. It would be foolish for an agency to judge the value of its programs without the representation of those whom their programs are designated for, as much as it is for the community to evaluate these programs without the agency being given its say (an occurrence that is, unfortunately, not always avoidable).

The consultant or agency evaluator must, therefore, ensure that both agency personnel and citizen participants are aware from the start of planning what their role will be. Even these earliest discussions are themselves a joint agreement among all concerned. The citizens and agency personnel are not told by management or by a consultant what is expected of them, but rather joint discussions are used to develop precisely what each group perceives as its most notable contribution, what it feels able to best lend to planning, and what it believes should definitely come from its group. Planning an acceptable procedure for evaluation follows almost the same steps as planning for the entire program.

The agency management or the consultant does not ask agency personnel and citizen groups if they think evaluation should proceed. Evaluation is, or strives to be, a precise methodology, a skill or area for professional application; its value is not something to be hashed out by a group. On the other hand, those professionals who believe they are skilled as recreation evaluators should not bring the "tyranny of the experts" to hang heavy about any joint discussions. Because evaluation research and methodology are in their youthful stage, there is a tendency for those who practice it to treat evaluation as a fragile instrument which they alone can handle. Its fragility in such cases is often related to its weaknesses and not to its sensitivity as an instrument of appraisal.

Evaluation, though practiced by few, must be open to the understanding and suggestions of others. Its value and necessity are accepted as intrinsic to planning by professional planners: That is not really the debatable point here. What is to be worked out with agency personnel and with community participants is not *how* to evaluate the programs under scrutiny, or not necessarily *why* to evaluate these programs, but *what* criteria will be used as measurements and guidelines for judging the efficacy of the comprehensive plan once it is in force. Reaching such criteria for evaluation is the purpose of this submodel within the comprehensive planning model.

The intention of the joint meetings on evaluation is to begin from the beginning again, since "the purpose of monitoring is to evaluate the outcomes of all other steps in the planning process."[26] Of course, since most of those involved in monitoring and feedback would be the same people who have been involved all along in comprehensive planning, we can expect some efficiency in covering the aspects of evaluation, rather than time-consuming duplication of planning.

The evaluator at first works separately with agency personnel and

[26]Perlman and Gurin, *Community Organization and Social Planning*, p. 227.

with program participants in determining whether the problem definition of the overall project had indeed been correctly perceived, whether the policies and programs that emanated from the problem definition were suitable, whether alternatives which were originally discarded might have been more effective, or if the programs that were implemented were carried out in the correct way. Such questions are not a sign of misgivings about past decisions, but a way of registering opinions to gauge whether the program in operation is effective, or of uncovering the source of a problem if difficulties have arisen since implementation. Evaluation must include a discussion of the ongoing programs as well as analysis of their impact. This dual concern requires the guidance of an evaluator or consultant to prevent either personnel or program participants from deviating into extraneous matters.

It is the responsibility and function of the evaluator to design report forms, quantitative or otherwise, that will enable these two groups to respond with the appropriate type of information. Evaluation is not open-ended brainstorming as earlier stages of planning often are; it is as precise a methodology as experience and the amorphous boundaries of the human services permit. Thus, the evaluator has to be very careful that early meetings with both groups do not become mere talk sessions. These two groups do not necessarily have to meet together often, or at all, if the evaluator is effective in obtaining the type of information necessary for evaluation. If the groups meet regularly for other purposes, it is wise *not* to add evaluation reports to their agenda. Such a tactic merely enumerates evaluation along with other issues, and its importance and need for thought-out information and statistical reports can be overlooked.

Evaluation data must be of the highest order possible in an agency and community setting, for not only are they to be used for appraisal of the present programs, they will serve as the basis for any further planning which may be necessary. Data "of the highest order" are far from sophisticated: in the human services it is often difficult to obtain even rudimentary data on, say, the characteristics of those who use our services, or the reasons people use or do not receive existing services. This is why it is essential that evaluation be part of planning from the start. The data sought for planning purposes, the nature of the record and accounting systems used by an agency, and the regularity with which these data are compiled and analyzed, must be directly related to the needs of evaluation. If evaluation is merely something tacked on to the end of planning, it would be most unlikely that the information would have much value for the evaluator. Planning and evaluation are not simply *related* functions, they are *interrelated*, and must be conceived as such throughout all planning work: "An important tool, whose absence is lamented . . ., is the capability to carry out evaluation research on programs that have already been implemented."[27]

27Ibid., p. 241.

One of the first probable conflicts experienced in evaluation research, presuming the above data are useful for evaluation purposes, is the invariable discrepancies between information obtained from agency staff and that from program participants. Analysis of discrepancies, a nice-sounding phrase, can be most difficult. It involves not only discarding the items of false conflict between these groups but reaching some sort of workable and agreeable compromise so evaluation can proceed. The fact that the model narrows abruptly at the analysis of discrepancies is not to illustrate that participant and personnel viewpoints are "squeezed" into a palatable ball; it merely indicates a suitable mix or blending, perhaps even unanimity, of viewpoint in order that an analysis of constraints on their joint suggestions can be made.

Any modifications or suggestions made for the leisure services plan currently in effect have to be submitted to the same analysis and scrutiny given to any goal or solutions submitted during planning. The limitations and constraints of a jointly agreed-on new or modified program, for instance, have to be determined. If these groups feel that an increase in the number of children served in a special program for the handicapped is necessary to make community leisure services truly comprehensive, it is not simply a matter of arithmetic. All the implications of even what appears as a simple increase have to be determined and analyzed, foreseen or projected. Even if a program were not to be changed but is simply being evaluated, a comparable scrutiny is made and a reiteration of the same steps made in planning are applied.

Let us say the program being evaluated is one that had been approved and implemented in the community a year before for handicapped children, in this case children who were judged mentally or physically retarded. At the time of planning it had been decided that one solution for the isolation of these children from community leisure services was to create a program expressly intended for them, a program designed for at least 1,000 participants. If out of the analysis of discrepancies which emerged from staff reports and citizen evaluations of this program came the suggestion that this particular program be expanded to include more children, evaluation research would then begin to focus on the implications of this recommendation. Furthermore, let us assume the overall known number of children in the community or cooperating communities who would "qualify" for this program is approximately 3,000, and that the staff and citizens feel any program that seeks to be comprehensive should aim to serve at least two-thirds of this population, or 2,000 handicapped children.

Before any consideration is made of increasing the program, an evaluation has to be made of how effective the present program is in terms of the goals and criteria established for it at the time of implementation, to what extent the goals and criteria may be shifting, and what new limitations and constraints are posed by the suggested new goals and criteria. To determine how effective the present program has been requires more than membership statistics, or even evaluation questionnaires obtained from parents and guardians, though these are critical parts of any evaluation or record-keeping system. The program has to be more intensively appraised beyond membership statistics, parental satisfaction or dissatisfaction, or even the observed responses of children to the program. If the purpose of the program was simply to offer these children a place to gather and to participate in various projects, then its evaluation would be less difficult. However, in this example is added the agreed-upon program goal of improving the social skills and behaviors of these children.

Observation is one way to determine whether these children have improved in predetermined skills in any perceivable way. But beyond even the observations of parents and professionals, volunteers and outside consultants involved in observational work, a firmer measurement of success would have to be built into evaluation research from the start. One obvious method is some sort of test, written, physical or manual coordination, any of the variety of tests which can elicit and measure change in these children. These tests can then be used to judge whether the goals and criteria of the program are being met, the extent to which they are not, the skills that seem intractable to program intervention (other than those that had been originally diagnosed as permanently intractable), and the realism of the original goals and criteria in view of such test results.

For new programs, once in operation, it is not unusual for the goals to be beyond the capabilities of those who offer them. This is especially so in handicapped programs where the aspirations of those who create such programs often lead to a belief that high hopes bring high results. If they do not bring the anticipated results, this does not necessarily belie the efficacy of the program but perhaps merely the tenor of the goals. Of course, if the test results are excellent, then program designers would have to set even higher goals and more exacting criteria if they wish the program to serve the broadest known potentialities of the children. Once such information is obtained on the present program, then the evaluation begins to concentrate on the effect the policy to increase the program is likely to bring.

An analysis of the various outcomes and constraints of the suggestion to increase program participation by 1,000 should lead next to a joint development of goals and objectives by both staff and community representatives: "To solve any problem realistically, and to know whether we have in fact reached a viable solution, we must have some prior measures for evaluation, we should have a very clear notion of what we actually want. These measures are known as a solution's goals or objectives."[28]

A joint development of goals and objectives follows from a separate consensus among agency personnel and among community representatives in view of various alternative ways to improve or modify the program.

[28]Bannon, *Problem Solving in Recreation and Parks*, "Defining Objectives," pp. 68–69.

These alternatives, in turn, came from an analysis of constraints and of supply and demand of all resources available for the program. That is, the alternatives were defined in terms of what was possible for the agency and the community to do within the limitations they had mutually agreed to. Once a joint agreement is reached on a statement of goals and objectives, agency staff and community groups then separately establish criteria to measure these goals and objectives. Again, most of these negotiations should be done separately in both groups; there seems little purpose in having groups with often divergent views determine what their preferences are in a potentially combative or confused atmosphere. Each group has to clearly define its wishes, aims, and criteria. This task would be greatly hampered and obscured by joint work sessions at inappropriate points. The points at which these groups collaborate is when consensus or mutual agreements are sought. Before that need arises, in this model, joint efforts would be misguided and fatiguing.

Whatever criteria the groups separately come up with for measuring their jointly agreed-upon goals and objectives, they now have to agree once more on their criteria for program evaluation. It should be remembered that all these steps would have been carried out a year earlier when evaluating the programs that existed before the comprehensive leisure plan was implemented. Presumably, therefore, these two groups would have a good knowledge of what criteria are meaningful for measuring goals and objectives, and what mutual agreement is likely to involve in terms of reconciliation and compromise. The evaluator or consultant is essential in aiding in these joint discussions by confining the group to measurable criteria, preferably criteria requiring quantifiable information. Broadly stated vague criteria are as worthless as vague goals and objectives, no matter how appealing they may sound.

It is a weak criterion to say that 50 percent of the handicapped children should show improvement in a particular social skill, without clear methods for observing and measuring this improvement, along with proficient research on what can be realistically expected from handicapped children. It may be a rule of thumb in some programs to accept a certain percentage of change or improvement as indicative of success. But rules of thumb are notoriously misleading if they are applied indiscriminately to programs with widely divergent purposes. If 50 percent of the children in a swimming class fail to learn to swim, we can be justifiably displeased. If 25 percent of the children in a special handicap program improve some specific social skill, we may have every cause for rejoicing. A criterion should concentrate not only on methods of measurement—be these tests, feats, or observation—but also on the degree of change that can realistically be obtained. The sky is not the limit in establishing criteria. A program director does not seek to startle the community with high aims, but to satisfy them with realizable, humane, and wholesome goals, measured by useful and meaningful criteria for future planning and evaluation.

The development of measuring instruments and procedures for administering these tests is the responsibility of the evaluator. The citizen representatives and agency personnel can, of course, be involved in their determination, but the design or selection of these instruments is basically the task of a specialist. There is such an array of psychological, intellectual, and manual dexterity tests, that one must be somewhat modest in the desire to involve oneself in test selection without the advice and involvement of specialists. In addition, one of the major areas of controversy in the social sciences today, both in terms of methodolgy and implications, is the entire area of testing. Community participants and agency personnel are likely to have firm opinions on the value of tests, whether they should even be part of a leisure service, and so forth. These views must be heeded and reflected in the program if they are sound. But once a testing approach is decided on, this is primarily the concern of testing specialists or those whom they will train.

The final stage of this model is to determine how often this program, and others in the leisure service plan, should be assessed and under what conditions. To a great extent, the type of activity being assessed determines how often it should be evaluated. Once a realistic period for evaluation is decided on, then the recreation evaluation process begins anew, from the start of the model, where feedback from previous assessments form the starting point for ongoing evaluation.

SELECTED REFERENCES

ARGYRIS, CHRIS. *Interpersonal Competence and Organizational Effectiveness.* Homewood, Ill.: The Dorsey Press Inc., 1962.

CAMPBELL, DONALD T. "Considering the Case Against Experimental Evaluations of Social Innovations." *Administrative Science Quarterly,* XV, No. 1, 1970.

ETZIONI, AMITAI. "Two approaches to Organizational Analysis: A Critique and a Suggestion." *Administrative Science Quarterly,* V, 1960.

FERRISS, ABBOTT L. "Application of Recreation Survey." *Public Opinion Quarterly,* XXVII, Fall 1973.

GROSS, BERTRAN M. *The Managing of Organization,* Vol. II. New York: The Free Press, 1964.

SNYDER, D. R., AND BLAESING BRAIN. "Methodology for Regional Recreation Site Evaluation." Land Use Working Paper #1. Detroit: Southeast Michigan Council of Governments.

TAGIURI, R., AND G. H. LITWIN, eds. *Organizational Climate: Explorations of a Concept.* Boston: Harvard University Press, 1968.

Tannenbaum, A. S., ed. *Control in Organizations.* New York: McGraw-Hill Book Company, 1968.

Taylor, J., and D. Bowers. *Survey of Organizations.* Ann Arbor: University of Michigan, Institute for Social Research, 1972.

Yuchtman, Ephraim, and Stanley Seashore. "A System Resources Approach to Organizational Effectiveness." *American Sociological Review,* XXXII, No. 6, December, 1967.

7

ORGANIZATION
AND ADMINISTRATION
OF LEISURE SERVICES

Intelligent planning on the part of management in setting up the formal structure of organization can do much to improve the quality of human relations. Horizontal, less complex structures, with a maximum of administrative decentralization tend to create a potential for improved attitude, more effective supervision, and greater individual responsibility and initiative among employees.

INTRODUCTION

To properly and effectively organize and administer leisure services, it is important for any parks and recreation administrator to be aware of theories and findings in fields that affect leisure planning. For instance, an enormous amount of work has been done studying organizations, especially over the past thirty years. If an administrator seeks to organize a large-scale, long-range leisure plan for a community, he or she will of necessity begin to search out materials, guidelines, and theories that bear on the establishment, survival, and success of social service agencies.

Since the bulk of research and analysis on organizational structures has been conducted on business firms, rather than on public organizations, the recreation professional initially leans quite heavily on such studies. The same is true for information, models, and guidelines on personnel and financial practices, though these are rapidly beginning to be dealt with more specifically in terms of practices and needs in the social services, especially in the area of values—value expertise, the setting of value objectives.[1] Nonetheless, a debt of thanks is owed to the enormous amount of theoretical and applied researches in other fields that preceded recognition by parks and recreation professionals that theoretical constructs and viewpoints were needed in their own work, especially as their viewpoint expanded more toward leisure science.

Recognition of the usefulness and possible applicability of theories or findings from other disciplines, say, sociology, business administration, or industrial administration, is not a call for the formulation of theories in recreation and parks itself. Emergent disciplines always run the risk, and some more disastrously than others, of feeling compelled to create a theoretical base for their profession, as if theory alone confers intellectual respectability to a discipline. There are worthwhile theories and there are worthless theories, and no mere accumulation of theories can ever in itself lend competence and substance to a field that is itself nonscientific or merely practical.

On the other hand, this is not a plea to steer clear of original theoretical efforts in recreation and parks. Rather it is an admonition to avoid the theoretical "bug," so to speak, until we have explored and judged, applied or discarded, the innumerable findings and insights of others in the many behavioral and social sciences directly affecting leisure concerns. Too many professions, especially in the social sciences, become pseudo-sciences in their rapid accumulation of theories. At this juncture, it is much more creditable for recreation and parks to set its aims toward a careful scrutiny and examination of the findings and experiences of the other social sciences, than toward the impatient acquisition, hit or miss, of its own theories. These are developing as a natural outgrowth and concern of field experiences and intellectual questionings by those practicing the profession and by their colleagues in universities.

Even though a planning consultant may have a surer grasp of the theories and practices in other fields, and may himself be a professional in one of these areas, the recreation and parks administrator must also be familiar with these disciplines.[2] Any intellectual and theoretical framework, a framework that might eventually yield building blocks for a firmer comprehension of leisure services as a broad field of study, is *not* a delegatable task. We can readily delegate to others the responsibility for a technique or procedure that we ourselves are not familiar with (e.g., computer programming), but we cannot delegate the responsibility

[1]Herbert A. Simon, *Administrative Behavior: A Study of Decision-Making Processes in Administrative Organization*, 2nd ed. (New York: The Free Press, 1965). Much of Simon's discussion on organizational values and objectives is based on those made in public administration.

[2]Gordon L. Lippitt, "Implications of the Behavioral Sciences for Management," *Public Personnel Review*, XXVII (July 1966), 184–91; William P. Sexton, *Organizational Theories* (Columbus, Ohio: The Bobbs Merrill Co., Inc., 1970); and Derek S. Pugh, *Organizational Theory: Selected Readings* (New York: Penguin Books, 1971).

for the intellectual comprehension of an organization to another, without seriously incapacitating ourselves and that organization's purpose.

It is our responsibility as administrators to formulate the premises of our agency and of the leisure services. Naturally, this does not mean an administrator should work in some sort of feverish solitude; however, if we do draw on the expertise of others, we should do so for the purpose of enlarging our own conception of the service we perform, the society and culture for whom it is performed, and the techniques and organizations, theories and constructs, aids and guidelines that exist or can be deduced to effectively perform that service.

It is important to stress the relevance to recreation and parks, not only of the scientific method, but of the research methods and findings from such fields as public administration, business administration, educational administration, sociology, social work, psychology, library science, and industrial management. This chapter attempts to cover some of the pertinent findings in these fields, as well as to discuss various studies and materials available within the recreation profession itself.

An administrator needs to be eclectic, drawing on the findings and implications of fields outside parks and recreation. This is crucial to our profession which for too long has maintained a fun-and-games philosophy, supplemented by traditional theories of play. We need to be less insular in our concerns, acquiring a broader conception of parks and recreation in relation to other disciplines and to social demands. We should pursue the use of more sophisticated methods of analysis and data compilation, most notably the use of computers. As one critic puts it:

> All the great social theories to date, including those of Marx, Weber, Durkheim, and behavioral social science, for example, are in fact false. They overextended categories appropriate only to a particular time and place; they offer us false predictions; they are deceived by the ideological structures of their own society; they formulate generalizations which they propose as laws where laws are inappropriate; they reify abstractions in misleading ways. But nonetheless all these great social theories have the power to incarnate and reincarnate themselves in social life, and by so doing give themselves a semblance of truth which they do not in the end possess. In order not to be deceived by them we have to become fully conscious of what they are saying to us and of why what they are saying has the power over us that it has.[3]

An obvious question still remains: "What is the value of organization and administrative theories for park and recreation professionals?" Most recreation organizations are directed by men and women with practical experience who use personal expertise or trial-and-error approaches in their work. While nothing can replace the value of on-the-job

[3]Alasdair MacIntyre, review of Steven Lukes, *Emile Durkheim: His Life and Work* (New York: Harper and Row, Publishers, 1974), in *The New York Review of Books*, March 7, 1974, p. 26.

experience in running an organization, theories permit a broader comprehension and sophistication of what that practical experience means, how it can be used to affect an organization, and what inferences might be usefully made to other organizational settings.

Many people think reading a book is not experience, that performing an action is more worthwhile. However, it is not a question of whether passive or active experience is more valid: both constitute experiences and both have valuable implications for how we live our lives. If academic knowledge is judged a form of passive experience, and on-the-job activity as more pertinent experience, then the need to interrelate and compare these types of experience seems crucial. Too often formal education is devalued and practical experience overvalued, to the detriment of both. Education, and the research that goes on in various educational institutions, is speculative, theoretical, contemplative, allowing perspectives on daily life and work to be examined from a multitude of angles. But it is also practical, applied, and pragmatic. The Ivory Tower houses the same kind of people as do most organizations.

It goes without saying that a great deal of educational material, and even more research, is not very useful. However, while on-the-job experience is the more practical for learning how to be an administrator, it is not necessarily the most useful. Education and practice are both important. If you are restless in a classroom, anxious to be on the job, you can be sure there are many practitioners longing to be in a seminar speculating and theorizing about their work experiences.

The two cultures, first depicted by Bronowski and later by Snow as the separation between scientist and humanist, are actually reflected in a much larger split between the cultures of the academician and the practitioner.[4] Many of the arguments on both sides are well known. Nevertheless, there is massive interdependence between these two "cultures," many people belong to and interact with both. It is a false dichotomy to pose the intellectuals on one side and the down-to-earth type on the other. As soon as something goes wrong in either world, it is always someone from the other culture that is called in! Practitioners supply information and data to theorists, who in turn offer perspectives and viewpoints on organizations. Each function is intrinsic to the other, though education comes under scrutiny and criticism more regularly, it seems.

Any administrator who does not quickly realize that formal education is simply a gateway to a career is in for a rude shock. As mentioned earlier, the value of education and practice is essential for achieving a wholesome approach to any career. If one relies too heavily on education to provide all the answers, that is as lopsided as believing the clues for

---

[4]Jacob Bronowski, *Science and Human Values*, rev. ed. (New York: Harper and Row, Publishers, 1965); and C. P. Snow, *Two Cultures*, 2nd ed. (New York: Cambridge University Press, 1965).

effective management lie solely in practical experience. Not only is education a part of what is needed for effective management, it also has to be updated regularly. Many a young business administration graduate has been brought in to replace an "old-fashioned" manager. Usually a fiasco develops as everyone quickly realizes the handicap of education alone without the guidelines and "reality checks" of practical experience.

If we accept the need for education in administration, then we also have to recognize the need to update such education. Except for those who have a penchant for self-education, most administrators will very quickly fall behind in management education. What is valid during one's years in school can quickly become outmoded. Some observers say that a trained or educated manager is out of date seven years after graduation. The seven-year itch can be the desire to return to school; it may soon become a necessity.

Theories allow the accumulated wisdom and experience of professionals and researchers to be shared, if only to sober the myth that personality alone determines the kind of administrator someone will be, or that experience, no matter how painfully or awkwardly acquired, is the key determinant of leadership skill. Organization theories, and the assumption underlying them, offer insights into the knowledge and speculations of those who have studied or who have worked in organizations.

Too often we begin to see the implications and dimensions of our work only after being immersed in it for some time. How often are we admonished to stand back and get the big picture, to perceive a situation from a broader viewpoint? Theories provide this perspective, while also allowing us to think about our own organizational and administrative setting. It can be chilling to study theory if one sees where lifeless theories often depart from reality; however, it *is* important to acknowledge when theory mirrors reality, or to paraphrase MacIntyre, when theories shape reality. We need to know enough to avoid any either/or approaches to the value of theories: Academicians have to understand the supreme value of on-the-job experience; on the other hand, professionals in the field should comprehend the possible *implications* of theory.

As noted, the more we know about theories and the assumptions on which they are founded, the less likely we are to be taken in by theoreticians expounding nonsense. To accept or reject anything, we should have substantive knowledge of it; otherwise we are merely prejudiced, casting aside or accepting the good with the bad without much reflection. When we argue that recreation and parks professionals need to be *more* professional, we don't mean some mindless affinity for theories; rather, an important attribute of any skilled administrator is the ability to *critically* evaluate theories in related fields.

It is something of a misconception to define theories as merely speculative, unrelated to everyday activities. Although some theories are intentionally comprised of visionary assumptions, others are intended as applicable, practical, and testable for organizational settings. Organization theorists and administrative scientists deal with both the theoretical *and* the practical in their models, elaborating on either the normative (how organizations *should* behave) or the descriptive (how organizations *do* indeed behave).

There is a popular tendency to criticize normative models as lacking practicality, or to attack descriptive models as lacking vision. Such criticism often stems from confusion about the *intentions* of such models. What need to be criticized or examined are the premises that underpin these models: What are the rationales used to describe the ideal or actual organizational behavior, and how operable are these intended to be?

In the formulation of knowledge and information about administering recreation and parks organizations, we draw on a great deal of information from the behavioral social sciences. From economics, we examine the Theory of the Firm and other behavior in market relations. For instance, if recreation is considered a service to consumers, we can readily see analogies from economics. Organization theory develops logically out of the Theory of the Firm to concentrate on the theory of the *business* firm or of *public* administration. As a matter of fact, some attention has been given to combining the study of economic and organization theories into one field.[5] Administrative science, on the other hand, examines social behavior in employment relations with a so-called "Administrative Man," whereas economics has long posited its more rational "Economic Man" in market relations, though this rational man is rapidly fading.[6]

The most serious drawback of the economic and the organizational models of behavior is the assumption that people in both situations manifest rational, utility-enhancing behavior. This assumption had been carried farthest in game-theory models, or statistical decision theory.[7] That people are not always rational, and how this affects recreation and parks administrators, is one of the concerns of this discussion.

Other social scientists have studied organizations and groups as well: social psychologists and sociologists have concentrated on small group theory; learning theorists have studied problem solving; and political scientists have examined power. All these disciplines have overlapped in their research on decision makers, decision making, and models and systems for decision making. Whether wished for or not, out of these social sciences—especially social psychology—has emerged "irrational"

---

[5]Herbert A. Simon, *Models of Man: Mathematical Essays on Rational Human Behavior in a Social Setting* (New York: John Wiley & Sons, Inc., 1957), p. 195. These quantitative theories examine the rational and nonrational aspects of human behavior in a social setting, combining both economics and organization theories.

[6]Rendigs Fels, ed., *The Second Crisis of Economic Theory*, Proceedings of the American Economic Association Meeting, December 27–29, 1971. The first crisis, of course, was the Great Depression of the 1930's. The second crisis is the inability of economic theory to deal with many contemporary problems related to income distribution, or how "Economic Man" can be so easily frustrated in many applications of his posited rationality.

[7]John von Neumann and Oskar Morgenstern, *Theory of Games and Economic Behavior* (Princeton, N.J.: Princeton University Press, 1944).

or nonrational man, the countervailing force to the too-perfect rational man of earlier theories.[8] The impact of irrational behavior on organizations, or at least that facet of irrational behavior that exists in administrators, has to be further examined. For instance, learning theories and psychological theories of perception and cognition "appear to account for . . . behavior rather better than do the theories of rational behavior."[9] Much of Simon's work has concentrated on contrasting rational and nonrational decision-making processes.[10]

ORGANIZATION THEORY AND STRUCTURE

One of the major areas for concentration in organizational studies, and most notably in administrative science, is analysis and explication of the duties and skills of an administrator or decision maker. Regardless of the type of organization, if it has already established leadership, then examination of leader activities, skills, responsibilities, and theories holds great value.

Illustration 7.1 is a simple model of the components of management or administration in any organization, regardless of its size or complexity. The function and activities depicted in the illustration have to be performed by someone—an administrator, director, manager, chief, or even a group performing in this capacity. Although our discussion touches briefly on each of these aspects of management noted in the model, brevity does not indicate a lack of importance.

As shown in Illustration 7.1, regardless of the type of organization—profit or nonprofit, public or private—there has to be a *need* for that organization, even if there is not a large *demand*. Especially in the case of parks and recreation, there has to be a need, perceived by the community, to create an organization. Too many organizations fail because of an inability to accurately determine the need for a product or service. Or, as Drucker reiterates in his latest book, too many organizations flounder or fail because they have no clear idea of what they should be doing.[11]

---

[8]Charles Hampden Turner, *Irrational Man: Processes of Psychosocial Development* (New York: Doubleday & Company, Inc., 1971). A broader philosophical discussion of man's creative irrationality can be found in William Barrett, *Irrational Man: A Study in Existential Philosophy* (New York: Doubleday & Company, Inc., 1958).

[9]Simon, *Models of Man*, p. 201.

[10]Simon, *Administrative Behavior*; and Herbert Simon, D. W. Smithburg, and V. A. Thompson, *Public Administration* (New York: Alfred A. Knopf, Inc., 1950). The original classic in administrative science is, of course, Chester I. Barnard, *The Functions of the Executive* (Cambridge, Mass.: Harvard University Press, 1936).

[11]Peter F. Drucker, *Management: Tasks, Responsibilities, Practices* (New York: Harper & Row, Publishers, 1974).

BASIC MANAGEMENT MODEL

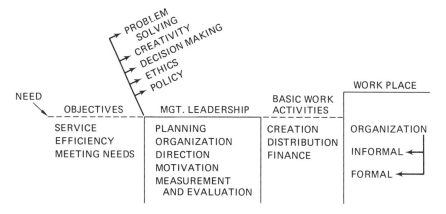

ILLUSTRATION 7.1

For the most part, determining the *need* for parks and recreation in a community has been completely nontheoretical, basically a trial-and-error method. A vulnerable point for any public organization is the inability to justify the need for new programs, additional funds, or even ongoing support. Models drawing on the expertise of organization and business theorists can be developed to help communities articulate the need for recreation and parks. Such models are by no means the goal, but are merely a step toward rigorous examination of the need for recreation and parks.

After the need for an organization has been established, there are three *objectives* an administrator has to attain: to provide service; to provide it efficiently; and to meet a need which has been previously determined. For example, how do we know the service we are providing is effective (not necessarily successful, but effective)?[12] In the past we have avoided examining why people use recreation and parks, or how effective we are in providing these services. Because of the ambiguity or complexity of the issue, we justify our continued existence merely by attendance records or the smile on a child's face, two justifications which can be readily slaughtered at a budget meeting, as many of us well know.

We cannot use vague philosophical justifications anymore, no matter how appealing; we have to be more precise in documenting what we do and whether it is valuable. The tax dollar is very tight: the public agency that can justify itself in a precise and documented form is the one that is likely to get tax monies. Even though there is more latitude

[12]Charles E. Ridley and Herbert A. Simon, *Measuring Municipal Activities* (Chicago: International City Manager's Association, 1943).

in public service than in business firms, with tax dollars coming in fairly regularly, there is no justification for complacency. We have seen too many social and human services decimated to ever believe we are somehow inviolable. As we know from experience, not everyone sees the clear need for recreation and parks, nor the necessity of financing such services.

As shown in Illustration 7.1, an administrator has *four basic tasks:* to plan, organize, direct, and motivate the staff, as well as to measure and evaluate the outcome of these four tasks. It is the responsibility of an administrator to justify the programs which evolve from the organization. To accomplish these four tasks, an administrator has to use problem-solving techniques and in general to be problem-oriented. So much of the parks and recreation curricula emphasizes the more mechanical aspects of management and too often ignores the techniques of problem solving and decision making.

An administrator also has to be *creative.* Unfortunately, most researchers and texts do not attempt to pinpoint or define creativity. One aspect of creativity in parks and recreation is offering programs for the 1970's and not for the 1940's. This point is especially crucial for those administrators who feel they can readily ignore services for the more intractable members of a community, e.g., teenagers, the handicapped, older citizens, racial minorities, and so forth.

In addition to creativity and problem-solving skills, an administrator has to be able to make decisions based on information obtained through application of these very skills. Of course, many good decisions are mere luck, but luck or not, an administrator has to be a decision maker, to be able to choose among various alternative solutions. A quick decision is not necessarily better than a more contemplative one. Nonetheless, an administrator who clearly defines a problem for a board, but who does not recommend a solution for their consideration as well, is failing in his advisory function.

If the basic task of management is perceived to be determining what the problems *really are* that confront an organization, then a natural concomitant of this crucial skill is the ability to perceive solutions, or to seek out those who are best able to recommend solutions (e.g., consultants). There is no need for an administrator to be both a problem definer and a problem solver (and there are those who see the first skill as the rarest of all among executives); but there is a definite need for an administrator to recognize the necessity for both skills in organizational decision making, especially in a service agency with a lay board.

All decisions affecting an organization should be made within the context of professional and personal ethics; decisions, that are made by choosing one alternative over another, are both practical *and* ethical. Attitudes toward patronage is a good example of where professional or personal ethics can affect a decision to hire someone. Or, an administrator's attitude toward traditional board-staff relations—that is, where the board makes policy and the director carries it out—is another example of both personal and professional ethics being involved, especially if an administrator wishes to modify such traditional approaches.

If an administrator disagrees with a policy because of personal values or ethics, then at some point there has to be a change either in those ethics or in the policy, or there will be a parting of the ways. An administrator can influence board policies to bring them more in line with ethical considerations. Although an administrator has to work within the policy constraints established by the board, this does *not* mean he cannot determine what that policy should be in the first place. It is a textbook fallacy in recreation and parks that the board decrees and the director carries out policies. There are many directors who submit final policies for approval to their board. Even though the board reserves the right to veto any policy recommendation, it is naive to believe directors do not directly create, affect, and influence policy. Board-staff relations are discussed further in a later section.

Some of the basic tasks of an administrator are developing work activity, distributing and assigning jobs among staff, and acquiring funds to finance such activities. The final component of Illustration 7.1 focuses on the workplace of an organization—the organization's structure. Structure is what determines how effective an organization will be in meeting its goals and the goals of its employees. Workplaces can be either formal, informal, or a combination of the two.

Formal and Informal Organization

Formal organization, as used in organization theory, means the hierarchical form of job relationships, the allocation of tasks from superior to subordinate, with responsibilities given to job positions rather than to particular individuals. People entering these positions are thought to be already prepared for the job—"predeveloped" is the term used in the training literature. That is, the formal organization concentrates first on positions to be filled and tasks to be formed, then on people to fill them. There are usually two familiar aspects in a formal organization: (1) a job-task hierarchy, and (2) a communications network. The best-known model of a formal organization is, of course, the organization chart. An organization chart establishes in normative terms what the structure of an organization *should be,* not what it may actually be in its daily operation. Even tightly structured organizations such as the U.S. Army or the Catholic church have developed an interminable maze of informal operations and channels to circumvent their formal structures; many of them are quite effective.

Organization theory has been generally concerned, first, with the conditions necessary for encouraging people to participate in an organization and, second, with the survival of an organization. In some organization theories, the administrator is the key "rational" person, with employees or consumers in a more passive role. Other theories stress all participants, not only the administrator, and are concerned with the overall environment which enhances participation and personal contribution. The first type of theory describes *authoritarian* organizations; the latter, *democratic* or *participatory* organizations.[13]

To most people, and unfortunately to some theorists, organization means only what is shown on the formal organization chart or included in operations manuals and job descriptions. Actually, organization is "the complex pattern of communications and other relations in a group of human beings."[14] A formal organization is prescribed by clearly delineated lines of authority and communication, by the responsibilities and activities of staff members, and by procedural rules and regulations. To a great extent these details are simply abstractions of the normative organization, with no reference to activities in the informal workplace. When a theory or model is intended as normative—something the organization *should* tend toward (such as our Western model of participatory democracy)—then the abstraction is a philosophy of organization, *not* a description. One cause of administrative failure is confusing normative and descriptive organizational structures; a springboard for theoretical failure is the same.

The formal organization structure is both a guideline and a limitation on organizational activities. As a lay board serves to set limits on a recreation director's authority, so a formal organization structure, if only on paper, sets limits to the informal activities that might develop within, especially if these threaten the organization's ability to survive. For the purposes of this book, it is irrelevant who actually controls organizations, most notably in corporate ownership. However, distinctions between *beneficial owners* of a corporation—those who get dividends and capital gains—and *operational owners*—those who control and run organizations—are important.[15] Although this is not a problem in public administration, there are always analogies from corporate experiences to be made.

Two early theorists concerned with formal organizations and their characteristics were Max Weber, a German political economist and sociologist interested in bureaucracy, and Luther Gulick, an administrative scientist concerned with the aspects of administrative science.[16] Illustra-

13Peter M. Blau and W. Richard Scott, *Formal Organizations: A Comparative Approach* (San Francisco: Chandler Publishing Company, 1962).

14Simon, *Administrative Behavior*, p. xvi.

15An excellent discussion of control and ownership can be found in Peter Barnes, "Absentee Owners of America," a six-part series in *The New Republic*, 1972–1973, available as a separate pamphlet.

16Luther Gulick and L. Urwick, eds., *Papers on the Science of Administration* (New York: Institute of Public Administration, 1937): and Max Weber, *Theory of Social and Economic Organization*, trans. A. M. Henderson and Talcott Parsons; ed. Talcott Parsons (Glencoe, Ill.: The Free Press, 1947).

CHARACTERISTICS OF FORMAL ORGANIZATION

Weber – Gulick

Unity of Command (A-B Concept)

Role-Playing

Dependency

Obedience

Discipline

Reward

Predictability

Rules and Regulations

Chain of Command

ILLUSTRATION 7.2

tion 7.2 is a composite of the traits these two researchers felt were necessary for a formal organization.

Undoubedly, the most indicative characteristic listed in Illustration 7.2 is the unity of command or A-B concept. As shown in Illustration 7.3, a formal organization bases its survival on A's authority over B, where B is a subordinate who accepts the responsibility to obey A. If B refuses to obey, the organization tends to become ineffective, according to Weber and Gulick. That is, A has influence of power only insofar as B legitimizes that power through consent. This is an extremely important concept for the strict authoritarian or autocratic bureaucracy.

With this command assumption, A has the right to direct B, with power then flowing from the top down. If B refuses to obey, A has the power to fire B, though if all replacements of B also refuse to obey, then A faces a power crisis. A refusal to obey need not necessarily be overt. An administrator can readily be sabotaged through passive resistance.

UNITY OF COMMAND

POWER FLOW

$$\frac{A}{B} \quad \downarrow$$

POWER-ACTION BY AUTHORITY

$$\frac{A}{B} \quad \uparrow$$

POWER-ACTION BY INFLUENCE

ILLUSTRATION 7.3

Some social scientists believe that power often flows from the bottom up, where B's consent to A's authority *permits* A to rule. However, the power to hire and fire still carries a great deal of weight no matter which power-flow concept we accept. The motivations which lead B to consent to A's authority are varied: tradition, fear, conformity, need for money, desire for career status, and so forth. We will return to these motivations in a later discussion on "Leadership Styles," as well as in a discussion of Maslow's hierarchy of need and its effect on the A-B Concept of organizational relations.[17]

Within most social structures, such as a family, or an organization, it is assumed everyone will play a certain role. There is a set of clear and stable expectations as to what is required of each member of a group; sociologists call this a role system.[18] Through a large number of rules and regulations, and a reward-punishment system, members in a formal organization are encouraged to conform. Discipline and obedience to organization goals are considered essential.

The stability of organization roles has a great appeal and logic. In fact, one could argue that the rationale for any organization is to compartmentalize and order a wide variety of supplementary and complementary roles. Thompson in *Modern Organizations* calls role-playing dramaturgy, where everyone performs a different role in a variety of organization settings.[19] Goffman, cited previously, calls it dramaturgical interaction. Role theory specifies types of behavior, with variation permitted among individuals, but not much deviation. Deviation brings in the punishment system, although many people continue to fight normative roles, developing rebel roles instead, which themselves can be just as confining.

Gulick and Weber further stress the key importance of the chain of command as depicted on a formal organization chart. Without this chain, the organization, they feel, is in jeopardy. Remember that the concern of organization theory is primarily with survival, *not* optimality. It is believed that the survival of an organization is enhanced by placing staff members in some specific hierarchical relationship of authority (chain of command), and that this formal relationship is necessary to maintain the unity of command, A → B.

Gulick states that although "rigid adherence to the principle of unity of command may have its absurdities, these are, however, unimportant in comparison with the certainty of confusion, inefficiency, and

---

[17]A. H. Maslow, *Motivation and Personality* (New York: Harper & Row, Publishers, 1964).

[18]Erving Goffman, *The Presentation of the Self in Everyday Life* (New York: Doubleday & Company, Inc., 1972).

[19]Victor A. Thompson, *Modern Organizations* (New York: Alfred A. Knopf, Inc., 1961).

irresponsibility which arises from the violation of the principle."[20] That is, to get fairly predictable results from organization activities, a strong chain and unity of command from the top down, A → B, are deemed essential; if A does one thing, B will do another, and so forth. It is felt that predictability is ensured with such formality.

The only acceptable deviation from this unity-of-command/chain-of-command dictum is that subordinates may properly affect power from the top down in an advisory capacity. The use of advisory positions, so prominent at the federal government level, is to avoid tampering with the formal command structures of entrenched bureaucracies. A circumvention of formal organization, through the use of advisors, was most evident in the Nixon Administration. Regardless of all Nixon's talk about bureaucratic reorganization, he created excessive staff-government positions, private men whom Congress rarely saw. Nixon's answer to the entrenched federal bureaucracy was to create his own informal organization.

Argyris in *Personality and Organization* presents a well-documented coverage of the logic behind formal organization, and lists the following assumptions of formal organization:

1. Relations in groups are clearly defined by an organization chart.
2. Behavior is governed by rational thinking.
3. Subordinates will always do as they are told.
4. An administrator knows best how to solve a problem.
5. The way to get things done is through use of authority.
6. People are merely instruments of production.
7. Man is isolated, unaffected by group pressures.[21]

McGregor's Theory X, which is a model of formal organizations, shows subordinates as passive, rather unimaginative, with higher-ups necessary to motivate them.[22] Theory X describes the premises which underlie most formal organizations: Workers are naturally lazy, the administrator must motivate them; they are dependent and passive, so the administrator directs them; their natural irresponsibility needs curbing by close supervision; their inbred hostility causes organization leaders to distrust them; finally, their lack of vision and imagination requires

20Luther Gulick, "Notes on the Theory of Organization," in Gulick and Urwick, eds., *Papers on the Science of Administration*, p. 9.

21Chris Argyris, *Personality and Organization: The Conflict Between System and the Individual* (New York: Harper & Row, Publishers, 1957); see also C. Argyris, "Individual Actualization in Complex Organizations," in Fred D. Carver and Thomas J. Sergiovanni, eds., *Organizations and Human Behavior: Focus on Schools* (New York: McGraw-Hill Book Company, 1969), pp. 189–99.

22Douglas McGregor, *The Human Side of Enterprise* (New York: McGraw-Hill Book Company, 1960).

administrators to outline and plan their work for them in detail. Illustration 7.4 summarizes this profile of workers in formal organizations.

A directive model of organization with a clearly defined hierarchy of authority, of course, has some advantages. It encourages order, predictability, control, and relatively stable relations. On the other hand, its disadvantages are ineffective communications, isolation among various levels of staff, dependency, and potential insurrection. If formal organization persists with little flexibility and variation, workers will become inefficient, there will be high staff turnover, hostility and aggression toward supervision will become evident, or apathy, selfishness; and loss of self-confidence among workers may develop. Some workers might become needlessly ambitious merely to rise to a position of leadership so they can affect decisions. One way subordinates can be involved in decision making is through more informal organizational structures and channels. Workers create many of these structures on their own.

Personal experience with organizations, as well as sociometric analysis of group interrelations, reveals that organization charts rarely reflect how organizations actually operate.[23] The chain of command is in reality a normative framework for how an organization should work, and for setting limits on uses of authority and power within the organization

An informal organizational structure depicts how things actually get done and challenges the various principles of formal authoritarian organization listed by Argyris. For instance, people do not always behave rationally, especially when their rank in an organization limits the reliable information they have access to. Rationality presupposes knowledge; what is irrational given one set of information may not be with another. It is not simply that people are irrational, the situations they find themselves in may be irrational: "Economic man" is too often operating in an irrational environment rather than in the rational environment in which he is depicted in economic theory.[24] We should avoid thinking

THEORY X

NATURALLY LAZY	MOTIVATE THEM
DEPENDENT	DIRECT THEM
IRRESPONSIBLE	CLOSELY SUPERVISE THEM
HOSTILE	MISTRUST THEM
LACK IMAGINATION	PLAN THEIR WORK FOR THEM
LACK VISION	OUTLINE THEIR WORK IN DETAIL

ILLUSTRATION 7.4

[23]See, for instance, Keith Davis, "The Organization That's Not on the Chart," *Supervisory Management*, July 1961, pp. 2–7.

[24]Richard C. Edwards, Michael Reich, and Thomas Weisskopf, eds., *The Capitalist System: Readings in Radical Economics* (Englewood Cliffs, N.J.: Prentice-Hall, Inc., 1972).

that people operate in some kind of rational vacuum. On the other hand, if we simply accept that people are irrational, this acceptance could justify use of rigid organizations to control people, just as much as it argues for latitude to allow for irrational responses.

Finally, contrary to Argyris's assumption, man is not an instrument of production, coming to some organization to perform merely a productive role. Employees are complex—with values, needs, frustrations, anxieties, and desires for success, and they have personal conflicts and aspirations as well. An employee's overall individuality, where this is knowable, has to be accounted for by the administrator in the Basic Management Model shown in Illustration 7.1. That simple model acknowledges that informal relations and subgroups in an organization exist and often nourish and enhance employees much more than any formal rankings. The worker is not isolated from group pressures: No man is an island in organizational life, nor is he a cog.

Modifications in theories of organization reflect a shift from the so-called "scientific" school of management toward a more human relations perspective, which emphasizes people in organizations much more than formal structures and normative behavior.[25] Although people require and appreciate some sort of organization framework, they are also capable of self-direction and imaginative problem solving. One of the most evident signs of informal organization are subgroups that form within a formal organization. Illustration 7.5 is a simple representation

INFORMAL ORGANIZATION

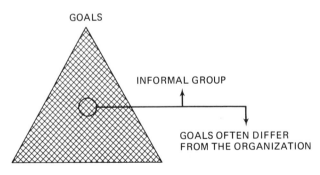

ILLUSTRATION 7.5

[25]William G. Scott, *Organization Theory; A Behavioral Analysis for Management* (Homewood, Ill.: Richard D. Irwin, 1967); Rensis Likert, *The Human Organization: Its Management and Value* (New York: McGraw-Hill Book Company, 1967); Chris Argyris, *Integrating the Individual and the Organization* (New York: John Wiley & Sons, Inc., 1964); and Ben B. Seligman, *The Revolt Against Formalism* (Chicago: Quadrangle, 1962). There is even speculation that the shift toward human relations in organization analyses might have been overdone, *viz*: Howard Baumgartel, "Too Much Concern With Human Relations?" in Amitai Etzioni, ed., *Readings on Modern Organizations* (Englewood Cliffs, N.J.: Prentice-Hall, Inc., 1969).

of this concept, where the administrator, or the specified goals of an organization, has theoretical primacy, yet informal groups and their goals often have equal impact.

Although such informal groups are not reflected on any organizational chart, nor are their goals in any bylaws, an administrator has to deal with them, for the simple fact that they exist and wield power and influence in an organization. These groups, both in nucleus and intent, are comparable to the development of labor unions, pressuring organizations from within the ranks and eventually organizing into formidable suborganizations to challenge the parent organization. Furthermore, these groups themselves then become formalized, with further subgroups developing from them, and so on. Again, this development is best seen in the labor movement, where groups excluded from or ignored in existing labor unions form caucuses of their own to agitate for reforms. That is, the original groups tend to become rigid even though they were initially the mavericks.[26]

An administrator who wishes to understand the role of informal organization has to rethink traditional conceptions of what employees actually want from their jobs. Illustration 7.6 is an example of what one study indicated supervisors felt workers wanted and what the workers themselves actually desired, rank-ordered from one to ten.[27]

Many of the rankings in this illustration might be a surprising departure from supervisors' traditional beliefs of employee wants. The

WHAT DO WORKERS WANT FROM THEIR JOBS?

	SUPERVISOR	WORKERS
GOOD WORKING CONDITIONS	4	9
FEELING THEY ARE IN ON THINGS	10	2
TACTFUL DISCIPLINING	7	10
FULL APPRECIATION FOR WORK DONE	8	1
MANAGEMENT LOYAL TO WORKERS	6	8
GOOD WAGES	1	5
PROMOTION AND GROWTH	3	7
SYMPATHETIC UNDERSTANDING OF PERSONAL PROBLEMS	9	3
JOB SECURITY	2	4
INTERESTING WORK	5	6

ILLUSTRATION 7.6

[26]For a discussion of the major subgroup that has recently developed in American labor groups, see William Lucy, "The Black Partners: Labor in '74," *The Nation*, September 7, 1974, pp. 177–80.

[27]Paul Hersey and Kenneth Blanchard, *Management of Behavior—Utilizing Human Resources*, 2nd ed. (Englewood Cliffs, N.J.: Prentice-Hall, Inc., 1972), p. 39.

only conditions that are closely matched for both groups are "management loyalty to workers," "job security," and "interesting work."

A 1973 Gallup Poll of U.S. workers indicated that 61 percent would be more productive if they were more satisfied with their jobs: "Enjoyment of one's work comes out ahead of 'good pay' as the chief reason given for job satisfaction. . . . 'Poor wages' is the reason given most frequently by those dissatisfied with their jobs. At the same time, a full list of their reasons shows that pecuniary reasons actually are outweighed by non-pecuniary reasons. . . ."

McGregor's Theory Y is the obverse of Theory X, the authoritarian model of organization already discussed. Illustration 7.7 indicates the precepts of Theory Y, which views employees as creative and self-directed:

THEORY Y

DYNAMIC, SELF-MOTIVATED	GUIDE OR PROVIDE GUIDELINES
INDEPENDENT	PROVIDE OPPORTUNITIES FOR SELF-DIRECTION
RESPONSIBLE	TRUST THEM
ALLIES	COOPERATE-COLLABORATE WITH THEM
CREATIVE	ESTABLISH ENVIRONMENT
IMAGINATIVE WITH VISION	PLAN WITH THEM

ILLUSTRATION 7.7

Theory Y reflects the more positive, participatory philosophy of management, involving both workers and administrators in organizational decision making and judgments. Illustration 7.6 indicated that workers highly value being "in on things," which they ranked second in importance while supervisors ranked this last. Involving staff in organizational decision making is, of course, not as easy as it sounds.[28]

If participatory management is considered, an organization's leadership has to educate its staff in all phases of administration and decision making. It is foolish to give expanded authority to subordinates, watch them flounder, then retrieve that authority, smugly "proving" that only administrators know how to administer. Conflict and confusion are bound to occur when staff are not adequately prepared to handle decisions which have heretofore been made for them. Employees will identify with an organization when they feel they have some involvement with decisions, recognizing of course that ultimately the administrator has to make the final decisions, or at least accept responsibility for them.

There are disadvantages for any organization implementing a

---

[28]Interesting discussions of the status of participatory management in business can be found in Paul Blumberg, *Industrial Democracy: The Sociology of Participation* (New York: Schocken Books, 1974); and David Jenkins, *Job Power: Blue and White Collar Democracy* (New York: Penguin Books, 1974).

participation-developmental model, but there are obvious advantages as well. Participation encourages employees to be creative, allows for flexibility in work patterns and styles, promotes greater cooperation among all levels of staff, and yields an increase in morale. The disadvantages of employee participation are a lack of clearly defined leadership, an initial drop in time efficiency, loss of authoritarian control, and a diminished ability by administrators to predict outcomes.

Another example of the gains or pitfalls of participatory management can be seen in education. The major finding of those involved in free school experiments is that liberalization of an organization can only develop from liberalization of a society or a community; otherwise any experiment with authority is insulated and destined to fail.[29] Free schools appear and die at very high rates. Before we agree that liberalization is a good thing in itself, we should ponder the conflicting and troublesome experiences of participatory management in other institutions. Informality is not simply doing away with structure and rules; that's license and disorder. Informal organization is also not possible in isolated instances, but must be related to more liberal trends in business and society. If these do not exist, or begin to change, the institution will invariably enter into periods of conflict and strain.

Organizational Conflicts

Even within the informal or dynamic organization, there are still separations between staff, or at least gradations of skills which are reflected in the organization. Those who wish to experiment with informal organizations sometimes feel that the removal of differences between staff—in concept at least—is the quickest method to ensure participatory management; it is probably the surest road to failure. The removal of so-called elitism between, say, line and staff members of an organization, without comprehension of why these differences exist in the first place is foolhardy.

The specialists or technicians within an organization are usually known as *staff* people, those who exist to aid others in the organization to do their job better. Those whom staff employees are there to help are commonly known as *line* people. There exists and always has existed friction between line and staff members of organizations, most notably because staff members consider themselves or are viewed as more intellectual, more scientific, hence more conceptual and broad-ranging in their skills. The line employees, on the other hand, are those who do the day-to-day work of an organization, often looking to staff employees for guidelines and specific technical and specialized help.

[29]Jonathan Kozol, *Free Schools* (New York: Houghton Mifflin Company, 1972); and Joseph Turner, *Making New Schools: The Liberation of Learning* (New York: David McKay Co., Inc., 1972).

A good analogy of the friction between staff and line positions can be seen, again, in the Army. Many of us are familiar with the young staff lieutenant who enters the service fresh from college and who depends almost totally on the old-line sergeant who knows the service inside out. The friction and resentment that can exist in such a relationship mirror the dilemma organizations face with technically trained staff employees who work with line staff having extensive practical experience. (In the case of the lieutenant, he may have neither technical skills nor practical experience, further amplifying the conflict.) In many ways, the conflict is similar to that which can exist between professionals and practitioners in any institution or field.[30]

Staff positions usually carry more prestige and income, hence there is likely to be more tension and anxiety in their interactions. This was evident in the Nixon Administration, where staff positions proliferated in an effort to circumvent old-line bureaucracies. Former President Nixon had even moved a high-ranking army officer (General Alexander Haig) to a presidential staff advisory position. This position had become so influential and powerful that some observers felt "General" Haig (for a short time retired from the army) became acting President in the last days of the Nixon Administration. There is no doubt that staff positions in any organization carry a great deal of prestige and a great deal of actual and potential power.

One of the major internal problems faced by organizations, and one which perplexes organization theorists as well, are the conflicts between staff and line, on the one hand, and functional authority on the other.[31] Functional authority is simply the influence and power exercised by staff specialists because of superior knowledge and skills:

> The multiplication of functional lines could result in disorganization, conflict, and lack of coordination. Nevertheless, it is impossible to abolish the influence of technical specialization. Any solution must be a compromise. The most helpful solution is to exercise functional authority without infringing on the administrative authority of the line. . . .[32]

Pfiffner and Fels, after the above quotation, simply suggest that the prevention of infringements of functional authority can be "accomplished by careful delineation of authority combined with a tactful, cooperative, and consultative approach to the exercise of all types of

[30]For some discussion of the struggles between staff and line employees, see Melville Dalton, *Men Who Manage* (New York: John Wiley & Sons, Inc., 1959), pp. 71–109; and Robert C. Sampson, *The Staff Role in Management* (New York: Harper & Row, Publishers, 1955).

[31]For a fuller discussion of this dilemma, see John M. Pfiffner and Frank P. Sherwood, *Administrative Organization* (Englewood Cliffs, N.J.: Prentice-Hall, Inc., 1960); and Thompson, *Modern Organizations.*

[32]John M. Pfiffner and Marshall Fels, *The Supervision of Personnel: Human Relations in the Management of Men*, 3rd ed. (Englewood Cliffs, N.J.: Prentice-Hall, Inc., 1964), p. 74.

authority. In modern large-scale organizations, the two must learn to get along together."[33]

Since the planning model in this text presumes the use of planning or other professional consultants, it seems necessary to comment here on the potential confusion or conflict that might arise when traditional staff-line dichotomies are complicated or even obscured by the introduction of outside consultants. Although we discussed the relationship of agency staff to outside consultants in Chapter 2, the simple hope that all workers will learn to "get along together" in an organization can be an invitation to even greater confusion.

There is no clear or simple solution to problems encountered between line and staff members in an organization. There can certainly be experimental modes of interaction, but as long as organizations put a higher value on staff technicians and professionals, the conflict will remain. This conflict can be further compounded by the introduction of outside professional consultants, who are in essence staff people. Consultants, especially if their expertise impinges on that of existing staff employees, can also readily cause resentments to develop, not to mention the probable further isolation of line employees from the sources of decision making and authority. A good example of this was President Nixon's use of Henry Kissinger as foreign policy advisor, initially outside of the State Department, though ultimately he was given the title Secretary of State, a job he had performed all along.

Line employees have good reason to be wary of staff employees, and it is not enough to hope for the best. As Pfiffner and Fels suggest, one way to decrease the possibility of conflict between line and staff, and between these and outside consultants (who themselves can be given functional authority for a time in an organization), is by a careful delineation of authority. An organization chart depicting line-staff positions, accompanied by job descriptions, organization manuals, or work flow charts, are useful, but these alone are not sufficient against potential abuses of authority or against day-to-day conflicts.

Pfiffner and Fels feel that the line-staff division of labor may no longer be useful for organizations, and that in many organizations these separations have broken down or will be modified:

> This will be the case because the line-staff concept is based on the assumption that authority and responsibility are delegated downward, which even if true, overemphasizes the *power* of officially constituted authority. Under newer theories of interaction-influence [e.g., small group research], the influence in the organization will be seen as moving upward and sideways as well as downward. Under such conditions separation of staff-and-line will tend to have no significance.[34]

Modifications in the management of organizations is one way in

[33]Ibid.
[34]Ibid., p. 355.

which line-staff divisions can change. However, power is power and mere modification of organizational relationships to tone down the *presence* of official power is not a philosophy of management that gets at the heart of the conflict. Many groups, in organizations and elsewhere, want to share power, not engage in organization experiments that pretend power has been relinquished when indeed it has not. Participatory management can be time-consuming and frustrating for workers if the element of power in organizations is not also scrutinized. As Kissinger was purported to have said, "Power is the ultimate aphrodisiac."[35] The *pleasures* of power are many; that is why it is rarely yielded.

The resolution of conflict as an organization moves toward greater informality is a real challenge. Illustration 7.8 shows some conflicts which can emerge in any organization. According to Maslow's hierarchy of needs, a person's first needs are physical necessities—food, clothing, shelter; then a need to secure these necessities; finally a need for status, esteem, and self-actualization. Alongside these needs, Illustration 7.8 lists Argyris's development characteristics of people, and then the traditional organizational concepts of Weber and Gulick.

Argyris suggests that humans grow from being passive to active, from dependent to independent, and so forth. The formal organization, as described by Weber and Gulick and depicted in McGregor's Theory X, does not reflect Argyris's development hypothesis. Furthermore, once we have achieved the first two essential needs in Maslow's hierarchy, we begin to desire the more elusive needs of self-esteem and self-actualiza-

SOCIOLOGY OF ORGANIZATIONAL CONFLICT

MASLOW	ARGYRIS	WEBER
Physical	Passive–Active	A–B Concept
Security	Dependent–Independent	Role Play
		Pre-entry Training
		Dependent
Status	Subordinate–Superordinate	Obedience
		Discipline
Esteem	Few Ways–Many Ways	Predictability
		Rules
Self–Actualization	Shallow–Deepening	Unity Command
	Lack Awareness–Awareness	Chain Command

ILLUSTRATION 7.8

[35]Ronald Steel, "All About Henry," Review of Marvin and Bernard Kalb, *Kissinger* (Boston: Little, Brown and Company, 1974), in *The New York Review of Books*, September 19, 1974, pp. 34–35.

tion. For the most part, these latter needs are often incompatible with highly structured organizations, where few people rise to top positions and few are allowed to expand or vary their role in order to achieve self-actualization.

Conflict arises when a subordinate wishes to gratify needs other than Maslow's subsistence needs. If these needs are not met and the employee is dissatisfied, the survival of the organization can be threatened. In the past generation there have been major shifts in attitudes toward work and serious challenge to our so-called work ethic. Most of this challenge came from high school and college students, minority groups entering the mainstream labor force in greater numbers, and women moving into higher levels of organization.

These groups, with the exception of those in lower-level menial jobs, often display less interest in status and income, stressing self-esteem and self-actualization as needs which an organization must satisfy. Status and money alone are no longer crucial to many workers, especially the young. This is especially ironic during a time of chronic and structural unemployment at all levels of society, as well as rampant inflation:

> There is, indeed, substantial evidence to prove that America, like other highly industrialized nations, does face a revolutionary attitude toward work.
>
> Today's workers have far higher educational achievements than their parents and grandparents; they are less fearful of permanent unemployment, more confident of their ability to find work when they need it.[36]

Nor is this liberalization in attitudes toward work confined to subordinates:

> Until the 1970's, the typical executive in the U.S. still concentrated on career advancement at any cost, almost to the total exclusion of family, health, and other considerations. While there still are many executives fitting this mold ... they are becoming much rarer. The executive on the rise now is unwilling to be so single-minded.[37]

Although commentators on the present economic crisis in the United States foresee, or already perceive, a reversion to more conservative viewpoints and behaviors by Americans as the result of economic pressures, there is not much likelihood that the pressure for jobs or for higher wages will reestablish a work-oriented attitude among workers; if anything, greater social programs for citizens at all levels are more likely than any return to a dominant work ethic among the labor force.[38]

[36]Harry Bernstein, "Changing Ethic: Work Alone Not Enough," *The Champaign-Urbana News Gazette*, Illinois, no date.

[37]"New Trend Seen in Executive Life-Style," *Los Angeles Times*, October 8, 1972.

[38]For a discussion of some of the social implications of the economic crisis, see Geoffrey Barraclough, "The End of an Era," *The New York Review of Books*, June 27, 1974, pp. 14–20.

If administrators are to run effective organizations, they will have to create environments where workers will want to work (and this does not mean plush environments), and will have to provide their staff with every opportunity for self-esteem and self-actualization. If individuals move from subordinate positions as children to superordinate positions as adults, as Argyris posits, we cannot deny this development by locking them into subordinate positions in organizations if they have the capacity for greater development.

If Argyris is correct in his notion of personal development, then formal organizations can thwart personal growth where someone is a responsible adult at home and a subordinate at work. This does not make sense; nor does it make sense to assume that if a person is effective at home, he or she is necessarily effective in an organization. But wherever our hierarchy of needs and our abilities and capacities clash with the formal organization, conflict is likely to emerge. There has to be some degree of latitude to allow staff to attain personal goals.

Another kind of organizational conflict develops from ambiguity or apparent conflict in the goals and objectives of an organization. The best example of this in the social services occurs in community outreach work. Outreach work—where a social agency, including recreation and parks agencies, sends workers out into the community to search for potential clients—inevitably brings tensions and conflicts to the existing organizational structure. "Some wish to avoid this conflict by avoiding outreach work lest it cause serious internal dissension. Others are fatigued at the thought that they must immerse themselves daily into the obvious ambivalences of outreach work in dynamic, changing communities.[39]

A real problem in the use of paraprofessionals, or professionals for that matter, as recreation outreach workers is the issue of loyalty. Is it possible to be loyal to the organization for which they work and also loyal to the clients they seek to represent and serve? For outreach workers to be effective, they have to have good relations with the community in which they work; in fact, many workers are chosen because of an established rapport with people in the park district or neighborhood. However, this rapport is often jeopardized when that person begins to work for the so-called "establishment." There then arises the dilemma of whether these workers can be effective representatives of clients while they are also employees of a social agency. Too often the agency avoids examining its basic goals and objectives in comparison with the goals and objectives of an outreach program. These are often in conflict, and it is the worker on the street who bears the brunt of this organizational duplicity. If an agency decides to practice what it preaches— to actually seek to serve the community through more informal organizational endeavors—it may find itself in direct conflict with city hall!

[39]Bannon, *Outreach*, Chapter 2, "Community Outreach in Recreation," and Chapter 3, "Role and Function of the Outreach Program."

The emphasis in this discussion is not so much on resolving these types of organizational dilemmas as in revealing them. Social services are seeking to diversify their services, to become more responsive to their clients, even to hire former clients as paraprofessionals. All these decisions bring new conflicts, raising serious questions about the true purposes of social agencies in the first place. These purposes often conflict with client needs, and employees are forced to solve what is in essence an organizational conflict by themselves. Outreach workers who clearly reveal this conflict are usually fired. It is a waste of resources to recruit or encourage outreach workers only to abandon them at the first sign of organizational conflicts which emerge from more liberal reforms.

Any change in an organization brings problems and conflicts. As administrators of outreach programs, we have to struggle with questions of power and of intent. Do we really mean to serve the community as best we can? Are we prepared to support a worker in his or her efforts, even if those efforts involve ultimately clashing with governmental or other powers? Or will we try to talk out of both sides of our mouth, hoping the conflict will disappear if we placate both sides? Ambiguity in goals and objectives is what brings about organizational conflict, not radical advocacy by an outreach worker.

Organizational conflicts need to be resolved, but in their resolution we need to also examine the roots of the conflict or these will rise again in another situation. For our purposes now, it is enough if this example underscores the type of conflict which can develop as organizations change, are forced to change, or change too abruptly without scrupulous preparation and examination.[40]

Another type of organizational conflict, by no means confined to organizations in transition, is communication problems. The informal communications system is, of course, the grapevine. We all are participants in the "grapevine-telegraph" in a number of organizational settings. Grapevines thrive on one type of communication to the exclusion of all others—rumor or hearsay.

No matter how inaccurate or misleading the information conveyed via the grapevine, the administrator has to recognize that it exists as a potent force in an organization. The administrator should, at the least, determine how it operates in order to feed it accurate information. It is fairly simple to determine who the key informal communicators are in an organization. Supply different information to several members of an

[40]George Hage, *Social Change in Complex Organizations* (New York: Random House, Inc., 1970); Garth N. Jones, *Planned Organizational Change: A Study in Change Dynamics* (New York: Praeger Publishers, Inc., 1969); Herbert Kaufman, *The Limits of Organizational Change* (University: University of Alabama, 1971); Paul R. Lawrence, *The Behavioral Sciences and Organizational Change* (Evanston, Ill.: Management Programs Office, Northwestern University, 1966); Gordon L. Lippitt, *Organizational Renewal; Achieving Viability in a Changing World* (New York: Appleton-Century-Crofts, 1969).

organization and see how swiftly each message travels and in what form. There are some co-workers who will not pass on a message-rumor, there are others who will guarantee you will hear your "secret" back, invariably in some distorted form, within 24 hours.

The best way to counter the grapevine is to feed it accurate information through such key communicators, offsetting any inaccuracies in transmission by a steady supply of good information. The grapevine must work *for* the administration not against it. Obviously, it is difficult to maintain a trustworthy key communicator or grapevine. The simple classroom exercise of one person telling another person a story, who in turn relates it to another, quickly reveals how innocent can be the art of fabrication and exaggeration.

Robert Hershey, a psychologist and personnel manager long interested in grapevine-type communication, studied the efficacy of such unofficial information. Using thirteen volunteer students from one of his evening courses, he asked them to collect the following information from their daytime jobs:

1. The number of employees at the work facility and the nature of the industry.
2. The definition of a rumor as information heard from an unofficial source. Information not to be considered as rumor included bulletin board announcements and information given by a supervisor or union representative in his official capacity.
3. Documentation of rumors heard over a two-month period and the dates heard.
4. Documentation as to whether the rumor proved to be accurate within a month after that two-month period.
5. Documentation as to whether the rumor was heard more than once.[41]

Of the thirty rumors recorded in this study, sixteen were groundless, nine accurate, and five partly accurate. "A partly accurate rumor, for example, may have it that an entire department of 200 men is to be transferred to a new location, whereas only 20 men actually are." All of the accurate rumors were circulated almost a month before they were effected, which explains why employees give some attention to grapevine rumors: some of the information is good.

Hershey defines two factors which contribute to the existence of a grapevine: (1) a lack of effective official communication, and (2) the position of employees in the organizational hierarchy. Formal organization retards the flow of information, so employees create information flows themselves. The conflict in most organizations is between what the leaders want *to tell* their staff and what employees want *to know*. Although there is no sure way to combat rumors and leaks, Hershey

[41]Robert Hershey, "The Grapevine . . . Here to Stay But Not Beyond Control," *Personnel*, January-February, 1966, pp. 62–66.

suggests five ways to at least subdue the grapevine and reduce communications conflicts:

1. Keep the channels of communication open. Rumors abound in the absence of reliable information, and although bulletin board announcements and house organs are helpful, there is no substitute for good supervisor-to-subordinate communication.
2. Defensive attempts to disprove the logic of a rumor have been found to be less than effective in discrediting rumors. The opposite tack—positive presentation of fact upon fact about the topic—will bring out the true story.
3. Guarding against idleness and monotony among the troops has long been a military technique to prevent rumors, and it is just as applicable to any other organization.
4. Faith in the credibility and source of management's communications is another important area to develop. A company attempting to present its story accurately and convincingly must have built a record of truthfulness and reliability in dealing with its employees.
5. I don't ever recall having seen the subject of rumor dynamics touched on in a supervisory training program, but it might be a good idea to consider the psychology of rumors in such a course. Managers, too, should be trained to question what anxiety or other attitude is coming to light behind a given rumor.

Another study, by a personnel officer at a Naval Ordnance Test Station in California, assessed the effectiveness of the various forms of communication used to reach the station's more than 4,000 employees.[42] The following question was asked of a sample of 100 employees:

Management made an important change in the way the station would be run—through what channel or means of communication would you most likely get the word first? Here's the response:

Channel	Percent
Grapevine	38
Supervisor	27
Official memo	17
Station newspaper	7
Station directive system	4
Bulletin boards	4
Other	3

The second question in this survey was: Which of these methods of communication was most effective? The order of preference changes, and the grapevine is not even included!

42Eugene Walton, "Communicating Down the Line: How They Really Get the Word," *Personnel*, July-August, 1959, pp. 78–82.

1. Station newspaper
2. Station directives
3. Bulletin boards
4. "All Hands" meetings
5. Employee-Management Council
6. Off-station newspaper

These ratings seem to show that while the grapevine is the fastest means of communication it is not necessarily the most effective. Walton recommends three conditions for good communications:

> First and foremost, the channel should *always* reach *all* employees. Second, it should be official—the employees should be confident that it comes straight from the horse's mouth. And, third, it should be closely associated with the established order; that is to say, the supervisory system. By adhering to these simple rules, any organization should be able to increase the effectiveness of its present employee communications system.[43]

In dealing with organizational conflict, and with organization structures, administrators need to examine their conceptions of leadership styles and behavior. For this, they need to be aware of the various types of leadership as practiced and researched in organizations. For this we examine a leadership continuum, which includes the authoritarian to the more participative forms of leadership.

Leadership Styles

Leadership style is simply how an administrator interacts with subordinates, the policy or philosophy of an organization toward interactions between staff of superior and subordinate ranks. As shown in Illustration 7.9, leadership styles can be traced along a continuum, from the authoritarian "boss-centered leadership" to the more egalitarian "subordinate-centered leadership." Some of these patterns have been also labeled as participative, authoritarian, task-centered, laissez-faire, or impression management (management by the role one assumes). The most notable and attractive has been the participative model which we have already talked about.

A brief look at this illustration shows the management-subordinate interactions posited by various theorists in concepts of leadership. It is important to remember that a management style is not necessarily rigid; there are always some decisions a leader makes in an authoritarian manner, depending on certain circumstances, and there could easily be others made in a more democratic style. Nonetheless, most organizations tend toward some point on the continuum, if for no other reason than to lend stability to their decision-making environment.

[43]Ibid.

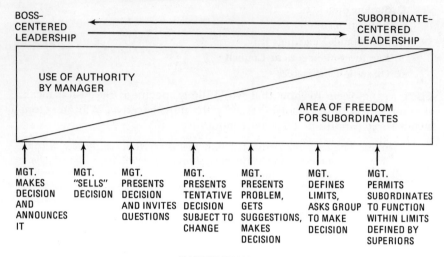

CONTINUUM OF LEADERSHIP BEHAVIOR

ILLUSTRATION 7.9

Source: Robert Tannebaum and Warren H. Schmidt, "How to Choose a Leadership Pattern," *Harvard Business Review*, March-April 1958, pp. 95–101.

There are basically four formal patterns or styles of administration with which we are most familiar, and which would be reflected on any continuum of leadership: (1) the absolute ruler, (2) the line-staff division of responsibilities, (3) multiple chief executives with no one with sole responsibility, and (4) the management-team concept, which is an executive committee form of leadership.[44]

Most of us are familiar with the excesses of authoritarian leadership, either in our own lives or through observation. We may not, however, be as familiar with the excesses of liberalization. To liberalize any organization without forethought and planning is foolish. To go back to the earlier example of free schools: free schools fail at an alarming rate not merely because they seek to radicalize education without also radicalizing the outside community, but because they apply simplistic notions of equality. To run an organization without leadership, whether of one person or a group, is a disaster. If group leadership is inaugurated without training and help for those unaccustomed to leadership, it will fail or become a sham of participatory management.[45]

[44]Alonzo McDonald, "Conflict at the Summit: A Deadly Game," *Harvard Business Review*, March-April 1972, pp. 59–68.

[45]A good example of where democratic styles of administration fail is when a previous leader attempts to play down his or her leadership skills in an equalitarian experiment with nonoppressive work arrangements. See, for example, Herbert Kohl, "Education: Trying Other Ways," *Ramparts*, August 1974, pp. 48–51, and in *Half the House* (New York: E. P. Dutton & Co., Inc., 1974).

If an organization desires to move away from authoritarian management, it makes more sense to move along the continuum to a slightly modified version of management, rather than completely shifting to the most extreme style. That was the mistake of free schools and other experiments with institutional management—the dramatic shift, the confusion and lack of direction, bringing demoralization, then failure. If a parks and recreation organization decides to modify its leadership style, it is more sensible to examine the experiences of other organizations who made comparable changes rather than rushing into change. For example, the four-day or three-day work week is quite popular. However, there is also controversy about its success because workers, after all, don't like working ten-hour days to get three days off. Before introducing such a policy, no matter how attractive it seems, an administrator should examine the findings of those who have already tried it. The same goes for liberalizing work hours, where workers come in and work their 35- to 40-hour week on a more flexible basis, not simply 9 to 5.

Unlike free schools, which were created without much deliberation about what a community or society desired in educational reform, organizational flexibility has many appeals: longer hours for services to be open to the public, less rush-hour traffic jams, workers with three-day weekends (reducing weekend crushes at entertainment and recreational sites), and so forth. If the conflicts that arise out of a change in leadership style seem irresolvable, then a modified style can be tried.

Our interest in participatory management is strongest because that is where most organizational modifications tend. McDonald believes companies move from stage 1 (absolute rule), to stage 2 (management by line-staff), to stage 3 (multiple chief executives), to stage 4 (the management team). Although "only a few organizations ever evolve through all four of these working relationship patterns . . . in my observation, this is the sequence in which any two or three of these options are most likely to be tried in a given company."[46]

Those of us with any organizational experience know that the concept of the sole decision maker is largely a myth, an ideal conception of the rugged-individualist executive. Decisions are made with the guidance and help of others. The *responsibility* is the leader's, but that is different from the decision process itself. Most organizations have included many forms of subordinate participation in decision making, without giving recognition (and rewards) to those who actually contribute. There are many weak leaders who have effective people working for them, "the brains of the organization." All participatory management does is attempt to reduce the hypocrisy and the inequalities of most decision making. For this reason, participatory leadership may not come as a jolt to some organizations, especially those who have been experimenting with modifying leadership styles all along.

One of the more sinister implications of participatory management

[46]McDonald, "Conflict at the Summit," pp. 63–64.

is giving workers a sense of importance, burdening them with more responsibility, without giving them the commensurate authority, rank, and salary for such expanded duties. This problem can be notorious with women, who are often as capable as their male boss, but who are used for all they are worth in the name of experimental work styles. We must be honest in whatever changes we seek to inaugurate in our organizations. Let us not merely change the name of exploitation and subordination to something less harsh.

Participatory management can also become as rigid and "authoritarian" as its opposite philosophy. How dreadful it can be to have to make every decision with a group of co-workers! One research organization designed an entire building to encourage a cluster-management philosophy, where workers' offices all lead into one another, with passageways leading to group workrooms, coffee rooms, and so on. The building structurally denied that anyone might enjoy working alone or having a solitary cup of coffee, not to mention making solitary decisions. The very walls of that informal research edifice "encouraged" one to interact—subordinate and executive alike. Individual worth can be denied as much by a liberal workplace as by the most repressive. We have to be careful when we talk about loosening up formal organizations, as if that were an end in itself, and as if liberality itself harbored no threats.

The traits of the effective participative manager are generally conceded to be as follows:

Counsels, trains, and develops subordinates.

Communicates effectively with subordinates.

Lets the members of the organization know what is expected of them.

Sets high standards of performance.

Knows subordinates and their capabilities.

Gives subordinates a share in decision making.

Stays aware of the state of the organization's morale and does everything possible to make it high.

Keeps subordinates informed of the true situation, good or bad, under all circumstances.

Is willing to make changes in ways of doing things.

Expresses appreciation when a subordinate does a good job.[47]

These characteristics were ranked in a study of 318 managers as being the most effective leadership characteristics for the participative manager. However, Greiner concludes that "participative leadership appears to be a sound concept, but only if presented as a general model within which individual leaders can exhibit a variety of actions to satisfy different personal and career needs." If the individual is subsumed to a philosophy of management, no matter how liberal a philosophy, the

[47]Larry E. Greiner, "What Managers Think of Participative Leadership," *Harvard Business Review*, March-April, 1973, pp. 11ff.

person will have reduced self-realization and self-actualization, not to mention the reverberations of his frustrations on other employees.

Earlier research on leadership tended to concentrate on the sole decision maker's personal traits. *Trait theorists* felt that some combination of individual qualities, be they inherent or acquired, was what constituted effective leadership. The remnants of trait theory are still evident in all discussions of leadership, including this one. If one stresses the value of the individual and concentrates on leadership, a list of traits is bound to emerge. In fact, the above list of characteristics of effective leadership cited by Greiner in 1973 grows directly out of trait theories, though they are more behaviors than isolated attributes.

The literature abounds in research on leadership traits. Researchers have concentrated on isolating traits as indicative of leadership ability: intelligence, aggressiveness, honesty, integrity, enthusiasm, energy, friendliness, or a sense of purpose. The leader with such traits is then examined in group interactions, where these traits presumably come into play, and we have the area of research known as group dynamics or small group theory.[48] All of that research is basically interested in the leader, regardless of what situation or organization he or she is in: that is, all effective leaders have these traits, so most group situations demand a leader with such traits if the group is to accomplish anything.

Another area of research, which we touched on somewhat already, deals with the type of organization or the type of leader in an organization. Again, *type theorists* concentrate on the individual leader. If the decision maker is democratic, then he or she will have some of the characteristics listed for the participative manager. A laissez-faire type of management allows subordinates to establish their own goals, with their decisions being task-oriented in terms of their own responsibilities and authority. If the leader is autocratic, then subordinates react out of fear, or a respect for authority. Autocratic authority is centralized, with little or no subordinate interaction in decision making, a boss-centered model. This type of leadership can be seen in dictatorial and autocratic institutions and states.

A good example of an autocratic, albeit unsettled, institution would be the Roman Catholic Church:

> The Roman Church is the world's largest nongovernmental bureaucracy. It employs 1.8 million fulltime workers—priests, brothers, sisters, and laymen. These employees work within a corporate structure which an American business consultant firm rates as among the most efficiently operated organizations in the world. The institutional Church functions on a par with the General Motors Company and the Chase Manhattan Bank. Recognition of this fact is accepted, sometimes, with pride. But to some, the machine-like smoothness itself seems to discredit the Church....

---

[48]Dorwin Cartwright and Alvin Zander, eds., *Group Dynamics: Research and Theory*, 2nd ed. (Evanston, Ill.: Row, Peterson and Company, 1960).

Wavering, doubt, and confusion reign among its directors, functionaries, and employees. The giant begins to totter before it collapses.[49]

In type theory, McDonald describes top-level executives as usually consisting of three types: leaders, followers, and neutralists:

> The leaders are typically capable, enthusiastic, and highly motivated. They seek power, willingly take risks, and need recognition and applause. In consequence, their motives may often be misunderstood.
>
> The followers at the top-executive level, although usually quite capable, are far less aggressive than the leaders. The follower wants to see himself as a superb "number two" who is respected by all and revered by many in subordinate ranks. Followers tend to be more conservative, standing back until the lead becomes reasonably visible and the risks have been assumed by the group.
>
> In between are the neutralists, who fall into two distinct types. Neutralists of the first type—thoughtful, objective, and open-minded— are invaluable to large, technology-based companies operating in an unstable environment. The second type of neutralist—the politician—resembles the objective neutralist superficially, but his motivation is very different. His whole policy is to remain uncommitted except in situations that he can exploit for personal gain. General de Gaulle, frustrated at the repeated personal maneuverings of some cabinet members and their supporters, referred disgustedly to this type as *les politichiens*.[50]

A final area of research on leadership styles has been *situational theory;* that is, a leader is not someone with inherent skills which are transferable to any situation, but rather leadership is relative to each situation. One can easily be a lord in the executive suite and a boob elsewhere. An executive can decide assertively to invest his firm's capital, but he may linger long over a decision whether to wear black or brown socks. This is a well-known and humorous caricature. Situational theory seeks to validate this homespun truism of relative abilities.

Consider an airplane pilot with a disabled plane in the desert: In the air he is the "natural" leader, even somewhat of a benign dictator to whose authority all willingly consent. In the desert, with injured, frightened passengers he may no longer be the best leader in the group. There may be someone among the passengers or crew who is a more natural leader in the changed situation. Only the narrowest of persons would argue for the pilot's continued supremacy when no longer in flight simply because he was the leader in the air. He may still have charisma, but you may die of thirst. Situational leadership posits a change in leadership by either a shift in persons or a shift in the role the leader performs.

Katz and Kahn studied successful organizational situations and found that effective leaders are more likely to be as follows:

[49]Ivan Illich, "The Vanishing Clergyman," in *Celebration of Awareness: A Call For Institutional Revolution* (New York: Doubleday & Company, Inc., 1969), p. 71.

[50]McDonald, "Conflict at the Summit," p. 61.

1. Are able to play many roles, change situations.
2. Spend more time planning, providing materials, initiating next step.
3. Delegate authority.
4. Check up less, support action.
5. Develop working team, group solidarity.
6. Ask for more information, and give more information. Are always reassessing the problem.[51]

What these three kinds of theories—trait, type, and situational— show is that there is no single quality or situation which determines effective leadership. Furthermore, it is probably more of a combination of such theories, rather than any theory by itself, that is nearer objective truth.

Simon, Smithburg, and Thompson give four aspects of authority or four reasons why people respond positively to authority:[52]

1. Authority of Confidence
2. Authority of Identification
3. Authority of Sanctions
4. Authority of Legitimacy

Or put another way, Simon, *et al.*, define the following five bases of power and authority in a leader:

1. Reward Power: reward for complying
2. Coercive Power: noncompliance, punishment
3. Expert Power: obey because of skills and knowledge
4. Referent Power: admiration, identity (e.g., President John F. Kennedy)
5. Legitimate Power: right to do so, elected or appointed

There are basically six ways in which an organization can adapt itself to enhance employee identification and rapport with the organization:

1. Seek consensus of all in the group regarding the means and ends of achieving goals and objectives.
2. Allow greater latitude to employees in the definition and achievement of personal goals.
3. Encourage a great amount of communication and interaction among all levels of staff (too many mechanisms are created especially to keep staff away from each other).
4. Ensure vertical mobility and job enhancements.
5. Offer general rather than close supervision.

[51]Daniel Katz and Robert B. Kahn, *The Social Psychology of Organizations* (New York: John Wiley & Sons, Inc., 1966).

[52]Simon, Smithburg, and Thompson, *Public Administration.*

6. Encourage participation, through established channels in decision making.[53]

In addition, there are six steps an administrator can apply to design a formal organizational structure so the informal organization within will work to achieve organizational goals:

1. Assign work in terms of *meaningful end products.*
2. Place people with skills as *close as possible to the point of action.*
3. *Set guidelines,* but leave as much control as possible for the group to set its own pace.
4. Provide mechanisms within organization that will involve *decision making.*
5. Understand and support the idea of *informal groups.*
6. Set up a *communication system of task forces.*[54]

To an administrator confronted with on-the-job dilemmas of working with subordinates, all these theories and styles of leadership and organization may seem of little direct value. Attempts to apply theories of decision making and administrative science to real-life situations led to use of the case study method of problem solving, with which we are all familiar. All of these theories and applications of theories are attempts by social scientists to enable those who manage organizations to manage them more effectively, more scientifically if you will.

There are several attributes of adaptive management which need to be discussed if we are going to effectively use the information offered so far. Perhaps the most evident quality of effective administrators is that they *have* a philosophy of management, or at least a philosophy of what they are attempting to do within their profession. Of course, most administrators are professionals interested in a subject or field outside of administrative science. Although the skills of an administrator are a separate area of inquiry and specialization, many administrators have professional goals and aspirations as well.

For instance, a director of a parks and recreation department may have a philosophy of management comparable to the participative model. This philosophy, to be effective, must be related to any purely professional philosophy the administrator may also have. The need for some integrated attitude toward a job becomes essential to avoid conflicts of interest. *Example:* A manager may have a philosophy of participation by all workers in decision making. However, because of a personal professional goal to succeed in recreation and parks, he may publish all project reports with only his name. An authoritarian approach to satisfying professional goals is in direct conflict with his management philosophy.

[53]Based on James G. March and Herbert A. Simon, *Organizations* (New York: John Wiley & Sons, Inc., 1958).

[54]Based on the work of Chris Argyris and Herbert A. Simon already cited.

A philosophy of management, or of professional development, need not be rigid or even consistent. If an administrator has to be adaptive to change in order to survive, his or her philosophy must be flexible as well. Flexibility does not mean one leans with every passing breeze; it means an ability to see the need for modification as situations or issues change. You may be an aggressive person in temperament, but have to recognize nonaggression as a trait useful in some situations. To accept personal aggressiveness, or any other trait, as somehow immutable and instinctive displays a lack of imagination and inventiveness.

Any philosophy is an *attitude* one assumes toward a given situation. Therefore, any viable philosophy is rarely a consistent one; to be consistent is to maintain a rigid attitude toward all situations. It is our ethics that remain fairly stable, and even they have to be reasserted periodically to give them new life. *Example:* If you have always been aggressive at board meetings, your philosophy (attitude) about board members may be that they are not really knowledgeable about parks and recreation and need a sure push from the director. This is a firm philosophy of board-staff relations. If the composition of your board changes, bringing in more sophisticated, knowledgeable members, will aggressiveness continue to serve you well or would a more collaborative spirit be better? If your philosophy of board-staff relations remains the same regardless of what kind of board you have, you *and* your consistency will sink together. However, if a board, knowledgeable or not, asks you to engage in something unethical, then your position should not shift. Flexibility in ethics is very unsure territory, regardless of the appeal of situational ethics. You may have to compromise, but that is a more overt decision.

Another fallacy, when we consider effective attributes for leaders, is that decisiveness is the ability to make *quick* decisions. How often we are impressed with someone who is quick on his feet, who reacts swiftly and cogently under pressure. This is an acquired skill, for the most part, and you can be certain that person has spent "slow" hours acquiring the wisdom and know-how to make rapid responses. It is completely nonsensical to be impulsive when time is not an issue, to be proud of being a fast decision maker for its own sake. Decisions are of varying types, priority, and implication. To be impulsive is not to be decisive.

An administrator has to be able to handle conflict, withstand pressure, and at times even abuse as the perennial "whipping boy" of all disaffected parties in and outside an organization. The pressure of administrative life is not only the workload, but all the extra pressures that are not in any job description. Here is where a philosophy of management or life is helpful. If you accept pressure as part of the job and can detach yourself from it somewhat, then you will be better equipped to succeed. How one deals with pressure is an individual matter; the *need* to deal with it is a professional matter.

Often an administrator has to stand alone on issues. This is a pressure that is difficult to share. Many theatrical dramas show one person against the mob; these plays always reveal the extreme tension, pain, and risk that come from defending one's beliefs even if one has to stand alone. If you want to be popular, well-liked, and a hail-fellow-well-met, don't be an administrator. The life of an administrator is not necessarily one of isolation and pressure, it is one of *anticipation* of these hardships and a willingness to endure them for some ethical or professional goal. The motivation may be sheer ambition, to endure all sorts of hardships and ridicule to get to the top. I do not want to suggest that the ability to rebound after assault is necessarily noble. It is simply necessary if one wants to be an effective leader.

Workers in an organization, no matter what the style of management, have to be evaluated for their work performance. Even if you yourself have a casual attitude about performance measurements, you can be certain someone else will raise the issue. It is much wiser to develop and apply your own standards of measurement than to have others foisted on you. It is no easy matter to evaluate worker performance and effectiveness once you get away from production quotas. However, an effective manager is one who has scrutinized available measurement methods, perhaps modifying them to his or her own use, but is in any event concerned about their use in an organization.

An important facet of worker performance is not only the measurement you use but what you seek to measure. It is possible to judge worker performance only if you have clearly stipulated standards for performance and goals to be achieved. Whether these are group-determined goals and standards is not important in this context. What is important is that they be clearly perceived by everyone in an organization and not be privately or vaguely held notions of productivity and efficiency.

As noted, an administrator has to be a diagnostician and a problem solver, rather than a curer of symptoms. Simple models, systems, processes, and graphs of how to solve problems abound in management literature.[55] These techniques are guidelines. They are not intended to replace individual ingenuity; they seek to guide it so that time and energy are not wasted. If one feels his individual judgment is ignored or threatened by a theoretical approach to management, then he can bypass it. For those who welcome such supplementary aids to problem solving, they are there to be used. These can save a lot of wheel-spinning. One can learn to bake cakes without recipes, but you can be certain that a lot of recipes were experimented with before that skill was perfected.

Nonetheless, whenever we draw inferences from the social and behavioral sciences, we must again caution that these are the most fad-ridden disciplines of all. For a behaviorist, the actions of men and animals are the result of measurable external and internal stimuli, which

[55]For instance, see Joseph J. Bannon, *Problem Solving in Recreation and Parks* (Englewood Cliffs, N.J.: Prentice-Hall, Inc., 1972).

are usually scrutinized with a zest for quantification. From such research we get all sorts of theories and activities. Although not a very impressive book, *The Human Nature Industry* does give some idea of the nonsense and the cranks who often flourish from behaviorism and popularizations of its findings. Cannel and Maclin attempt to reveal "how human nature is manufactured, distributed, advertised, and consumed in the United States and parts of Canada."[56] As stated at the beginning of this chapter, one reason to become familiar with theories is to be able to judge their usefulness as well as to detect nonsense.

As we concentrate on more humane forms of organization and management, we must remain aware of the profusion of theories and findings that are an utter waste of energy and time. Although none of us can be foolproof, and admittedly a lot of behavioral-like theories are plausible and attractive, we still have to be scrupulous in our examination and application of such findings. Otherwise we are merely trying to go along with fads rather than selecting useful and applicable models of administration.

The behavorial and especially the social sciences have shown the relative aspects of leadership; that is, a leader in one setting may be an incompetent in another. Locking a person into a leadership role, regardless of the situation, also prevents others from assuming leadership. If we accept the situational focus on leadership, which has been validated by many of our own experiences, then we are able to have both education and workplaces reflect the more variative nature and capacities of people.

Perhaps the most important implication of this discussion of organizational and administrative theories is that if an organization is to succeed, the objectives of the employees and the organization must be compatible, though they are not necessarily identical. Of course, this presupposes a predetermined need for the organization. The aims of employees and organization may be compatible to the highest degree, but if there is no need for what they provide, then it is to little avail. However, it would be naive to ignore all the pressures—good and bad—which exist to encourage employee goals to be compatible with the aims of an organization.

If we desire recreation and parks organizations to be adaptive to the changes in the demands of employees and citizens, we need to examine the theoretical findings of other sciences and consider their applicability and relevance to our profession. Even though recreation and parks is a relatively young profession, it can be remarkably conservative and traditional in the face of social and cultural changes. The profession needs to be more aware of organization theory and administrative science, and of the data such theorists draw on from other social sciences, to permit a more sensitive adaptation to the 1970's.

[56]Ward Cannel and June Maclin, *The Human Nature Industry* (New York: Doubleday & Company, Inc., 1973).

PERSONNEL: PRACTICES AND POLICIES

Personnel Administration

To many involved in the study and practice of personnel administration, management and personnel administration are the same thing.
However, in an organization of any size the manager is aided by a personnel administrator. This should not be treated as a nice-sounding but
not really essential position. Personnel administrators are staff people;
they influence the policies made by top management although they
themselves may not have policy-making authority. Like organization
theory, personnel administration theory has focused on formal and
informal modes of administration, on person-centered approaches and
policy-centered approaches. However, in personnel administration the
focus on the individual never loses sight of the policies which have
determined the presence of that person in the organization in the first
place, because:

> exclusive emphasis on the person-centered approach would be misleading.
> It needs to be combined with the approach in which generally valid
> principles of behavior are formulated as guides to action in specific types
> of situations, i.e., policy-centered thinking.[57]

Human relations and personnel administration are closely related
but are not one and the same. Human relations is an essential part of
personnel administration but not the only part. Human relations is a
viewpoint or method that draws on various techniques and sciences and
is applied in professions such as administration, personnel relations, or
labor relations.[58] Therefore, when discussing personnel administration it
is necesssary to distinguish between people-centered approaches and a
human relations viewpoint; one is necessarily more encompassing than
the other. An early book by Pigons and Myers first attempted to relate
personnel relations and human relations.[59]

Personnel administration focuses on the specific areas of (1) em-

[57]F. J. Roethlisberger, *Man-in-Organization* (Cambridge, Mass.: Harvard University Press, 1968), p. 75.

[58]Norman R. F. Maier, *Principles of Human Relations: Applications to Management* (New York: John Wiley & Sons, Inc., 1955).

[59]Paul Pigons and Charles A. Myers, *Personnel Administration*, 6th ed. (New
York: McGraw-Hill Book Company, 1969); or B. M. Selekman, *Labor Relations and
Human Relations* (New York: McGraw-Hill Book Company, 1947); Chester Barnard's,
The Functions of the Executive, already cited at the start of this chapter, made an
excellent first attempt at relating human relations to administration. More recent
works are Robert Saltonstall, *Human Relations in Administration* (New York: McGraw-
Hill Book Company, 1959); and Ralph M. Hower and John D. Glover, *The Adminis-
trator: Cases and Human Relations in Business*, 4th ed. (Homewood, Ill.: Richard D.
Irwin, Inc., 1963).

ployee recruitment, selection, and placement; (2) selection and training of supervisors; (3) employee induction, training, and motivation; (4) employee rating and promotion; (5) transfer, downgrading, and layoff; (6) discipline and discharge; (7) wages and hours; and, finally, (8) employee services, programs, and benefits. Although these areas are all of concern to management and lie clearly within the purview of management, because of the specialization and details which have developed in most of these areas the need is clear for a special person or department to handle these matters. For example, the area of recruitment and training of personnel has so burgeoned in the past decade or two that it now represents a rather formidable specialization in its own right.[60]

Personnel administration, a relatively new field of administration, received (and still does) a great deal of its impetus from federal legislation and the growth of labor unions, not to mention the disruptions caused by the Great Depression. Federal, state, and local legislation proliferate with regulations that affect almost every phase of personnel administration, and these are likely to increase greatly as more and more groups agitate for equal opportunities in the job market. For example, affirmative action (getting jobs for minorities and other groups discriminated against) is itself an area of concentration in personnel administration. For an administrator to keep up with the legal issues of employee relations alone requires technical assistance and staff in personnel and labor relations:

> These events of the past thirty years have resulted in personnel administration being firmly established as an essential function of business, government, and other organizations. Perhaps the most difficult problems facing administrators today lie in the area of personnel administration. For these reasons, personnel administrators have achieved top management status and recognition.[61]

The personnel administrator, or the personnel department, acts in a staff capacity to assist supervisors and other leaders in the organization in solving problems.[62] The basic task of personnel administration is to enhance employee relations, whether these employees are organized by unions or not. In small organizations, personnel administration can be a part-time responsibility; again, this does not mean it is an unimportant activity. Since many park and recreation organizations are small, initial part-time duties in personnel administration are more likely. Many of the case studies in personnel administration texts concentrate on problems in selection, training, and ongoing appraisals of employees.

[60]One example of training needs in recreation and parks is discussed in Phyllis Grunauer, "Training for the Outreach Function," in Bannon, *Outreach*, pp. 103–28.

[61]Alva F. Kindall, *Personnel Administration: Principles and Cases* (Homewood, Ill.: Richard D. Irwin, Inc., 1969), p. ix.

[62]Louis A. Allen, "Personnel Staff and the Line Organization," *Personnel*, XXXIII, 3, November 1956, 236–41.

Most of these concerns are found in any organization regardless of its size, function, or service.[63]

Job Placement and Development

Job placement and training functions are often closely related personnel activities, but job development is often left unspecified. This is an especially critical situation when people are being hired for sensitive positions (e.g., outreach work in the human services), or when those being hired are members of groups who have been denied natural access to the job market.

If an organization is small, then the task of hiring, training, and placing staff may be done by one or only a few people. In such cases, the separations between these tasks are minor. It is in larger agencies and organizations where recruitment, training, placement, and any job enhancement or development are performed by separate people or sections that oversights and conflicts can develop.

Recruitment of personnel is but the entryway to an organization, though there is logically a great deal of attention given to it; however, without equal emphasis given to all other ongoing aspects of personnel relations, excellent recruiting attempts are wasted. This is especially the case when hiring persons an agency has long overlooked for employment, notably minority groups:

> The personnel director of a light manufacturing firm in a midwest city noted that 10 percent of the disadvantaged youth employed by the company quit after the first day of employment, an additional 15 percent left by the end of the first week, and fully 66 percent of those hired left at the end of the first month.[64]

The conflicts that have arisen in minority group employment are indicative of a more general difficulty encountered to some degree with all workers. One affirmative action officer, in discussing job placement for blacks, said that the problems black workers encounter are the same as those experienced by most workers—the problems are aggravated by racism but they are basically the same.

A recognition of the sameness of workers' problems, regardless of their race or their position in an organization, has long been the argument of insightful labor leaders and observers.[65] This recognition of

[63]Michael J. Jucius, *Personnel Management*, 6th ed. (Homewood, Ill.: Richard D. Irwin, Inc., 1967); Herbert J. Chruden and Arthur W. Sherman, Jr., *Personnel Management*, 2nd ed. (Cincinnati: Southwestern Publishing Company, 1963); and, especially, Glenn O. Stahl, *Public Personnel Administration*, 3rd ed. (New York: Harper & Row, Publishers, 1962).

[64]Louis A. Ferman, "Job Placement, Creation, and Development," in *Breakthrough for Disadvantaged Youth*, U.S. Department of Labor, Manpower Administration (Washington, D.C.: Government Printing Office, 1969), p. 181.

[65]Jenkins, *Job Power: Blue and White Collar Democracy*.

sameness is becoming evident in labor unions, where racial conflicts are reduced by efforts to understand that *all* workers encounter the same difficulties to some extent, that attempts to focus on racial or other differences among workers are merely divisive. For this reason, in our discussion of employment relations we concentrate on minority employment issues as indicative of labor problems generally.

It is often in the extremest cases that the truth of a situation is revealed. When one begins to examine the difficulties inherent in affirmative action programs—where specific and legal attempts are made to employ neglected minorities and women—what actually begins to surface is the entire area of employer-employee relations, not merely racial or sexist conflicts. The affirmative action officer referred to above felt that to solve problems in the employment experience of blacks, one must first solve the overall problems and dilemmas of labor relations generally; attempting to concentrate on the successes or failures of one group ignores that blacks are entering a white job market, and it is the majority of white workers who are involved as well as a minority.

A good example of this broader viewpoint could be applied to labor unions. Blacks are presently joining unions in far greater percentages than other groups:

> Only one of four American workers belongs to a union; thirty years ago it was better than one in three. The one exception to this slippage is to be found in the black community. Three million blacks make up 15 percent of the organized work force, and union membership draws increasing numbers.[66]

Much of the history and experience of white unions are of value to blacks in unions, even though it is the former who have tried almost without exception to keep blacks out of unions, out of jobs, and out of decision-making positions in the unions once they are permitted to join. The experiences are of value nonetheless because whites have encountered, and still do, problems comparable to those of black workers, albeit of less intensity.

When recruiting minority workers for an agency, especially young people, organizations have to rely less on "passive" job placement—that is, the presumption that workers have been prepared for their jobs by formal education or vocational training. That this is not the case is a daily reality in many organizations. In fact, this situation is in no way confined to minorities, but is the case with most workers: all of us are educated to some extent, few of us are prepared for work.[67]

Even in cases where one is sufficiently educated and trained for a job (notably in the professions), one may not be *prepared* for a job, and time is needed to be able to adjust to and handle the job. For example,

[66]William Lucy, "The Black Partners," *The Nation*, September 7, 1974, p. 177.

[67]Ivar Berg, *Education and Jobs: The Great Training Robbery* (New York: Praeger Publishers, Inc., 1970).

in the 1972–1973 deliberations about modifying the U.S. Supreme Court to reduce the workload of its justices, Justice Douglas, arguing against formation of any national court of appeals to review cases submitted to the Supreme Court, said it took him ten years to learn how to handle his job as a justice.[68] Admittedly, this is an extreme example, but it does show that jobs do require adjustment, a growing into, an acquiring of skills and expertise before one can feel at ease in performing duties. The attention of personnel administrators is turned to efforts to prepare people for work, to help them find the kinds of positions they want, and to ensure that the positions continue to be a source of not only income but satisfaction.

Recruitment, training and/or placement, follow-up, longevity, termination—all of these areas have become specializations within personnel administration. In situations where these critical aspects of employment are treated mechanically, without regard for individual differences, or separately without regard for continuity, problems are going to arise. One of the simplest rules to follow in employment situations where some form of training is to be used is to bring the job placement staff and the training staff together before recruitment begins. Not only should job placement personnel be involved with trainers, they should be personally involved in training and counseling activities as well. If these employment functions are separated for purposes of efficiency, there should be as much interaction between them as possible.

For this reason, those who will be training new employees have to have ready access to placement files and vice versa. It is surprising how quickly one unit of personnel becomes attached to their records and resents other units having equal access to them. Those in training programs have complained about several members or departments of an organization seeking the same information, each setting up its own file on the worker, in some cases even giving duplicate tests! This not only is time-consuming but gives the new or potential worker impressions of confusion and disorganization, if not outright abuses.

For example, the giving of repetitive tests to an interviewee for a job was a good tactic for discouraging that worker from pursuing a job opening any further; this tactic became very effective in preventing "undesirable" people from entering an organization. Who is undesirable, of course, varies from organization to organization. The covert methods used to keep these people out are astounding—for example, putting a black dot on application forms from blacks once race could no longer be overtly recorded. Some large agencies have required interviewees to fill out application forms at several stages of the interviewing process. One department in a university desired its own application form for all interviewees; its application form was badly constructed and contained in-

    [68]Arthur J. Goldberg, "One Supreme Court," *The New Republic*, February 10, 1973, pp. 14–16.

formation requests that had long been banned from such forms—such as race, any arrests, and so forth. Not only was the use of this form unnecessary (since department heads had easy access to central personnel files), but it flew in the face of recent legal protections of workers' civil rights; all of these tactics were carried on without the knowledge of the personnel administrators, or regrettably, with their tacit approval.

When several units or areas of personnel work together, they should be very specific about who is to perform what in terms of new employees (we are assuming now that recruitment has been accomplished). It is one thing to say that both placement and training staff are interested in the welfare of the new worker; it is quite another to plan and decide how such welfare is to be achieved. In one recent training program, one person designed the program (for a semi-technical job), another administered it, and a third recruited the minority person for the job. Needless to say, confusion abounded, with the not unexpected result that the new employee left the organization within the first month and could not be encouraged to return. The three involved in this "affirmative" action realized how quickly it became "negative" action, and the person to really suffer was the trainee: she was out of work, and still not formally trained for a field in which she possessed clear potential; the agency was left with an unfilled position, a bewildered (frustrated) personnel staff, and charges of not attempting to fulfill the demands of affirmative action.

The person who wrote the training program was pleased with it, but the supervisor who was to administer the training did not have any say in its preparation, nor did she see the program until after the trainee had been hired. Needless to say, the supervisor also had nothing to say about who was hired for the position, even though they were going to share the same office! It is felt by many that the key determinant of success in a job lies with the supervisor; if the supervisor is unprepared, hostile, or in any way resistant to a new worker—no matter how carefully the worker has been selected or prepared—a breakdown is bound to occur. In the supervisory literature this relationship between worker and supervisor is viewed as the supervisory matrix, one of the more critical matrices in internal organization.[69]

In efforts to bring new minority workers into an organization, most of the attention was focused on the worker. Very little was done to prepare supervisors for these new workers. More recently, especially in very large organizations, work with supervisors to prepare them for minority and other new workers has become more commonplace. But for the most part, supervisors were either overlooked in the early stages of employee introduction or were felt to have some inexplicable quality, as supervisors, which would enable them to handle the situation. This was not and is not the case. Since most of the early efforts to bring

---

[69]Pfiffner and Fels, *The Supervision of Personnel*, Chapter 10, "The Superior-Subordinate Matrix."

minority workers into organizations had taken place under enormous time pressures, it is somewhat understandable that grievous and unnecessary errors were made.

A case in point: A young trainee was hired for a beginner's position in a research laboratory. The supervisor had no involvement in designing the training program, was resentful of blacks getting "a break" when she and others had to compete for such positions, and so forth. The earliest stages of the training program called for familiarizing the trainee with basic laboratory procedures. This was interpreted by the supervisor in the most rudimentary manner—she put the trainee to work washing Petri dishes for a week; the trainee quit the job. Where lies the fault in this all-too-common failure? It occurred at virtually every stage in the employment process, coming quickly to a head when the trainee began work. The trainee had been recruited by a black personnel officer, one totally empathetic to the denials and denigration in employment suffered by his people. The trainee was then placed in a job with a white supervisor who had never worked with blacks, who might or might not harbor racial resentments, and both are greeted with a training program they have literally seen for the first time.

To intensify this particular situation, the trainee had previous laboratory experience (all those Petri dishes to haunt him) but, because of lack of a college degree, had to enter the organization as a trainee, a not-too-pleasant avenue for eventually waiving an educational requirement. In other words, the worker is purposely downgraded in the first place to get the job, but the training program is in no way modified to reflect this previous experience. The trainee had nothing to say about how he was trained, how he preferred to learn, and the generalized program is tediously followed step by step.

Illustration 7.10 shows two methods of adult teaching, the more traditional and the more experimental, the latter approach more likely to be successful in training programs. These divisions of pedagogy and andragogy are similar, of course, to the authoritarian and participatory methods of management discussed under management philosophies earlier. In fact, in all areas of organization, administration, and management, we again and again see the division between formalized traditions and more contemporary demands for accommodation and reform at all levels of employment relations.

In her discussion of training minority and other groups for sensitive outreach work in recreation or other human services, Grunauer suggests that trainers (in our case supervisors) have, *at least,* the following traits:

- Several years of experience working with minorities
- A warm personality, interest in, understanding of, and respect for the cultures of minorities
- An ability to communicate and to listen well, to be supportive and nonjudgmental
- A nonauthoritarian manner, open about personal feelings

LEARNING AND BEHAVIOR STRATEGIES

	Pedagogy	Andragogy
Climate	Authority-oriented Formal Competitive	Showing mutuality Respectful Collaborative Informal
Planning	By teacher (trainer)	Mutual planning
Diagnosis of needs	By teacher (trainer)	Mutual self-diagnosis
Formulation of objectives	By teacher (trainer)	Mutual negotiations
Design (or plan)	Logic of the subject matter Content units	Sequenced in terms of readiness Problem units
Activities	Transmittal technique	Experiential techniques (inquiry)
Evaluation	By teacher (trainer)	Mutual rediagnosis of needs Mutual measurement of program

ILLUSTRATION 7.10

Source: Phyllis Grunauer, "Training for the Outreach Function," in Joseph J. Bannon, *Outreach: Extending Community Service in Urban Areas* (Springfield, Ill.: Charles C Thomas, 1973), p. 111, based on Malcolm S. Knowles, *The Modern Practice of Adult Education; Andragogy vs. Pedagogy* (New York: Association Press, 1970).

- A knack for involving individuals in group tasks and responsibilities
- An orientation to the agency and its objectives, as well as an attitude that is supportive toward trainees[70]

The approach most commonly used to meet criteria such as these has been for organizations to train the trainer and not to leave supervisors floundering alone with their confusions, hostility, or just simple ignorance about what is expected of them. When we speak of employee relations we must include all employees and not assume that because someone has reached the supervisory level he is suddenly immune to the problems encountered by the newest of workers. In many ways, bringing in new types of workers is a fresh situation for supervisors and should be handled accordingly; assailing them for racism is not the way, though their racial attitudes will have to be handled in any training devised for them. And to be consistent (and wise) let them have a say in their own training, what they feel they need help with, how they can best be guided, and so forth.

Preparation and follow-up are the keys to successful, meaningful employment relations. If anyone in an employment situation is not prepared for events and experiences that one can be trained for, or if an employee is left on his or her own after job placement, then personnel administration and employment relations become unnecessarily intractable:

Job placement should not end with entrance to the job, but should include

[70]Phyllis Grunauer, "Training for the Outreach Function," in Bannon, *Outreach*, p. 108.

a follow-up procedure that includes an assessment of job adjustment (satisfaction, wages, training opportunities) and some feedback of difficulties in bridging the gap between training [or recruitment] and placement.[71]

That is, job placement is always more than finding or giving a job to someone; job preparation and follow-up are integral parts of the process.

Unfortunately, too many agencies have no formal follow-up procedures for ongoing evaluations of an employee or for job enrichment. Although a pat on the back occasionally for a job well done is pleasing, it is hardly sufficient to pass as employee relations. One must also offer substantive rewards, give workers a sense that they have not been placed and forgotten. Agencies that experience high turnover know this is not all there is to effective employee-employer relations. Some early training programs in affirmative action left follow-up to be done on an informal basis or confined it to ritual calls and reports from the supervisor on how the trainee "was doing." The trainee was never contacted to see how the supervisor "was doing"! It is obvious now how one-sided and authoritarian such a procedure is. The trainee was contacted only when an employment situation had seriously deteriorated. Most serious and direct contact with these workers took place when they had already become ex-workers. Then the problems were perceived quickly and accurately.

Even formal follow-up procedures, which either stress complaints or are interested basically in supervisory evaluations of an employee, are perhaps not worth the efforts to apply: only failures or problems are followed up on, nothing is learned about successes, nor about potential areas of modification or improvement. These are so prevalent in training situations that many of the expectations, on both sides, have already become stereotypes: the trainee is not able to adapt to a work situation, the supervisor or trainer is a racist (or sexist), the training program is "Mickey Mouse."

> the administrator . . . will understand these stereotypes and know how they were arrived at and conditioned. Above all, he will be aware of the fact that he has a stereotype of his own, and in his dealings with others he will be tolerant of theirs.[72]

Job development must include follow-up *services* to workers to ensure their adjustment to the position as well as later promotion or mobility within the organization. The line between job placement and job development is not so evident as might seem the case. *Job placement* is concerned with assessing interviewees for positions, and helping them to overcome any deficiencies that may deny them access to a job. Working with interviewees to prepare them for a job is admittedly a new concept, or at least one that challenges more traditional forms of passive

[71]Ferman, "Job Placement, Creation, and Development," p. 182.
[72]Pfiffner and Fels, *The Supervisor of Personnel*, p. 182.

placement, but is nonetheless essential not only with minority group members but most entry-level applicants.

Job development, on the other hand, is concentrating more on the atmosphere of the workplace, where this might come into conflict with workers' desires, aspirations, and expectations. Improvement in job conditions, a whole area of concern reflected in unions, is the task of job development. Personnel administrators thus reach out from the organization toward potential workers and into the community, helping to discover and prepare workers for employment in a substantive way; they also reach into the working units of the organization to ensure that on-the-job conditions will increase employee retention. It makes little sense to concentrate only on job placement to the neglect of job development, since without the latter concentration, the efforts of even excellent job placement are weakened.

Ferman found three basic conclusions from his experience with government programs in job placement, job development, and job creation for disadvantaged youth: (1) that training should be available to both employee and supervisors; (2) that outside community services should be coordinated (health, housing, education, etc.) to bring forth truly employable workers; and (3) that training programs must ensure other than dead-end or menial jobs:

> These three postulates must be at the core of any job development program. They mark a radical departure from the passive approach to job placement, in vogue only 10 years ago. In essence, they point to a manpower policy that is client rather than employer-oriented.[73]

I would go further and say that job development reflects a more community-oriented rather than organization-oriented philosophy of personnel administration, one that is particularly useful and applicable to the human services. Recreation and parks, both in its services and in its employment policies *and* practices, must serve the community. A job development philosophy is based on the premise that the individual is part of a community (large or small) and that unemployment or underemployment in that community is a problem of the labor market, not an individual problem.

This sort of thinking permeates many of the social services today, as well as other professions, where the individual is not faulted for problems that are woven into the very fabric of our social life and culture. Of course, reflecting such a philosophy in the policies of an agency is but the first step to offering this vital service far from the parks and playfields of our communities. One of the major demands made of the social services in the past decade was not only for better services, but for employment in the social agencies that serve a community, and a say in the decisions and policies that shape the agency. Improved personnel

[73]Ferman, "Job Placement, Creation, and Development," p. 208.

policies are an excellent sign that a social agency stands to practice what it preaches when it says it seeks to serve the whole man.

Board-Director Relations

Another aspect of internal organization relations, and one that is peculiar to the social services, is the relationship of agency staff, notably the director, to members of a lay board. Although this is not exactly an employee-employer relationship, there are ingredients of the relationship that make it a very sensitive area. This board-staff relationship is a major and critical one in recreation and park agencies.

To ensure that every citizen is aware of and has access to recreation services, the men and women who advise, administer, and operate recreation organizations, and their relationships to each other, are critical forces in enhancing the quality of recreation. Through an understanding of these relationships, their potentials and shortcomings, recreation professionals and interested laymen can together achieve the successful offering of leisure services.

The quality and strength of the relationship between a lay board and the director of a recreation organization have always been vitally important. It is even more critical today in a society experiencing sudden massive social changes, which directly affect the behavior and responsibilities of the recreation profession. The increase in the demand and importance of recreation, especially in urban areas, has brought a host of organizational, administrative, and staff problems. People are becoming significantly more leisure-oriented, and their recreation sophistication must be met with a comparable concept of leisure greater than that of the more traditional uses of parks, centers, and playgrounds. Recreation professionals, and their lay boards, must expand their image and abilities as leaders of broad and complex leisure-oriented programs.

Two significant changes have occurred in recreation in response to the social and economic forces at work in American cities. First, and perhaps more important, it is now generally accepted that providing recreation for the nation's residents is basically a *local* responsibility. Second, recreation must be considered as essential a municipal service as sanitation, fire, and police protection. Recreation activities must be organized and promoted, with progressive supervision and leadership provided. Park areas dominated by swings and slides, programs emphasizing basketball and football, or programs excluding minority youth, are clearly insufficient.

Recreation officials must design programs for everyone and be sensitive to all neighborhood needs. Officials and boards in recreation and other social services must devise new, creative approaches to health, employment training, education, and recreation that will aid in the maximum use of existing resources and in their coordination with other services. The only way for a board and staff to achieve this is by a thorough knowledge of both the community and the profession, and by a constant application of this knowledge to improving the recreation organization they represent.

However, our concern here is primarily with the organizational relations between the board and staff of recreation organizations in their attempts to serve a community. Board experiences with recreation directors, and both their experiences with the community, have not been the best, nor always the most likely to benefit the organization. The effective interaction of these groups is imperative. The relationship of the lay board to the director or administrator is a strategic one that has to accurately reflect the needs and realities of all involved, especially the community. Experience with lay boards has shown that there is no way to ignore discussion of breakdowns in these relationships, or of the need to confront them candidly.

Of course, the relationship between the director and the agency staff is crucial to the workings of an organization. If, for example, the director does not inform the board of ongoing administrative issues, or keeps the agency staff in ignorance of potential policy changes, the probability of such an organization being successful in its aims is greatly reduced. Such breakdowns in relationships cause serious disruptions in the organization and in the community.

The scenario is usually as follows: The lay board representing the beliefs and aspirations of the public, with a professionally trained director supplying technical competence and know-how, has been deemed the most effective organizational arrangement for offering recreation to a community. Inherent in such an arrangement is the assumption that the board represents the public in establishing the goals of the organization, and generally determines the direction which recreation programs should take. The technically trained director, through his abilities and those of his professional staff, assists the board with policy making, implements the policies and directions of the board, and generally operates the recreation organization. The director assumes responsibility for all activities designated by the board, and is expected to perform them in such a way as to assure their success. However, this neat scenario rarely occurs. Relations between board and director, director and staff, and the organization and the community often deviate from such a pattern, and in some cases to the benefit of all.

There are basically two types of boards or park commissions that recreation and park departments work with: (1) semi-independent boards who function basically as policy-making bodies, and (2) advisory boards who serve the director at his or her discretion. In some cases, the board is actually a blend of both types. Where statutes do not prohibit, an amalgam of both types is more preferable. Professionals feel that a lay advisory board is the least desirable form of organization for recreation:

"It is difficult to make work meaningful to a body that is confined to an advisory role. Hence, such boards are not considered the most desirable for effective recreation management."[74]

A semi-independent board in a municipality would generally be appointed by the mayor and city council, with delegated policy-making and administrative authority. This type of board would have full authority and responsibility over recreation programs, service, and facilities, as well as over internal personnel matters to a great extent. The advisory board, on the other hand, is basically powerless to act with any degree of authority unless it develops some policy-making agreement with the director. Advisory boards are, therefore, only effective if the director provides clear leadership and allows them to contribute to the formulation of policy.[75]

Generally speaking, boards of five or seven members are most common, and most workable, although it is not unusual to have from three to eleven members. A recreation board is either elected or appointed: appointments to a municipal board are usually the responsibility of the mayor and the city council. Recreation boards are elected if the provisions establishing them call for such a selection; boards for district operation are usually elected. In most communities, board members serve for overlapping terms of three or five years without compensation, except for out-of-pocket expenses.

How might a lay advisory board be encouraged to make significant contributions to organization policy making? And how might a director work best with a semi-independent board which has final say on policy? Some lay advisory boards provide excellent guidance for the organization on specific objectives. This is generally because of the expertise and interests of individual board members, combined with a sure leadership from the director. While this is not a policy-making function as such, it does enable advisory lay boards to provide an extremely worthwhile and pertinent service to the organization, thus eliminating or reducing any possible rubber-stamp function for itself.

Therefore, to make a distinction between a lay board in an advisory capacity, and one in a more precise policy-making capacity, is not to demean the advisory function. It is capable of achieving great strength when properly used and skillfully directed by an administrator. All boards are created for specific functions. The function of the lay advisory board, or the semi-independent board to a greater extent, is to help establish the objectives of recreation services for a community, and to formulate plans and policies for achieving these.

A board is responsible for advising on basic policies recommended by the director which shape the organization. The administration of

[74]Lynn S. Rodney, *Administration of Public Recreation* (New York: The Ronald Press Company), p. 85.

[75]Ibid., Chapter 4.

policy—the actual operation of parks and recreation services—is a professional problem which requires recreation professionals for implementation. Thus, the basic scenario offered above begins to shift toward more policy-making responsibility for the director, as it actually exists in many recreation organizations today.

From this basic advisory function for the board develops a need for the board (1) to maintain or improve the quality of recreation services in a community, (2) to keep the community informed of the existence and value of such services, (3) to keep other civic and public persons informed of the recreation and leisure needs of a community, (4) to hire or fire the recreation director, as well as to initially inform him of his duties and responsibilities if the present board precedes a director's appointment.[76]

In addition to these responsibilities, the board is concerned with overall budgetary aspects of the organization, with providing adequate community facilities and programs, and with the sustained and critical evaluation of the organization in view of the community's recreational needs and aspirations. Some boards, especially those assigned specific administrative responsibilities, are also involved in personnel matters and some less-pressing nonpolicy concerns as well. These latter involvements, even where stipulated by local preference, are far from suitable and in many ways hinder successful interaction between board and director.

These basic responsibilities and duties of boards can vary, of course, by limitations or expansions given to boards in specific situations. They also vary by the tractability or strength of the board or director in relinquishing or acquiring power from each other. More specifically, the typical responsibilities and duties of a recreation board would be:

1. Establish a sound financial plan and seek to achieve the budgetary goals of the organization. The board must plan the expenditures it will permit in advance and set aside money for such plans. It is also the board's responsibility to give final approval on any plans made and give approval to the director for application.
2. Provide adequate working areas, and safe, hygienic facilities for the organization staff. If the organization is to maintain good staff relations, the board must be concerned with these facility problems.
3. Evaluate the organization's objectives on a regular basis. Any organization that fails to reevaluate its policies, rules, finances, etc., may find itself in unexpected difficulty.
4. Study and analyze the recreation and park needs of a community.
5. When necessary, seek to raise funds and elicit donations for recreation services and other related programs.
6. Serve as a forum for the director and staff to consider new policies and programs.

[76]Ibid., p. 96

7. Interpret recreation policies to the community and encourage their interest and participation in policy and program matters.
8. Cooperate with other civic and private groups or agencies for the advancement of recreation in the community.
9. Advise on the development of recreation areas, parks, and programs for improving leisure services.
10. Coordinate community recreation programs with other communities, schools, and civic and private organizations.

Thus, "the board proposes and disposes, approves and reviews policies and regulations. The superintendent [director] nominates, co-ordinates, and recommends; and once a decision is made by the board, he directs, evaluates, and reports back to the board and the community."[77] The difficulties and confusions encountered by professionals and board laymen in recreation are comparable to those of superin-tendents and boards in school systems. For instance, in a nationwide study of school boards, 21 percent of the responding school districts listed problems in board-superintendent relationships as being of most concern. Further, a large majority of the problems listed "pertained to the need to distinguish clearly between board functions and administra-tive responsibilities."[78]

The board is concerned with decision making, policy making (general legislation), evaluation of practices and programs, advising a director on any items in which the board members have a greater exper-tise, representing the will of the community, and determining the needs of the community and how it can best be served. The director, on the other hand, is basically concerned with program development, financial management, policy recommendations and design, personnel and staff morale, as well as spearheading any public relations or public informa-tion programs.

When evaluating ideal board members for election or appointment, therefore, it is important to have in mind persons who can meet these major responsibilities and duties. The person should first be one inter-ested in parks and recreation and its potential for meeting the leisure and physical health needs of a community. He should also be willing to serve without remuneration (except for expenses) and to avoid using the board for achieving other "business" or personal ambitions. That is, the board should not be a vehicle for other interests of a board member. Board members need to be sensitive to the residents of a community, especially to youth, and the multitude of problems and concerns they raise.

In addition to a clear understanding of the community, board

[77]California School Boards Association, *Boardmanship: A Guide for the School Board Member* (Sacramento: California School Boards Association, 1969), p. 48.

[78]Alpheus L. White, *Local School Boards: Organization and Practices* (Wash-ington, D.C.: Government Printing Office, 1971), p. 82.

members must be capable of formulating and achieving policy recommendations they feel are of value to a community. A board member must seek accurate information on the structure of the total community, so he or she has a clear notion of the part recreation performs in the community members' lives.

Although the theoretical duty of a semi-independent board is to devise and formulate policy for the recreation administrator to implement, this strict form of leadership is fortunately changing, enabling the director to perform a stronger, clearer leadership role rather than merely following unilaterally determined policy. Of course, this pattern will take time to fully emerge, since most semi-independent boards are established by public law or statute and are not easily modified or circumvented.

Where strict policy power is held by the board, the genuine leadership role of the director becomes even more strategic. Policy gives an administrative framework to the director; it does not lead him by the nose. Thus, the interpretation and application of such policies are to a great extent at the discretion of the administrator and staff. His ability to aid the board in formulating policy can add to his organizational leadership. The policies should be jointly discussed, with an agreed-on conception of what is meaningful for the recreation needs of a community. In many cases this ideal is far removed from the atmosphere in which policies are made. It is therefore stressed that a director should work closely with his board whenever policy is considered, so that such policies may reflect his judgment and professional evaluation. The director is most often the one who proposes and formulates much of the program and administrative policies, even when this function is not clearly stipulated by statute or bylaws.

The point is not that a director should wrest control from a legally designated board, but that he have a substantive and formal role in the formulation of policy, as directors actually do in many recreation organizations. The same precept applies to the director's staff. If his staff members' views are not considered along with policy concerns of the organization, there is little likelihood of any organizational effectiveness.

Both staff and board must be seriously involved in policy design, even though ultimate responsibility invariably lies with the board. There is, of course, no certainty that legally decreasing the functions of a board, or of a director, for that matter, will immediately lead to a well-balanced interaction of viewpoints. The board must be alert to its function of advising and guiding the director; the director must be alert to his responsibility to design or suggest policy for board consideration; the staff must be conscious of its role in feeding information to the director from the bottom up, of participating in policy decisions for improved organization decision making.

Most policies include basic guidelines that do not usually impinge on the administrative functions and duties of the director. For example, a director might not have a substantive say in whether a new recreation center is needed; but how he will run it, or how his staff will choose to establish their role with the community in such a center, is generally left to the director's discretion and professional know-how once the policy decision on building is made. Thus, when we talk about policy constraints on the director, we have to be clear about the degree of latitude between policy stipulations by the board, and the daily operation of an organization by its director. The director needs to be involved in the policy considerations of the board, even to assume leadership in such deliberations where useful.

A close and cooperative relation should exist between a director and the recreation board. Such a cooperative policy-making relationship does not imply an infringement on each other's responsibilities, but a sharing of knowledge and experience, and an overlap of functions for the benefit of the organization. Board members are most often laymen; the director and his staff, professionals. The combination of interested and concerned laymen and a professionally astute staff can be a powerful one for effecting quality recreation in a community.

Nonetheless, it should not be the prime concern of *any* board member to administer or implement policies for the organization. Reliance on the director and staff for these functions is a sign of the board's confidence in them to adequately interpret and implement policy:

> The board has neither the time nor the knowledge to carry out policies. In fact, this is not their function. Therefore, it can be seen that the policy-making bodies provide the guidelines, the purposes, and the goals while the implementation of these purposes rests with the executive and his staff.[79]

Such confidence is enhanced when the director and his staff have had some involvement in policy formulation. There is no firm demarcation between policy and administrative responsibility; lines of responsibilities should and do overlap between board and director, and between the director and staff. Such an overlap, when initially understood and agreed on, can be exceedingly stimulating and rewarding.

If a board spends time on policy application and implementation, or if the director spends too much time in policy formulation, their *prime* functions will suffer. They each serve two different purposes, and it is to these purposes that the bulk of their time should be devoted. The overlap in functions should be natural and encouraged, but certainly not disproportionate to their main responsibilities: "In all matters of recreation operation, the board should look to its executive officer for leadership and guidance. But a reciprocal relationship exists in that the executive looks to the board for the direction the recreation system will take."[80]

[79]Rodney, *Administration of Public Recreation*, p. 99.
[80]Ibid., p. 110.

The difficulty arises only when any person in the organization steps out of his or her prime area of responsibility and begins to seriously hamper or decrease the function of another. Yet there is no justification for discouraging overlap simply because abuses might occur.

Another way of viewing the division of responsibility, and one that is often cited in theories of public administration, is that the board generally makes *value* decisions and the director makes *factual* decisions formulated on these values.[81] That is, the policies of an organization, because they are broad, primarily reflect the values that city officials and community leaders view as essential to their public charge. The factual decisions or judgments made by a recreation director generally draw on the fields of recreation and management, with the agreed-on values serving as a base.

Directors' recommendations to boards are often based on value positions, in that they represent their conception of the expected outcome of the recommended action. It is thus apparent that serious misunderstandings can occur if board members interpret these recommendations from different value positions. "When individuals first come together in a group, their expectations may or may not be similar but there is one condition which can be reasonably assumed: They will not know what the expectations of the others are."[82]

On the other hand, board members might interpret the director's recommendations correctly enough, but oppose them because they are in conflict with conceptions which they believe desirable. Unless the director understands the bases on which his recommendations are opposed, the board opposition might be misinterpreted as simply an indication of lack of confidence. A person's value-orientation has been shown to have a significant influence on his perceptions of the values held by others.[83] Persons who are "emergent" in their values perceive others as holding emergent values, while those who are traditional in their values perceive others as holding traditional values.

Boards and directors must resolve value differences and differences in expectations regarding the degree of participation of the director in board decision making. Difficulties frequently result from the divergent values of lay citizens and professionally trained administrators. However, an awareness that differences may exist is a first step toward resolving them. Similarly, varying expectations as to the director's role in decision making and policy making must be thoughtfully analyzed. Decision making works best when neither the board nor the director dominates, and when the technical competence of the director blends with the viewpoints of the board in a synthesis of discussion and action.

[81] March and Simon, *Organizations.*

[82] Neal Gross, *Who runs Our Schools* (New York: John Wiley & Sons, Inc., 1958), pp. 124–25.

[83] Max Abbott, "Values and Value-Perceptions of School Superintendents and Board Members," unpublished Ph.D. thesis, University of Chicago, 1969.

Whatever philosophy of decision making one subscribes to, it is important to avoid defining the responsibilities and duties between the board-staff functions too narrowly. When it is of value to have the director recommend policy, this should be done. When the board has some insights into administrative development, its views should be heard. But these should occur with some perspective of the main concerns and responsibilities of each. One of the understandings that can exist between a board and director, as well as a director and his staff, is not for a thorough involvement in each other's responsibilities, but the sense that each can comment and make recommendations on the other's prime area of responsibility.

The major difficulty encountered by a board and director is usually a vague conception of what each one should be doing. If a board is matched by a strong, independent director, who ignores the advice of that board, or if a board lacks confidence in their director, confusion rules, for neither are clear about what they should be doing or should be primarily concerned with. To assure a better understanding of their respective roles, it is the task of the director to educate his board on recreation issues. It is also preferable to have the functions of each clearly stated in job descriptions, policy statements, or by statute and bylaws. A clear understanding at the start can help eliminate much confusion about roles and responsibilities. The same naturally applies to director-staff relationships.

In recreation, as with other public service agencies with lay boards, it is often said that it is the responsibility of the director to carry out policy. But, as we discussed, this is never as straightforward as it might seem. For instance, many school boards and superintendents have stumbled over the problem of where policy making ends and administration begins:

> No board and superintendent should attempt to conduct the affairs of the public without first reaching agreement on a division of duties and responsibilities. Such agreement should be reached through a process of study and discussion and should have as its major objective the efficient, professional operation of the system. The agreement should cover every major area of responsibility and be expressed in terms of the functions to be performed.[84]

This need for prior agreement on the allocation of duties and responsibilities seems logical. The difficulty lies not in the need for preplanning, but in the determination of who exactly provides the leadership for the organization and what patterns develop over time.

The leadership should come from or be encouraged to develop from the director rather than the board. The board should act as an instrument of social policy in its representation of the public. The

[84]James J. Harmon, "Principles of Governing School Board—Administrator Relationships," *School and Community*, November 1969, pp. 40–41.

board's purpose and function are to represent the public and to review and analyze the feasibility of suggestions and programs made by the director. The board does not become a rubber stamp of the director's wishes, but a working relationship is established which clearly indicates the primacy and leadership of the director in the actual workings of the organization. That is, the board helps the director to be more responsible to the special needs of the community.

Lack of understanding or a misconception of what is expected of both the administration and the board is a serious obstacle to achieving good board-director relationships. Disagreements and misunderstandings arise when expectations are not met. Moreover, the feeling of teamwork, which should permeate board-staff relationships, cannot exist in an atmosphere of uncertainty and ambiguity. For these reasons, a board and a director seeking to improve their relationships, and desiring to secure an atmosphere where issues and problems may be met directly and honestly, will find prior understanding of expectations invaluable.[85]

Strong leadership does not mean dictatorship. There is certainly the risk of disproportionate power developing in either the board or director, but this can be anticipated and offset by a prior agreement of their roles.

As noted, one fear that comes from having a powerful director is that the board would perform in a rubber-stamp capacity, simply agreeing with everything the director presents and offering little or no opposition to any decisions or policy recommendations. Is it good or bad? One gets as many answers to this question as there are recreation directors. At first glance, it would seem to be a good situation for a director. However, the role of the board is to define the organization's objectives and make plans and policies for harmonizing them. If the board became nothing more than a rubber stamp, it would be denying the director a most vital asset and not fulfilling the prime purpose for which it was originally instituted.

It is possible for a board and director to have so much harmony that there is rarely a dissenting voice. It is often felt that unanimous votes are indications that a board is in good working order. If the director makes all the decisions, he had best be certain he is always correct. However, if the board members have some say as to what the final decisions are, then there is greater latitude. The director is wise to make use of his board, both to gain valuable insights and to be "protected" somewhat in cases of poor decisions.

If a board lacks confidence in the director, there is no way that director will ever genuinely acquire leadership in the organization. The board will not yield power or control to someone about whom it is not certain. If such lack of confidence is a serious impediment to analyzing

[85]Archie R. Dykes, *School Board and Superintendent: Their Effective Working Relationships* (Danville, Ill.: The Interstate Printers & Publishers, 1965).

the structure of an organization, and the preferable roles for those in it, it is perhaps better to simply replace the director, rather than circumvent or distort the true source of leadership.

When a board looks to the director for leadership, this does not mean this leadership is not carefully scrutinized and evaluated by the board continually. Once leadership is decided on, the board does not relinquish the necessity and responsibility to criticize and weigh the accomplishments of a director. This is best achieved by establishing open communications between the board and the director, and between the director and staff. The necessity for this is obvious, but it bears repeating.

The achievement of open and candid communications between the director and the board can be planned for; it cannot be left to chance. We should purposefully design the lines and channels of communication, when they will occur, how often, with whom, and in what form. It might be an achievement to have spontaneous channels of communication develop over time between the board and the director, and the director and his staff, but this does not often happen, and it is better to prepare proper channels to ensure such communications.

It is stated later in this chapter that public relations is the need for both internal and external communications: we deal externally with the public and internally with those involved in the organization. All the precepts of good public relations apply equally well to the organization staff, the board, and the community. We must be sensitive to the interests and needs of all and seek to satisfy these by full and open discussion of matters of concern to every member of the organization.

A flow of communications should not be simply random; when confusion exists, the board and director should seek to clarify the issue jointly. Communications between a board member and the director should occur through designated channels, with no sidestepping authority, going behind another's back, or political manipulation and pressure. Further, a "superintendent [director] should expect board members to unify and organize themselves around him. When this is not possible, it should be communicated and the relationship should be changed accordingly."[86]

The director should be the spearhead of communications. He should expect to be the core of the organization, to receive information from the bottom (his staff) and from the top (the board), and to keep this flow of communication and information open and directed toward the problems and concerns of the organization.

Sometimes a policy of free and open communications among all levels can actually frustrate the purpose of such an open policy. If the policy serves no function other than to allow people to speak their minds, with no real impact on decision making, the superficiality of such a

[86]Harmon, "Principles Governing School Board—Administrator Relationships," p. 40.

policy is eventually revealed. In addition to speaking their minds, people must be able to affect the decision of an organization for communication to be worthwhile. Open communication means nothing if the substance of communications is neither directed nor heeded.

The director many times uses the board as a virtual "sounding board" to test ideas. If the board is indiscreet and leaks information on the plans of the organization, this is as damaging as if the director leaked information on board deliberations. There is a need for mutual discretion and confidence in the handling of policy and personnel discussions. The same applies to staff members in their relations with the director. The organization needs to encourage the flow of information among all levels, but this should be accompanied by a sense of awareness of what items might be sensitive to public exposure or misunderstanding.

One of the prime functions of the director's leadership, and one which justifies the need for leadership, is to keep the board thoroughly informed on all matters that concern the organization. If the board is not well advised, or is ignorant of some aspect of an issue it is called to advise on, the person responsible for this omission is the director. It is up to him to be sure the board receives as much background and information as he can provide them. A good administrator will also provide time for consideration of matters the board will need to decide on.

To assure a board is properly used, there should be no unexpected items on the agenda, no deception about what the director has in mind for policies or programs, and no administrative policy making of which the board is ignorant. The board is an instrument to aid in policy formation, and to be effective it has to be knowledgeable about all facets of the organization. The fact that the board members change every few years is no reason for the director to abuse their function in the organization. To do so jeopardizes his own position. It therefore behooves the director to make the best use of the board for both himself and the community.

How does the director develop a well-informed and helpful board? The simplest manner is to channel all pertinent information on a given subject to the board by verbal comments, written reports and statements, films, outside specialists, conferences, and meetings. In addition, board members, when possible, should be encouraged to attend professional meetings and conferences to keep themselves abreast of happenings in recreation and related fields. When this is not possible, the board members should receive copies of materials distributed at such conferences, or reports by the director of the activities at these conferences, as well as recent findings of interest in recreation.

The participation of the board in such activities serves not only to keep them informed about the recreation profession, but links them more closely to the director and staff. Such a mutual interest is more than a simple desire for *esprit de corps,* but an essential ingredient for a successful board-administrator relationship. Of course, the director will be more informed about the issues and specialty of his profession than the board, since this is a career and professional concern. However, a lay board need not be a group of amateurs. Information should be made available for board members; there is no point in cultivating or sustaining an ignorant board.

The board, on the other hand, should expect valid and substantial information for making decisions. They should never determine or evaluate policy without a thorough comprehension of the issue. An effective director will always see that information of such quality is available well in advance of board meetings. The administrator should assure the board that, good or bad, "they will always receive complete information. There is no way a board can effectively exercise its policy-making function without valid information."[87]

As representative leaders of public interest in recreation, the board must be thoroughly aware of the real needs of its community. They will have to establish strong links with the community to assure that they have accurate sources of information. Part of this is a public relations task, as we will discuss, but part is a genuine attempt by the board to understand the needs of those they were selected to represent.

The modes of forging such links with the community will undoubtedly vary by board member. However, they must make attempts to discover true community "leaders." Many actual leaders of communities do not have a high profile, especially in urban communities, or are not readily identifiable by our usual standards of leadership. These persons can be highly useful for board members in understanding and comprehending the needs of a community. The board jeopardizes its purpose if it fails to elicit and support recommendations that benefit rather than ignore the community.

Discussions with practitioners, board members, and others interested in recreation and parks have uncovered other problems prevalent in board-staff relations. All felt that a long term of office did not allow for much efficiency. Boredom in board members seemed to be a common experience after the fourth year, and the organization suffered because of it. All agreed that a shorter term would be better, but there was no agreement as to a preferred length. However, the election of board members, as opposed to appointment, was felt to be a strong point in favor of obtaining the best board.

Some practitioners favor the "caucus candidate," a person selected to represent a group and to a certain extent obligated to follow the policy set by that group. Such an arrangement would enable the director at least to understand each member's policy and, therefore, be better prepared to deal with the persons ultimately elected. The public would also have a clearer understanding of what to base their votes on. How-

87Ibid., p. 41

ever, this could lead to election of several different interest-group representatives and lead to a breakdown in smooth board-staff relations.

Those in recreation have a somewhat unique problem with boards when the lay leadership are small interest-group representatives, e.g., Little League, who try to pressure the board into making decisions beneficial to one group at the expense of others. Since it is the duty of recreation to serve all, interest groups are contrary to the philosophy of the profession. If a director faces a small interest-group supporter on the board, he must tread softly to avoid alienating any faction of the city's power structure. A strong director should have the complete support of his board, and should make it known early in his association with any board member that the organization is a public service agency for offering comparable services to all groups under its jurisdiction.

Some feel this type of board member is the most troublesome one a director has to deal with. If this interest-group member makes too strong a push for a pet project, the other board members might be able to control him with their voting power. This is, of course, only possible if the interest-group member is not the leader of the board, and if the other board members are responsible persons interested in making the best decisions for the community. The director under such conditions must strive to avoid decisions that will adversely affect the interest group. His failure to do so will almost certainly force the other board members to choose sides, and the administrative needs of the organization will be endangered. So might the director's job!

However, if the interest-group member is the board leader and affects the decision of the board in his favor, at the expense of other groups, the director must attempt to control this problem. The best solution to this situation was stated in the concept that a strong director should have the complete support of his board and should make it known early in his association with any board member that the organization is a public service agency. The board members must accept what the proper intentions and responsibilities of the organization and director are. Few board members enter an election for financial profit and, in fact, would strive to avoid such situations. However, this is often not the case in large cities where the opposite tendency exists. Business dealings with a board member, in any form, represent a conflict of interest, and so this practice is a poor one.

A recreation director is primarily a trained professional, capable of making responsible decisions under the most stringent conditions. However, a major problem that most directors face at some time is the credibility gap, when the director finds himself working with a board hesitant to accept his expertise on major decisions. This is often the case when a board consists primarily of businessmen who have knowledge of financial and business practices. It becomes particularly vexing when such a group is led by a retired park professional. Under such conditions, the best a director can do is maintain close touch with his professional associations at both the state and national levels, and to encourage other board members to obtain their own knowledge of the profession and its concerns.

A director in this dilemma should keep in touch with colleagues in the profession to obtain their opinions on any situation before suggesting a final decision. In this way, the director can be more aware of recent developments in the field and be informed about changes or innovations that may affect a particular situation. Should there be any disagreement on a solution, the director can allude to the opinions of professional colleagues and professional associations for added support.

On the other hand, the director should not discredit the board's opinions merely because they have no professional background in recreation and parks. It is best to get board opinions, since this interaction can keep professionals from developing a one-sided "recreator's philosophy." A director should encourage board trust by making good decisions and by using their advice and suggestions whenever possible.

The director must exercise strong, directive leadership in planning, advising, and making recommendations to the board, as well as in implementing board decisions. Some boards have been forced to assume administrative responsibilities because of a laissez-faire attitude by their director. If the director is unwilling or unable to make a responsible decision on some issue, he may choose to force the board into a decision-making role by refusing to provide the expected leadership. In such situations, the director may be using the board as a "security blanket." By shifting the responsibility for decision making to the board, he can exonerate himself should a decision prove faulty.

The security blanket board can also appear in another form, where the director neglects to provide adequate public relations to the community. Directors of this type often use boards as buffers to the community. This is not necessarily bad. Boards can be, if properly used, an excellent advertising or public relations medium. However, when the director uses a security blanket board as a crutch to mask failures, then it becomes detrimental to the organization.

Abbott found the following aspects affecting the relationship between school boards and superintendents:

- Length of professional association was not found to be a significant factor in determining value perception.
- Board members who were most similar to their superintendent in value orientation were found to express slightly higher confidence in those superintendents.
- Board members were significantly more traditional than superintendents of schools, also than parents and citizens.
- Board members were significantly less confident in their superintendents in areas of school-community relations, school-plant planning, and

management than in curriculum development, staff relations, business and finance, and management.[88]

Personnel management provides the setting for many public controversies that grow out of board-director relations. Too often personnel problems reach a point where they must be discussed in public. The harm to an organization is incalculable when this happens, particularly if the problems are serious and persistent. Both the board and the director carry heavy responsibility for proper handling of personnel matters. Not only must adequate staff be provided to run the organization, but an atmosphere conducive to productivity must be maintained.

Supervision of personnel matters should be confined to the director and should not be discussed in public. If the board has criticism of a staff member this should be communicated to the director discreetly and in a straightforward manner. The director should then decide what response the criticism requires. The board should not directly resolve personnel matters, except when it involves the director. In turn, the board holds the director responsible for handling personnel matters.

It is only in board meetings that a board can legally act. Much of the board's effectiveness, therefore, is determined by the quality of its meetings. Properly planned, well-organized, and efficiently conducted meetings are essential for effective board operation. All official acts of the board must be recorded in minutes and these maintained in a manner befitting legal documents.

As far as director-staff relations, there is no one organizational structure that will ensure successful interaction between director and staff. Basically, the internal organization of a recreation department is to provide an avenue for meeting the organization's objectives and for carrying out policies and directives of the board.[89] Each organization varies in design according to the kind of objectives the organization wishes to attain. In general, the internal workings of a recreation organization are concerned with program services, special facilities, construction and maintenance, business and finance, and public relations.

The internal structure of a recreation organization should be patterned not only to augment the needs and abilities of staff members, but to reflect the needs of the community, and to offer the broadest set of programs possible within staff and resource constraints. The new impact of social issues on the recreation profession, and more expanded concepts of recreation, should be reflected in the organization design. Once a structure is selected which best represents the staff and community, it should be flexible enough to change with the times.

[88]Abbott, "Values and Value-Perception."

[89]Harold D. Meyer and Charles K. Brightbill, *Recreation Administration* (Englewood Cliffs, N.J.: Prentice-Hall, Inc., 1956).

To achieve an optimum relationship between director and staff, a clear understanding has to exist about the duties and responsibilities of both. If not, ambiguity and misunderstanding will arise as to who is responsible for what, and to what extent their duties and functions overlap. To enhance interactions between the staff and director, and among staff members themselves, a lateral form of organization structure should be encouraged rather than a vertical. One cause of difficulty between an administrator and staff is the lack of consultation with the staff on important issues. Even if the director seeks staff involvement in the decision and policy concerns of the organization, partially or poorly communicated information to staff members can do more harm than no information. The director must desire and act on the need for open and full disclosure.

If it is not possible to modify the structure of an organization, there should be plans to optimize communications between director and staff. Although there are not many layers of authority intervening between a director and staff in a recreation organization, this does not mean their communications are good. The director must be sure that the flow of information *up and down* is of the best quality. The director must do more than voice the desire for an interactive organization; he must build and maintain it. Certain signs of organization weakness might indicate the need for reorganization to encourage the relationship between director and staff. It is not suggested that reorganization occur immediately, but that it be carefully discussed with the board and staff and, if both groups are amenable to change, that it be done gradually over time.

Some organization traits that negatively affect the relationship of staff and director are:

- An incompetent director
- Too many layers of management, i.e., a long chain of command
- Inadequate communications among organization levels
- Poor interdepartment coordination
- Lack of consistent policy
- Slow or poor decision making
- Failure to meet organization objectives
- Excessive budgetary and personnel constraints
- Personality clashes, line-staff conflicts

Considering these problem areas, organizational change is obviously complex and difficult to initiate. However, it becomes clear that to avoid many problems, it is wise to keep the following organization and management guidelines in mind:

1. The role of the director in a recreation institution is to create an organization within which decision making can operate effectively and democratically. The director and board should encourage decisions to be made as *close* to the source of effective action as possible.

2. The administrative staff of a recreation organization should be established to provide staff members with as much chance for initiative as is consistent with existing policies and efficient operation of the organization. For example, the administrative functions of decision making should be designed to encourage democratic operation and decentralized decision making as much as possible.

3. Authority and responsibility delegated by the director to staff should create unitary decision making at all levels. The purpose of the organization is to clarify and distribute the responsibility and authority among individuals and groups in an orderly fashion. A structure of an organization is determined by its form of decision making and its policies. The functions of the staff should be established to ensure the most effective reflection of these.

4. The administrative structure should provide for a continuous and cooperative evaluation of the organization on how its goals are being obtained.

In other words, a system of "management by objectives" for the staff assigned to carry out objectives should be encouraged: "the system of management by objectives can be described as a process whereby the superior and subordinate managers of an organization jointly identify its common goals, define each individual's major areas of responsibility in terms of the results expected of him, and use these measures as guides for operating the unit and assessing the contribution of each of its members."[90]

PUBLIC RELATIONS AND INFORMATION

A good relationship between a recreation and parks agency and a community is best achieved by a wide range of programs and services suited to the true needs of the community residents. One way of attaining such a relationship, and maintaining it, is through a well-conceived public relations program reflecting the needs of the community. Special attention is given here to the importance of an effective public information program, because it can greatly aid the agency in fulfilling one of its civic obligations—to keep the community informed, involved, and interested in the objectives and goals of the organization. Naturally, the best public relations that any agency can achieve is effective performance

---

[90]George S. Odiorne, *Management by Objectives* (New York: Pitman Publishing, 1965), pp. 55–56; see also R. L. Sheely, "An Analysis of Staff Participation in Policy Formulation," unpublished Ed.D. dissertation, Teachers College, Columbia University, 1970; Paul Goodman, *People or Personnel: Decentralizing and the Mixed System* (New York: Vintage Books, 1968); John W. Humble, ed., *Management by Objectives in Action* (New York: McGraw-Hill Book Company, 1970); and Charles H. Granger, "The Hierarchy of Objectives," *Harvard Business Review*, XLII, May-June 1964, 63–74.

of their responsibilities. Public relations flows from that performance to the community, with little attention given to promotions or the "puffery" of public relations.

It is regrettable that public relations often suggests public distortion, or even deception and pressure. Public relations, if properly used, becomes public information, a means of accurately informing the public of the activities and plans of an organization in a stimulating yet candid manner. Announcements by the board or director which distort or amplify the achievements of either serve little purpose. Public relations has been discredited by its abuse and misuse, its confusion or overlap with press agentry. "Press-agentry, with its emphasis upon image, betrays an ignorance of what constitutes effective public relations—which is, of course, telling the truth."[91] An administrator has to anticipate critics who find any information given to the public in a planned and coordinated manner suggestive of distortion or commercialism. A distinction must be drawn between high-pressured salesmanship and direct, candid, yet not necessarily dull publicity releases. The public is not best informed through suggestion and speculation, but through intelligent, reflective media releases about matters that interest and affect them.

The public needs and wants to be informed; if it does not receive its information directly from the board or organization, it will obtain it through other means. Before discussing the preparation and presentation of information, we must first determine whether the agency is meeting its responsibilities to the community. It makes little sense to prepare elaborate releases on organization activities and programs if the recreation and civic responsibilities of the organization have not been met in the first place.

A public recreation agency exists to serve the community; thus its achievements, or what it is aspiring toward, are of interest to the people it serves. Everyone involved in the organization can to some extent be a public relations representative, as long as the information released, the manner in which it is released, and when it is released are clearly understood by board members and by the director and staff.

Although the best and most natural public relations program consists in doing a good job, it is conceivable that an agency may be doing a good job and the public may not be truly aware of it. Then, the need for a public relations program becomes necessary to inform the public about the organization, its achievements, programs and activities, as well as plans for the future, and how these all involve community residents. On the other hand, if an organization and its board are doing a discreditable job for the community, no public relations program—no matter how slick or formidable—can long delay the community's awareness of the situation.

A good director realizes he must develop outstanding rapport with the media in his area in order to be able to receive adequate coverage.

[91]Mark Singer, "The Editors Reach Out," *The Nation*, October 5, 1974, p. 306.

Newspaper photos, speeches at lunches, ribbon-cutting and dedication ceremonies, golfing dates with public figures, and the like are some of the events which a director can arrange for his board members. On the other hand, there are some who may maintain this is not a duty for the director. There is much difference of opinion on this point. A director must decide how to handle all aspects of public relations. Admittedly, it can be time-consuming, but it can be beneficial to the agency and the board, while pleasing to various community groups.

In addition to the genuine achievements of the agency, another natural source of good public relations is board members. If election or appointment to a park board is considered a prestigious achievement, the caliber of person attracted to these positions can often enhance the agency. Nonetheless, if the board does not represent the community, the achievements of individual members are irrelevant. If the recreation agency serves a black community with all-white board members (no matter how prestigious), the public relations earned will be practically nil. In such instances, the agency is ignoring their public; any concept of public relations built on the negation of equal community representation is bound to be spurious and an insult to the community.

Perhaps this fact is not fully appreciated: Many times when board members are challenged with demands for true community representation, they defend themselves by parading their credentials, their recreation interests and social convictions, and so forth. Of course, the qualifications of any board member are important (especially if they are appointed to the position), but the board member primarily exists to serve the public. If they are unable to effectively do the job because they do not actually represent their constituency, the value of personal qualifications fades. There has to be a blending of qualifications and representation for a board to be successful in its public relations. The need for representation applies also to all social classes, sex, and age, as well as to race. Representation of the public the agency serves, rather than paternalistic leadership, often yields excellent public relations and support for an agency.

If overall community representation on the board is desired but an agency does not really want equal representation for all community segments, the strength of a "token" appointee can be disproportionate to the actual qualifications of that individual. The token board member may seem to be a community's only link with the agency and sought as the only person representing the organization. Thus, by attempting to avoid representation of all segments by tokenism, an agency may actually diminish the public relations strength of its board.

The director must be sensitive to the composition of board membership. He needs to be sensitive to community and staff criticisms of even the most "prized" board member, for there may be some truth in what is being voiced. The community to be served is not static, and the administrator can never assume he has an ideal board to represent that community. On the other hand, the director must be judicious about criticism, and avoid overresponding to every chance accusation against a board or staff member. He needs to have some concept of what the board is capable of achieving, and what the limitations of the staff are; he should not assume an ability to respond quickly to criticisms is necessarily a good thing. Sometimes a delayed response can mitigate or more clearly reveal an issue in question.

Even with an "ideal" board, the members can still detract from the public relations of an agency in several ways: if they have served too long on the board, or have lost interest in or sight of the needs of the organization and the community; or if they have become rigid in their trusteeship role and begin to identify more with the organization's viewpoint than with the community's. This can happen to any board member, no matter how responsive he or she may initially have been. The agency should not pride itself on a well-balanced board and ignore hardening of the arteries. It must be alert to the *ongoing* qualifications and abilities of a board to meet its responsibilities and duties. Otherwise, the board becomes a facade, no matter how impressive.

If a public relations activity is well handled, one problem with board members can be avoided: boredom. Since many of the appointments or elections to the board are rather long terms for advisory positions, the board member may get restless with performing familiar tasks for several years. If with public relations the director can highlight not only the activities of the agency but other relevant activities of the board members as well, he can satisfy their need to be recognized and admired. A progressive and knowledgeable recreation director will see the possibility of achieving two objectives with one strategy in such a situation: to get exposure for the programs the agency offers and for its board members as well.

There are persons who run for public office with the idea of getting publicity for some other personal ambition. Often the "publicity hound" will leak priority information before an agreed release date in order to be a source of information and garner much sought-after public exposure. The publicity hound may give an impression of disharmony among the board members or between the director and the board. This could lessen public respect for the organization. A good director must be aware of this possibility and attempt to control it through sound policy and decision making on the origin, content, and planning of *all* publicity releases and events. It should be a general policy that any release or event relating to agency affairs must be formulated and issued by the director and/or the board at a date agreed on by both.

Each board member can counter poor public images or opinions of the board or agency by dealing with them informally, though with the knowledge of the director to prevent any confusion. A board member can be sensitive to pending community or organization problems and attempt to alleviate them before they are a real issue. Thus, board members can be more than trustees of the organization; since they usually live in the community, they can be an excellent source of informal information for formulating an effective public relations program.

The director and staff can also be useful in public relations activities. Through social connections and activities, they can promote the agency's programs and objectives. If the administrative staff are well informed about the policies and objectives of the organization, they can be most useful in conveying messages to the community: "A whispering campaign can be good as well as bad, and people are impressed when they get the 'low-down' from those on the inside."[92] To achieve this, everyone promoting the interests of the agency, informally or formally, must be aware of the overall organization "plan" for public relations. Staff or board members should avoid offhand comments about pending programs or plans if these statements might precipitate premature responses to organization goals.

The manner in which public announcements are made has much to do with the quality of board-community, board-staff, and director-staff relations. The board should clearly authorize the board president, the director, or both to act as spokespeople for the organization: "Many boards have found their superintendents [directors] to be in the best position to handle this responsibility effectively. Once a spokesman has been designated, public announcements should originate with him, and individual board members should not release statements to the news media. . . ."[93]

It is important once a person has been designated for handling the public relations function, that this designation be relatively constant. If the director is selected, the board should avoid making the more important public announcements and relegating the less important ones to the director on an arbitrary basis. This is especially important when staff or personnel matters are to be announced. If the staff sees that all major personnel announcements are made by the board, they may look to the board to promote their career, bypassing the director. This tendency to overlook the director can confuse the administrative relationship of the director to his staff, as well as negatively affect organization morale. All personnel matters should be handled by the director, including public announcements. If the director is permitted to make only the less important announcements, the community and agency staff may come to view the director as less important than the board.

To ensure a higher level of public relations for an organization, the board must carefully determine who (other than the director) may be best suited to handle releases of information, under what circumstances, to what media, and how often. These decisions in essence constitute a

[92]Roy Sorenson, *The Art of Board Membership* (New York: Association Press, 1950), p. 53.

[93]Dykes, *School Board and Superintendent*, p. 144.

formal public relations plan, and are one way of ensuring that informal communications do not undermine or detract from the formal public relations.

There is no intention to prevent informal information from going to the community. What an agency wants to prevent are unreliable sources of information who might distort the aims of the organization. Any "whispering campaign" that exists should either be positive or be curtailed if possible. This is, of course, an exceedingly sensitive area of public relations, especially for social service agencies.

If the community has no sure source of information about an agency, they will seek whatever sources exist, regardless of their validity. If the staff is not clearly informed about the intentions of the board or of the director, it too will convey or seek erroneous information. Obviously, an effective public relations program, both external and internal, is virtually mandatory for an effective social service organization. An agency's administration must be sincere and persistent in its efforts to formulate clear policies about public relations, and to follow these with ongoing releases to the staff and community. In addition to the informal social and business connections of the staff and board, annual reports, agency newsletters, speeches, special conferences and meetings, community-staff committees, newspaper, television, and radio releases, as well as organization open houses, can all aid in keeping everyone sufficiently and accurately informed.

If an organization can afford it, it can retain a public relations consultant, especially if it is encountering serious problems with public information. Before hiring such a consultant, however, it should be certain the problem is actually one of poor public relations and not something else. Whether an agency plans its own public relations program or seeks professional assistance, the board and the administration need to critically evaluate it periodically, as follows:

• Discover what the community thinks of the organization, and what they believe its function to be
• Interpret the organization to the community and vice versa
• Develop the most effective means of communication, involving the greatest number of people, and use all media available
• Stimulate public interest in the organization and its programs
• Develop and maintain community confidence in the board and professional staff
• Anticipate and circumvent problems caused by poor community relations
• Constantly evaluate past public relations to improve future plans[94]

[94]Suggested by Robert R. Luse, *Public Relations Primer* (Trenton, N.J.: New Jersey State Federation of District Boards of Education, 1967), p. 9, in Lloyd W. Ashby, *The Effective School Board Member* (Danville, Ill.: The Interstate Printers & Publishers, Inc., 1968), pp. 93–94.

These precepts for enhancing public relations externally can also be extended to internal public relations. The board must seek to know and understand the administration, and the administration, its staff. Otherwise, the external public relations program will have no bearing on the internal realities of the organization and the people who run it. The response of the board to administrative demands, the director to staff needs, and the response of all agency personnel to the community entail the use of public relations skills and techniques. Many issues arise for all these relationships which have considerable public relations consequences, good and bad. All persons in an organization weaken or improve public relations by their wisdom or indiscretion, their tact or arbitrariness, their care or neglect of these matters, which are sensitive and open to wide repercussions.[95]

FINANCIAL ADMINISTRATION

A Fiscal Framework

Recreation and park services, no matter what one's philosophy of leisure might be, are essential services for any community. Yet this social service, like so many others, is threatened by the declining amount of resources available for community services, especially in urban areas. According to the National League of Cities, central cities "are burdened with more than their share of welfare costs, education costs, and regional facility costs. They are burdened with costs so far beyond their own present revenue-raising powers that many mayors spend far too much of their time begging grants-in-aid from the state and/or federal governments. . . ."[96]

There is some question whether revenue-sharing arguments from states, in terms of their impoverished fiscal condition, are indeed the case:

> The fiscal crisis of state government, a staple of revenue-sharing rhetoric of last summer, has suddenly vanished. . . . For the states the fiscal crunch at the end of the '60s was more of a cyclical than a permanent problem. . . . There was an "explosion" in state welfare costs as more of the poor learned they were eligible for a whole range of benefits. That explosion appears to have simmered down, partly as a result of recent social security increases.[97]

The necessity for ensuring a flow of government resources to recrea-

---

[95]Sorenson, *The Art of Board Membership*, p. 53.
[96]"Financing Our Urban Needs," *Nation's Cities*, March 1969, p. 21.
[97]"State Gravy," *New Republic*, March 10, 1973, p. 9.

tion and parks programs, therefore, becomes the province of the parks and recreation profession. There is no way that recreation and parks agencies can expect an already beleaguered mayor to concentrate on obtaining more funds for their particular service.

Since the services to be provided are for an entire community, the people of the community carry the burden for financing such services through their taxes. As we all know, taxes are already burdensome for many groups. The financing of what are considered essential human services, of which recreation and parks is one, through taxes has become intractable if not impossible. Whether or not there will be a taxpayers' revolt, it is clear the tax base of a community is not an inexhaustible cistern that keeps up with accelerating social demands for municipal services.

Furthermore, even when federal monies are given back to the states via revenue-sharing programs, there is no assurance that all social services will be well served. Local authorities tend to be much more conservative and tight-fisted than the federal government, especially when it comes to social services:

> A Tax Foundation questionnaire, sent to 409 cities with populations greater than 50,000 . . . showed that the revenue-sharing moneys were spent in five main categories: environment, 12.7 percent; law enforcement, 11.5 percent; street and road repair, 10.9 percent; fire protection, 10.4 percent; parks and recreation, 7.4 percent. Only 1.6 percent went to social services and 1.1 percent to health.[98]

One can see that the services which receive the least amount of money are those that are *perceived* as less important, while the reverse operates for the municipal services receiving higher proportions of local monies. These perceptions of greater or lesser importance are basically political perceptions. That is, the elected representatives of communities respond to pressure from special-interest groups or wealthier taxpayers to finance services these feel to be important. A taxpayer with a good income is more likely to desire better police protection, environmental control, and improved roads than he is to fight for expanded leisure services, and he is more likely to make campaign contributions and to vote.

Many recreation and parks specialists see the status of their professional services in serious jeopardy in the public sector. The amount of money put into recreation and parks in many areas has been steadily declining and will continue to do so. It seems no longer possible to ignore the necessity for acquiring improved public and private revenues and support:

> The jeopardy represented by present inadequacies in fiscal resources is affecting every area of services specialization perpetuated by the Recreation and Park Profession. Public recreation services, institutional recreation

[98]Michael Harrington, "Grass-Roots Needs," *The Nation*, January 19, 1974, p. 69.

programs, state, county, and city park systems, and special facilities such as zoological parks are experiencing varying degrees of difficulties in maintaining services at a level equal to the needs and expectations of their clientele.[99]

Recreation and parks straddles the fence between being an "acceptable" social service and one that is linked with welfare or free health programs; this is why it has usually received a relatively decent slice of the municipal pie. However, we must not forget that our profession for a long time did not serve all members of a community, that it was essentially a middle-class service and hence likely to obtain unquestioned support. But as it began to reach out to serve all segments of a community, especially the poor and minority groups without political or financial power, it began to experience itself what these people had been enduring—neglect, distrust, uncertainty, ambiguity.

For recreation and parks agencies situated in middle-class neighborhoods, money is certainly tight; for those in urban or poorer communities the funds are becoming nonexistent. Part of the struggle within recreation and parks, by so-called traditionalists, is not so much to keep the profession and its services unchanged as to prevent it from acquiring the "taint" of the other human and social services. With this taint, recreation loses importance as an essential service, and becomes one that is useful to keep minorities and poor off the streets, but far from essential. Our society in less than a decade has swung from serious concern for the poor and other repressed groups to an inordinate concern with law and order against these very groups; such a society is not likely to display much patience with social services.

The choice for the profession, it seems, then becomes whether recreation and parks will strive to be a broad social service or whether it will focus on offering traditional services, without the taint of welfare, in more stable communities. Or more to the point, perhaps this issue has already been decided by the location of a recreation and parks agency: those in established communities will have to struggle to maintain or increase their budgetary allotments; those in urban areas, especially in the inner cities, will have to beg. They will have to go begging to the mayor who purportedly has gone begging to the federal government. And the taint of welfare accompanies the attempt to serve those too poor to offer an adequate tax base for their services. One of the tenets of recreation and parks is that funds for programs shall be derived primarily from taxes paid by those who participate in or benefit from the programs and facilities. What is not clear is how to finance such services for those groups whose tax base is too low to support even minimal services; are these groups going to receive support through sufficient budgetary allocations regardless of their personal wealth?

[99] National Recreation and Park Association, "Draft of Position Statement on Fiscal Resources," mimeographed, October 1971.

The prime responsibility for providing fiscal resources for parks and recreation belongs to the people benefiting at the local level. However, additional help will be needed in high density, low economic areas. Elected and appointed officials at the national and state level are urged to assure that grants-in-aid for parks and recreation include provisions for funding facility management, programming and maintenance, as well as capital development. They are also urged to stipulate that parks and recreation be a facet of all state, county or municipal level public service programs using federal funds; to eliminate requirements and regulations that strain the fiscal resources or restrict the expenditures of grants inhibiting the quality and quantity of programs.[100]

In addition, special tax levies for improvements in cities and special districts can be modified to use for facilities and services at the neighborhood level. When citizens become aware of the values of recreation and parks facilities in their neighborhoods, they are willing to pay for them. Poorer neighborhoods would then need the help of the parks and recreation agency to seek additional resources to make up any deficit in neighborhood assessments. Model Cities and urban renewal are two examples where outside funding was sought.

The financial situation of state and local governments is in a period of uncertainty—either because we do not understand the financial situation or because it is being overdramatized by local government officials. There is no easy way to find out: those closest to local government say the budgets are excessively tight; those more removed, who look at the state versus the federal revenue situation, say that not only are states in better shape than the federal government, but many states report or anticipate surpluses. As Representative John Anderson (R, Ill.) pointed out in late 1972:

> Now we find the federal budget facing an inflationary $10 to $15 billion full-employment deficit while the state and local sector is accumulating a $15 billion surplus this fiscal year. If the trend continues, it could reach $24 billion in 1975.[101]

It is difficult to speculate on any trends at this time in our economic history. What is a surplus situation for local government at one point can quickly become a deficit situation, especially if unemployment levels continue to rise and inflation continues to increase. Whatever our opinions on general revenue sharing as a fiscal measure, it has raised the right questions for providing a framework for financial administration:

> What kind and how much revenue should state and local governments be allowed to raise? Is more revenue sharing the way to go, or should the states make more vigorous use of the state income tax? How can the federal government enforce national standards, yet leave state and local

[100]Based on "Statements of Position on Fiscal Resources," National Recreation and Park Association.
[101]"State Gravy," pp. 9–10.

government free to experiment? Is it fair to reward governments that reform their tax structures and consolidate their government operations or put their revenue shares to some "progressive use"? And what is a progressive use? Property tax relief may be just as "progressive" and much more popular than a clumsy expansion of the state bureaucracy. These are not nuts-and-bolts questions of public administration; they are the political issues at the heart of the New Federalism.[102]

The point of this discussion is that we should not assume that states and local governments are experiencing fiscal crises if indeed they are not. The clarion call of all public agencies, governments, and institutions is that they are always broke. "In fact, most park and recreation administrators and specialists learn early in their careers to accept the reality of limited budgets, restrained expenditures, and an ongoing disparity between their service capabilities and the needs and desires of those who expect to receive their services."[103] We can see how easily we would begin to accept the argument of "tight funds" without reassessing this for ourselves on a fiscal-year basis.

Anyone in public service, be he the dispenser of funds or the recipient, is well advised to gain some skill or acumen in financial analysis, or have access to those who do. Scepticism is probably the best response to any financial cliche. Money may be tight for recreation and parks, while not for law enforcement services. It is the responsibility of the recreation agency to determine what precisely is the community's financial situation (in terms of a formal governmental budget), what is being spent for particular services, what is not, and the rationale behind the entire budgetary process. We should not concentrate merely on what is appropriated or should be appropriated to recreation and parks, but how this service is handled relative to other municipal services, and what trends might exist in overall budgetary allocations. The most effective observers are those who comprehend and assess the total picture.

If we wish to obtain greater public awareness and support for recreation services, we cannot present our arguments in some theory-of-play vacuum; we must present recreation and parks as a vital human service in the framework of all municipal services, not within the framework of how good and healthy it can be for people. This latter approach is a justification for the service, the former is the presumption that it is a necessary municipal service and we thus pursue the necessity for its balanced representation in the budget. No one seeks to justify garbage pick-up, police protection, or other local services; rather they attempt to gain increased allocations for these services. As long as recreation and parks professionals continue to justify their programs and services, they will be on the defensive in public and budgetary hearings.

[102]Tom Geoghegan, "Reversing the Flow of Power: Big Brother's Little Spoons," *The New Republic*, March 31, 1973, p. 17.

[103]National Recreation and Park Association, "Draft of Position Statement on Fiscal Resources."

Professionals should not be arrogant and assume the need is so self-evident for leisure services that they will not reiterate it; such a tactic will unnecessarily antagonize everyone. On the other hand, assuming there is a need to justify recreation services in budget hearings will only lead to self-aggrandizement or defensive statements about the value of recreation. If, as professionals believe, recreation opportunities are a basic need and right of all the people, then the issue becomes one of ensuring that right, not justifying its existence; presumably this has already been agreed on. If time and public opinion reshape the value of recreation and parks, the profession should be adequately prepared to justify its continued existence.

An administrator with an attitude that confidently presumes (and believes) that recreation and parks is a basic right, and proceeds from there, is in a much stronger position than one of defensive posturing. If a city council or mayor asks for justification of a new program, don't parade the rationale for recreation and parks in general; be specific about a program or a facility. It is surprising how often recreation professionals and practitioners will assure each other in private meetings and conferences how important their services are. We know they are, otherwise we would not be working in the field. If we have to convince anyone of recreation's value, it should be the people we serve, not each other. These people can at least hope to affect their government officials in allocating sufficient funding for the services.

Fiscal Resources

The recreation and parks profession must put pressure on all levels of government—federal, state, and local—as well as on citizens, to decrease the ignorance or apathy that surrounds the provision of public funds for leisure services. With almost all their resources coming from government funds, recreation and park agencies are totally dependent on public support for their survival. This recognition of dependency, as argued above, should not lead to passivity by professionals, practitioners, or even citizens, but:

> should be the stimulus for alert and aggressive actions in the public arena to protect and satisfy the fiscal interest and needs of the park and recreation field. New and broader strategies designed to overcome and counterbalance the circumstances or problems that threaten the fiscal security and capabilities of the parks and recreation delivery system must be developed and applied.[104]

By necessity, then, recreation administrators will have to take on the concerns of fiscal management; they cannot afford to passively wait

[104]Ira J. Hutchinson, "Fiscal Resources—Statement of Position," National Recreation and Park Association, "Statements of Position on Human Resources, Natural Resources, Fiscal Resources," mimeographed, October 1971.

for budget appropriations: "This means being able to look at local and national trends in . . . fiscal resources and promptly executing those responsive actions that will be to their fiscal advantage."[105] Until recently, most administrators have been waiting for some change or impetus to emerge from other directions and solve their problem. It has been evident for some time that it is up to the profession itself to ensure its own life in the competition for public monies.[106]

Taxes remain the prime support for parks and recreation agencies. Although other public and private special-assistance programs are valuable for land acquisition, solid tax support is essential for local services. Unfortunately, taxes at the local level have not kept up with the demand, need, and cost of public services. Recreation and park agencies must actively seek or develop methods of obtaining "special" tax dollars—i.e., revenue bonds, and so forth—to supplement funds available for the general tax fund.

Although state budgets for recreation and parks have been comparatively modest, the demand for funds is increasing. In the past, state legislatures were reluctant to appropriate funds for recreation and parks at levels comparable to other state services. Because of increased public demand and federal incentives, states have begun to recognize their responsibility to support parks and recreation services in a more substantive way. Ongoing pressures from citizens, the cities, counties, and the federal government can bring even larger and more regular state tax revenues for parks and recreation. Since a substantial share of special recreation services are for state institutions and agencies (education, ill and disabled, the aging, the mentally and physically retarded), state tax revenues have been a key resource for administrators and specialists handling these programs. Nonetheless, because of the "squeeze" on the tax dollar, even these services are being reduced.

County taxes have been more productive in developing recreation and parks. The independent taxing authority of many county recreation and park systems has increased the number of well-developed and coordinated county programs. This authority reduces the competition county officials usually endure over limited funds. With such independent tax authority, the funding necessary for parks and recreation can be better assured.

In addition to public funds, the parks and recreation profession should give more attention to private contributions. Foundations, business corporations, industry, and individual donors are all possible sources of money and other resources, if these are ethically acquired. Unlike grants or tax money specifically for parks and recreation, private contributions can be used for a variety of broader causes and purposes, such

[105]Ibid.

[106]Much of the following discussion is based on ideas presented in the National Recreation and Park Association, "Statement of Position on Fiscal Resources."

as outreach programs. In obtaining private contributions, well-organized planning is required for initial contacts and ongoing communication. Some recreation and park agencies have found that private contributions are enhanced once the private donor or a representative is given a policy role or involvement in program development. Even though industry and corporations have been a minor source of funds in the past, this need not be the case. In communities where an industry is dominant, and recreation and parks can offer it a service, the chances for support are excellent. Parks and recreation administrators are also attempting to establish such relationships with corporate leaders locally to encourage contributions.

Foundations and other nonprofit groups are essentially geared to therapeutic recreation needs. Vocational rehabilitation, special education, and many others fields already obtain substantial support from foundations. Private contributions all can assist in developing special park and recreation facilities. Funds from zoological societies, and the Junior Leagues in their support of nature centers, are examples of private contributions that are used for maintaining and operating special facilities and programs.

Park and recreation administrators are also using fees and charges as one alternative to their funding problems. As self-sustaining programs and facilities are created, much more money is available to maintain or expand overall services. For the use of fees and charges to be a worthwhile funding source, there has to be a change in the philosophy of many recreation and parks agencies. For example, what has to be reconsidered is the premise stated earlier, that recreation and parks is a basic public service that should be tax supported, without fees and charges to users. Within this premise lies the welfare concept of recreation, that these services will be free to those whose tax support is minimal and who are unable to pay for recreation services. Another presumption against fees and charges is that they would put public recreation facilities in unfair competition with private recreation services. Finally, some administrators fear they will lose tax support if some services appear to be self-supporting.

The public has come to expect fees for other public services, such as charges for textbooks in public schools, tolls on public highways, parking fees for most public property and streets. If fees can enrich the quality or quantity of recreation services, people are likely to pay for them. State parks charge a camping or parking fee, a charge for boat or other equipment rental, plus an additional charge for any swimming pool or other special recreation they might have. There has been little complaining from users, and as the demand increases, the more and better services there are. These fees have also helped to ease somewhat the financial restrictions of the state park systems. Any administrator who can improve services through use of a fee should do so.

Public grants from all levels of government have represented the most readily accessible monies in the past decades, with federal grants by far the most important; those available at the state, county, or local level have involved less money and have been more competitive. Because of financial difficulties and the low priority given to recreation and park programs, there seems little likelihood that state, county, or municipal grants will increase significantly in the near future. Again, objections to grants as a source of funding have been several: (1) the funds offered do not match the needs they seek to serve; (2) often there are too many strings or excessive controls attached to grants; (3) when matching funds from the local level is a federal stipulation, obtaining even minimal amounts becomes untenable for budget-constrained communities; and (4) at this point of environmental concern, a disproportionate share of grants are for land purposes over human services. Furthermore, federal grants are likely to become even scarcer, with fewer categorical grants available to help the local recreation agencies.

With these various sources of funding in mind, the agency must have an overall fiscal strategy to ensure that resources reach a worthwhile and productive level. With three factors in mind—that service claims for money are highly competitive, that there is little likelihood of gaining much more fiscal support from state and local governments, and that federal grants are decreasing—parks and recreation agencies should resolve to:

1. Identify those public and private resources that are now directly or indirectly available for the use of parks and recreation
2. Determine what new sources of public and private fiscal resources are needed and launch actions to make them available to parks and recreation

Although these are clear-cut approaches to stimulating the flow of additional resources, the drawbacks to their success are several:

1. Lack of familiarity with sources of public and private resources
2. Limited time, money, skill, and personnel for acquiring public and private resources
3. Limited cooperation among recreation agencies in acquiring and disseminating information regarding public or private resources

One way of reducing these three problems is for recreation and parks agencies to work in concert on the entire issue of funding, primarily through pooling their information and fiscal experiences. For example, are there any methods of acquiring or stimulating fiscal resources that might be useful to other recreation and parks agencies? What changes in policies, procedures, or philosophy are needed to encourage the flow of monetary resources? What additional staff or consultants are useful for acquiring outside funding? Finally, what political barriers exist to the acquisition of private and public funds, and how can these be legally and ethically circumvented? There is enough diversification among agencies that the above questions, in order to yield a useful fiscal strategy, must be answered broadly or specifically as the case may be. Those staff within the agency who will be concentrating on fiscal plans must be able to elicit the type of information they require from those with experience in fiscal management, as well as to be superbly informed of all laws, directives, ordinances, and policies that bear on any fiscal tactic or plan.

Fiscal Administration[107]

Fiscal management of a recreation and parks agency is similar to that of any enterprise—it involves an annual budget of ongoing expenditures and capital financing. The annual budget, as mentioned, is usually obtained through tax sources or levies of one kind or another, as well as from agency fees and charges for their services (where used). Capital improvements are usually financed by a bond issue. In some cases, capital improvements may be financed by gifts or bequests. The central tool of fiscal administration is, of course, the budget.

> Other than the primary reason of a plan of services, a budget is necessary for fiscal control. Division and department heads are able to fix responsibilities for their particular activities and become accountable within the boundaries established by the budget. The plan is as flexible as the legislative body sees fit.[108]

Since the emphasis in parks and recreation is on services, annual budget preparation does not begin with a forecast of revenues as other budgets do, but starts with the services an agency needs or desires to perform. If additional taxes or revenues are impossible to generate, only then should the budget be viewed from a revenue viewpoint, with services being reduced or eliminated to match what is available. Thus, the administrator presents the budget in terms of services.

Preparation of a budget for capital improvements states the sources of revenue, as well as the times and phases for the items to be developed. This budget would indicate which projects are to be developed from what particular funds—bonds or tax levies—and also include stipulations for ongoing support in maintaining and operating the new facility. Capital improvement planning and budgets must, of necessity, look well beyond the scope of an annual budget, with any changes in the economic situation requiring a reassessment of the entire capital improvement program, at least every five to ten years if not more often. Planning for capital improvements involves preparing (and updating) a schedule of facilities or related equipment to be built or purchased over a period of years. The only difference between an annual capital budget and a capital improve-

---

[107]Many of the suggestions in this section are taken from Illinois Association of Park Districts, *A Manual for Park District Commissioners in Illinois* (Springfield: IADD, 1968).

[108]Ibid., p. 22.

ments program is that the latter involves projections of needs for several years instead of a one-year period. Once accepted, however, a capital improvements program becomes part of the annual capital budget for the duration of the project.

The value of having capital improvements plans is that they enable agency administrators to look beyond the annual budget survey and decide what future improvements should be made. Capital improvement planning also "enables officials to avoid the exhausting impact that unplanned capital expenditures often have on local resources."[109] Six years is generally considered to be the best, because any shorter period does not afford the time needed to plan and finance major facilities. On the other hand, planning for a period of more than six years in advance may be impractical.

To be successful, a capital improvements program should be compatible with the overall objectives of a community, and should relate to the building plans of all other overlapping jurisdictions. By focusing on overall community needs and capabilities, capital projects can reflect these objectives, enhancing their probability of being constructed. Good planning of future needs can help save taxpayers' money—for example, in the acquisition of land well in advance of any critical need: "Sharp changes in the tax structure and bonded indebtedness may be avoided when the projects to be constructed are spaced over a number of years. Where there is ample time for planning, the most economical means of financing each project can be selected in advance."[110]

Any realistic capital improvements program must be related to the fiscal capacities of the local agency or government. This capacity is related to the financial history of the agency in terms of trends in taxation and assessment, as well as what the expenditures have been in other units of government of comparable size and financial resources. In many communities the capital improvements program is included in a comprehensive or a master plan for a community or region. "Although each city, county, or special district may develop its own capital improvements program, there is a growing recognition that on such matters as streets, highways, schools, parks, and water and sewer facilities there is a need to coordinate planning among all the major agencies."[111] This is a viewpoint stressed throughout this book; indeed comprehensive planning involves other agencies, whether it be for effective capital improvements or for any other community projects.

There are several methods of financing capital improvements. The first method is to finance the project(s) out of current revenues which

109U.S. Department of Housing and Urban Development, "Capital Improvements Programming in Local Government" (Washington, D.C.: Government Printing Office, 1970), p. iii.

110Ibid., p. 2.

111Ibid., pp. 7–8.

come from general taxes, fees and charges for services, or special funds and assessments. The prime advantage of such funding is, of course, the saving of interest charges on borrowed money and greater budget flexibility. Reserve fund financing is another pay-as-you-go method, with funds set aside each year in anticipation of capital improvements spending. The disadvantage of these two methods is the necessity for having cash available, often reducing the possibility of extensive projects in a small community.

General obligation bonds can be used to finance permanent expenditures such as schools, parks, and recreation facilities, where the taxing body is pledged to pay interest on and retire the debt. In many states, however, these bonds require the approval of the electorate. Revenue bonds are often used for revenue-producing projects, such as swimming pools, golf courses, and so forth. Interest rates are usually higher than on general obligation bonds because these are not totally backed by the local jurisdiction, nor is voter approval necessary. To make this method feasible, great care must be taken to ensure that earnings projected for the new facility are realistic.

The lease-purchase method of financing involves having a private company build a facility; this facility is then leased by a municipality or other jurisdiction. The rental paid over a period of years will include the original cost of the project plus interest. At the end of the leasing period the title to the facility is granted to the lessee. However, this method can prove very costly, especially if for any reason the lease has to be renegotiated and the interest rates increased.

Authorities and special districts (e.g., park districts) have the power to tax, issue bonds, and construct facilities that may not be self-supporting. Even though special districts are not constrained by any debt limit of a local government, these expenditures still are part of a community's financial obligation. Special assessments are usually made for public works programs, such as paving streets, sewers, and water mains; or joint financing may be arranged among other jurisdictions and government agencies to share the costs of projects that might be too expensive for one government or agency. The outside financial sources already mentioned (state and federal grants-in-aid) are a final method for a capital improvements program, though these can vary greatly with the political climate.

Since accounting procedures used for municipal agencies are different from traditional business accounting, the principles recommended by the Illinois Association of Park Districts are suggested:

1. The accounting system must make it possible to show that legal provisions have been complied with, to reflect the financial condition of the district, and to reassure the results of operations.
2. If legal and sound accounting provisions conflict, legal provisions must take precedence. It is, however, the finance officer's duty to seek

changes in the law to keep the law in harmony with accepted accounting principles.

3. The accounting system must be kept on a double-entry basis and subsidiary records provided where necessary.

4. Every governmental unit should establish whatever funds are called for either by law or by sound financial administration. However, funds introduce an element of inflexibility in the system, and accordingly, consistent with legal provisions and requirements of sound financial administration, as few funds as possible should be established.

5. Depending on the legal and financial requirements, the following funds are recognized: (1) General, (2) Special Revenue, (3) Working Capital, (4) Special Assessment, (5) Bonds, (6) Sinking, (7) Trust and Agency, and (8) Other Enterprises. These classifications, to the extent required, should be followed in the budget document and in the financial reports.

6. A complete self-balancing group of accounts should be maintained for each fund, including all accounts necessary to set forth financial condition and results of operations of each fund and to reflect compliance with legal provisions.

7. A clear segregation should be made between the accounts relating to current assets and liabilities and those relating to fixed assets and liabilities.

   With the exception of Working Capital, Other Enterprises, or Trust Funds, fixed assets should not be carried in the same fund with current assets, but should be set up in a self-balancing group of accounts known as the General Fixed Assets Group of Accounts.

   Similarly, except in Special Assessment, long-term liabilities should not be carried with the current liabilities of any fund, but should be shown in a separate self-balancing group of accounts forming part of the General Bonded Debt and Interest Group of Accounts.

8. The fixed asset accounts should be maintained on the basis of original cost, or the estimated cost if the original cost is not available. In the case of gifts, the appraised value at the time received is used.

9. Depreciation on general fixed assets should not be computed unless cash for replacements can legally be set aside. Depreciation on these assets may be computed for unit cost purposes even if cash for replacements cannot be legally set aside. These depreciation charges are used for memoranda purposes only and are not reflected in the accounts.

10. The accounting system should provide for budgeting control for both revenues and expenditures, and the financial statements should include budgetary information.

11. The accrual system in accounting for revenues and expenditures is recommended. Revenues, partially offset by provisions for estimated losses, should be taken into consideration when earned, even though not received in cash. Expenditures should be recorded as soon as liabilities are incurred.

12. Revenues should be classified by fund and source. Expenditures should be classified by fund, function, department, activity, character, and by main classes of objects, in accordance with standard classifications.

13. Cost accounting systems should be established wherever costs can be measured. Each system should provide for the recording of all the elements of costs, those incurred to accomplish a purpose, to carry on an activity or operation, to complete a unit of work or a specific job. Although depreciation on general fixed assets may be omitted in the general accounts and reports, it should be considered in determining unit costs.

14. A common terminology and classification should be used consistently through the budget, the accounts, and the financial reports.

In addition to following these principles of accounting, an agency has to have sufficient internal control to safeguard assets, generate reliable accounting data, promote efficiency, and encourage adherence to policy. Internal control includes both accounting and administrative controls. Accounting controls are those that relate to asset protection and reliability of data; administrative controls relate to methods of encouraging adherence to policy and of promoting efficiency. A successful set of organizational controls would include the segregation of functional responsibilities—for instance, records existing outside of the department or unit serving as a control over the activities of that department. However, for a small parks and recreation agency this separation may not be as possible as in larger agencies. In any event:

> There must be always someone charged with the responsibility of ascertaining the integrity of a transaction after it has been effected. Bank reconciliations, trial balances, and other records are all examples of post transactions or procedures that are not only sound practices, but basic to the efficient operation of a bookkeeping system.[112]

An effective financial system for helping administrators allocate their resources more effectively in terms of agency objectives is the Planning-Programming-Budgeting System (PPBS). "Its essence is the development and presentation of relevant information as to the full implications—the costs and benefits—of the major alternative courses of

---

[112]Illinois *Manual*, pp. 28–29.

action."[113] What PPB does not include are such areas as budget implementation, efficiency of work groups, manpower selection, or the cost control of *current* operations. Although cost accounting data and other nonfiscal data are important for PPB analyses, they are supplementary to and not a part of the system. The main characteristics of the system are:

1. The objectives of an agency or any other decision-making level are identified, and all activities are related to these objectives.
2. Future implications are carefully considered.
3. All pertinent costs are considered, capital as well as noncapital.
4. Systematic analysis is undertaken to (1) identify agency objectives, (2) identify alternative ways of meeting these objectives, (3) estimate cost of each alternative, (4) estimate results of each alternative, and (5) present cost/benefit data on each alternative.

There is nothing new about PPBS, since it uses a basic problem-solving approach to fiscal management; what is unique about it, however, is the combination of several management techniques into a systematic program for financial planning. Automatic data-processing equipment is usually considered essential for this system of standardized functional accounting, enabling the analysis to be more complex and presumably more realistic:

> PPBS potentially can help state and local governments deal with public problems ahead of time, in a comprehensive manner, and can place in much improved perspective the principal issues on resource allocation. The visibility of relevant information (on costs and benefits of pertinent alternatives) provided by PPBS is the key element.[114]

PPBS enables an agency to shift its attention to individual services rather than maintaining an agency orientation. The introduction of functional accounting and budgeting, which examines the income and expense of each service or function in detail, permits accurate costing for services. Functional accounting is a system that allows an administrator to relate costs to services as well as to *units* of service, if needed.

> Funding bodies now want to pay for specific services. No longer are they prepared to grant a sum of money to an agency solely on the premise that the agency enjoys a good reputation and is said to be doing good work. The funding bodies will now say, and rightly so—"We are prepared to grant x dollars for this and x dollars for that service according to the priority rating of such services." Therefore, . . . agencies are expected to

113State-Local Finances Project, "What Is PPB? Planning, Programming, Budgeting for City, State, County Objectives" (Washington, D.C.: George Washington University, 1967), p. 1; based on Harry Hatry and John Cotton, *Program Planning for State, City and County Objectives* (1967).

114Ibid., p. 8.

be able to identify the total cost of each service they are providing and the cost of each unit of such service.[115]

The functional accounting or service cost accounting used in PPBS makes this possible.

The PPB system does not contradict the advice given earlier that recreation and parks agencies should concentrate first on the services they wish to provide, then on the costs of these services. PPBS is an internal budgeting system; it permits accurate appraisal of costs and alternatives which in no way precludes the services-first approach to budget formulation. In fact, it clearly states in order: Planning, Programming, then Budgeting. By using a standardized functional budgeting and accounting format, the agencies are able to clearly identify the precise cost of services and programs in a community:

> The functional accounting procedures ... have proven to be of considerable value to many agencies on the system. For the first time they are able to identify clearly program and service costs and are in a position to negotiate meaningfully with government and other funding bodies in offering their services at realistic prices .... standardized functional accounting and unit cost figures are extremely valuable in comparing similar programs provided by different agencies.[116]

This information forms one of the first components of a PPBS model (see Illustration 7.11). This does not mean because good budgeting information is available that budget concerns should precede planning and programming.

The general Planned Program Budget Model developed by Vancouver's United Community Services offers a framework for identifying and assessing needs, determining priorities, setting objectives, planning services and programs, and evaluating results. Again, this "systematic" approach is similar to that used in systems analysis and in problem-solving techniques. Although PPBS is basically thought of as a budgeting system, it is really a more integrative management technique such as systems analysis. The focus of this model is to consider planning, programming, budgeting, and even evaluation in view of the primary goals and objectives of the agency.

The *data bank* should store and provide information, as needed, to identify and measure social problems, needs, or trends in the community. Of course, where there is only one agency involved, a data bank may be somewhat pretentious or redundant if the agency has access to these

[115]Allan R. Fitzpatrick, "Computerized Functional Accounting for Health, Welfare and Recreation Organizations" (Vancouver, British Columbia: United Community Services of the Greater Vancouver Area, June 1971), p. 1.

[116]A. R. Fitzpatrick and R. W. Patillo, "Vancouver Planned Program Budgeting Systems: Progress Report" (Vancouver, British Columbia: United Community Services of the Greater Vancouver Area, March 1972), p. 5.

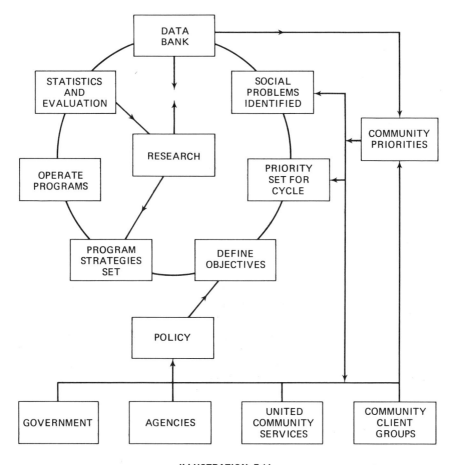

ILLUSTRATION 7.11

PPBS Model Cycle

Source: United Community Services of the Greater Vancouver Area, "Vancouver Planned Program Budgeting Systems Project" (Vancouver, B.C.: UCS, March 1972), p. 7.

data from other sources. The *identification of social problems* (or needs) can proceed from these data or from persons outside the agency with relevant information. The *development of priorities* should then be made in terms of the relative importance or urgency of each need and the available resources. After establishing priorities, specific *objectives* should be established for each of the problems or needs identified. "These objectives should clearly and definitively spell out the expected outcomes to be achieved during the planning-budgeting period, and should be stated in quantifiable terms. For example—to reduce juvenile delinquency by 20% in a certain area of the community."[117] In both determining priorities and in setting objectives, policies of the agency must be reflected.

Once these objectives are clearly stated, *strategies* of programs or services to achieve the objectives should be selected or determined. After these program/service strategies have been agreed upon, then funds should be allocated (or sought) to *operate the programs,* to offer these services to the community or neighborhood. The program strategies selected will, of course, be affected by ongoing evaluative research, experience, or data from other communities or agencies. The Vancouver Project staff suggests that *statistics and evaluation* be part of the data bank to provide a self-monitoring system. That is, these statistics and financial information should be available to any group or organization in the community, as well as for agency use in the next planning-programming-budgeting cycle. The value of this cycle, as depicted in the model, is that financial decisions can be related to earlier stages of decision making and to previous years.

Each of the phases of this model are likely to take a long time to develop. This is not a simple system. PPBS is designed for the highest levels of public decision making. The system requires time, patience, and cooperation to work well for any agency hoping to reap the benefits of an integrated public decision-making technique. The value of PPBS as a system of planning-programming-budgeting for social services is that it attempts to allocate public funds more realistically among competing public demands. In essence, for a group of agencies PPBS offers:

1. An improved process for decision making.
2. A systematic method of exploring alternative ways (more effective or less costly) for getting the public business done.
3. A procedure for coordination of governmental programs in the light of identified common or single objectives.
4. A better method of selection among federal aid offerings and of integrating federal aids into the jurisdiction's own service program.
5. A strengthening of the initiative of the state and local government in policy formulation.[118]

On the agency level, the short-range advantages of PPBS are:

1. An examination of fundamental objectives of the jurisdiction and the role of individual programs in meeting those objectives.
2. Better guidelines for policy formulation on one or two major issues on which decisions must be taken immediately....

[117]Ibid., p. 9.

[118]State-Local Finances Project, *Planning, Programming, Budgeting for City, State, County Objectives* (Washington, D.C.: George Washington University, June 1968), Note 1, p. 2.

3. More information on the present budgetary allocations existing among program expenditures. . . .[119]

If an agency or a commission or park district is considering the introduction of PPBS, a top-level staff member or a consultant should be assigned to explore its feasibility. One of the considerations to be examined is whether existing staff could handle such a system of program evaluation or whether new personnel would be required. Although a decision to take on PPBS as a permanent system may be too onerous for some agencies, the system could be tried on a trial basis. Initially, whether PPBS is to be permanent or temporary, it should not interfere with the ongoing operating and budgeting activities. For a while the system can be handled parallel to the regular budget procedures, or the regular budget system can be converted to a program budget. The decision to convert, though desirable for the long run, is optional until PPBS is fully operational since such a conversion requires considerable effort. Whatever approach is selected, a close relationship to the annual budget is, of course, necessary.

Some sort of PPBS central analysis group, as part of the administrator's office or in a budget or finance department, should have full responsibility for the system. Each department or unit head in an agency would be a member of a task force to work with the central analysis group in setting up the system:

> A department would develop a comprehensive program plan for the areas assigned to it, drawing upon other departments as needed. The central analysis staff would review all program analyses to provide the needed perspective for the chief executive. It would also perform selected program analyses that are not appropriately assigned to individual departments.[120]

Needless to say, whatever organizational format for handling PPBS is used, there are bound to be pros and cons, gains and losses.

Appendix F is a model of instructions for establishing a PPBS system at the state or local governmental level suggested by the State-Local Finances Project.

SELECTED REFERENCES

ARGYRIS, CHRIS. *Personality and Organization.* New York: Harper & Row, Publishers, 1957.
EREILICH, R. H. "A Model Statutory Proposal for the Regulation of Municipal

---

[119]Ibid., p. 2.
[120]Ibid., p. 8.

Regulations." University of Missouri at Kansas City. *Law Review*, XXXVIII (Spring 1968), 373.

HALPIN, A. W. *Theory and Research in Administration*. New York: The Macmillan Company, 1966.

HERYBERG, FREDERICK. *Work and the Nature of Man*. New York: World Publishing Company, 1972.

JUCIUS, MICHAEL. *Personnel Management*. Homewood, Ill.: Richard D. Irwin, Inc., 1967.

KOONTZ, HAROLD. *The Board of Directors and Effective Management*. New York: McGraw-Hill Book Company, 1967.

LIKERT, R. L. *New Patterns of Management*. New York: McGraw-Hill Book Company, 1961.

NEGGISON, LEON C. *Personnel: A Behavioral Approach to Administration*. Homewood, Ill.: Richard D. Irwin, Inc., 1967.

STRAUSS, GEORGE, AND L. R. SAYLES. *Personnel: The Human Problems of Management*. Englewood Cliffs, N.J.: Prentice-Hall, Inc., 1967.

TAYLOR, J. C., AND D. C. BOWERS. *Survey of Organizations*. Ann Arbor, Mich.: Institute for Social Research, 1972.

GLOSSARY OF TERMS
FOR PLANNING
RECREATION AND PARKS

Access Road. A roadway or street paralleling a freeway or limited access highway for the purpose of conducting traffic from the abutting property to ingress, egress, and crossover points. Also called a frontage road.[e]*

Acre. A unit of measure for land, used in the United States, Canada, and Great Britain. An acre is equal to 160 square rods or 43,560 square feet. 640 acres is equal in area to one mile square.[e]

Acre Foot. A quantity of water sufficient to cover an area of one acre to a depth of one foot. One acre foot is equal to 43,560 cubic feet or 325,851 gallons. A flow of one cubic foot of water per second (cfs) is equal to approximately two acre feet per day (24 hours).[e]

Active Files. Records and nonrecords needed for conducting current business or pertaining to specific uncompleted cases.[f]

Administrative Files. Files created as a result of the general administra-

---

*Footnotes are listed at the end of the Glossary.

385

tion of responsibilities and in support of specific transactions relating to operations.[f]

Aerial Photography.   The art of making photographs of the earth's surface and features thereof, from aircraft at various altitudes.[c]

Air Pollution.   The presence of contaminants in the air in concentrations that prevents the normal dispersive ability of the air and that interferes directly or indirectly with man's health, safety, or comfort or with the full use and enjoyment of his property.[e]

Air Pollution Episode.   The occurrence of abnormally high concentrations of air pollutants, usually due to low winds and temperature inversion and accompanied by an increase in illness and death.[e]

Air Quality Control Region.   An area designated by the federal government where two or more communities—either in the same or different states—share a common air pollution problem.[e]

Air Quality Criteria.   The levels of pollution and lengths of exposure at which adverse effects on health and welfare occur.[e]

Air Quality Standards.   The prescribed level of pollutants in the outside air that cannot be exceeded legally during a specified time in a specified geographical area.[e]

Annexation.   The process by which a municipality or other governing authority absorbs surrounding land and brings it under its jurisdiction. The great cities of the United States achieved their present size primarily through this mechanism, which was more commonly used before 1900 than it is today. Acquisition by annexation is now usually only of unincorporated territory. It is accomplished under a special act of the legislature, by action of the governing body where so authorized, or by a combined vote of the electorates concerned. Although Detroit and Los Angeles both annexed substantial territory during the twentieth century, and although there was a revival of annexations after World War II, fringe areas surrounding existing cities now generally resist it either through exertion of political pressures or by "defensive incorporation." The growing problems of the big cities have made its neighbors reluctant to share in them.[b]

Arboretum.   A place where trees are grown for scientific or educational purposes, either by themselves or in association with other plants. Arboretums are botanical gardens in which trees and other woody plants predominate. Much of our knowledge regarding the culture of trees and shrubs has originated in arboretums.[c]

Arterial Highways.   Major transportation highways of the community. They are used primarily for intercity or cross-city traffic, depending upon the size of the community. Their purpose is to carry the greatest amount of traffic without interference to adjacent land use.[d]

Backfill.   The material used to refill a ditch or other excavation, or the process of doing so.[e]

Base Map.   A map that indicates the existing street systems, railroads, rivers, or other community features that are part of the development of the city. This map is used for preparing other maps shown throughout the comprehensive plan.[d]

Beach.   A sandy or gravelly strip of gently sloping land on the shoreline of a sea, lake, or other body of water. The term is generally applied to the strip of land between high and low tide, or to the strip subject to the action of waves.[c]

Bond, Public.   A bond issued by a public agency. The agency may be the federal government, a state, county, city, township, borough, school or special district, special-purpose authority, or any one of numerous subdivisions of government. A *municipal bond* is a bond issued by any political subdivision of the state, usually a city. A *tax-anticipation bond* is a bond issued in anticipation of tax receipts. A *special assessment bond* is one issued for a special improvement re-payable out of earmarked assessments levied on designated persons or property. Municipal bonds must be issued for a public purpose. They may be general-obligation bonds to which the full faith and credit of the issuing agency is pledged, or revenue bonds payable from specified revenues. They may also be bonds of federal agencies payable out of their own assets and income but having the moral backing of the federal government. Public-housing bonds are bonds issued by local housing authorities. In the case of federally aided projects, they will be backed by federal subsidies pledged to the authorities. State and local government bonds usually yield a lower interest rate to the buyer than federal bonds, but they are exempt from federal levy because the states are viewed as the original sovereignties and the federal government as the states' creation. Since the power to tax carries the power to destroy, the federal government has been held to be unable to tax its creators or subdivisions and instrumentalities. This immunity from taxation has encouraged a steadily increasing stream of tax-exempt obligations for a growing variety of purposes. The purchasers are usually holders of larger aggregations of wealth seeking escape from federal levy.[b]

Bond, Revenue.   A bond issued by a public agency payable from earmarked revenues, as distinguished from a general obligation bond in which the general credit of a city or state is pledged. Revenue bonds have become common devices for financing such public works as water and sewer systems, bridges, tunnels, highways, public garages, and similar improvements. The charges, assessments, or tolls derived from the improvement are pledged to pay the interest and sinking-fund requirements of the bonds. Since the general revenues of the issuing government are not pledged to the bonds, and since their security depends on the sufficiency of the earmarked revenues to pay them, they will be priced somewhat higher than general-obligation bonds. Defaults, however, are few on well-rated bonds issued by the responsible investment houses. The reasons a state or municipality will issue revenue bonds instead of general-obligation bonds are unwillingness to pledge the general revenues or inability to pledge them due to legislative limitations on the amount of general revenue bonds issuable, and fear of impairing the general credit by the issuance of too many general bonds.[b]

Borrow Pit. An excavation for the purpose of obtaining earth materials for fills or earthworks. They often become serious landscape problems.[c]

Bridle Path. An improved right of way for horseback riding, or a riding trail in a suburban area.[c]

Building Area. The total area covered by buildings. Taken on a horizontal plane at mean grade level, exclusive of uncovered porches, terraces, and steps.[a]

Capital Budget. A statement of proposed public expenditures together with a plan for financing them, usually prepared annually. A municipality's capital budget generally provides for the financing of its schools, parks and playgrounds, public offices, and other nonrecurrent expenditures; these may be financed out of revenues, borrowings, or both.[b]

Capital Improvement. Any substantial physical facility built by the public, or any major nonrecurring expenditure of government. The construction of schools, highways, sewer and water systems, the landscaping of a park, the purchase of land for a municipal hospital, the architectural restoration of a city hall—these are all capital expenditures as distinguished from *operating costs,* which can be expected to recur annually as long as a program or service is offered. One of the great defects of federal aids to urban areas is that the great majority are limited to capital costs. The much-vaunted federal program for multi-service centers, for example, makes no provisions for the cost of the services housed in a center or even the money to sweep the floor. Often the more capital improvements a city accepts from the federal government, the more impoverished it becomes trying to use and maintain them.[b]

Capital Improvement Program. A governmental schedule of permanent improvements budgeted to fit financial resources. A city's planning commission is sometimes given authority to budget the city's program, thereby linking planning to function and giving the commission more prestige and independence. Despite this optimistic effort to strengthen the commission's hand in the city's development, experience has shown that the mayor's support still gives the muscle to the agency he favors. In contrast to the capital budget, capital improvement programs are usually projected five or six years in advance and updated annually.[b]

Channelization.   The straightening and deepening of streams to permit water to move faster, to reduce flooding or to drain marshy acreage for farming. However, channelization reduces the organic waste assimilation capacity of the stream and may disturb fish breeding and destroy the stream's natural beauty.[e]

Chlorination.   The application of chlorine to drinking water, sewage, or industrial waste for disinfection or oxidation of undesirable compounds.[e]

City Planning.   The planning of future development, or redevelopment, of cities, towns, and urban areas, usually under the supervision of a local planning board or commission. City planning is largely preoccupied with the problems of zoning and land use regulations, the redesign of areas to alleviate traffic congestion and the space problems created by the predominance of the automobile as a mode of transportation, the opening or reservation of space for recreation and other public uses, and the design of civic centers. Because city planning is limited by jurisdictional boundaries, long-range planning objectives cannot be achieved except as the plans are integrated with the planning of the natural region of which the city, town, or urban area is a part. . . . The literature on the subject is extensive, but is mostly concerned with pleading the necessity for city planning, and with city building history, rather than with the solution of specific problems.[c] (See Comprehensive Plan, Planning.)

Civic Center.   A more or less unified assemblage of public buildings which house local governmental functions and other public or semi-public uses. American cities have been engaged in the development of civic centers since the beginning of the twentieth century. Early plans were sometimes elaborate, formal, grandiose, or even baroque. Modern taste favors more modest architecture arranged on appropriate campus-like sites, and integrated with the economic and social requirements of the community.[c]

Collector Streets.   Highways that carry traffic from minor streets to arterial highways. They perform the function of gathering traffic from local streets and distributing it to other local or major highways.[d]

Community.   A population of organisms sharing a common area and a common environment. The human community fits this definition. We complicate it by limiting areas with political and other artificial boundaries. (See Neighborhood.)[c]

Community Center.   A neighborhood building for social, recreational, and cultural activities. The term came into general use about 1915 as a new name for the social center with which the churches and settlement houses had become involved. Initially school buildings were used for adult education and recreational programs. Community houses, churches, and other institutions supplemented the educational centers. Community centers have become more important in suburbs, where recreation is receiving emphasis, but have lost some of their influence in the central cities. As earlier generations of urban immigrants left for the suburbs and central-city church activities declined, many of the privately organized centers weakened. Lately, the resurgence of community emphasis among minorities and the growth of publicly assisted programs have given them new strength, particularly in the slums and ghettos where the loss was mostly felt.[b]

Community Facilities.   Facilities used in common by a number of people. Often used to connote particularly nonprofit facilities such as educational, recreational, social, religious, etc.[a]

Comprehensive Plan.   An official document adopted by a local government setting forth its general policies regarding the long-term physical development of a city or other area. The plan should be broad enough to include all aspects of a development or redevelopment program as distinguished from sporadic, isolated, or piecemeal planning. It is used interchangeably with the terms *general plan* and *city plan* and is probably most familiarly or notoriously known as a *master plan.*[b]

Comprehensive Planning.   An effort to involve all those individuals and groups likely to be affected by some contemplated action in the decision making which precedes that action. The aims of comprehensive planning are to shape the environment or to affect the future. It includes functional and project planning but is necessarily broader than both. Comprehensive planning usually involves planning for the nation, a larger region, or a city or metropolitan area.[f]

Cost-Benefit Analysis.   An analytical method which enumerates and evaluates all the costs and benefits associated with a program or a project. If the benefits exceed the cost, then the program or project is economically reasonable and can then be ranked according to some other criteria. If, however, the program or project benefits are less than costs, it should be rejected on economic grounds, if economy is a prime criterion.[f]

County Planning.   Planning within a county but with aims broader than community planning; its primary focus is usually governmental. As with area, state, national, or even international planning, while each may be considered a type of community planning, the difference for each lies in the level and the complexity of the situation.[f]

DDT.   The first of the modern chlorinated hydrocarbon insecticides whose chemical name is 1, 1, 1-tricholoro-2,2-bis (p-chloriphenyl)-ethane. It has a half-life of 15 years, and its residues can become concentrated in the fatty tissues of certain organisms, especially fish. Because of DDT's persistence in the environment and its ability to accumulate and magnify in the food chain, the Environmental Protection Agency has banned the registration and interstate sale of it for nearly all uses in the United States effective December 31, 1972.[e] (See Pesticide.)

Demography. The study of population and population change. The basic interests of the demographer are the size, composition, and distribution of peoples. Once thought of as simply a matter of births, deaths, and other vital statistics, demography now records patterns of marriage and divorce, consumer expenditures, educational attainment, and distribution of wealth. Demographers are the source of a mass of other information vital to understanding urbanization and the problems that beset urban life.[b]

Development Area. A physically defined area for proposed housing development. It may be of any size, as long as the development is to be carried on under single or coordinated direction. This report deals primarily with development areas ranging in size from a small group of dwelling units (25 to 50 houses) to complete neighborhoods.[a]

Diatomaceous Earth (Diatomite). A fine siliceous material resembling chalk, used in waste water treatment plants to filter sewage effluent to remove solids. May also be used as inactive ingredients in pesticide formulations applied as dust or powder.[e]

District. The larger locality or geographic area in which a neighborhood may be located; usually composed of several neighborhoods. Districts often contain substantial commercial and industrial land uses. In the case of a small city, the district and the city may be coterminous. District . . . describes that part of the city which is large enough to support a high school and a substantial shopping center.[a]

Dump. A land site where solid waste is disposed of in a manner that does not protect the environment.[e]

Easement. An acquired right of use, interest, or privileges (short of ownership) in lands owned by another, such as an easement of light, of building support, or of right of way. Easements are often acquired by highway departments because they entail smaller payments than would be required for outright purchase yet satisfy a road's land requirements. They may be permanent or limited in time, depending upon the easement agreement.[b]

Ecology. The study of the interrelationships among living organisms and their environments. As a branch of the biological sciences, ecology is concerned with the way plant and animal species distribute themselves and how they adapt to one another and to their total environment. The high degree of complexity and mutual interdependence that characterizes the natural world has suggested analogies to students of the city, who have borrowed a number of terms and concepts from ecology to describe urban processes.[b]

Ecosphere. The biological sphere that contains life on land, in the waters, and in the air. It includes the various levels of the atmosphere as well as all life therein.[f]

Ecosystem.   The relationships between all living things and the earth's environment of land, air, and water.[f]

Effluent.   Gases or liquids containing pollutants expelled into the environment. *Effluent fees* are dues paid by industrial polluters for the right to continue to pollute, usually based on the damage done by their discharge, or on the cost of cleaning up the pollution.[f]

Eminent Domain.   The concept of the power of the state to acquire, for public use, privately owned real estate, by means of legal processes and adjudicated compensation to the private owner. Eminent domain proceedings are instigated in the public courts by properly authorized officers of the state. The courts determine the proper compensations. States may, and frequently do, delegate the right of eminent domain to cities and counties and other subdivisions of the state government. The right of eminent domain and the legal procedures are commonly called *condemnation.*[c]

Emission Inventory.   A list of air pollutants emitted into a community's atmosphere, in amounts (usually tons) per day, by type of source. The emission inventory is basic to the establishment of emission standards.[e]

Emission Standard.   The maximum amount of a pollutant legally permitted to be discharged from a single source, either mobile or stationary.[e]

Enabling Act.   Legislation authorizing cities, governmental agencies, and sometimes private groups to carry out an undertaking or project— for example, the state statute empowering a housing authority to build, manage, and finance public housing.[b]

Encroachment.   An unauthorized extension of a building or part of a building upon the land of another. Depending on its seriousness, and on whether it has been authorized or acquiesced in, it may or may not justify a rejection of the title by a prospective purchaser.[b]

Environment.   The sum of all external conditions and influences affecting the life, development, and ultimately the survival of an organism.[e]

Environmental Impact Statement.   A document prepared by a federal agency on the environmental impact of its proposals for legislation and other major actions significantly affecting the quality of the human environment. Environmental impact statements are used as tools for decision making and are required by the National Environmental Policy Act.[e]

Erosion.   Man-made erosion occurs when natural surfaces used for normal run-off are cemented or in some other way interfered with. As a result, water has to carve new paths, thus causing erosion.[f]

Feasibility Study.   A survey to determine the practicality of an enterprise before a commitment is made. It is often undertaken in advance of urban renewal and other federally assisted projects.[b]

Files. Any papers accumulated or maintained in filing equipment, boxes, or on shelves, and occupying office or storage space. The term has the same meaning as "records" except that it has a more limited connotation and is used to designate assemblages of papers resulting from specific transactions, operations, or processes. (See Active Files, Administrative Files, Operating Files.)[f]

Filling. The process of depositing dirt and mud in marshy areas to create more land for real estate development. Filling can disturb natural ecological cycles.[e]

Frontage Road. See Access Road.

Game Fish. Those species of fish sought by sports fishermen—for example, salmon, trout, black bass, striped bass. Game fish are usually more sensitive to environmental changes and water quality degradation than "rough" fish.[e]

Green Belts. Certain areas restricted from being used for buildings and houses; they often serve as separating buffers between pollution sources and concentrations of population.[e]

Habitat. The sum total of environmental conditions of a specific place that is occupied by an organism, a population, or a community.[e]

Housing Code. Local regulations setting out the minimum conditions under which dwellings are considered fit for human habitation and putting certain limits on their occupancy and use. Overcrowding, unsanitary conditions, vermin, inadequate heat, and structural hazards are the kind of deficiencies housing codes are designed to prevent or remedy.[b]

Implementation Plan. A document of the steps to be taken to ensure attainment of environmental quality standards within a specified time period. Implementation plans are required by various laws.[e]

Impoundment. A body of water, such as a pond, confined by a dam, dike, floodgate, or other barrier.[e]

Lagoon. In waste water treatment, a shallow pond, usually man-made, where sunlight, bacterial action, and oxygen interact to restore waste water to a reasonable state of purity.[e]

Land Use Map. A map that shows the existing land uses in the community. It maps each parcel in accordance with the current type of use. Land uses are usually divided into several different categories—residential, commercial, industrial, public, semi-public.[d]

Land Use Plan. The official formulation of the future uses of land, including the public and private improvements to be made on it and the assumptions and reasons for arriving at the determinations.[b]

Land Use Survey. A survey of the uses to which land is put in a particular area, usually summarized both in map form and statistically, that shows developed and vacant land, streets, parkland, public buildings, etc. Acreages are often summarized in terms of percentages for the developed portions and for the area as a whole.[b]

Land Value.   The value of a parcel of land is determined by two factors: (1) The productive use to which the parcel can be put; i.e., its suitability as a site upon which to grow a crop, mine a mineral, build a residence or a factory, perform a service, or construct some device essential to human welfare or economy. (2) The density of the population; i.e., the number of people residing within a given distance from the location of the land parcel.[c]

Major Traffic Street.   A street connecting cities or major parts of a single city, serving large volumes of comparatively long-distance, fast moving traffic (includes highways, freeways, etc.).[a]

Management by Objective (MBO).   Where the effectiveness or appropriateness of an institution's or agency's activities are tested against a hierarchy of aims and objectives, such as the agency's prime purpose, its specific projects, strategies, and resources.[f]

Metropolitan Area.   The Standard Metropolitan Statistical Area (SMSA) is one city with 50,000 people or more, or two contiguous cities with a combined population of 50,000, plus the adjacent counties which are functionally integrated with the central city; or functionally integrated areas of 100,000 or more composed of an urban area or central city of at least 50,000 people, and the surrounding counties.[f]

Minor Streets.   Thoroughfares that provide access to individual properties.[d]

Minor Traffic Streets.   Streets connecting neighborhood feeder streets to major traffic streets, to local shopping districts and centers. Preferably outside the neighborhood, serving district traffic.[a]

Model.   The essential characteristic of any model is that it should represent those aspects of the real-life situation which may significantly affect the outcome of a plan. If data cannot be obtained for some part of a model, it is possible to treat this as a "black box" to be noted for future study.[f]

Multi-Family.   Three or more units in one structure, usually with common access, services, and use of land.[a]

Neighborhood.   A local area whose residents are generally conscious of its existence as an entity and have informal face-to-face contacts and some social institutions they recognize as their own. They may or may not have a formal neighborhood organization. There is no clear line between a neighborhood and a community. Sociologists, however, say a community has a socially conscious population working together as a body to meet its common needs and objectives. Often the term "neighborhood" is used to mean nothing more than the geographic area within which residents conveniently share the common services and facilities in the vicinity of their dwellings.[b]

Neighborhood Density. The number of persons, families, or dwellings per acre of neighborhood land area, including all land uses for neighborhood activities (net residential land plus land used for streets, schools, recreation, shopping, and other neighborhood community uses), but excluding non-neighborhood land uses or unusable land within the neighborhood boundaries.[a]

Neighborhood Feeder Street. A street connecting residential service streets to each other, to community facilities, and to minor traffic streets; it serves only neighborhood traffic.[a]

Neighborhood Shopping Facilities. Those stores and commercial service establishments used frequently by most of the inhabitants of a neighborhood which should be easily accessible to the home. Types of services and facilities will vary in different neighborhoods. Minimum facilities are considered to include stores for the purchase of food and drugs. Maximum facilities include those stores and services which can economically be supported without drawing on the district outside the neighborhood for customers.[a]

Nonrecords. (1) Extra copies of papers preserved only for convenience of reference. A paper will be considered as an extra copy when an identical copy is maintained as the official file record copy by the responsible office of record, or the official file copy is filed elsewhere in another department or agency. (2) Routine requests for information and publications; tracer letters, letters directing the correction of records and reports; letters of transmittal; daily, weekly, monthly, and feeder reports. (3) Registers, control cards, and auxiliary documents which control work in progress and which act in support of the official record.[f]

Open Space. Land and water area left open or undeveloped as an element in planning and design processes.[d]

Operating Files. Files created as a result of fulfillment of functional responsibilities of a department or other agency.[f]

Operations Research (OR). Usually includes a series of advanced mathematical techniques and computer simulations for use in decision making. Involves linear programming techniques applied to a problem, where the relevant variables are assigned sequences of values until their most desirable configuration becomes apparent and the best alternative selected. Its main purpose is to analyze, forecast, and select alternatives.[f]

Pesticide. An agent used to control pests. This includes insecticides for use against harmful insects; herbicides for weed control; fungicides for control of plant diseases; rodenticides for killing rats, mice, etc.; and germicides used in disinfectant products, algaecides, slimicides, etc. Some pesticides can contaminate water, air, or soil and accumulate in man, animals, and the environment, particularly if they are misused. Certain of these chemicals have been shown to interfere with the reproductive processes of predatory birds and possibly other animals.[e]

Plan.   A formalized statement of goals, objectives, and policies; an assemblage of management directions; a predetermined course of action.[d]

Planner.   Anyone engaged in planning, especially in a professional capacity. Architects, engineers, and landscape architects are recognized professionals engaged in planning. There are others engaged in city planning, business planning, etc., who are not yet recognized as professionals, although some of the practitioners may have achieved professional competence.[e]

Planning.   (1) The act of deciding in advance what to do; a dynamic effort to use decisions to guide future actions and decisions; a means of solving future problems by intent; one step in the process of guiding the future.[d] (2) Recognition of an existing or anticipated need with specific steps for meeting that need. The primary motivation for planning is dissatisfaction with conditions as they exist and a desire to change them. Planning usually encompasses everything from initial recognition of a problem to taking an action or actions to resolve the problem. (See City Planning.)[f]

Planning Agency.   A general term for any public body authorized to prepare or to approve plans for the development or extension of public projects. Planning agencies may be designated as "planning boards," "planning commissions," or by a variety of other names, some of which may not be descriptive of their functions with reference to planning. A check of the roster of one of the larger states reveals that it has eighteen permanent boards, commissions, or committees which are primarily engaged in planning activities. Only two of these agencies have a word in their title which refers to their planning functions. There is no agency in this state with the responsibility for overall planning, or coordination of planning at the state level. This situation exists in various degrees in many other states and in cities, counties, and other subdivisions of government. The most important function of any planning agency is its role as client representing the public interest.[e]

Planning Board.   A planning agency authorizied by law to prepare and recommend plans for the development of physical, social, economic, and cultural resources and facilities within a political unit of government. Also called a "planning commission" and sometimes by other titles.[e]

Planning Consultant.   A planner of professional competence employed to plan or to assist in planning public or private projects.[e]

Planning-Programming-Budgeting Systems (PPBS).   (1) The planning by objective, (2) the selection of programs following an evaluation of alternatives using sophisticated measurement techniques, and (3) the appropriate allocation of resources—all done within a single structured, management framework.[f]

Policy. A guide or limit to actions and decisions; criterion; a means of perpetuating continuity and stability of management; a definition of constraints within which administrators handle problems quickly and with greater freedom.[d]

Pollutant. Any introduced gas, liquid, or solid that makes a resource unfit for a specific purpose.[e]

Pollution. The presence of matter or energy whose nature, location, or quantity produces undesired environmental effects.[e]

Population Density. The number of units, be these persons, families, or dwellings, per acre or per square mile.[f]

Procedure. A series of related steps to be carried out in performing an activity.[f]

Project Planning. Usually part of agency or organization planning concerned with the planning and carrying out of some part of an overall program.[f]

Record Group. The all-inclusive title of similar or related papers which accumulate in various forms but which are related to the same functional or administrative phase of an agency or agencies—for example, "Procurement Records," i.e., requisitions, purchase orders, etc.[f]

Records. *City records* include all books, papers, maps, photographs, reproductions, or other documentary materials owned, made, or received by any governmental agency of the city in connection with the transaction of public business and preserved for evidence of the organization, functions, policies, procedures, operations, or other activities of the city or because of the informational value.[f]

Reservoir. A pond, lake, tank, or basin, natural or man-made, used for the storage, regulation, and control of water.[e]

Residential Facilities. Facilities devoted exclusively to dwellings and directly to accessory uses. These include residential buildings and the immediately surrounding land for gardens, drying yards, driveways, garages, tool sheds, etc.[a]

In areas developed for one- or two-family houses where each family will own or rent an individual plot of land, the land devoted to residential services will normally be the dwelling lot. This will include the front, back, and side yards used for driveways, private gardens, and for such auxiliary buildings as private garages, tool sheds, etc.[a]

In areas developed for multi-family dwellings where the surrounding open space is used in common by all families, residential facilities will include also the land used for parking areas, playlots for small children, and landscaped areas considered to serve the residential structures.[a]

Residential Service Street. A street providing direct access to residential structures, serving only those vehicles going to a comparatively small number of dwellings.[a]

Rural Population. Includes people living in the open country or in towns of less than 2,500; subdivided into *rural farm population,* which comprises all rural people living on farms, and the *rural non-farm population,* which includes all others in the rural population.[f]

Sanitary Landfiill. A site for solid waste disposal using sanitary land-filling techniques.[e]

Sanitary Landfilling. An engineered method of solid waste disposal on land in a manner that protects the environment; waste is spread in thin layers, compacted to the smallest practical volume, and covered with soil at the end of each working day.[e]

Sketch Plan. A quick and incomplete plan drawn early in the planning process after only limited observation and study. Its purpose is to test preliminary ideas, capture hunches and first impressions on paper before they fade, elicit response from a client or collaborator, and guide subsequent stages of work.[b]

Smog. Generally used as an equivalent of air pollution, particularly associated with oxidants.[e]

Strip Mining. A process in which rock and top soil strata overlying ore or fuel deposits are scraped away by mechanical shovels. Also known as *surface mining.*[e]

Subcontractor. A contractor who performs a specific portion of a project, under the supervision of a general or principal contractor.[c]

Subdivision. A parcel of land divided into blocks, lots, or plots for im-mediate or future use or sale, or for building developments.[a]

Systems Analysis. A method for systematically analyzing a system in its context and for identifying the component parts or operations of the overall system. Systems analysis attempts to measure the effectiveness of the entire system relative to the objectives and restraints of the parent organization or the system itself.[f]

Tax, Ad Valorem. A tax based on a property's value, as distinguished from a tax on income, sales prices, etc. The value fixed by local governments is not always or even usually the market value but only a valuation for tax purposes. In some cases the rate is high and the valuation low; in other cases the rate may be low and the valuation high, low, or near the market level.[b]

Topography. The configuration of a surface area, including its relief, or relative elevations, and the position of its natural and man-made features.[e]

Transit System Map.   A map that, ideally, shows the streetcar, bus, and high-speed transit system in relation to employment, shopping, residential, and recreational areas served. The map should indicate express routes and terminal exchange facilities (such as bus, truck depot, major transfers, and connection points).[d]

Urban Population.   Includes all people living in areas that have at least one city of 50,000 and a surrounding closely settled area of 2,500 or more people outside of urban areas.[f]

Urban Regions.   Areas of one million people or more in a continuous metropolitan zone or system of metropolitan areas which may include a few enclosed or connecting nonmetropolitan counties.[f]

Vital Records.   All documents which must be maintained permanently for reference purposes in the conduct of business.[f]

Water Pollution.   The addition of sewage, industrial wastes, or other harmful or objectionable material to water in concentrations or in sufficient quantities to result in measurable degradation of water quality.[e]

Water Quality Criteria.   The levels of pollutants that affect the suitability of water for a given use. Generally, water-use classification includes public water supply, recreation, propagation of fish and other aquatic life, agricultural use, and industrial use.[e]

Water Quality Standard.   A plan for water quality management containing four major elements: the use to be made of the water (recreation, drinking water, fish and wildlife propagation, industrial, or agricultural); criteria to protect those uses; implementation plans (for needed industrial-municipal waste treatment improvements) and enforcement plans; and an anti-degradation statement to protect existing high-quality waters.[e]

Watershed.   The area drained by a given stream.[e]

Zoning.   In general, the demarcation of a city by ordinance into zones, and the establishment of regulations to govern the use of the land (commercial, industrial, residential, type of residential, etc.), and the location, bulk, height, shape, use, and coverage of structures within each zone.[b]

[a]Committee on the Hygiene of Housing, *Planning the Neighborhood-Standards for Healthful Housing* (Chicago: American Public Health Association, n.d.).

[b]Charles Abrams, *The Language of the Cities—A Glossary of Terms* (New York: The Viking Press, 1971).Copyright © 1971 by the Estate of Charles Abrams. Reprinted by permission of The Viking Press, Inc.

[c]Warner L. Marsh, *Landscape Vocabulary* (Los Angeles: Meramar Publishing Co.), 1964.

[d]*Forest Service Handbook, FSH*

[e]Gloria J. Studdard, *Common Environmental Terms: A Glossary* (Washington, D.C.: U.S. Environmental Protection Agency, 1973).

[f]Definition developed by the author.

APPENDICES

A suggested agreement for comprehensive planning for recreation and parks.

AGREEMENT

THIS AGREEMENT entered into this _____ day of _____,
197__, by and between the City of _____(Name)_____, hereinafter referred to
as the "Local Public Agency", and ____(Name of Firm)_____, a corporation
organized and existing under the laws of the State of ___(Name)____, of the
City of ____(Name)____, State of ____(Name)____, hereinafter referred to as the
"Contractor".

WHEREAS the Local Public Agency desires to engage the Contractor to render
certain technical advice in accordance with such undertaking of the Local Agency.

NOW, THEREFORE, the parties hereto do mutually agree as follows:

A. SCOPE OF SERVICES. The Contractor shall perform the necessary services
under the Contract in connection with and respecting the City of_(Name)___
Planning Program and shall do, perform and carry out, in a satisfactory and
proper manner as determined by the Local Public Agency, so much of the work
activities as detailed in the Work Program, appearing in this agreement.

B. TIME AND SCHEDULE OF PERFORMANCE. The services of the Contractor are to
commence upon the execution of a Contract Agreement and will be undertaken and
completed in such sequence as to assure the expeditious completion of all work
items set forth in this Agreement on or before (month)   (day)   (year) .

C. COMPENSATION AND METHOD OF PAYMENT. The Local Public Agency will pay to
the Contractor the sum of ___(amount)_ which will constitute full and complete
compensation for the Contractor's services as set forth in this Agreement. This

sum shall be paid in two (number) equal monthly installments of (amount). The final payment shall be paid upon satisfactory completion of all work items shown in this Agreement.

Specifically, the study and plan will include:

PHASE I

1. Natural Resources and Geological Study

    A natural resources and geological study will be prepared covering the physical characteristics of the planning area including general topography, soils, minerals, woodlands, historic landmarks and water resources.

2. Population Profile

    The population profile will analyze various socio-economic characteristics of the population of (name) including growth trends, age and sex distribution, income and educational levels and occupation groups. These characteristics will be reviewed as they relate to the park and recreation plan and, where applicable, projections will be made of expected future conditions.

3. Public Facilities Inventory & Analysis

    An inventory shall be undertaken to determine the extent of park and recreation facilities available within the community which are owned and/or operated by a public agency. This inventory shall include the facilities of the Park Board, the recreation facilities of the local school district and other public agencies which may be providing recreation services. This data will be presented in both map and text form.

4. Private Facilities Inventory & Analysis

    A survey will be made of all existing private facilities within the City which provide recreation facilities. These facilities might include golf courses, tennis courts, ice skating, sledding and tobogganing, playgrounds, playfields or athletic fields, recreation centers, swimming facilities, boating access sites, marinas and boat clubs, fishing, camping and picnicking areas.

    The analysis of both the public and private park and recreation facilities shall include the determination of the following characteristics or attributes:

    a. Seasonal consideration and the possibility of multiple uses to attain the maximum possible annual user days;

-2-

403

b. Ownership, public or private, and the degree of availability of
the supply to meet the estimated total demand;

c. Geographic implications including availability in terms of access
by roads, highways, paths, trails, etc.;

d. Sectors of demand served by community or neighborhood;

e. Qualitative rating of setting in terms of natural scenic beauty or
potential developed scenic beauty, number of park area acres in terms
of land area, water area and total area;

f. Parking and interior access features.

5. Inventory & Analysis of Community Resources

a. Generalized Existing Land Use Analysis

The existing land use study prepared as a part of the Comprehensive
Plan shall be analysed in terms of the relationship of residential
areas to existing park and recreation facilities.

b. Natural Resources Inventory & Analysis

From existing data, an analysis will be made of the relationship
of existing and proposed park and recreation facilities to soil
conditions, drainage, ground cover, and topography.

c. The Potential of Vacant Land for Use as Park or Recreation Areas

A survey will be made of all major vacant sites within the City to
determine their suitability and applicability to recreational use.
Characteristics to be considered include:

1) Topography, water areas, and ground cover

2) Location to residential areas

3) Size and scenic beauty

6. Future Need for Park & Recreation Land & Facilities

a. Park and Recreation Standards

For the purpose of coordinating demand and supply information, a
statement of standards of use will be made for each activity which
relates expected user population to each type and size of facility.
This set of standards will be used to evaluate present and forecast
recreation supply in terms of present and expected demand. The demand
standards will specifically include acreage requirements by type of
facility and will be related to locational needs.

-3-

b. Future Park and Recreation Acreage Requirements

Based on the projected population growth and acceptable park and recreation standards, future park and recreation acreage requirements will be determined.

7. Sample Attitude Survey

A recreation and leisure time questionnaire will be prepared and distribured to a portion of the City's population in order to determine current and projected demands for park and recreation acitivities.

PHASE II

8. Park & Recreation Plan

a. Site Location Study

An overall City-wide program for park and open space development will be prepared which reflects the prospective recreation demand as determined by the previous analysis. This study shall result in a statement of recreation facility needs at present and for the future to   (year) . It shall also result in the preparation of alternative sketch plans which present both general locational recommendations and specific area recommendations for meeting the recreational needs of the present and future population.

b. Site Development Planning

For specific proposed park sites, detailed preliminary site plans will be developed which shall indicate topography, wooded areas, and related physical characteristics as well as proposed roadways, building construction, and recreation facilities. This series of detailed site plans shall be developed over United States Geological Survey Maps or aerial photography.

c. Cost Estimates and Acquisition & Development

Cost estimates and methods of financing the recommended plans for recreation land and facilities to be developed will be outlined.

9. Action Program

a. Review of Financial Assistance Programs and Local Financial Resources

A comprehensive survey of Federal and state financial assistance will be made to determine its applicability to the local park and recreation program. This nonlocal financial assistance will be coordinated with the local financial capability to determine the most feasible financing of the park proposals.

b. Establish Timetable for Capital Expenditures based upon Need, Land Availability and Financial Resources.

-4-

405

This study will summarize the recommendations in terms of parks
to be developed, timing and financial recommendations and will
relate these findings to the existing and proposed capital expenditures
program of the City.

10. Reports

Throughout the development of the park and recreation study and plan,
working papers will be developed which will present the various findings
of the proposed work activities. Upon complete review and concurrence
by the City, these papers will be summarized in a final report which
will be printed with text, tables and maps. One hundred (100) copies of
this report will be prepared for distribution.

The proposed Park and Recreation Plan will be developed under the guidelines
of the ___(state)__ Department of Natural Resources in order to qualify for
financial assistance under the Land and Water Conservation Fund Program and
other Federal programs benefiting local park and recreation programs.

IN WITNESS WHEREOF, the Local Public Agency and the Contractor have executed

this Agreement on the date first above written.

                                    CITY OF __(Name), (State)____
                                    Local Public Agency

                                    _____
                                    Mayor

ATTEST:

_____   (Name of Firm)
                                      Contractor

                                    _____

ATTEST:

_____

-5-

City of Wooster

DEPARTMENT OF PARKS AND RECREATION

Wooster, Ohio

Leisure Behavior, Attitude, and Opinion Study

Student Questionnaire

Christopher R. Edginton
Director of Parks and Recreation

Consultant
Joseph J. Bannon, Ph.D.
Chief, Office of Recreation and Park Resources
University of Illinois

STUDENT QUESTIONNAIRE
DEPARTMENT OF PARKS AND RECREATION
WOOSTER, OHIO

1. What is your age? _____

2. What grade in School are you in? (circle) 7 8 9 10 11 12

3. Are you a male ☐   female ☐

4. How many <u>hours</u> per day on the average do you watch television?

   ☐ None   ☐ 3 hours

   ☐ 1/2 hour   ☐ 4 hours

   ☐ 1 hour   ☐ 5 hours

   ☐ 2 hours   ☐ 6 or more hours

5. Do you participate in after-school programs (Bands, Intramurals, clubs, etc.) sponsored by school authorities?   Yes ☐   No ☐

6. How many years have you lived in Wooster? _____

7. Check the items you personally own

   ☐ T.V.   ☐ Boat

   ☐ Car   ☐ Bicycle

   ☐ Stereo or tape   ☐ Motor Bike

   ☐ Musical Instrument   ☐ Telephone

   ☐ Radio   ☐ Other (Specify) _____

8. In the average day, how many <u>hours</u> do you spend in school?
   Include traveling time and <u>time</u> spent doing school homework.

   ☐ 5 hours   ☐ 9 hours

   ☐ 6 hours   ☐ 10 hours

   ☐ 7 hours   ☐ 11 hours

   ☐ 8 hours

9. In an average week, how many <u>hours</u> do you spend working?
   Include both the hours you work at home and when working at outside jobs.

   ☐ None to 3 hours   ☐ 10 to 14 hours

   ☐ 4 to 6 hours   ☐ 15 to 19 hours

   ☐ 7 to 9 hours   ☐ 20 or more hours

10. How much allowance do you receive each <u>week</u> to spend as you choose (do <u>not</u> include money used for lunch, transportation, school supplies and the like)? _____

1

11. How much money do you earn each week from jobs performed outside of your home? _____
    (during school year)

12. How much money did you earn last summer? _____

13. How do you most often hear about the City of Wooster parks and recreation programs?

    _____ Family   _____ Newspaper   _____ Flyers or Bulletins   Others

    Specify _____

14. Who, of the following, would you prefer to have as supervisors of recreation activities?

    ☐ College age students   ☐ Parents

    ☐ Volunteers (other than parents   ☐ Park & Recreation Personnel

    ☐ School teachers working for the Park and Recreation Department

    ☐ Others (Specify) _____

15. Do you know where the Parks and Recreation Department is located?   Yes ☐   No ☐

16. When is the last time you called the Parks and Recreation Department for information about
    recreation activities?

    ☐ Yesterday   ☐ Month ago

    ☐ 3 days ago   ☐ Last summer

    ☐ Week ago   ☐ Don't ever call

    ☐ 2 weeks ago

17. What additional facilities would you like to see in Wooster?

    _____ More swimming pools   _____ More gymnasiums

    _____ Youth Center (centrally lo-   _____ Rifle-Pistol range
              cated for all to use)

    _____ More neighborhood parks   _____ Nature Center

    _____ Lighted basketball courts   _____ Indoor tennis courts

    _____ Indoor/outdoor year-around   _____ Lighted tennis courts
              pool complex

    _____ Cultural arts center   _____ Others (specify)

    _____ Lighted softball and   _____
              baseball fields

    _____ Ice Rink   _____

                                                     _____

2

18. To which Radio Station do you listen most often?

- ☐ WCUE-FM
- ☐ WKYC
- ☐ WHLQ
- ☐ WCWS-FM

- ☐ WHLO
- ☐ WDBM-FM
- ☐ WWST
- ☐ WMMS-FM

- ☐ Other

19. Do transportation problems limit participation in after-school or evening recreation activities?

_____ Yes _____ No

20. On what nights do you prefer recreation programs sponsored by the Parks and Recreation Department during the school year? Please rank the days listed in the order of your preference using numbers 1–7.

_____ Sunday _____ Tuesday _____ Thursday _____ Saturday

_____ Monday _____ Wednesday _____ Friday

21. On what night do you prefer recreation programs during the summer? Please rank the days listed in the order of your preference using numbers 1–7.

_____ Sunday _____ Tuesday _____ Thursday _____ Saturday

_____ Monday _____ Wednesday _____ Friday

22. Are you allowed to attend parties in the homes of your friends? ☐ Yes ☐ No

23. Do you give parties in your home? ☐ Yes ☐ No

24. If yes, how many parties do you give?

- ☐ 1 or more a month
- ☐ 1 every three months

- ☐ 1 every six months
- ☐ 1 per year

25. Which of the following facilities do you and your family use most? Place a 1 next to that facility. The next most place a 2 next to that one. Continue ranking through 5.

- ☐ Freedlander Park
- ☐ Christmas Run Park
- ☐ Schellin Park
- ☐ Knight's Field
- ☐ Cohan Park
- ☐ Jaycee Park
- ☐ Snow Trails
- ☐ Wooster Skate Land

- ☐ Y.M.C.A.
- ☐ Freedlander Pool
- ☐ Knight's Field Pool
- ☐ Christmas Run Pool (City Park)
- ☐ Youth House (Trinity Church)
- ☐ Public Golf Courses
- ☐ Clear Fork
- ☐ Churches

- ☐ Wayne Co. Historical Society
- ☐ Wooster College Facilities
- ☐ Mohican State Park
- ☐ Stark Wilderness Area
- ☐ Pleasant Hill
- ☐ Charles Mill Lake
- ☐ Out-of-Town Facilities
- ☐ Others (Specify)

_____ _____

3

410

26. What other recreation and park facilities similar to those listed in question No. 25 do you use other than those provided by the City of Wooster (i.e. YMCA)? List in order of greatest use first. (Do not limit yourself to the City of Wooster).

_____   _____

_____   _____

_____   _____

27. On the day you do not participate in "after-school activities", what do you do? Put a 1 before that activity you are most likely to do and 2 before that activity next most likely to do, etc. (continue to rank through 5).

☐ Go home   ☐ Methodist Church Gym   ☐ Dairy Isle

☐ The Shack   ☐ YMCA   ☐ Drive-in Restaurant

☐ Hall Loitering   ☐ McDonald's   ☐ Plaza Lanes

☐ Friend's home   ☐ Dairy Queen   ☐ The Parlor

☐ Go downtown   ☐ City News   ☐ Others (specify)

☐ Public Library   _____

                                                 _____

28. What percent (%) of your leisure time do you spend with

   Friends? _____ %   Organized group? _____ %

   Family? _____ %   Alone? _____ %

29. Here is a list of activities which many people do during their free time.

How often do you:		Not at all	Less than once a month	About once a month	Several times a month	Several times a week	Almost every day
Dance?	During Summer	☐	☐	☐	☐	☐	☐
	During School Year	☐	☐	☐	☐	☐	☐
Read a book or part of a book (do not include magazines or school homework)?	During Summer	☐	☐	☐	☐	☐	☐
	During School Year	☐	☐	☐	☐	☐	☐
Swim (Outdoors)?	During Summer	☐	☐	☐	☐	☐	☐
	During School Year	☐	☐	☐	☐	☐	☐
Play games such as cards, checkers, monopoly, chess, etc.?	During Summer	☐	☐	☐	☐	☐	☐
	During School Year	☐	☐	☐	☐	☐	☐
Play Billiards or pool?	During Summer	☐	☐	☐	☐	☐	☐
	During School Year	☐	☐	☐	☐	☐	☐

Continued on next page

4

411

		Not at all	Less than once a month	About once a month	Several times a month	Several times a week	Almost every day
Listen to records?	During Summer	☐	☐	☐	☐	☐	☐
	During School Year	☐	☐	☐	☐	☐	☐
Paint or draw?	During Summer	☐	☐	☐	☐	☐	☐
	During School Year	☐	☐	☐	☐	☐	☐
Spend time on crafts such as model plane or car building, etc.?	During Summer	☐	☐	☐	☐	☐	☐
	During School Year	☐	☐	☐	☐	☐	☐
Participate in dramatics?	During Summer	☐	☐	☐	☐	☐	☐
	During School Year	☐	☐	☐	☐	☐	☐
Play a musical instrument?	During Summer	☐	☐	☐	☐	☐	☐
	During School Year	☐	☐	☐	☐	☐	☐
Attend plays or concerts?	During Summer	☐	☐	☐	☐	☐	☐
	During School Year	☐	☐	☐	☐	☐	☐
Go to the movies?	During Summer	☐	☐	☐	☐	☐	☐
	During School Year	☐	☐	☐	☐	☐	☐
Go to the shopping center?	During Summer	☐	☐	☐	☐	☐	☐
	During School Year	☐	☐	☐	☐	☐	☐
Play softball or baseball?	During Summer	☐	☐	☐	☐	☐	☐
	During School Year	☐	☐	☐	☐	☐	☐
Go Boating?	During Summer	☐	☐	☐	☐	☐	☐
	During School Year	☐	☐	☐	☐	☐	☐
Play tennis?	During Summer	☐	☐	☐	☐	☐	☐
	During School Year	☐	☐	☐	☐	☐	☐
Water ski?	During Summer	☐	☐	☐	☐	☐	☐
	During School Year	☐	☐	☐	☐	☐	☐
Play Golf?	During Summer	☐	☐	☐	☐	☐	☐
	During School Year	☐	☐	☐	☐	☐	☐
Go snow skiing?	During Summer	☐	☐	☐	☐	☐	☐
	During School Year	☐	☐	☐	☐	☐	☐
Play football?	During Summer	☐	☐	☐	☐	☐	☐
	During School Year	☐	☐	☐	☐	☐	☐
Go tobogganning or sledding?	During Summer	☐	☐	☐	☐	☐	☐
	During School Year	☐	☐	☐	☐	☐	☐
Play volleyball?	During Summer	☐	☐	☐	☐	☐	☐
	During School Year	☐	☐	☐	☐	☐	☐
Ice skate?	During Summer	☐	☐	☐	☐	☐	☐
	During School Year	☐	☐	☐	☐	☐	☐

Continued on next page

5

		Not at all	Less than once a month	About once a month	Several times a month	Several times a week	Almost every day
Swim (indoors)?	During Summer	☐	☐	☐	☐	☐	☐
	During School Year	☐	☐	☐	☐	☐	☐
Fish?	During Summer	☐	☐	☐	☐	☐	☐
	During School Year	☐	☐	☐	☐	☐	☐
Hunt?	During Summer	☐	☐	☐	☐	☐	☐
	During School Year	☐	☐	☐	☐	☐	☐
Hike or walk for pleasure?	During Summer	☐	☐	☐	☐	☐	☐
	During School Year	☐	☐	☐	☐	☐	☐
Go on a picnic?	During Summer	☐	☐	☐	☐	☐	☐
	During School Year	☐	☐	☐	☐	☐	☐
Camp out overnight?	During Summer	☐	☐	☐	☐	☐	☐
	During School Year	☐	☐	☐	☐	☐	☐
Play basketball?	During Summer	☐	☐	☐	☐	☐	☐
	During School Year	☐	☐	☐	☐	☐	☐

30. In what other recreational activities do you participate? List activities which were not previously mentioned.

How many days during a year?

_____   _____

_____   _____

_____   _____

31. Are there any activities in which you do not now participate but would like to? Major reason for not participating now. (check one)

Activities (specify)	Do not know how	Facilities not available	Program not offered	High Cost	Other (specify)
_____	☐	☐	☐	☐	_____
_____	☐	☐	☐	☐	_____
_____	☐	☐	☐	☐	_____

Continued on next page

6

32. Now we would like to know how you feel about your community, its park and recreation system, and other related items. Here are a few statements. Check the box which corresponds to how you feel. (Answer every question as best you can.)

	Completely disagree	Partially disagree	Partially agree	Completely agree
I am satisfied with the park facilities in the City of Wooster	☐	☐	☐	☐
There are sufficient opportunities to use free time constructively	☐	☐	☐	☐
The number of activities offered by Parks and Recreation Department for teenagers is adequate	☐	☐	☐	☐
The quality of the activities now offered by Parks and Recreation Department is good	☐	☐	☐	☐
There are activities offered by Parks and Recreation Department in which I cannot now participate because of admission charges	☐	☐	☐	☐
There is sufficient outdoor space in the Parks and Recreation Dept. for me to enjoy	☐	☐	☐	☐
The quality of leadership provided by the Parks and Recreation Dept. is good	☐	☐	☐	☐
There is a need to coordinate the existing recreation programs being offered by various organizations in Wooster	☐	☐	☐	☐
The type and quality of activities for teenagers in Wooster is good	☐	☐	☐	☐
I would like to see an ice rink constructed in Wooster	☐	☐	☐	☐
The City of Wooster should acquire additional open space for park and recreation purposes	☐	☐	☐	☐
Public park and recreation programs are well worth the cost	☐	☐	☐	☐
Wooster has better park and recreation facilities than most other communities its size	☐	☐	☐	☐
I would like to live all my life in the City of Wooster	☐	☐	☐	☐

Continued on next page

7

414

	Completely disagree	Partially disagree	Partially agree	Completely agree
More competitive athletic activities for females should be offered by the Parks and Recreation Dept.	☐	☐	☐	☐
I would be willing to volunteer my time for services in the community (Lewis Sr. Center, tutoring, Candy Striper, etc.).................................	☐	☐	☐	☐

33. What additional facilities would you like to see in the City of Wooster?

\
\
\
\

34. What improvements or changes would you recommend for existing park and recreation facilities and programs in the City of Wooster?

\
\
\

35. Is there any other information you would like to give us regarding the recreation and park services offered by the City of Wooster?

\
\
\
\

36. In which area of Wooster do you live?

     1   2   3   (Circle one)   See map next page

8

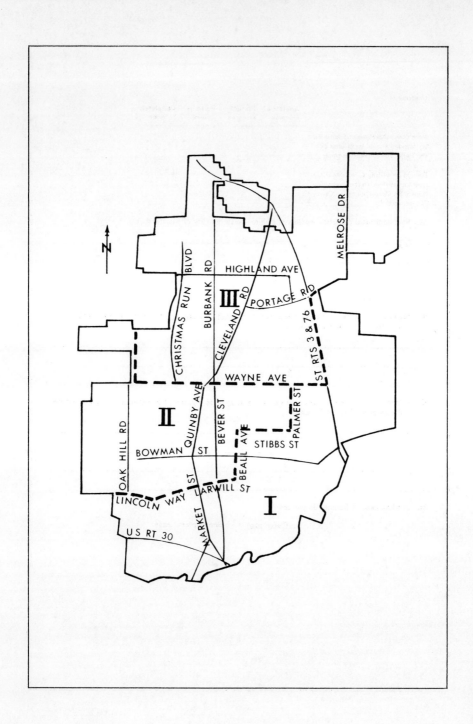

City of Wooster

DEPARTMENT OF PARKS AND RECREATION
Wooster, Ohio

Leisure Behavior, Attitude, and
Opinion Study

Adult Questionnaire

Christopher R. Edginton
Director of Parks and Recreation

Consultant
Joseph J. Bannon, Ph.D.
Chief, Office of Recreation and Park Resources
University of Illinois

417

ADULT QUESTIONNAIRE

DEPARTMENT OF PARKS AND RECREATION
WOOSTER, OHIO

1. Are you ☐ Married ☐ Single

2. Are you ☐ Male ☐ Female

3. What is your age _____

4. Are there children living in your home _____ Yes _____ No

   A. How many under 6 years of age _____   C. How many 12 years to 14 years _____

   B. How many 6 years to 11 years _____   D. How many over 14 years of age _____

5. How many years of education have you completed (circle number of years)

Grade School	1 2 3 4 5 6 7 8
High School	9 10 11 12
College	1 2 3 4
Graduate School	1 2 3 4

6. What is your occupation _____

7. What is the occupation of the chief wage earner of the household (if not same as above)

   _____

8. Do you work in Wooster or within a 5 mile radius of Wooster ☐ Yes ☐ No

9. How much was earned by all the adult members (husband and wife) of the household

   last year _____

10. Do you belong to a Country Club ☐ Yes ☐ No

11. Do you belong to any other clubs that sponsor recreation, example, Tennis Club or

    Swim Club ☐ Yes ☐ No

12. How many hours do you work in an average week? If you do some work at home related to your job, include those hours, too. Housewives should figure time spent doing household tasks or managing the home (Check one)

    ☐ 0 to 14 hours   ☐ 25 to 34 hours   ☐ 45 to 54 hours   ☐ 65 +

    ☐ 15 to 24 hours   ☐ 35 to 44 hours   ☐ 55 to 64 hours

13. How many hours, in an average week, do you spend attending meetings which you feel you are obligated to attend. (Check one)

    ☐ None   ☐ 1 to 5 hrs.   ☐ 6 to 10 hrs.   ☐ 10 to 15 hrs.

    ☐ over 15 hrs.

1

14. How many hours in an average week do you spend doing volunteer work and attending meetings which you attend only because you wish to. (Check one)

☐ None   ☐ 1 to 5 hrs.   ☐ 6 to 10 hrs.   ☐ 10 to 15 hrs.

☐ over 15 hrs.

15. On the average how many hours per day do you watch T.V.

☐ None   ☐ 1 hr.   ☐ 3 hrs.   ☐ 5 hrs.

☐ ½ hr.   ☐ 2 hrs.   ☐ 4 hrs.   ☐ 6 or more

16. How much vacation time do you usually have each year. (Check one)

☐ 1 week   ☐ 2 weeks   ☐ 3 weeks   ☐ 4 weeks

☐ more than 4 weeks   ☐ Other (specify) _____

17. When do you usually take your vacation. (Check one)

☐ Jan.   ☐ March   ☐ May   ☐ July   ☐ Sept.   ☐ Nov.

☐ Feb.   ☐ April   ☐ June   ☐ Aug.   ☐ Oct.   ☐ Dec.

18. What part of your vacation time last year was spent in Wooster, Ohio.

☐ None   ☐ 1/4   ☐ 1/2   ☐ 3/4   ☐ All

19. Do transportation problems limit your participation in Recreation activities   ☐ Yes   ☐ No

20. On what nights do you prefer recreation programs. Please rank the days listed in the order of your preference using numbers 1 – 7.

☐ Sunday   ☐ Tuesday   ☐ Thursday   ☐ Saturday

☐ Monday   ☐ Wednesday   ☐ Friday

21. In what recreation activities do you engage during your vacation period.

_____ Camping   _____ Snowskiing

_____ Swimming   _____ Sightseeing

_____ Fishing   _____ Loafing

_____ Boating   _____ Home Improvement

_____ Golf   _____ Touring or Traveling

_____ Water Skiing   _____ Other (Please list)

_____

_____

22. If you are a housewife do you have time during the day which you might use to participate in a recreation program sponsored by the Department of Parks and Recreation   ☐ Yes   ☐ No

2

419

23. If the answer is yes to question 22, what time would be most convenient for you to participate.
- [ ] 9 a.m. to 11 a.m.
- [ ] 3 p.m. to 5 p.m.
- [ ] 1 p.m. to 3 p.m.
- [ ] 7 p.m. to 10 p.m.

24. If you are a housewife, would the unavailability of a babysitter prohibit your participation in daytime recreational activities. [ ] Yes [ ] No

25. Is there a need for pre-school recreation activities for children in Wooster. [ ] Yes [ ] No

26. Is there a suitable place for children to play in your home. [ ] Yes [ ] No

27. Is there a suitable place for children to play in your yard. [ ] Yes [ ] No

28. Do your children feel that parks should be located closer to your home. [ ] Yes [ ] No

29. What do you feel should be the maximum distance that your children should have to walk to a park. _____ blocks.

30. Existing fees charged for Parks and Recreation programs are not too expensive. [ ] Yes [ ] No

31. How close do you live to a park.
- [ ] Less than two blocks
- [ ] 5 to 7 blocks
- [ ] 2 to 4 blocks
- [ ] 8 or more blocks

32. Which of the following facilities would you like located in your neighborhood. (Place a 1 next to that facility, the next most place a 2, next to the one third place a 3, etc. and rank through 5.)

_____ Grocery Store   _____ Shopping Area

_____ Gas Station   _____ Library

_____ School   _____ Parks

_____ Church   _____ Others (Specify)

_____ _____   _____

33. What percent (%) of your leisure time do you spend with

Friends? _____ %   Organized group? _____ %

Family? _____ %   Alone? _____ %

34. Would you financially support the development of a park in your neighborhood through special assessment. [ ] Yes [ ] No

35. The Wooster Memorial Park (Spangler) should be developed as follows:
- [ ] Left in its natural state
- [ ] Limited Development (nature paths, roads, picnic areas, etcl)
- [ ] Extensive Development (Golf courses, ski slope, skeet range, etc.)

3

36. Do you feel that existing parks are located too far from your home. ☐ Yes ☐ No

37. Do you consider that living near a park is an asset to the value ($) of your property.

☐ Yes ☐ No

38. Which of the following are representative of your opinions. (Check one or more)

☐ Parks should be used for active recreation only

☐ Parks should be used for active and passive recreation and should have beautiful qualities

☐ Some parks should be constructed that are conducive to passive recreation only.

39. Which of the following facilities do you or your family use most. Place a 1 next to that facility, the next most, place a 2, third most place a 3, etc., and rank through 5.

☐ Freedlander Park	☐ Y.M.C.A.	☐ Wayne Co. Historical Society
☐ Christmas Run (City Park)	☐ Freedlander Pool	☐ Wooster College Facilities
☐ Knight's Field	☐ Knight's Field Pool	☐ Mohican State Park
☐ Jaycee Park	☐ Christmas Run Pool (City Park)	☐ Stark Wilderness Area
☐ Schellin Park	☐ Senior Center	☐ Pleasant Hill
☐ Cohan Park	☐ Youth House (Trinity Church)	☐ Charles Mill Lake
☐	☐ Public Golf Courses	☐ Clear Fork
	☐ Snow Trails	☐ Wooster Skateland
☐ Other (Specify)	☐ Country Club	☐ Out-of-Town Facilities

40. What other recreation facilities similar to those listed in Question 39 do you use other than those provided by the Department of Parks and Recreation, i.e. YMCA – Girl Scouts – School Activities. (List in order of greatest use first.)

41. Now here are some questions concerning specific recreation activities.

How often do you:	Not at all	Less than once a month	About once a month	Several times a month	Several times a week	Almost every day
Visit friends?	☐	☐	☐	☐	☐	☐
Go swimming outdoors (in season)	☐	☐	☐	☐	☐	☐

Continued on next page

4

421

	Not at all	Less than once a month	About once a month	Several times a month	Several times a week	Almost every day
Read a book or part of a book (do not include magazines)?	☐	☐	☐	☐	☐	☐
Paint or draw?	☐	☐	☐	☐	☐	☐
Spend time on crafts such as woodworking, model building, etc.?	☐	☐	☐	☐	☐	☐
Play a musical instrument?	☐	☐	☐	☐	☐	☐
Go dancing?	☐	☐	☐	☐	☐	☐
Work on the lawn, garden or around the house?	☐	☐	☐	☐	☐	☐
Play games such as cards, chess, monopoly, etc.?	☐	☐	☐	☐	☐	☐
Others (Be specific, but do not name more than five?	☐	☐	☐	☐	☐	☐

42. The following activities are some which you might do throughout the year.

How often do you:	Not at all	Less than once a month	About once a month	Several times a month	Several times a week	Almost every day
Go shopping for pleasure?	☐	☐	☐	☐	☐	☐
Go swimming indoors?	☐	☐	☐	☐	☐	☐
Attend movies?	☐	☐	☐	☐	☐	☐
Attend plays and concerts?	☐	☐	☐	☐	☐	☐
Attend art shows or museums?	☐	☐	☐	☐	☐	☐
Play tennis?	☐	☐	☐	☐	☐	☐
Play golf (in season)?	☐	☐	☐	☐	☐	☐
Go bowling?	☐	☐	☐	☐	☐	☐
Attend sports events?	☐	☐	☐	☐	☐	☐
Attend adult education classes for enjoyment?	☐	☐	☐	☐	☐	☐

43. The following activities are more oriented to the outdoors.

How often do you: (in season)

	Not at all	Less than once a month	About once a month	Several times a month	Several times a week	Almost every day
Play softball?	☐	☐	☐	☐	☐	☐
Go fishing?	☐	☐	☐	☐	☐	☐

Continued on next page

5

Continued

	Not at all	Less than once a month	About once a month	Several times a month	Several times a week	Almost every day
Go ice skating?	☐	☐	☐	☐	☐	☐
Go overnight camping?	☐	☐	☐	☐	☐	☐
Go driving for pleasure?	☐	☐	☐	☐	☐	☐
Bicycle for pleasure?	☐	☐	☐	☐	☐	☐
Go boating?	☐	☐	☐	☐	☐	☐
Go snow skiing?	☐	☐	☐	☐	☐	☐
Go on picnic?	☐	☐	☐	☐	☐	☐
Go hunting?	☐	☐	☐	☐	☐	☐
Go jogging?	☐	☐	☐	☐	☐	☐
Hike and walk for pleasure?	☐	☐	☐	☐	☐	☐

44. In what other recreation activities do you participate. List activities which were not mentioned in the questions.

How many days during year

_____   _____

_____   _____

_____   _____

45. Are there any activities in which you do not now participate but would like to.

Major reason for not participating now

Activities (Specify)	Do not know how	Facilities not available	Program not offered	Cost	No baby-sitter	Other (specify)
_____	___	___	___	___	___	___
_____	___	___	___	___	___	___
_____	___	___	___	___	___	___

46. Which of the following items does the family own at least one of

☐ Stereo or Hi Fi   ☐ Tape Recorder

☐ Automobile   ☐ Bicycle

☐ Home   ☐ Boat

Continued on next page

6

423

Continued

☐ T.V.   ☐ Camping Equipment

☐ Camera   ☐ Golf Clubs

☐ Ice Skates   ☐ Snow Slide

☐ Skis   ☐ Toboggan

☐ Archery Equipment   ☐ Fishing Equipment

☐ Snowmobile   ☐ Hunting Equipment

47. Is there a need for the Recreation and Park Department to provide instruction in the use of this equipment

_____ Yes   _____ No Specify _____

48. Now we would like to know how you feel about your community, its Park and Recreation System and other related items. Here are a few statements. Check the box which corresponds to how you feel.

	Completely disagree	Partially disagree	Partially agree	Completely agree
I am satisfied with the Parks and Recreation facilities in Wooster	☐	☐	☐	☐
The quality of leadership provided by the Department of Parks and Recreation is good	☐	☐	☐	☐
There are sufficient opportunities for children to use their free time constructively	☐	☐	☐	☐
There is a need to coordinate the existing Recreation Programs being offered by various organizations in Wooster	☐	☐	☐	☐
The type and quality of activities for teenagers is good	☐	☐	☐	☐
I would like to see an ice rink constructed in Wooster	☐	☐	☐	☐
The City of Wooster should acquire additional open space for Park and Recreation purposes	☐	☐	☐	☐
The quality of maintenance of Park and Recreation facilities is good	☐	☐	☐	☐
The City of Wooster should update and install imaginative new playground equipment in the neighborhood parks	☐	☐	☐	☐

Continued on next page

7

	Completely disagree	Partially disagree	Partially agree	Completely agree
The Department of Parks and Recreation should expand its service to meet the demand of Wooster Citizens	☐	☐	☐	☐
I would be willing to pay additional taxes to provide more park and recreation services	☐	☐	☐	☐
Public park and recreation programs are well worth their cost	☐	☐	☐	☐
The Department of Parks and Recreation is spending its money wisely	☐	☐	☐	☐
There are not enough senior citizen activities	☐	☐	☐	☐
Wooster has better park facilities than most other communities its size	☐	☐	☐	☐
For activities which are expensive to provide and in which few people participate, those participating should pay a fee	☐	☐	☐	☐
I am properly informed about the activities offered by the Dept. of Parks and Recreation	☐	☐	☐	☐
More competitive athletics for females should be offered by the Department of Parks and Recreation	☐	☐	☐	☐
I would support the acquisition and development of a Green Belt (A park around the City)	☐	☐	☐	☐
If more Recreation Programs were offered in the City of Wooster, it would decrease Juvenile Delinquency	☐	☐	☐	☐
I would be willing to volunteer my time to help supervise Recreation Programs	☐	☐	☐	☐
Family recreation is important to our family	☐	☐	☐	☐
It is more important to me to have privacy than neighborliness	☐	☐	☐	☐

8

49. What additional facilities would you like to see in the City of Wooster?

_____

_____

_____

_____

50. In your opinion what are the major inadequacies or problems with the Department of Parks and Recreation

_____

_____

_____

51. What improvements or changes would you recommend for existing Park and Recreation facilities and programs in the City of Wooster

_____

_____

_____

_____

52. Is there any other information you would like to give us regarding the Park and Recreation Services offered by the City of Wooster.

_____

_____

_____

_____

_____

426

Appendix D

SUGGESTED PROVISIONS FOR MANDATORY DEDICATION
AND FEES-IN-LIEU REQUIREMENTS

ORDINANCE NO. _____

AN ORDINANCE OF THE CITY COUNCIL OF THE
CITY OF_____ESTABLISHING
REGULATIONS FOR DEDICATION OF LAND PAY-
MENT OF FEES, OR BOTH FOR PARK AND
RECREATIONAL LAND IN SUBDIVISIONS.[1]

THE CITY COUNCIL OF THE CITY OF _____DOES ORDAIN AS FOLLOWS:

SECTION 1. RECITALS. That the City Council of the City of
_____, does hereby find, determine and declare as
follows:

(a) In 1965, the Legislature of the State of California,
amended the Subdivision Map Act (Section 11500 et seq. of the
Business and Professions Code) so as to enable cities and counties to require either the dedication of land, the payment of
fees, or a combination of both, for park or recreational purposes as a condition of approval of a subdivision map; and

(b) Before a city or county may avail itself of said Act,
it must have a general plan containing a recreational element
with definite principles and standards for the park and recreational facilities to serve the residents of the city or county;
and

(c) The City Council of the City of _____ has
(adopted a general plan containing such recreational element)
(amended the City's general plan to include such recreational
element).

SECTION 2. SUBDIVIDERS MUST PROVIDE PARK AND RECREATIONAL FACILITIES.

Every subdivider who subdivides land shall dedicate a portion of such land,

---

This sample ordinance is taken from League of California Cities, Report
and Suggested Ordinance for the Dedication of Park Land in Subdivisions (Los
Angeles: Los Angeles County Division of the League of California Cities,
1966).

[1] The form of this sample ordinance is for a city and must be altered for
counties, or for a city which has a municipal code.

37

427

pay a fee, or do both, as set forth in this ordinance for the purpose of providing park and recreational facilities to serve future residents of such subdivision.

SECTION 3. APPLICATION. The provisions of this ordinance shall apply
to all subdivisions, as that phrase is defined in Section 11500 et seq. of the
Business and Professions Code of the State of California, except subdivisions
for which tentative subdivision maps have been filed within thirty (30) days
after the effective date of this ordinance and industrial subdivisions.

SECTION 4. RELATION OF LAND REQUIRED TO POPULATION DENSITY. It is hereby found and determined:

(a) That the public interest, convenience, health, welfare
and safety require that four (4) acres of property, for each one
thousand (1,000) persons residing within this City, be devoted to
park and recreational purposes;

(b) That said requirement will be satisfied in part by cooperative arrangements between the City and (the local school districts) (local park and recreation districts) to make available
one and one-half (1-1/2) acres of property for each one thousand
(1,000) persons residing within the City for park and recreation
purposes;

(c) That the remainder of the required four (4) acres shall
be supplied by the requirements of this ordinance and the recreation program of the city.[2]

SECTION 5. POPULATION DENSITY. Population density for the purpose of
this ordinance shall be determined in accordance with the 1960 Census of Population on Housing: Final Report PHC (1)-82 Los Angeles, Long Beach SMSA, to
wit:

(a) Single family dwelling units, and duplexes = 3.1 persons
per dwelling unit; and

(b) Multiple family dwelling units = 2.1 persons per dwelling
unit.

The basis for determining the total number of dwelling units shall be the number of such units permitted by the city on the property included in the subdivision at the time the final subdivision tract map is filed with the City
Council for approval.

SECTION 6. AMOUNT OF LAND TO BE DEDICATED. The amount of land required
to be dedicated by a subdivider pursuant to this ordinance, shall be based on

---

[2] In the event a local jurisdiction does not follow the recommendation
contained on pages 12 and 13 of this report, that subdivisions provide 2-1/2
acres of the 4 acres required per 1,000 people, it will be necessary for the
local jurisdiction to adjust (b) and (c) of Section 4.

38

the gross area included in the subdivision, determined by the following formula:

Net density per dwelling unit	Percentage of the gross area of the subdivision required when park land is dedicated
1 D.U. per acre or more	0.60%
1 D.U. per 1/2 to 1 acre	1.20%
1 D.U. per 10,000 sq. ft. to 1/2 acre	1.73%
1 D.U. per 9,000 to 9,999 sq. ft.	2.70%
1 D.U. per 8,000 to 8,999 sq. ft.	3.01%
1 D.U. per 7,000 to 7,999 sq. ft.	3.40%
1 D.U. per 6,000 to 6,999 sq. ft.	3.90%
1 D.U. per 5,000 to 5,999 sq. ft.	4.58%
10 to 19 D.U.'s per acre	5.79%
20 to 29 D.U.'s per acre	9.30%
30 to 39 D.U.'s per acre	12.56%
40 to 49 D.U.'s per acre	15.58%
50 to 59 D.U.'s per acre	18.40%
60 to 69 D.U.'s per acre	21.05%
70 to 79 D.U.'s per acre	23.54%
80 to 89 D.U.'s per acre	25.85%
90 to 99 D.U.'s per acre	28.00%
100 D.U.'s and over per acre	29.07%

SECTION 7. <u>AMOUNT OF FEE IN LIEU OF LAND DEDICATION.</u> Where a fee is required to be paid in lieu of land dedication, the amount of such fee shall be based upon the fair market value of the amount of land which would otherwise be required to be dedicated pursuant to SECTION 6 hereof. The amount of such fee shall be a sum equal to the fair market value of the amount of land required in accordance with the following formula:

<u>FEE FORMULA</u>

Net density per dwelling unit	Sq. ft. of park land required per gross acre of subdivision
1 D.U. per acre or more	262
1 D.U. per 1/2 to 1 acre	527
1 D.U. per 10,000 sq. ft. to 1/2 acre	767
1 D.U. per 9,000 to 9,999 sq. ft.	1,209
1 D.U. per 8,000 to 8,999 sq. ft.	1,350
1 D.U. per 7,000 to 7,999 sq. ft.	1,532
1 D.U. per 6,000 to 6,999 sq. ft.	1,768
1 D.U. per 5,000 to 5,999 sq. ft.	2,090

FEE FORMULA (Continued)

Net density per dwelling unit	Sq. ft. of park land required per gross acre of subdivision
10 to 19 D.U.'s per acre	2,680
20 to 29 D.U.'s per acre	4,466
30 to 39 D.U.'s per acre	6,257
40 to 49 D.U.'s per acre	8,039
50 to 59 D.U.'s per acre	9,825
60 to 69 D.U.'s per acre	11,611
70 to 79 D.U.'s per acre	13,408
80 to 89 D.U.'s per acre	15,185
90 to 99 D.U.'s per acre	16,969
100 D.U.'s and over per acre	17,851

'Fair market value' shall be determined as of the time of filing the final map in accordance with the following:

(a) The fair market value as determined by the City Council based upon the then assessed value, modified to equal market value in accordance with current practice of the (city) (county) assessor; or

(b) If the subdivider objects to such evaluation he may, at his expense, obtain an appraisal of the property by a qualified real estate appraiser approved by the City, which appraisal may be accepted by the City Council if found reasonable; or

(c) The City and subdivider may agree as to the fair market value.[3]

SECTION 8. CREDIT FOR PRIVATE OPEN SPACE. Where private open space for park and recreational purposes is provided in a proposed subdivision and such space is to be privately owned and maintained by the future residents of the subdivision, such areas shall be credited against the requirement of dedication for park and recreation purposes, as set forth in SECTION 6 hereof, or the payment of fees in lieu thereof, as set forth in SECTION 7 hereof, provided the City Council finds it is in the public interest to do so, and that the following standards are met:

(a) That yards, court areas, setbacks and other open areas

---

[3]Procedures for determining value of land should be developed to meet local conditions. The above suggestions are intended to be only a guide.

40

required to be maintained by the zoning and building regulations shall not be included in the computation of such private open space; and

(b) That the private ownership and maintenance of the open space is adequately provided for by written agreement; and

(c) That the use of the private open space is restricted for park and recreational purposes by recorded covenants which run with the land in favor of the future owners of property within the tract and which cannot be defeated or eliminated without the consent of the City Council; and

(d) That the proposed private open space is reasonably adaptable for use for park and recreational purposes, taking into consideration such factors as size, shape, topography, geology, access, and location of the private open space land; and

(e) That facilities proposed for the open space are in substantial accordance with the provisions of the recreational element of the general plan, and are approved by the City Council.

SECTION 9. CHOICE OF LAND OR FEE

(a) PROCEDURE. The procedure for determining whether the subdivider is to dedicate land, pay a fee, or both, shall be as follows:

(1) SUBDIVIDER. At the time of filing a tentative tract map for approval, the owner of the property shall, as part of such filing, indicate whether he desires to dedicate property for park and recreational purposes, or whether he desires to pay a fee in lieu thereof. If he desires to dedicate land for this purpose, he shall designate the area thereof on the tentative tract map as submitted.

(2) ACTION OF CITY. At the time of the tentative tract map approval, the City Council shall determine as a part of such approval, whether to require a dedication of land within the subdivision, payment of a fee in lieu thereof, or a combination of both.

(3) PREREQUISITES FOR APPROVAL OF FINAL MAP. Where dedication is required it shall be accomplished in accordance with the provisions of the Subdivision Map Act. Where fees are required the same shall be deposited with the City prior to the approval of the final tract map. Open space covenants for private park or recreational facilities shall be submitted to the City prior to approval of the final tract map and shall be recorded contemporaneously with the final tract map.

(b) DETERMINATION. Whether the City Council accepts land dedication or elects to require payment of a fee in lieu thereof, or a

41

combination of both, shall be determined by consideration of the following:

(1) Recreational element of the City's general plan; and

(2) Topography, geology, access and location of land in the subdivision available for dedication; and

(3) Size and shape of the subdivision and land available for dedication.

The determination of the City Council as to whether land shall be dedicated, or whether a fee shall be charged or a combination thereof, shall be final and conclusive. On subdivisions involving fifty (50) lots or less, only the payment of fees shall be required.

SECTION 10. TIME OF COMMENCEMENT MUST BE DESIGNATED. At the time the final tract map is approved the City Council shall designate the time when development of the park and recreational facilities shall be commenced.

SECTION 11. LIMITATION ON USE OF LAND AND FEES. The land and fees received under this ordinance shall be used only for the purpose of providing park and recreational facilities to serve the subdivision for which received and the location of the land and amount of fees shall bear a reasonable relationship to the use of the park and recreational facilities by the future inhabitants of the subdivision.

SECTION 12. The City Clerk shall certify, etc.[4]

---

[4]This ordinance has been drafted to apply only to subdivisions under the State Subdivision Map Act. It can be altered or amended to permit the city to require the payment of fees for park or recreational purposes as a condition to the approval of minor land divisions (i.e., lot splits).

42

APPENDIX E

A suggested agreement for the cooperative use of school and community facilities.*

THIS AGREEMENT made in Quadruplicate this _____ day of _____.

A.D. 1965.

BETWEEN:

> THE CITY OF EDMONTON, a Municipal
> Corporation (hereinafter called
> the "City"),

> > OF THE FIRST PART,

> > - and -

> THE EDMONTON SCHOOL DISTRICT NO. 7,
> (hereinafter called the "Public
> School Board"),

> > OF THE SECOND PART,

> > - and -

> THE EDMONTON R.C. SEPARATE SCHOOL
> DISTRICT NO. 7 (hereinafter called
> the "Separate School Board"),

> > OF THE THIRD PART.

WHEREAS it is the purpose of the City of Edmonton through the Parks and Recreation Department to develop, construct, operate and maintain Park and Recreation land and facilities, for Park and Recreation purposes and to organize and administer public recreation programs; and

WHEREAS the Public School Board and the Separate School Board (herein called the "Boards") have adopted a policy of making school buildings and grounds available for community recreation purposes provided there is no conflict with the operation of school activities; and

WHEREAS it is the wish of the City and the Boards to use the facilities for the maximum benefit of the community; and

WHEREAS maximum use of land and facilities should result in the most economical provision of school and public recreation facilities and programs; and

---

*The author wishes to thank the city of Edmonton, Canada, the Edmonton School District No. 7 and the Edmonton R.C. Separate School District No. 7 for permission to use this agreement.

433

WHEREAS it is the opinion of the City and the Boards that the gross cost of providing school and recreation facilities and programs will remain similar to the present costs under existing programs and conditions;

NOW THEREFORE THIS AGREEMENT WITNESSETH that the parties hereto agree together as follows:

1. That the Boards shall purchase outright and hold title to that portion of a senior high school grounds upon which school buildings are located together with the area necessary for lawns and landscaping immediately adjacent to the school buildings and that (the portion of the grounds required for school sport and athletics and public recreational purposes shall be purchased and held jointly by the City and the Boards.)

2. (a) That on junior high and elementary school sites the Boards shall purchase outright and hold title to the site required for all school purposes and the grounds required for school sports and athletics.

   (b) That the City shall purchase outright and hold title to all lands required for public park and recreational purposes to be acquired whenever possible adjoining such Junior High and Elementary School sites.

3. (a) That the Boards shall construct, operate and maintain school buildings and facilities at their expense and shall make available such buildings and facilities or parts thereof to the City on weekends, holidays and on school days after 6 p.m. until 11:30 p.m. or such time as may be regulated by the Joint Planning Committee; provided that arrangements may be made for Cubs, Brownies and other young children's activities at certain schools after 4:00 p.m. on any school day or at such times on other days as the Joint Planning Committee deems proper.

   (b) That the City shall receive use of such buildings, facilities or parts thereof free of charge in the operation of its public recreation programs whether operated directly or through the agency of City sponsored or approved volunteer, non-profit associations, clubs or groups.

4. (a) That the City shall construct, operate and maintain Park and Recreation areas, buildings and facilities at its expense and shall make such areas, buildings and facilities or parts thereof available to the Boards on

2

434

school days from 8 a.m. to 6 p.m. except in the case of outdoor
hockey rinks and arenas which shall be available from 8 a.m. to
4 p.m.; provided that the periods available to the Boards and the
City in a manner such as the Joint Planning Committee deems proper.

(b) That the Boards shall receive use of such areas, buildings and
facilities or parts thereof free of charge in the operation of their
programs;

5. That the City shall pay the cost of planning, developing and maintaining
school grounds including boulevards, excepting the cost of ornamental
front and side yards and boulevards which abut the school building;

6. That in planning school buildings the Boards shall provide for maximum
community use and the City shall pay the cost of those portions of new
buildings and additions to existing buildings which provide for specific
City recreational purposes as approved by the parties hereto;

7. That the City and the Boards shall continue to carry public liability
insurance under their various policies;

8. That the cost of property damage arising out of the use of the buildings
and facilities of any party to this agreement shall be assessed to and
paid by the party responsible for the activity from which damage results;

9. (a) That a Joint Planning Committee is hereby established and shall consist
of two officials from each of:

The City Parks and Recreation Department,

The Edmonton Separate School Board, and

The Edmonton Public School Board

to be appointed by the respective Superintendents.

(b) That the duties of the joint planning committee shall be:

1) to implement the terms of this agreement and to
co-ordinate all matters related thereto;

2) to recommend policies and develop regulations with regard
to the use of facilities, both buildings and sites.

10. This agreement shall be in effect for a period of one year from January 1st,
1966 provided that at the end of six months any of the parties may request
a review and revision of the agreement. Thereafter this agreement shall

3

continue in effect from year to year unless any of the parties gives thirty days notice in writing to the other parties requiring a review of this agreement.

IN WITNESS WHEREOF the parties hereto have executed this Agreement on the day and year first above written

SIGNED SEALED AND DELIVERED]
   in the presence of:]

THE CITY OF EDMONTON

_____
MAYOR

_____
CITY CLERK

THE EDMONTON SCHOOL DISTRICT NO. 7

_____
CHAIRMAN

_____
SECRETARY-TREASURER

THE EDMONTON R.C. SEPARATE SCHOOL DISTRICT NO. 7

_____
CHAIRMAN

_____
SECRETARY-TREASURER

4

APPENDIX F

MODEL FOR INITIAL INSTRUCTION TO ESTABLISH A PLANNING-
PROGRAMMING-BUDGETING SYSTEM IN A LOCAL OR STATE
GOVERNMENT

To   :   _____

Subject: A Planning-Programming-Budgeting System for the City (or
         State or County) of _____

I. Purpose

        This instruction announces the establishment of a Planning-Programming-
Budgeting System (PPBS) for the purpose of bringing all planning, programming,
and budgeting activities for the city (state or county) into a coordinated system
for year-round use by top management throughout the city's executive branch. It
should lead to more informed and coordinated budget recommendations.

        To this end, I have directed the establishment of a central analysis unit
which will report directly to _____, and have appointed a Task
Force to work with it in developing and introducing the new concepts and procedures
that form the basis for a productive PPB System. Their responsibilities and those
of the heads of departments and agencies are broadly outlined below.

        It should be clearly understood that, while the government-wide PPB System
and the comprehensive program structure may cut across organization lines of the
several departments and agencies, these have been developed strictly for purposes
of facilitating a coordinated approach to governmental issues and policy decisions.
The arrangement of functions under program areas and categories for purposes of
the PPB System has in itself no bearing on the pattern of administrative responsibility.

II. Background and Need

        A budget is a financial expression of a program plan. Under present
practices, however, program review for decision making has frequently been concentrated within too short a period; objectives of programs and activities have
too often not been specified with enough clarity and concreteness; accomplishments have not always been specified concretely; alternatives have been insuf-
ficiently presented for consideration to top management; future year costs of
present decisions have not been laid out consistently or systematically enough;
and formalized planning and program analysis have had too little effect on budget
decisions.

        To help remedy these shortcomings, our planning and budget systems should
be made to provide more accurate information to assist line managers, department
and agency heads, and the chief executive (or chief administrative officer) in

437

judging needs and in deciding on the use of resources and their allocation among competing program claims. The establishment of a PPBS will make needed improvements possible.

III. Basic Concepts and Design

    A. A PPB System is based on three concepts:

        1. An Analytic capability which carries out continuing in-depth analyses, by permanent specialized staffs, of the government's objectives and its various programs to meet these objectives.

        2. A Multi-year Planning and Programming process which incorporates and uses an information system to present data in meaningful categories in relation to necessary major decisions.

        3. A Budgeting process which can take program decisions, translate them into an implementing financial plan in a budget context, and present the appropriate program and financial data for executive and legislative action.

    B. Key procedures and "tools" of the System are:

        1. The Program Structure. An early and essential step is the determination of a series of output-oriented categories which, together, cover the total work of the governmental unit. These will serve as a basic framework for the planning, programming, and budgetary processes (including work on program analysis, reporting and evaluation of accomplishments) and for relating these processes to each other. (See Attachment I.)

        2. The Multi-Year Program and Financial Plan. A principal product of the System will be a multi-year program and financial plan (systematically updated) which will set forth, on the basis of the program structure, the activities and operations designed to reach program objectives in stated time periods.

        3. Summary Program Analysis Documents. Program analysis, prepared annually for major program categories, will summarize the recommended multi-year program and present an evaluation on the basis of the needs to be met in future years and an appraisal of the adequacy and effectiveness of the previously approved plan for the category. This will identify the governmental objective, costs, benefits, and major uncertainties of the proposed program and its principal alternatives.

2

C. Overall the System is designed to:

    1. Make available to top management more concrete and specific data relevant to broad decisions;

    2. Spell out more concretely the objectives of governmental programs;

    3. Analyze systematically and present for (chief executive or chief administrative officer) review and decision possible alternative objectives and alternative programs to meet those objectives;

    4. Evaluate thoroughly and compare the benefits and costs of programs;

    5. Produce total, rather than partial, cost estimates of programs;

    6. Present on a multi-year basis the prospective costs and accomplishments of programs;

    7. Review objectives and conduct program analyses on a continuing, year-round basis, instead of on a crowded schedule to meet budget deadlines. (An illustrative annual cycle of activities is presented in Attachment II.)

IV. Relation of the PPB System to the Budget Process

The introduction of the PPB System will not, by itself, necessarily require any changes in the form in which budget appropriation requests are made. Program decisions resulting from the information presented by the summary program documents and the multi-year program and financial plans will be used as guidance for preparation of annual budget requests. Over the years, budgetary procedures and controls will be brought into closer harmony with the basic program structure and the multi-year programs and financial plans.

V. Responsibilities for the PPB System

The major responsibility for the institution of the PPB System will rest with the PPB System Task Force consisting of representatives from designated departments and agencies. The Director of the central analysis unit will act as chairman. */ Departments and agencies will have a major part in the continuing operation of the PPB System.

---

*/ The membership and size of the Task Force presumably would be determined by the chief executive of the jurisdiction and a separate attachment would be inserted on these designations.

3

More specifically---

A. The ad hoc PPB System Task Force will:

1. Block out the major initial steps for instituting a PPB
    System, and establish a tentative time schedule for their
    completion. (See Attachment III for an illustrative time
    schedule.)

2. Formulate an initial government-wide program structure,
    including preliminary working descriptions of governmental
    objectives, and of the specific types of activities to be
    included, in each program category.

3. Prepare initial operating procedures for the PPB System and
    identify responsibilities for the preparation of PPB System
    materials (with resolution of jurisdictional overlaps) and
    provision for appropriate linkage to budget preparation
    procedures.

4. Prepare instructions for development of the initial multi-
    year program and financial plan.

5. Provide guidelines, instructional materials, and counsel to
    participating agency personnel.

6. Identify major issues facing the government in the near
    future that call for special analysis in the initial period,
    and arrange for selected program analyses by teams made up
    of personnel from the central analysis unit and from the
    departments and agencies involved.

7. Make recommendations for a continuing administrative frame-
    work for the PPB System based on the experience during the
    initial period.

8. Begin the process of identifying data required for program
    evaluations and make recommendation regarding additional data
    collection.

B. The Central Analysis Unit will:

1. Provide leadership to the ad hoc PPB System Task Force (by
    providing its chairman) and arrange for its adequate staff-
    ing. (The remaining responsibilities listed below pertain
    also to the continuing role of the central analysis unit
    after the close of the initial task force phase.)

4

440

2. Provide overall direction, coordination and review of the PPB System.

3. Arrange for orientation and training of personnel in PPB System operations as needed.

4. Perform individual analyses as appropriate.

5. Work with departments and agencies on individual analyses as work priorities indicate.

6. Establish and keep current a schedule of needed program analyses, with designation of the departments and agencies that will lead, or participate, in each study.

C. Department and Agency Heads. In addition to participation by designating major departments in the PPB System Task Force, all department and agency heads will:

1. Identify appropriate personnel for participation in the various PPB System activities which will become the continuing responsibilities of the department or agency.

2. Identify, within the agency's sphere of interest, major governmental objectives, criteria for evaluating performance in relation to these objectives, major policy issues expected to require decision in the next few months, and ways to improve data information systems in relation to the continuing requirements of program analysis.

3. Assume continuing responsibility for analytical tasks involved in planning, programming, and budgeting for operations within his agency; for appropriate participation in special in-depth analysis of issues related to program categories under his supervision; for seeking, coordinating, and reviewing recommendations by his principal administrative aides and managers on program plans and the findings of analytical studies for submission to the chief executive (or chief administrative officer); and for maintaining organizational arrangements that make his department or agency an effective participant in the PPB System.

VI. Timing

A. Since it is the primary ingredient for productive effort by all concerned, I shall expect the Task Force to report to me by (4 weeks) its preliminary schedule of major activities, with tentative completion dates for each. (See Attachment III for an example.)

5

B. The System should be in operation within a year, and I shall therefore expect the Task Force to present to me by (1 year) its recommendations for
a continuing administrative framework for, and the general operating procedures
necessary to, the ongoing PPB System.

It is my conviction that the establishment of an effective planning-
programming-budgeting operation holds great promise for sharpening the issues
involved in the allocation of available resources and for improving program development generally, but particularly for assuring that important policy decisions
are made only after full exploration of the relevent factors and within a longer-
term perspective than has been customary. Therefore, each department and agency
head should feel a personal responsibility for seeing that adequate staff effort
is addressed, not only to the initial exploratory work in support of the Task
Force, but to the agency's continuing responsibilities after the procedures have
been worked out by the Task Force.

The major part of the analytical work (the backbone of the PPB System)
will have to be carried by departmental staff. The long-run effectiveness of
this effort will therefore depend upon the energetic support of each of you.

From time to time, I shall meet with you as the work progresses.

Mayor or City Manager (or Chief Executive or Chief Administrative Officer
of the State or County)

6

INDEX

Chicago, recreation needs, 234–37
China, population, 87, 99, 180
Chubb, Michael, 210n, 211
Citizen involvement:
  in administration, 342–57
  advisory boards, 67–81 *passim*
  in evaluation, 285–92
  in planning, 4–9, 16–18, 22–25, 29, 43–45,
    187, 214–15
  and public relations, 359–65
  as volunteers, 151–53, 163–64, 165
City:
  land use, 168–73, 177–90 *passim*, 193
  leisure resources, 249–52, 363–76
  life, 105–14, 171
  planning, 8, 21, 79, 389, 396
  population, 119, 394, 399
  recreation:
    areas 193–208
    standards, 208–25
    demand, 225–44
City Demonstration Agency, 66, 74–75
Clavel, Pierre, 46
Clawson, Marion, 213
Client-agency relations (*see* Citizen
    involvement)
Close-ended questions, 140, 146 (*see also*
    Questionnaires)
Code of ethics:
  personal, 302–3, 329, 330
  planners, 51, 53, 57
  survey researchers, 161
Coding, 144, 162, 163
College towns, growth of, 111
Colorado, Aspen, 125–26
Columbia (Md.), 112, 173
Command, organizational, 304–8
Commercial recreation, 18, 119, 125, 213,
    371–72, 373
Commission on the Year 2000, 97
Commoner, Barry, 85, 92
Communication:
  board-staff, 352–54, 358
  in planning, 76–79
  problems, 318–21, 327, 328
  public relations, 359–65
Community:
  defined, 389
  need for, 108
  parks, 196–97, 229–30
  school cooperation, 254–65
Community Action Programs, 5–6, 66–69
Community involvement (*see* Citizen
    involvement)
Community planning (*see* Planning)
Community research (*see* Survey research)
Commuting, 113
Compensable regulation, 183
Comprehensive planning (*see* Planning)
Computer analysis:
  financial, 379
  leisure resources, 251
  recreation demand, 225–50 *passim*
Condemnation, 180–81, 392

Confidentiality, of data, 130, 134, 163
Conflicts, organizational, 312–31
Conservation:
  land use, 167–76 *passim*, 180–86
  preservation/conservation, 176–80, 187,
    188–208
  wilderness, 22–23
Conservation Foundation, 86
Consultants:
  and citizens, 43–45, 58, 67
  contracts, 51, 57, 59–61
  data needs, 47–48, 56, 59
  ethics, 51, 53, 57
  evaluation, 47, 280–82, 287–88, 291, 292
  fees, 49–51, 52–53
  financial, 373, 383
  need for, 37–39
  public relations, 77, 364
  responsibilities, 45, 295, 309
  selection, 39n, 51–57, 58
  and staff, 57–58, 60, 314
  survey, 161–64
  types, 39–42, 48
Contracts, for planning, 51–57, 59–61
Cost accounting, 378, 379–80 (*see also*
    Accounting)
Cost-benefit analysis, 81, 379, 390
Country:
  life, 105–14
  population, 398
  recreation needs, 232–34
Crabbe, George, 105–6
Creativity, 302
Crime, and recreation, 273–74
Critical Path Method (CPM), 158–65

Dade County (Fla.), Department of Parks
    and Recreation, 194–99 *passim*
Dallas (Texas):
  recreation needs, 239–44
  recreation standards, 221
Dangerous Classes of New York, The, 64
Data:
  bank, 249–52, 380–81, 382
  collection, 47–49, 130, 133–35, 137–38,
    150–58
  for evaluation, 288
  processing, 162–63, 164, 165
Decision making (*see also* Problem
    solving):
  financial, 378–83
  lay boards, 342–57
  staff, 358
  styles, 321–30
Dedication, of land, 183
Demand:
  estimating recreation, 225–50
  outdoor recreation, 19–20, 48, 49, 107,
    114–19, 210–12
Demography (*see also* Population):
  defined, 391
  recreation and, 211, 212, 232–49 *passim*
  survey data, 131, 133–34